Contents

SAGE was founded in 1965 by Sara Miller McCune to support the dissemination of usable knowledge by publishing innovative and high-quality research and teaching content. Today, we publish over 900 journals, including those of more than 400 learned societies, more than 800 new books per year, and a growing range of library products including archives, data, case studies, reports, and video. SAGE remains majority-owned by our founder, and after Sara's lifetime will become owned by a charitrust that secures our continued independence.

Los Angeles | London | New Delhi | Singapore | Washington DC | Melbourne

UNDERSTANDING VULNERABILITIES IN CONTEMPORARY SOCIETY

Thank you for choosing a SAGE product!
If you have any comment, observation or feedback,
I would like to personally hear from you.

Please write to me at **contactceo@sagepub.in**

Vivek Mehra, Managing Director and CEO, SAGE India.

Bulk Sales

SAGE India offers special discounts
for purchase of books in bulk.
We also make available special imprints
and excerpts from our books on demand.

For orders and enquiries, write to us at

Marketing Department
SAGE Publications India Pvt Ltd
B1/I-1, Mohan Cooperative Industrial Area
Mathura Road, Post Bag 7
New Delhi 110044, India

E-mail us at **marketing@sagepub.in**

Subscribe to our mailing list
Write to **marketing@sagepub.in**

This book is also available as an e-book.

UNDERSTANDING VULNERABILITIES IN CONTEMPORARY SOCIETY

Psychological Insights
and Reflections

Edited by
Nandita Babu
Anand Prakash
Ishita U. Bharadwaj

Los Angeles | London | New Delhi
Singapore | Washington DC | Melbourne

First published in 2021 by

SAGE Publications India Pvt Ltd
B1/I-1 Mohan Cooperative Industrial Area
Mathura Road, New Delhi 110 044, India
www.sagepub.in

SAGE Publications Inc
2455 Teller Road
Thousand Oaks, California 91320, USA

SAGE Publications Ltd
1 Oliver's Yard, 55 City Road
London EC1Y 1SP, United Kingdom

SAGE Publications Asia-Pacific Pte Ltd
18 Cross Street #10-10/11/12
China Square Central
Singapore 048423

Published by Vivek Mehra for SAGE Publications India Pvt Ltd. Typeset in 10.5/13 pt Bembo by Zaza Eunice, Hosur, Tamil Nadu, India.

Library of Congress Control Number: 2021941153

ISBN: 978-93-91370-85-5 (HB)

SAGE Team: Amrita Dutta, Shipra Pant and Anupama Krishnan
Cover Image: Gaurav Bharadwaj

List of Figures

List of Tables

Foreword

The perennial search for happiness through maximization of pleasure, evasion of pain and avoidance of negative emotions constitutes a key concern in the post-global era. The dominance of divisive cultures seems imperative in the emerging paradigm of human development. In this scenario, the nature and sources of vulnerability too are emerging as a major concern in the fields of economics, sociology, psychology, mental health, climate studies and disaster management, though practitioners from these disciplines use the term with different connotations and distinct foci for analysis.

Psychological literature conceives vulnerability as a latent trait endogenous to individuals, situating its roots in dysfunctional learning or genetic endowment. Intuitive viewpoints about vulnerability implicate an increased susceptibility to emotional pain and loss to welfare at an individual and/or collective level. The colloquial expressions in Hindi for this use such terms as *bebasi, becharagi, lachari* and *vivashata*. The conventional approaches to the study of the conditions such as poverty, marginality and illness among individuals/groups/communities often fail to understand 'their' experiential world.

The present volume moves beyond the 'trait view' of vulnerability, endeavouring to offer an experiential account of vulnerability in diverse areas of life. It problematizes vulnerability across some 'distinct' sites, capturing 'latent' experiences in the lived realities. The contributions to this volume illustrate vulnerability in a wide range of conditions and attend to the constraining psychological, social, cultural and economic factors varying along the spatio-temporal continuum. Caste-related stigma, womanhood, desires growing up as a girl, the status of refugees, the life of transgender individuals, provision of care for patients of Parkinson's disease, child sexual abuse and the enigma related to infertility are some of the issues and concerns taken up in this volume.

Insecurity and a sense of victimization and marginalization are found to be prominent in most of the narratives shared by the authors. It has been documented that the nature and extent of vulnerability and outcomes depend on the characteristics of the specific risk involved and the individual's sensitivity and ability to respond to that risk.

While the sites of vulnerability vary across contributions, all of them involve the probability of experiencing a loss to welfare caused by identity threat, uncertainties and norm violations. However, the chapters enable the readers to appreciate the 'inevitability' of 'being vulnerable', which holds a potential insight into the phenomenon. By bringing into focus the moments, stakes and forms of encounters in real life, the contributors make vulnerability intelligible in the lived personal and social contexts. Deploying qualitative methods, the authors attend to intrapersonal and interpersonal processes, cultural and social norms, interactions and relationships. The socio-symbolic processes uncovered suggest that vulnerability needs to be understood with respect to its social, political, economic and historical context.

The present volume is a groundbreaking endeavour to understand the phenomenon of vulnerability through the mobilization of myriad factors and processes that enable us to understand how individuals or groups become vulnerable. Taken together, the contributions help determine the complex system of relations with oneself, with others and with the world, which creates intersecting spaces of vulnerability. By demystifying the processes that render people vulnerable at work, the volume draws attention to the multiplicity of levels of the lifeworld involved. The vulnerabilities implicit in daily life do need further probe. The volume reflects the need to appreciate reality as it emerges in real life and invites critical thinking about the issues addressed and the engaging subjectivities in the construal of reality. I congratulate the editors and authors of the volume for the incisive analysis of this ubiquitous phenomenon traversing the life domains encompassing social, as well as intimate zones of lived experiences.

Girishwar Misra
Former Professor, Department of Psychology
University of Delhi

Preface and Acknowledgements

The compilation of this book is interposed with a sense of responsibility to an initiative undertaken by the Department of Psychology, Delhi University, under the University Grants Commission–Special Assistance Programme (UGC-SAP). The inception of this book culminated as an afterthought of the National Seminar (2017) on *Psychological vulnerabilities* held by the department. The idea behind the seminar was to create a common forum for discussions and sharing by psychologists, health practitioners, academicians, teachers and activists. Psychosocial vulnerability appears to be a serious concern of our times. A perceptive approach towards the concept inspired us to delve into the nuances and shades of vulnerability, positioning it as one of the thrust areas for our teaching and research. It also inspired us to conceive this book and invite colleagues with similar interests to write essays on various topics in the domain of psychological. As the editors, we wish to share our labour of joy with a note of remembrance and gratitude for all those who have been part of the incredible journey of this book.

First, we would like to express our sincere gratitude to Prof. Girishwar Misra for being a source of inspiration, facilitating the genesis and evolution of the book. We are immensely grateful to him for composing the Foreword of this volume. We would like to offer our gratitude to all the authors who have invested their time, creative thoughts and persistent efforts in shaping the various chapters of this book—without which the book would not have taken the form that it has. We sincerely appreciate the collaborative trust vested in us by our colleagues for this project. Their inputs, suggestions and support have been a valuable source of inspiration for this book.

We would especially like to offer our gratitude and accolade to the efforts of our dear students Aritra, Radhika, Supreet, Pradakshina, Nidhi, Annie and Sohini who have been the backbone of this entire project. Through their devout dedication, enthusiasm and active engagement, they have been a key instrument in driving this project to its successful culmination.

We are thankful to the editorial team of SAGE Publications, especially Abhijit Baroi for accommodating us throughout the process of publication and for his invaluable insights at every step of the way. We are grateful to Amrita Dutta for her sincere and prompt help in compiling the book.

Finally, we owe this work to the seen and unseen contributors who have been ardently with us on this journey.

Introduction

Vulnerable, as a term, originated from the Latin noun *vulnus* ('wound'), which led to the Latin verb *vulnerare,* meaning 'to wound'. The late Latin adjective *vulnerabilis* became 'vulnerable' in English by early 1600. What initially meant 'capable of being physically wounded or having the power to wound' transitioned to a figurative use indicating being defenceless against physical attacks. In other words, someone (or something) can be vulnerable to criticism or failure, as well as to literal wounding. When it is used figuratively, 'vulnerable' is often followed by the preposition 'to'.

'Vulnerability' has chiefly remained a significant concept in the context of 'disaster risk' and 'climate change adaptation'. For instance 'vulnerability' has been looked at as the propensity of exposed elements, such as human beings, their livelihoods and assets, to suffer adverse effects when impacted by hazard events (UNDRO, 1980). It has also been seen as the 'state of susceptibility' to harm from exposure to stresses associated with environmental and social change and from the absence of the capacity to adapt. In the natural sciences, thus, vulnerability is seen as the degree to which a system is exposed to, becomes sensitive to and is yet unable to cope with adverse impacts of global change stimuli (Downing et al., 2003).

Borrowing from this context, over the years, the concept of vulnerability found its pitching in other areas—economic, political, social and psychological, and cultural as well. It came to be studied in relation to predisposition, susceptibilities, fragilities, weaknesses, deficiencies or lack of capacities that favour adverse effects on the exposed elements. However, despite being extensively researched for the past three decades, across disciplines in social sciences, the concept of vulnerability remains primarily explored and cognized in limited terms of its literal meaning of 'being at risk' (Havrilla, 2017). It was not until the path-breaking work of Rose and Killien (1983) that the essence of vulnerability as a critical–meaningful psychological experience inherent in the everyday life of every individual was captured.

VULNERABILITY FROM A PSYCHOLOGICAL LENS

Studies on vulnerability with respect to 'psychological frailties' helped in identifying the 'at risk' population as well. From being used to describe those individuals harmed and wounded due to geographical and economical insufficiencies, the term vulnerable has been reconceptualized to also encompass those individuals who 'are susceptible' to 'emotional' and 'psychological injury'.

Furthermore, with the advent of cultural–historical transitions, the collective adjectival term of vulnerability has been undergoing constant transformations, emphasizing the need to acknowledge the omnipresence and significance of 'convolution', a mathematical concept used by Cardona (2003) to describe the 'concomitance and mutual conditioning between hazard and vulnerability'. In other words, one feels vulnerable when one is threatened, and one is threatened when one is exposed and vulnerable. Since the possibility of modifying the hazard and reducing the risk is negligible or zero in many contexts, research and intervention focused towards modifying the conditions of vulnerability of the exposed elements become the need of the hour.

With the onset of globalization, thrust on modernity and nostalgic adherence to local culture, the imagery of inhabiting an otherwise 'liberal' 'independent' and 'developed' India seems to be in dissonance to what one gets to experience. The sociopolitical inequalities, regional ethnicities, cultural eccentricities, economic disparities and notions of (un)wellness are some of the macro concerns enmeshed in our social fabric. Our social systems, still in transition, on the one hand, struggle to save the girl child, with slogans like *beti bachao beti padhao*, while, on the other, wish to reiterate the rhetoric of gender empowerment through its existing education system. Such psychological paradoxes hold potential insights for understanding the dynamicity of social structures.

Additionally, with regard to mental health and wellness, a very narrow and adversative meaning has been associated with the notion of vulnerability. Since the bio-medicalization of mental health from the second half of the 20th century (Clarke et al., 2003), a biogenetic explanation for all psychological phenomena has created a split between the inner and outer, the abled and ailed and the psychological and social domains. Further, in the 1980s, the social stigma and the shame associated with victim identity urged social movement activists (feminists and survivors of sexual abuse) to emphasize being a survivor and promote a resilience model of thriving (Samelius et al., 2014). Hence, there emerged a thrust to distance the self from vulnerability, creating dichotomous categories, such as victim/survivor, vulnerable/invulnerable, vulnerable/resilient, passive/agentic, in the narratives of individuals.

Hence, with the changing times, the concept of vulnerability seems to be 'hegemonized' into a singular meaning, by various stakeholders, failing to capture the experiential essence of the concept in the lived world of an individual. Hence, in the existing academic discourses, it becomes increasingly important to accommodate the issues that an individual is subjected to.

The dominant models of 'resilience and coping', emphasizing denial of one's vulnerability, further incentivize adherence to the position of shunning it. There is often an implied consensus on 'who can' be 'categorized' as 'vulnerable'. The elderly, the ill, the homeless, single parents, young children or individuals who are unable to fend for themselves—these are the ubiquitous categories of vulnerability. However, they are also the 'known' and 'seen' categories. In addressing the explicit, the bigger picture is seldom accounted for. In that case, what happens to the vulnerabilities that exist in the blind spots of policymakers and health workers?

A PLAUSIBLE GAP: THE 'WHY' OF THE BOOK

Although it is being investigated across various branches of knowledge, ranging from the economic and political to the psychosocial, little is known about the intersectional impact systems and individuals could have while experiencing vulnerability.

Vulnerability is not a static phenomenon. It changes within the eco-cultural and biological system of human life. The dynamic nature of vulnerability makes it inevitable for everyone. It could be that one is less or more vulnerable, but the absence of vulnerability is a myth. The sociocultural–temporal dimensions of one's experience of vulnerability are clearly evident during the current COVID-19 pandemic. This crisis has exaggerated inequalities, and it has also pushed previously less vulnerable groups across capability and opportunity thresholds, creating unexpected, new vulnerabilities. For instance, social isolation has exacerbated personal and collective vulnerabilities while limiting accessible and familiar support options. Reports of domestic abuse and family violence have increased around the world since social isolation and quarantine measures came into force (Usher et al., 2020). Crises, in other words, give rise to new kinds of vulnerabilities (or older ones that are now visible) that take us by surprise, which might create new sensitivities in the memories of those affected—new kinds of awareness that will last beyond post-crisis recovery periods.

This book takes up the challenging task of exploring vulnerability on a spectrum, especially in a context as diverse as that of India. Here, vulnerability is always a relevant topic owing to the wide range of intersecting identities of individuals: social, economic and caste-, gender- and disability-based. A precise attempt has been made to touch upon the intersection between the macro and micro issues in which the individual gets to encounter his/her vulnerability. The attempt is not to question the existence of vulnerability but rather to examine the ways in which collectively and individually, one's vulnerability is reinforced for one's ensured survival.

BRIEF OVERVIEW: THE 'WHAT' OF THE BOOK

The chapters in this book cover on a wide spectrum of issues around psychological vulnerability. The diversity of the chapters enabled us to map the context and situatedness around the experience of vulnerability. Caste discrimination in India has been existing as an imperceptible phenomenon encompassing the life of a large sector of the population. Chapter 4 in the book, 'Voicing Vulnerabilities Around the "Caste" Stigma: A Qualitative Study' focuses on the experience of vulnerability among marginalized groups because of social discrimination. In the case of systemic violence (associated with caste, gender, sexuality), individuals are constructed to experience said violence in the context of neoliberal market rhetoric and logic, such as bootstrapping, competition and entrepreneurship. This creates personal responsibility that renders agency to the burden of suffering, effectively obfuscating the significance of systems of oppression (Samelius et al., 2014).

In India, despite strong evidence of the fact that vulnerability is experienced differently by men and women, research to understand the experience of women vis-à-vis men is yet to come under the limelight. There are four chapters in this book that deal with vulnerability as experienced by women in India. Chapter 8, 'Women and Work in Post-reform India: Reality of Vulnerability and Exclusion', describes an extensive analysis of how employment and the workforce in India have been gender-biased to a large extent irrespective of the emphasis on the state policy of gender equality at all levels. The authors comment that the economic gender gap runs deep in Indian society.

Chapter 11, 'The Experience of Vulnerability and Resilience of Adolescent Girls in Slums', explores the factors contributing to their perceived vulnerability and resilience from a gendered, economic lens. It traces the concerns of adolescent girls regarding their financial instability, employment, career, health, etc. Further, it seeks to explicate the dynamics of navigating an urban slum set-up. The chapter also throws light on the issue of gender intersectionality, especially in the complex context of a slum dwelling.

With both these chapters delving into the explicit facets of vulnerability, what intrigued us was: How does one address the implicit vulnerabilities—the vulnerabilities felt in intimate relationships while giving care to a loved one or while tapping into the felt experiences of (in)fertility? The themes around these have been explored through a process-driven approach in Chapters 9, 6 and 10, 'Vulnerabilities of Desire: A Qualitative Study with Indian Housewives', 'Invulnerable Parkinson's Caregivers: An Existential Phenomenological Perspective' and 'Reflections on Psychic Pain Around (In)Fertility and "Being" of a Woman', respectively. Through these chapters, we wish to bring forth that usually, with every explicit vulnerability, its implicit shade remains unaccounted for, and while focusing on those implicitly vulnerable, their explicit vulnerabilities are taken for granted. Thus, it is critical to move beyond binaries and emphasize how the various forms of vulnerability coalesce into one another. Chapter 6, 'Invulnerable Parkinson's Caregivers: An Existential Phenomenological Perspective', explores the lived experiences of Parkinson's disease caregivers. Using an existential phenomenological method of analysis, the chapter explores the temporal aspect of vulnerability, as well as the relational dimensions of a patient–caregiver dynamic. By focusing on the intricacies and perplexities inherent in the life of caregivers, it tracks their journey of embodying the caregiver identity. Touching upon the elements such as emergence of parenthood among the caregivers, blurring of identity as an individual and experience of choicelessness, as well as alienation, in the known structures of one's family, this chapter brings to light the usually silent and concealed shades of vulnerability.

Chapter 9, 'Vulnerabilities of Desire: A Qualitative Study with Indian Housewives', undertakes an in-depth inquiry into Indian womanhood and its psychological complexities. Using a focus group discussion, the author explores the narratives of four female friends individually and collectively encountering the desire of the other/another woman. The analysis reveals the psychological processes of 'identification' and 'othering' as the participants reflect on and legitimize the protagonist's silence and loss and become distant when they encounter her desirous self.

Chapter 10, 'Reflections on Psychic Pain around (In)Fertility and "Being" of a Woman', revisits the conceptualization of female desire in modern times and how it continues to be a site where there is a continuous tussle in establishing and understanding notions of womanhood, motherhood and infertility in the Indian cultural context. Through a different lens, the author explores the disruptions in psychic structures experienced by these women on the unending cycle of hope and disappointment. The chapter taps on their experiences to reveal and voice the array of emotions encountered while struggling to develop coherence in the face of persistent fear of potential loss, unceasing socio-culturally imposed stagnancy and a perpetual state of isolation.

Chapter 1, titled 'Everything That We Could Carry: Understanding Vulnerabilities in Refugees', attempts to understand the experience of Tibetan refugees through the lens of existing definitions by policymakers, and other markers like age and stage, of refugee experiences. In this study, one gets to see vulnerability as a dynamic experience, which appears to change within the eco-cultural and biological system of human life. Vulnerability as an ineviexperience gets reiterated through this study.

Chapter 2, titled 'Growing Up Asian-Indian in USA: Identity Development and Psychosocial Adaptation', looks into the experiences of second-generation Asian-Indian adolescents in the United States. This chapter examines the layers of vulnerability while using the theoretical framework for multiple worlds, US societal context, home and parental factors, schools and ritualistic practices of Hinduism. Using a mixed-method approach, it explains the experience of vulnerability in the context of cultural invisibility and parental regulation of interpersonal relationships.

Chapter 3, titled 'Mental Health Vulnerabilities of the Third Gender Community', is a rather theoretical chapter capturing the plight of third-gender or transgender individuals in the Indian context. The authors examine the third-gender community's sense of victimhood in the context of identity. The sense of marginality felt by them and its impact on their mental health has been an important concern. These experiences, over the years, have been predisposing the members of the third gender community to mental and physical illnesses, such as anxiety, depression, mood disorder, substance use and high prevalence of HIV/AIDS. The road of suffering does not end here, as seeking quality healthcare has also been a challenge for the community. However, the landmark judgement of 2014 by the Supreme Court of India and the Transgender Persons (Protection of Rights) Act (2019) brought a ray of hope for the community.

On the other hand, Chapter 5, titled 'Psychological Trauma in Child Sexual Abuse: Withstanding Vulnerability and Nurturing Resilience' highlights the dynamics of sexual abuse in the Indian context. Using a bio-psychosocial model of child sexual abuse under relevant theoretical frameworks, it explicates the experience of vulnerability. The chapter also explores multidimensionality in the effects, key challenges in the assessment of dynamic vulnerabilities (child-/family-/culture-specific), major factors in strengthening resilience within and outside home, legal frameworks and healing of the trauma.

In contrast, Chapter 7, 'Positive Deviance: Use of Phenomenon in Vulnerability to Depression', gives a detailed account of the concept of positive deviance, where the authors look into the case of a resilient community in which people have never experienced depression.

Chapter 12, 'Managing Vulnerabilities of Institution-Building and Organizational Change: The Role of Trust', has been written with a slightly different perspective. It brings forth the fact that institutions represent structural configurations in an organization, which are often taken for granted but have far-reaching impacts on the behaviours of members of the organization. Institutions help preserve stability but at the same time may also lead to obsolescence and possibly imminent chaos, particularly if the nature of these structural configurations is not dynamic. Organizations, therefore, are vulnerable to a complex range of stability- and change-related issues in view of the institutions they carry. One of the fundamental factors in the emergence and mainte-nance of these structural configurations and organizational institutional arrangement is trust, which in turn is associated with exposure to risks and acceptance of vulnerability.

This book has tried exploring the myriad circumstances, contexts and issues through which vulnerabilities are created, fostered or shunned. The purpose of writing this is actually to initiate a dialogue around the conception and perception of vulnerability. With this book, we hope to move past the facile meaning associated with the notion of vulnerability and sensitize our readers to its intricate embeddedness.

REFERENCES

Cardona, D. O. (2003). The need for rethinking the concepts of vulnerability and risk from a holistic perspective: A necessary review and criticism for effective risk management. In G. Bankoff, G. Frerks, & D. Hilhorst (Eds.), *Mapping vulnerability: Disasters, development and people* (p. 254). Earthscan.

Clarke, A., Shim, J., Mamo, L., Fosket, J., & Fishman, J. (2003). Biomedicalization: Technoscientific transformations of health, illness, and U.S. biomedicine. *American Sociological Review, 68*(2), 161–194. http://www.jstor.org/stable/1519765

Downing, T., Patwardhan, A., Klien, R. J. T., Mukhala, E., Stephen, L., Winograd, M., & Ziervogel, G. (2003). Vulnerability assessment for climate adaptation. In B. Lim, & E. Spanger-Siegfried (Eds.), *Adaptation policy framework for climate change: Developing strategies, policies and measures* (Technical Paper 3, p. 24). Cambridge University Press.

Havrilla, E. (2017). Defining vulnerability. *Madridge Journal of Nursing, 2,* 63–68. https://doi.org/10.18689/mjn-1000111

Rose, M. H., & Killien, M. (1983). Risk and vulnerability: A case for differentiation. *Advances in Nursing Science, 5*(3), 60–73.

Samelius, L., Thapar, B. S., & Binswanger, C. (2014). Turning points and the 'everyday': Exploring agency and violence in intimate relationships. *European Journal of Women's Studies, 21*(3), 264–277.

Usher, K. M., Bhullar, N., Durkin, J., Gyamfi, N., & Jackson, D. (2020). Family violence and COVID-19: Increased vulnerability and reduced options for support. *International Journal of Mental Health Nursing, 29*(4). https://doi.org/10.1111/inm.12735

UNDRO. (1980). *Natural disasters and vulnerability analysis* (Report of Experts Group Meeting of 9–12 July 1979). UNDRO.

Chapter 1

Everything That We Could Carry
Understanding Vulnerabilities in Refugees

Pallavi Ramanathan and Nandita Babu

VULNERABILITY AND REFUGEES

When one thinks about refugees, the terms 'vulnerability' and 'vulnerable/at-risk group' are not far away. Given a situation where one is bereft of a home and all the social, emotional and economic resources that it encompasses, it is natural to connect the term 'vulnerable' with the term 'refugee'. It is, however, critical to understand what it means to be a refugee and in fact what it means to be a vulnerable refugee. How does the experience of being a refugee impact the experience of vulnerability? What makes a refugee vulnerable? Further, what comes after vulnerability? The present discussion seeks to explain the nuances of vulnerability in the context of refugees. It is undeniable that refugees face myriad challenges that are spread across most of the major arenas in life and thus need to be considered a vulnerable group, particularly one which could develop chronic illness (Bittenbinder, 2010). However, it is also important to acknowledge, in the same breath, those refugees who have faced hardships and have been successful in rebuilding their lives; Tibetan refugees are a significant example of this. This chapter discusses the refugee experience and vulnerability through a qualitative study on Tibetan refugees living in India. The study was done to examine specifically the identity negotiations and interactions of the Tibetans with the host community (India); however, this chapter highlights the vulnerability experienced by the Tibetan refugees. Prior to discussing the study and the consequent experiences, a theoretical understanding of refugees and vulnerability is established.

AN OVERVIEW OF REFUGEES AND VULNERABILITY

Refugees are part of a group called involuntary migrants. Refugees and other asylum seekers (now called 'forced migrants', collectively; Ager, 1999) are often faced with the greatest obstacles, as they are usually not keen on leaving their homelands, and if they are impelled to do so, it is not always possible for them to be able to stay and settle into the new society. The 1951 Geneva Convention is the key instrument of international refugee law, clearly demarcating who a refugee is and the kind of legal protection, assistance and rights refugees should receive from the countries who are party to this convention. As they cannot return home safely, refugees are owed specific protections under international law. Those refugees who arrive at the border of a country that is party to the 1951 Geneva Convention have a right to be admitted and given sanctuary. If they are granted admission as refugees, much of their uncertainty is reduced; however, this is not usually the case. According to this protocol and its 1967 amendment, a refugee is an individual who:

> owing to well-founded fear of being persecuted for reasons of race, religion, nationality, membership of a particular social group or political opinion, is outside the country of his nationality and is unable or, owing to such fear, is unwilling to avail himself of the protection of that country; or who, not having a nationality and being outside the country of his former habitual residence, is unable or, owing to such fear, is unwilling to return to it. [Article 1A(2)].

The convention also identifies refugees' obligations to their host governments. Initially, the convention was set up to mainly protect European refugees in the aftermath of World War II; however, the 1967 protocol expanded the scope of the convention as displacement became more and more widespread the world over. It should be noted that according to the United Nations High Commissioner for Refugees (UNHCR), by the end of 2017, 68.5 million individuals were forcibly displaced the world over as a result of 'persecution, conflict, violence or human rights violations'. This includes:

- 25.4 million refugees in the world—the highest ever seen;
- 40 million internally displaced people; and
- 3.1 million asylum seekers.

According to Berry et al. (1992), 'most refugees live with the knowledge that "push factors" (rather than "pull factors") led them to flee their homeland and settle in their new society' (p. 349). Further, most refugees have experienced extremely traumatic events and have lost family members, as well as material possessions. As per the 1951 Convention outlined previously, refugees are in danger of conflict or persecution, which is not usually the case for all migrants. Legal rights have been defined for refugees, whereas no such rights have been outlined for migrants. Again, evidences of vulnerability are everywhere within the narrative of refugees and their circumstances. But what do we really mean when we say vulnerability? How are refugees vulnerable?

Refugees: A Vulnerable Group

Vulnerability is defined as an individual, group or system's capacity to 'anticipate, cope with, resist, and recover from' the impact of a disruption or adverse event (Blaikie et al., 1994). Further, Guidry-Grimes and Victor (2015) explain that a person is vulnerable when he/she is 'in a position which threatens the holistic person as an agent for developing and achieving the most fundamental dimensions of well-being'. They also explain that vulnerability can be caused or in fact worsened by 'both internal and external variables including, but not limited to, a person's mental state, economic independence, political standing, physical security, or physical health'. In this sense, a refugee is especially vulnerable, given that they have little economic independence as they are dependent on the country of asylum for everything, and nor do they have any political standing to speak of. Looking at it from a larger perspective, vulnerability, even if understood in terms of disasters and crises, is never purely the result of natural processes but rather is a social product (O'Keefe et al., 1976), with social outcomes. The very fact that recent theory includes considerations of physical vulnerability—environmental and geographic conditions—and social vulnerability—the historic, sociocultural, economic, political and other conditions that structure adaption and coping for individuals and societies (Cardona, 2003)—is indicative of the vast applicability of vulnerability and its consequent relationship with refugees. Adger (2006) emphasizes some key parameters that are helpful and crucial for understanding vulnerability, such as exposure to external stresses or perturbation, sensitivity to these stresses and the capacity to adapt to and/or cope with perturbation and external stresses. As a refugee, an individual is constantly confronted by external stresses more than anyone else. These constant experiences of stress and anxiety certainly make the refugee highly vulnerable. In addition, the lack of documentation is a critical concern and can make refugees even more susceptible to disadvantage and negative experiences. However, since it is critical to understand the kinds of factors that make refugees particularly vulnerable, the following section illuminates the refugee experience with a specific emphasis on their vulnerability.

Blended Vulnerabilities

Many of the factors that make refugees vulnerable are the same for any other population, such as age, mental health, gender, socio-economic status and health. However, the crucial point in this discussion is the fact that the degree of vulnerability is much more for a refugee who is already surrounded by uncertainty regarding all his/her circumstances. It is an unfortunate fact that these various vulnerabilities do not occur in isolation. It is very possible that there may be many factors that make an individual even more vulnerable than others. For example, a young child may have a physical disability, or an older person may have a mental illness. These blends of various factors occur very frequently and should be noted as factors leading to additional vulnerabilities within a refugee. Some of the key factors that contribute to blended vulnerabilities are the age and physical and mental health of a refugee.

Age of a Refugee

The two ends of the age spectrum are of most relevance here, that is, children and adolescents (under 18), and older people (above 60).

1. **Children and adolescents:** According to UNHCR (2002; Westermeyer, 1991), approximately half of the world's 20 million refugees are children. They are an extremely vulnerable group, who are also prioritized for resettlement by the UNHCR resettlement categories, due to the high-risk nature of their vulnerability.
2. **Older people:** According to the World Health Organization (WHO), the definition of an older person is a person over 60 years old. Further, according to the UNHCR Policy on Older Refugees (2000), this group makes up a large proportion of the UNHCR caseload. It is also commonly assumed that 'older people are more likely to choose to stay in their place of origin, or, more tragically still, to perish in flight or to pine away and die in exile' (preliminary observations of the UNHCR Policy on Older Refugees, 2000). This policy also notes that older refugees make up 8.5 per cent of the overall population of concern to UNHCR, and the figure can be more than 30 per cent for some. It is also interesting to note that the majority of older refugees are women.

Mental Health of a Refugee

Very many studies have been done on the mental health of refugees over a period of time, in attempts to explore the impact of being a refugee on the individual's mental health. Trauma was considered a particularly relevant variable in this regard. Holtz (1998) conducted a study on 70 Tibetan refugees, of which 35 had experienced torture in Tibet and 35 whohad not been arrested, living in India. He administered the Hopkins Symptom Checklist-25, which assessed anxiety, affective disturbances, social impairment and somatic complaints. It was found that the torture survivors had a higher proportion of elevated anxiety scores as compared to the non-tortured control group. This study by Holtz (1998) emphasizes the long-term consequences of trauma and torture on mental health beyond the pre-existing effects of being uprooted, fleeing one's country and living in exile. This study additionally found that social support and prior preparedness, as well as political commitment, appeared to foster resilience in the group. The author further elaborated upon the highly effective role of Buddhism and spirituality in developing coping mechanisms and resilience in the group of Tibetan refugees.

Persons with Disabilities

The physical health of a refugee is a factor crucial to consider for this discussion. Pre-existing physical disabilities of an individual make them vulnerable no matter what their situation may be. Further, in the situation of a refugee, their life is already very difficult due to dangerous circumstances and fear of persecution. For a person with disability, this exponentially increases the issues faced. Thus, a person with disability is extremely vulnerable, and a refugee with disability even more so.

In addition to all these factors that make a refugee vulnerable, one key factor is the very 'label of being a refugee'. For an individual who was a permanent citizen with material and non-material possessions, a life, a career and a family to now become a refugee, to be 'called' a refugee, can be an extremely traumatic experience as well. Zetter (1991) has commented extensively on this topic, emphasizing the vulnerability of refugees to such imposed labels and, further, the powerlessness of the refugees themselves in this process of labelling.

Keeping in mind the above-mentioned notions of vulnerability, the following section elaborates the vulnerability in the refugee experience through the exemplar of the Tibetan refugees, describing the background of this population and their specific experiences.

RESILIENT REFUGEES: THE CASE OF THE TIBETAN REFUGEES

Approximately 70 years ago, in 1949, People's Republic of China started moving its troops into Tibet. As a result of this act of war, and the consequent imprisonment, labour camps and executions (and other equally appalling actions), approximately 1.2 million Tibetans died in

Tibet. The Dalai Lama attempted but was unable to find a peaceful solution to the violence, and his personal security was threatened. His call for help to the international community went unheeded, and His Holiness was forced to flee. The Dalai Lama's flight was followed by an exodus of Tibetan people unable to live under Chinese oppression. India granted refuge to the Dalai Lama when he fled Tibet in 1959 and permitted him to set up a government in exile in Dharamshala. Approximately 80,000 Tibetans followed His Holiness and fled to India (the first wave), with a steady flow filtering into India in the years that followed. According to the 2009 census of Tibet, up to 150,000 citizens were estimated to be living in exile. Now, after more than half a century of Chinese occupation, it is said that approximately 3,000 Tibetans continue to leave their homeland each year, undertaking the dangerous trek across the Himalayan mountains into Nepal and India (International Campaign for Tibet, 2006). Most of the people escaping from Tibet travel directly to Dharamshala, India, the seat of the Tibetan Government in Exile and Tibet's spiritual and political leader, the 14th Dalai Lama, before resettling in the surrounding regions. There are now even certain programmes and people in place to receive the people fleeing. According to a CTA (Central Tibetan Administration) survey in 2009, 127,935 Tibetans were registered as living outside of Tibet, with India hosting the largest number (94,203) of refugees.

How have they managed in these 70 years? In terms of vulnerability, the Tibetans did not know the language being spoken in India, were not accustomed to the climate and the geography and were also unfamiliar with the food! At a very fundamental level then, the Tibetans were and still are at a huge disadvantage. Such difficulties make it extremely tough for one to get a job to support oneself and one's family under normal circumstances, and even more so under circumstances wherein one is a refugee. Today, there are more than three generations of Tibetan refugees living in India across approximately 39 settlements. They have certainly identified strategies to overcome their disadvantage in order to survive and, in fact, to thrive. The Tibetans present a case of resilience and the ability of a human being to come through difficult circumstances successfully. There are myriad sources of the vulnerability faced by refugees, which is certainly faced by the Tibetans as well, but as a population that has lived successfully, and peacefully, in settlements for the past 70 years, the Tibetan-refugee story can certainly be considered a success story.

Today, there are many non-governmental organizations (NGOs) and Tibetan organizations that support this population and create opportunities for them. Very many schools have been built which teach the Tibetan culture and its rich history as an attempt to preserve the culture in exile. There is a Tibetan Government in Exile, installed purely for the benefit of the Tibetan people, in order to take decisions and create better opportunities for Tibetans as a people. Although the Tibetans went through enormous amounts of trauma and extremely difficult situations, theirs is a success story to be proud of. Of course, their journey is not over, as for a refugee there is always the hope to go back home. This is a very real and tangible feeling among the Tibetans, and they are always up for the cause of Tibet, fighting to go back home; after all, it is infinitely preferable to be a Tibetan in Tibet than be a Tibetan anywhere else. Considering this background, the next segment describes a study that was conducted among Tibetan refugees seeking to understand identity and acculturation. The study is described in a fair bit of detail, with a specific emphasis on the vulnerabilities that emerged through the narratives obtained.

Exploring Acculturation and Identity Concerns: An Intergenerational Study of Tibetan Refugees Living in Delhi

A study was done by Ramanathan and Babu (2018), the primary focus of which was to explore issues regarding identity and the process of acculturation among Tibetan refugees living in Delhi, across three generations of the refugees. The study aimed to explore the social and ethnic identity and its impact on the personal/psychological identity of the population in question. The possibility of a balance between identities in the form of a bicultural, multifaceted identity was investigated. The study also explored the level and intensity of acculturation (with reference to the model by Berry [1980]). The main catchment area was Majnu-ka-tilla, a Tibetan colony located within Delhi. In-depth, semi-structured interviews were conducted with three groups of participants divided as per their age. A thematic analysis (Braun & Clarke, 2006) was then done to analyse the data. Although the emphasis of this study was different, many instances of vulnerability (as discussed previously) emerged. The study showed that the experiences vary across age groups, highlighting the importance of exploring the notion of age. It was also found that vulnerability is not just the factors listed earlier; for the Tibetans, their very identity emerged as a kind of vulnerability. What are these vulnerable identities? How do we understand them, particularly in the context of Tibetan refugees?

According to Joseph Thompson, co-founder of AID: Tech (a software company dealing exclusively in digital identities), refugees in long-lasting dire straits are particularly vulnerable in terms of their identity. He articulates that 'not only do refugees need to reformulate their personal identity to secure a sense of belonging, but also it's imperative from a legal, social, and political perspective'. The complexity of this situation becomes self-evident then, considering the myriad refugee experiences across the world and the situation of these refugees in the various countries. In today's world, improper identity documentation can be a very significant avenue for disadvantage. In addition, according to Currion (2018), 'the individual is "born" into a new life as a refugee, often with little continuity between the new life and the old'. Being born into a life, it is of utmost importance to have documentation for the same; however, if the documents are lost or destroyed, the element of rebirth takes on a new meaning, as a refugee must make great efforts in order to either re-establish their old identity or create a new one in their new environment. For instance, in the study conducted, a 38-year-old participant who was born in India, when asked about documentation, shared the following:

I: so, uhh...what about any documentation? Do you have any documentation, like for example something which states that you have refugee status or something?

I2: no nono. See even, even Indian government don't recognise as a refugee....

I2: = Indian government is...you know Tibetans are not a refugee. Tibetans are foreigners.

I: okay. They're not a refugee. They're foreigners?

I1: yes yes

I2: if they recognise us as a refugee and give us refugee status, they have to give us [I1: every facilities] every facilities.. that refugees get…so… the Indian government they cannot give us [I1: recognise us] give us all the facilities..

I: so as foreigners, what, what is it that you get access to and what is it that you don't get access to? Is there a, is there a limitation?

I1: we have, we have a…we are holding a RC. [I: okay] RC is residential certificate. [I1: hmm]. So we have to renew it [I1: every year] we have to renew it every year…we have to go to FRO and extend it every year. [I1: future also]

This narrative gives a glimpse into the effort that goes into the establishment of a new identity. The vulnerability of the participant is also evident in this conversation, as he shares that he must 'renew' his old identity every year. On the other hand, the Indian state has a provision in place for providing citizenship to Tibetan refugees; however, many Tibetans have chosen not to take up this offer, despite the potential advantages it may bring. In this sense then, they would rather make the effort to re-establish their old identity rather than carve a new identity for themselves. This is just one example of the experiences of refugees, and the following section discusses their experience of vulnerability through three stages, attempting to highlight the significant issues in each.

UNDERSTANDING REFUGEE VULNERABILITY THROUGH THREE STAGES OF THE REFUGEE EXPERIENCE

According to Lustig et al. (2004) and Gonsalves (1992), there are three broad stages of refugee experience, each of which come with their own sets of issues and vulnerabilities; these are the pre-flight, flight and resettlement stages. The authors further suggest, citing Fazel and Stein (2002) and Papadopoulos (2001), that 'among refugees, four broad responses to the stressful experiences have been described: anticipation, devastating events, survival, and adjustment', which fit into the three phases previously mentioned. Although the authors talk primarily about children, adults also experience being a refugee across similar stages and are vulnerable to a different set of issues at each stage. The following sections describe each of these three stages in more detail, also substantiating the literature with evidence from the Tibetan refugee population.

Refugee Vulnerability: Pre-flight Stage

The pre-flight stage describes the time before an individual escapes from his/her country of origin. In this phase, according to Rumbaut (1991), refugees face plenty of social upheavals and increasing amounts of chaos and strife in and around their home. The children have limited access to schools, which disrupts their education and social development. Adults are unable to go to work and are often forced to quit their jobs, which leads to a decrement in their financial status and paucity in the resources available for the family. Elderly refugees are unable to access appropriate healthcare, leading to difficulties of another nature. Lustig et al. (2004) further remark that at the family and individual levels, refugees face threats to their safety and to that of their family members, which leads to increases in stress levels and anxiety. Lustig et al. (2004) propose that before their flight, refugees anticipate and then are eventually forced to cope with the devastating events they are confronted by. In this pre-flight stage, refugees may witness and/or engage in violence, further leading to depletion in their mental health.

Many studies indicate the harrowing experiences undergone by children who have not been able to flee as yet and are surviving in their current circumstances. A study by Boothby (1994) found that in Mozambique, 77 per cent of around 500 children surveyed had witnessed murders or mass killings. Another study by Kinzie et al. (1986) found that among a sample of 40 adolescent Cambodian refugees who had survived 4 years in a so-called work camp, 98 per cent were forced into labour, 90 per cent lived in camps, segregated by age, and 83 per cent lacked sufficient food for long periods of time. This is just a small example of the kind of turbulence experienced by refugee children. Of course, it is important to note that these are the children who were unable to escape from their circumstances and were still in a situation that was fraught with peril for them. Also, in these situations, the children were separated from their caregivers, for one reason or another, and thus forced to undergo such brutal conditions. Further, it is evident that these children were obviously not going to school. In the pre-flight situation, often, the country of origin, or the homes of refugee children, is extremely dangerous for the children. Thus, they are often unable to even step out of their homes, much less live a life close to normal. Additionally, the experience of combat is also unfortunately common among refugee children before or during the flight stage. According to an article in a website on child soldiers (2001), an estimated 300,000 children have participated in armed conflicts around the world, and many more are enrolled in the armed forces in countries not presently facing conflict. Some participants of the study shared that due to the dangerous situation, while planning to flee, they were often troubled by thoughts of their young children and struggled to plan how they would flee. Thus, it is difficult for young children to handle the situation at hand, because they may be unable to grasp the seriousness of the circumstances due to their age and their parents may be either unavailable or unable to explain it to them.

The pre-flight stage is no less traumatic for the elderly, who are also extremely vulnerable to the pre-flight stress. An older person would have spent essentially all their life in the context that they were living in. Having to uproot themselves from a place that was their home, where they grew up and made a life for themselves is an extremely taxing and traumatic experience. According to WHO, individuals who are aged 60 and above are considered as older or elderly people. Along with this age comes myriad problems, of which health problems and lack of financial resources are just two, with cognitive decline and serious, debilitating health issues being much further down the line. In the pre-flight stage, an older refugee must first get into a frame of mind wherein he/she understands that it is no longer safe to life in their home of many decades. Often, elderly people may not consent to leave their home, either for sentimental or for health-related concerns. Once a decision to move is arrived at, the packing and assembling of a life's worth of possessions must be done. Often there is no time to do so, and they must pick up whatever they can in a very short span of time. For the elderly, it is thus a very traumatic experience to leave behind an established life, family, culture and memories in search of a safe haven. Some participants in the present study shared that often, they were unable to bring their parents with them while attempting to escape, due to the latter's age and physical limitations; thus, the pre-flight stage is fraught with difficulties for elderly refugees.

The third refugee group that is extremely vulnerable consists of people having a pre-existing mental or physical disability. When one thinks of refugees, often one does not consider how hard it is for someone with a mental or physical disorder to make the transition from their hometown to a resettlement camp. Not much research has been conducted on such refugees either. In the pre-flight scenario, depending on the severity of their disorder, it is often very difficult to explain to the individual in question that there is a need to escape from their country of origin. Such individuals are often unable to understand the seriousness of the situation and thus are unable to escape the unpleasant outcomes associated with not removing oneself from the situation at hand. Also, it must be noted that an individual with a physical disability is sometimes unable to remove himself/herself from the situation due to the nature of the disability.

In the context of Tibetan refugees, the pre-flight stage was no less a struggle, as is observed from the journey of a 70-year-old man who escaped from Tibet and came to India in 1959, who also shared some of his experiences in Tibet:

G: *tibet se aaya that to usi time mein China ka kabza tha ussi time mein...*[I came from Tibet, at that time China had occupied Tibet]

...

G: *wahan toh humare mei china aayatha, sab tang karta that, sab ko tang karta tha, koi koi log paisa de nhi rha tha unko toh tang krta hi rehta tha uska baad fir 59 mein phir maa baap ne fir le gya tha ussi ne... pata nhi tha na kya... kya... darr se wahan se nikal lia tha...* [China had come there and they would trouble everyone. If people didn't give money they would trouble them. After 1959 my mother and father were scare so they took me out of there then]

I: *haan... haan... acha... toh aap fir 59 mein kaise aae aap?* [okay so how did you come here in 1959]

G: *paidal hi aae the* [we came walking]

...

G: *raat ko gaya, din ko soya, raat ko nikla din ko soya raat ko nikla... raat ko nathu la mein pohoch gaya mein... fir border haina china ka border pohoch jaate na fir wahan se india govt ne entry kar dia...* [we came in the night, slept during the day. Reached Nathula at night, then when we reached the china border, we entered India from there. The Indian govt gave us entry]

I: *acha toh apko yaad hai voh matlab voh kaise travel kiya tha Tibet se?* [okay so you remember how you travelled from Tibet?]

G: *ha wahan se to pure raat ko chalet rhe chalet rhe the napta nhi tha na kahi baraf tha bilkul jungle jungle se nilkte niklte karib 15 din karib laga hoga. Khana khana toh bahut mushkil hai...* [yes, we used to walk the whole night and we did not know where we would find snow or jungles... we walked through everything for about 15 days.. food was very difficult to find]

I: ha ha

G: *aur khana lene jaega to fir bago mein jana pdhta fir wahan pe china ki china ka aadmi tha... pakad lega badhi mushkil si thi* [to look for food we had to go into the forests and there were Chinese soldiers there... if they caught us it would be very difficult]

These experiences show a glimpse of the hard times that some of these people have gone through. This is part of the personal struggle of their lives and the thoughts and experiences they went through while taking the decision to flee and escape persecution.

Refugee Vulnerability: Flight Stage

In this stage, according to Lustig et al. (2004), 'refugees must survive displacement from their homes and transit or transitional placements (e.g., refugee camps) amid great uncertainty about the future' (p. 25). In such a scenario, the refugees are at the mercy of the destination country or the available camp resources in order to meet their basic needs, and they evaluate the alternatives available to them. They often have no idea about how long this transitional phase would last, and in fact refugees often spend many years in refugee camps. Jobs are few and far in between, and children, adults and the elderly are all equally affected, though in a variety of ways. Children often get separated from their caregivers, causing depression and anxiety in the adults and developmental delays and reduction in access to education for the children.

The flight stage is full of turmoil for a refugee child. The two key events that lead to vulnerabilities in refugee children are their separation from their caregivers and temporary placement in refugee camps. The impact of separation from caregivers on children has been extensively explored. Researchers have also noted the relatively greater impact of war-related separation between children and their parents than that of separation due to exposure to war-related atrocities (Freud & Burlingham, 1943). Often, due to war-/strife-related atrocities, whole villages/cities are wiped out, leaving just a few survivors; often, these are children without their caregivers. Sometimes, unsafe circumstances at home or the locality may also lead to separation. Parents may also send their children to safety, rather than themselves, again leading to separation between the two. A study by Loughry and Flouri (2001) compared 455 unaccompanied Vietnamese refugee children in camps in Hong Kong and Southeast Asia to a matched sample of local children who had never left Vietnam, on their internalizing and externalizing behaviours and perceived self-efficacy. The unaccompanied minors had lower scores on externalizing behaviours when compared to the local children. Sourander (1998) further studied unaccompanied minors and found that younger children displayed more behavioural problems and emotional distress than older children/adolescents. These studies imply that refugee children are especially vulnerable, and care must be taken to ensure their development and well-being. In terms of refugee camps, Harrel-Bond (2000) poignantly describes the harrowing experiences a refugee may go through while in a camp. She explains that refugee camps are ' "total institutions," places where…the inhabitants are depersonalized and where people become numbers without names'. Often, camps do not have access to proper water, food and similar essential resources, which leads to difficulties for the refugees living in them. Children in particular are especially vulnerable, as they are in a crucial period of growth and development and require adequate and appropriate food and nutrition. Schooling is another concern, and often refugee children lose out on their education, as they have higher priorities than education, such as food, water and shelter.

For the elderly as well, the flight stage is very difficult. For an individual over 60 years of age to be able to reach a resettlement camp is a tough task in itself. The transition from a permanent citizen to a refugee is also psychologically damaging. Further, in the flight stage, there is often a separation of family members, leading to other difficulties, such as an older person being left without their caretaker who is familiar with their needs. Once an elderly individual arrives at a refugee camp, it is difficult for them to find a place to live temporarily till they find a relatively more permanent place to stay. Further, some older people require a lot of assistance, and this is something they may not find in a temporary lodging like a refugee camp. The other issue that often comes up is that of finances. Older people are not usually financially solvent, particularly those who are seeking refuge from a war-stricken or otherwise-difficult situation. This makes the matter more difficult, especially as older people often have serious, life-threatening health concerns and require regular medication for the same. Such medication may not be easily available in the temporary lodging they are at. Some participants in the present study shared that when they fled from Tibet in 1959, some of them had to bring their elderly parents along with them, and they carried them through the mountains, as the elders were unable to walk for such a long distance. In this sense then, the experiences of the elderly are more complex and make them more vulnerable.

It is similarly difficult for a disabled individual to successfully flee from a situation of strife and war. Two groups are discussed in this section: people with mental disorders and people with physical disabilities. For people with mental disorders, it is almost essential to travel with a caretaker, which is often not the case, as there are many separations that occur during flight. An individual with a mental disorder is often unable to make it to a safe haven, due to lack of support in reaching there. For the ones that do make it, life is extremely difficult, as they suffer from many conditions requiring active and lifelong medication, which is frequently unavailable in refugee camps. Further, poor mental health conditions can get exacerbated by lack of social support, familiarity and comfort, which can be provided by family members or close friends but most of whom are generally nowhere to be found due to the circumstances of the escape and arrival at the refugee camp. For people with physical disabilities, the situation is equally difficult, as they too require a caretaker or some kind of constant support in order to reach a refugee camp. Many other individuals may not be available or interested or able to help out, which would certainly reduce this individual's chances of reaching a safe haven successfully. Further, at the camp, such individuals might require additional support and resources that may not be available at the camp. Another issue relates to the carrying of personal belongings; such individuals, due to the nature of their disability, might find it difficult to carry personal effects, leading them to discard the latter, which may cause trauma of a different kind altogether.

For the Tibetan refugee population, the flight stage was very difficult as well. As is evidenced from some of the narratives obtained during the study, the participants experienced a great struggle during their flight to India. A 73-year-old participant who came to India in 1960 shared the following:

> N: *aane ke time toh musibat mei aaaya na, humara apna desh chorh karke fir aaya na, samaan lekar aaya hai paidal aaya hai ghar milta nhi hai.. aise aise krte krte Nepal se hokaraayahai.* [it was very difficult when we came.. we had left our country.. brought our luggage and come walking not knowing whether we will find a place to stay.. slowly we walked and eventually came through Nepal.]

> I: *acha...* [alright]

> N: *Nepal mei 1 saal baitha hai* (I: hmm... hmm) *fir humare guruji ka kripa se letter dia ke india mei chorh do, fir hum log india mei aaya. Fir india mei aaya pehle wahan pathankot... pathankot aap janta hai na? Himachal ke neeche hai mein hai... idhar hi hai* [we stayed for 1 year in Nepal, then thanks to the blessings of our Guru (His Holiness the Dalai Lama), we were sent a letter allowing us into India. Then we came into India, we went first to Pathankot, you know Pathankot right?]

Another participant, a 65-year-old female, shared the following:

Hum to paidal aaye the 2 km–3km chalet chalet khana khuni ke liye ek baksa, peeth mein uthake, fir zyada hoega fir thoda aage pohocha do fir uthakar le aao aise aise uss time par huat ha. Uss time mein ma baap buzurg tha na ab hum log thoda jawan tha.. utha sakta tha jo kapde wagaira toh 1–2-km uthakar ek do km aage gaya, samaan rakha, fir dusra samaan lene gaya... vo buzurg log the na sath mei aayatha. Raste mei agar joota fatt gya toh kuch nhi hai... [we came walking... we walked for 2–3 km at a time and carried a box on our backs for food... we would carry a box for 2–3 km, set it down, then carry it again... that's how it was at that time.. we were young but we had elderly parents at that time... we could lift the heavy boxes... so we would carry one box full of clothes etc for 1- km, set it down, then go back and bring the other boxful... our elderly parents came with us.. if our shoe broke on the way nothing could be done...]

These narratives demonstrate the great struggle and strife experienced by this particular population in their attempt to escape persecution. It is important to acknowledge these experiences and note how far the Tibetans have come, from being the nomads who escaped to achieving their current status of a well-established and resilient refugee population. These excerpts bring us closer to their hardships but also throw light upon their ability to bounce back and survive despite all odds.

Refugee Vulnerability: Resettlement Stage

Once a refugee arrives at the country of destination, also called the host country, he/she has to wade through a whole new world, often navigating through a new language, culture, customs and belief systems (Papadopoulos, 2001). Family roles and patterns are often disrupted by resettlement, and resettlement in turn disrupts such roles and patterns (Foner, 1997). Children may find it easier to acclimatize to the new environment due to their faster development and ability to acquire language and belief systems. Coll and Magnuson (1997) suggest that children may even act as 'cultural liaisons' for the older refugees. This phase also involves acculturation, as described by Williams and Berry (1991), which occurs in four phases, namely contact, conflict, crisis and, ultimately, adaptation. Acculturative stress is one key struggle at this stage of the refugee experience.

At the resettlement stage, children are extremely vulnerable, because, as mentioned previously, many of them are separated from their primary caregivers and have to adjust to a life without that support. Further, it is a difficult task to decide whom to trust with your own well-being and to assess whether someone has your best interests at heart or not. According to Berry (1991), resettlement systems are underlined by the loss of a homeland, family, friends and possessions, as well as by being faced with the challenge of a new culture. Many refugees hope for a safer and more prosperous and fortunate life in the destination country, which, according to Keyes (2000), may 'initially offset losses and temporarily postpone grief'. According to Tobin and Friedman (1984), for refugee children, resettlement is more difficult, as they are torn between the culture of their homeland (as they or their parents remember it), the culture of the new country and also the prevalence of a refugee culture within the resettlement camp.

In this resettlement phase, the elderly also face a lot of difficulties. It is a well-documented fact that it is difficult for older people to pick up new languages and gain a strong handle on them. Thus, for an older refugee, resettlement is a big problem, especially when he/she is confronted by a completely new culture, new language and a new way of being, and he/she does not know how to adapt to the new situation. In this regard, children are relatively better off, as they are more resilient and able to acquire newer cultures fast. The other problem faced by older people in the resettlement phase is that of finances. Older people are usually retired and have little to no access to money, especially when carrying a refugee status. The latter makes their life even more difficult, as they are dependent on the destination country for resources and also require caretakers for healthcare assistance. Finances are a serious concern, as older people usually have lifelong health concerns whose treatment is often expensive. Also, families are often separated, and the consequent lack of social support is often very traumatic for elderly individuals as well. This results in older refugees being left at care homes, as they are often too old to gain access to jobs.

It is also a complicated process to resettle persons with disabilities and those with mental illnesses. Again, they too require much support and often also require round-the-clock care, which is difficult to procure in a resettlement situation. Further, if the severity of their illness is high, they may not be able to find jobs, which puts an additional financial strain on their already-finite resources. It is already difficult for a person with disability or mental illness to mingle with the larger society, due to pre-existing taboos and negative perceptions, and the label of being a refugee is an additional burden for such an individual.

The Tibetan refugees have also experienced difficulties in resettlement and issues when trying to earn money. A 65-year-old female participant who came to India in 1959 along with her aged parents shared the following:

I2: *pehle toh yahan aesa pakka ghar nahi hota tha...* [I: *acha...*] *pehle sab jhopdi hota tha...* but Tibetans, they know how to make money... so... within few years... you know, they make money, they build houses... now all over you can see, all over you can see they build, they build big buildings... [earlier we did not have permanent houses like these, earlier it was all temporary houses and shanties]

I: hmm... so initially how did they make money? Like you were saying woollen clothing...?

I2: yes. Yes. See, woollen clothing is very seasonal. It's a season business.

I: hmm yeah it's a seasonal business.

I2: only in winter they can make good money. On that season in December. Only in Tibetans, most of Tibetan people they went so far. Like if I stay in Delhi, I could go to Calcutta for the winter season ... and ... some you know ... as I told you many of the guest houses, and hotels, many of them are run by monasteries. It's like they're fund, uhh, fundraisers or something... [I: hmm yeah] and all the money... it go to the monasteries ... so like that ... monasteries build the hotel and they make the money... and give back to monastery ... their rooms are cheap ... rooms are easily available ... are good...

From this exchange, one gets an understanding of the vulnerability experienced by the Tibetans. Resettlement is a tough phase for these refugees; however, as is evidenced by the number of Tibetan refugee settlements in India (39, major and minor settlements), this group seem resilient. It is evident that that they have been able to create a space where they can sustain for a while. Many Tibetan schools also exist, called Tibetan Children's Villages (TCV) schools, where the students learn based on a Tibet-specific curriculum, while also studying the basic subjects required. In this sense then, the resilience of this group is remarkable. Although it is not in the purview of this chapter to do so, it must be noted that the resilience of the Tibetan refugees is extraordinary. As has been evidenced in the excerpts and the study discussed through the chapter, it is exceptional to note how this group have survived since they fled from Tibet in 1959. Perhaps, future studies can endeavour to explore their experiences in more detail, in order to understand their resilience and how it came about.

CONCLUSION

What does it mean to be a Tibetan refugee? What role does vulnerability play in being a refugee? This chapter opens a small window into the lives of hundreds of Tibetan refugees residing everywhere but in Tibet. Some of these excerpts display their vulnerability, indicating to the world the need to acknowledge refugees as a vulnerable group requiring specific attention. This chapter describes the experiences of Tibetans and throws light upon their vulnerability, in a bid to highlight their specific issues and the need to attend to these. It is important to understand where their vulnerability lies in order to work towards its amelioration. The chapter notes the specific definition of refugees as given by the UNHCR, displaying the attention to detail when it comes to refugees. It further identifies the concept of blended vulnerabilities, explaining that while there are certain groups within refugees who are more at risk, such as children, the elderly, people with mental illnesses and people with physical disabilities, such vulnerabilities often occur in tandem with one another. It must, however, be observed that research in these specific domains has been limited. The chapter also describes a study done in this area, with Tibetan refugees, seeking to understand the challenges faced by them. Although the primary objective of the study was not to specifically explore vulnerability, it established that the experiences of vulnerability vary depending upon the age of refugees. This chapter explores the study more thoroughly, through the lens of vulnerability, and displays that variations in vulnerability depend not just upon age but also upon the stage of the refugee experience. What has emerged eventually is a comprehensive idea of the refugee experience, explored through the exemplar of the Tibetan refugee population.

The chapter also notes that vulnerability is not a static or unchangeable parameter; refugees, and in fact everyone, pass through phases wherein they are more or less vulnerable. The current scenario depicts Tibetan refugees as the 'ideal' [sic] refugee population, as they seem to have adapted fairly well to their circumstances; however the excerpts in the chapter depict their vulnerabilities and the hardships they have faced. In this sense, one may note that they have become resilient and have confronted their vulnerabilities well. This is perhaps an interesting and important avenue for future research: how can vulnerability transform into resilience? This line of thought also lends hope to refugees of ameliorating their situation. It is however an undeniable fact that all refugees are vulnerable, and this situation must be addressed with haste.

We are refugees here.

People of a lost country.

Citizen to no nation. (excerpt from "My Tibetanness"; Tsundue, 2010, p. 13)

REFERENCES

Adger, W. N. (2006). Vulnerability. *Global Environmental Change, 16*(3), 268–281.

Ager, A. (1999). Perspectives on the refugee experience. In A. Ager (Ed.), *Refugees: Perspectives on the experience of forced migration* (pp. 1–23). Pinter.

Ahmed, S. (1999). Home and away: Narratives of migration and estrangement. *International Journal of Cultural Studies, 2*(3), 329–347.

Berry, J. W. (1980). Acculturation as varieties of adaptation. In A. M. Padilla (Ed.), *Acculturation: Theory, models and some new findings* (pp. 9–25). Westview.

Berry, J. W. (1991). Understanding and managing multiculturalism: Some possible implications of research in Canada. *Psychology and Developing Societies, 3*(1), 17–49. https://doi.org/10.1177/097133369100300103

Berry, J., Poortinga, Y., Segall, M., & Dasen, P. (1992). *Cross cultural psychology: Research and applications.* Cambridge University Press.

Bittenbinder, E. (2010). *Good practice in the care of victims of torture.* von Loeper Literaturverlag.

Blaikie, P., Cannon T., Davis I., & Wisner, B. (1994). *At risk: Natural hazards, people's vulnerability, and disasters.* Routledge.

Boothby, N. (1994). Trauma and violence among refugee children. In A. Marsella, S. Bornemann, J. Ekblad, & J. Orley (Eds.), *Amidst peril and pain: The mental health and well-being of the world's refugees.* American Psychological Association.

Braun, V., & Clarke, V. (2006). Using thematic analysis in psychology. *Qualitative Research in Psychology, 3*(2), 77–101. https://doi.org/10.19744/j.cnki.11-1235/f.2006.09.027

Cardona, O. D. (2003). The need for rethinking the concepts of vulnerability and risk from a holistic perspective: A necessary review and criticism for effective risk management. In G. Bankoff, G. Frerks, & D. Hilhorst (Eds.), *Mapping vulnerability: Disasters, development and people* (p. 17). Earthscan.

Child Soldiers. (2001). *About child soldiers: Questions and answers.* http://www.child-soldiers.org

Coll, C. G., & Magnuson, K. (1997). The psychological experience of immigration: A developmental perspective. In N. Landale (Ed.), *Immigration and the family: Research and policy on US immigrants* (pp. 91–131). Erlbaum.

Currion, P. (2018, March 14). *The refugee identity.* https://medium.com/caribou-digital/the-refugee-identity-bfc60654229a

Fazel, M., & Stein, A. (2002). The mental health of refugee children. *Archives of Disease in Childhood, 87,* 366–370.

Foner, N. (1997). The immigrant family: Cultural legacies and cultural changes. *International Migration Review, 31,* 961–974.

Freud, A., & Burlingham, D. T. (1943). *War and children.* Medical War Books.

Gonsalves, C. (1992). Psychological stages of the refugee process: A model for therapeutic interventions. *Professional Psychology: Research and Practice, 23*(5), 382–389.

Guidry-Grimes & Victor. (2015). *Mental illness and compounded vulnerability: Understanding compounded vulnerabilities.* https://guides.library.georgetown.edu/c.php?g=75563&p=490648

Harrel-Bond, B. (2000). *Are refugee camps good for children?* (Working Paper No. 29). New Issues in Refugee Research: UNHCR.

Holtz, T. (1998). Refugee trauma versus torture trauma: A retrospective controlled cohort study of Tibetan refugees. *The Journal of Nervous & Mental Disease, 186*(1), 24–34.

International Campaign for Tibet. (2006, September 11). *Refugee report: Dangerous crossing—2005 update.* https://savetibet.org/2005-refugee-report-dangerous-crossing-2005-update/

Keyes, E. F. (2000). Mental health status in refugees: An integrative review of current research. *Issues in Mental Health Nursing, 21*(4), 397–410. https://doi.org/10.1080/016128400248013

Kinzie, J. D., Sack, W. H., Angell, R. H., Manson, S., &, Rath, B. (1986). The psychiatric effects of massive trauma on Cambodian children: I. the children. *Journal of the American Academy of Child Psychiatry, 25*(3), 370–376. https://doi.org/10.1016/s0002-7138(09)60259-4.

Loughry, M., & Flouri, E. (2001). The behavioral and emotional problems of former unaccompanied refugee children 3–4 years after their return to Vietnam. *Child Abuse & Neglect, 25*(2), 249–263. https://doi.org/10.1016/S0145-2134(00)00240-4

Lustig, S. L., Kia-Keating, M., Knight, W. G., Geltman, P., Ellis, H., Kinzie, J. D., Keane, T., & Saxe, G. N. (2004). Review of child and adolescent refugee mental health. *Journal of the American Academy of Child & Adolescent Psychiatry, 43*(1), 24–36.

O'Keefe, P., Westgate, K., & Wisner, B. (1976). Taking the naturalness out of natural disasters. *Nature, 260,* 566–567.

Papadopoulos, R. (2001). Refugee families: Issues of systemic supervision. *Journal of Family Therapy, 23,* 405–422.

Ramanathan, P., & Babu, N. (2018). *Exploring notions of identity across generations in the Tibetan refugee population in Delhi* (Unpublished manuscript).

Rumbaut, R. (1991). The agony of exile: A study of the migration and adaptation of Indochinese refugee adults and children. In J. Athey (Ed.), *Refugee children: Theory research, and services* (pp. 53–91). Johns Hopkins Press.

Sourander, A. (1998). Behavior problems and traumatic events of unaccompanied refugee minors. *Child Abuse & Neglect, 22*(7), 719–727. https://doi.org/10.1016/s0145-2134(98)00053-2

Tobin, J. J., & Friedman, J. (1984). Intercultural and developmental stresses confronting Southeast Asian refugee adolescents. *Journal of Operational Psychiatry, 15,* 39–45.

Tsundue, T. (2010). 'My Tibetanness,' In T. Tsundue (Ed.), *Kora: Stories and poems* (6th ed., pp. 13). Tibet Writes.

UNHCR (date unknown). *The refugee convention, 1951.* https://www.unhcr.org/4ca34be29.pdf

UNHCR (date unknown). *Refugee statistics.* https://www.unrefugees.org/refugee-facts/statistics/

UNHCR. (2000). Policy on older refugees April 2000 (Annex II of the Draft Report of the Seventeenth Meeting of the Standing Committee [29 February–2 March 2000], EC/50/SC/CRP.13). UNHCR.

UNHCR. (2002). *Refugees by numbers*. http://www.unhcr.ch/cgi-bin/texis/vtx/ home/+cwwBmeLqZw_wwwwMwwwwwwwmFqtFEIfgIhFqoUflfRZ2It-Fqtxw5oq5zFqtFEIfgIAFqoUflfRZ2IDzmxwwwwwwww1FqtFEIfgI/opendoc. htm#World%20Refugee%20Overview.

Westermeyer, J. (1991). Psychiatric services for refugee children: An overview. In J. L. Athey (Ed.), *Refugee children: Theory, research, and services* (pp. 127–162). Johns Hopkins Series in Contemporary Medicine and Public Health. Johns Hopkins University Press.

Williams, C. L., & Berry, J. W. (1991). Primary prevention of acculturative stress among refugees: Application of psychological theory and practice. *American Psychologist, 46*, 632–641.

Zetter, R. (1991). Labelling refugees: Forming and transforming a bureaucratic identity. *Journal of Refugee Studies, 4*(1), 39–62.

Chapter 2

Growing Up Asian-Indian in USA
Identity Development and Psychosocial Adaptation

Revathy Kumar and Sarita V. Shukla

Culture provides the framework for our lives. It makes us who we are and is the prism through which we view the world and make sense of our experiences. Not surprisingly, therefore, cultural discrepancies between heritage and host cultures and inter-generational value discrepancies between parents and children play a significant role in shaping the lives of immigrant adolescents and youth (Suarez-Orozco & Suarez-Orozco, 2001). Attitudes and stereotypes associated with specific immigrant groups among members of the host society add another layer of complexity to the adjustment and acculturative efforts of immigrant first- and second-generation youth, living as they do in the contact zone of their home and host cultures (Sachdev & Bourhis, 1991; Schwartz, 2007; Ward, 2013). While these issues have been studied in depth among several immigrant groups in the United States, such as Latinx and other immigrants from South America, Chinese, Korean and Japanese from Asia and Arabs from the Arab nations in the Middle East, there is surprisingly little research involving the experiences of Asian-Indians in the United States. A search, based on keywords (ethnic/racial/national groups, immigrants to the United States, adolescence, adaptation), of the Psych Info database revealed that since the turn of the century, the number of peer-reviewed published articles regarding the experiences of Asian-Indians in the United States is a very small fraction of the number of research studies on Latinx (0.04) and Asian-American (0.12) adolescents. Indeed, relatively little is known about the Asian-Indian experience in the United States (Sheth, 1995).

Like most other immigrants, Asian-Indians also face the challenge of maintaining their cultural and personal integrity while at the same time fitting into the larger society. Even though the Asian-Indian population in the United States has doubled since 2000, with over 1.5 million adolescents and youth of Indian origin residing in the United States (Ruiz, 2018), Asian-Indians represent less than 1 per cent of the overall US population and likewise a very small percentage of the total student population in US schools and colleges. This is one of the reasons for the dearth of research on Asian-Indian adolescents' and youth's adjustment in the United States. If Asian-Indian adolescents and youth are at all included in research studies, they are either part of a very heterogeneous Asian/Asian-American sample or, as is customary in most studies, dumped into the 'Other' category. In this chapter we propose to utilize a mixed-method approach to highlight the experiences of a sample of Asian-Indian Hindu (AIH) adolescents reported in 2005 and the retrospective reflections from some of these adolescents on factors that helped or hindered their adjustment and identity development when they participated as young adults in a focus group interview in 2017.

This chapter examines the interplay of perceived risk and protective factors at home, school and the community (Garmezy & Masten, 1991; Kumar et al., 2012) and personal acculturative patterns that can potentially ameliorate or exacerbate AIH adolescents' and youth's (AIHA&Y's) experiences of cultural dissonance—the psychological cost associated with feeling caught between two cultures—marginalized, powerless and socially alienated (Rosenberg, 1962; Ward et al., 2001). As demonstrated in an earlier study with a culturally diverse sample, adolescents who experience cultural dissonance reported feeling angrier, were more self-deprecating, had lower self-esteem, were less hopeful about the future, felt less academically efficacious and had a lower GPA (grade point average) than adolescents who did not experience dissonance (Arunkumar [Kumar] et al., 1999). Because of poor intercultural adjustment, AIHA&Y may be vulnerable to the mental health problems like anxiety and poor emotion regulation (Buddington, 2002). Closely associated with problems of intercultural adjustment is their vulnerability to experiencing belonging uncertainty in school and social contexts where they are likely plagued by a sense of being the perpetual 'Other', of feeling that 'people like me do not belong here' (Walton & Cohen, 2007, p. 83). Therefore, the purpose of this chapter is to examine factors in different contexts—societal, home, community, school and peer—which function as risk and protective factors for AIHA&Y's experiences of cultural dissonance and development of a holistic sense of self and identity.

BOUNDARIES AND BORDERS BETWEEN ADOLESCENTS' MULTIPLE WORLDS

Working out of an anthropological framework, Phelan and her colleagues developed a typology to examine and interpret adolescents' perception of borders and boundaries between the different contexts of development, and the strategies adolescents employ to negotiate these borders daily. This model aims to examine how aspects of these different contexts, which the researchers refer to as 'multiple worlds', combine in the day-to-day lives of adolescents to affect their actions and interactions in the different settings. In their ethnographic work with high-school youth, these researchers (Phelan et al., 1994) examined how adolescents construe their realities as they navigate their way across their different social worlds.

The term 'boundary' refers to 'behavioral evidence of culturally different standards of appropriateness that are politically neutral' (Phelan et al., 1998, p. 10). Boundaries get transformed into borders when cultural differences are not politically neutral, and the knowledge, skills and behaviours in one context are more highly valued and rewarded than those in another (Erickson, 1993; Phelan et al., 1998). Based on their work, Phelan and her colleagues describe the psychosocial, sociocultural, socio-economic and structural borders that adolescents perceived between their worlds of home, school and peers. This model explains how adolescents' identities and feelings about the self are shaped and moulded as they negotiate the borders and boundaries between their multiple worlds (Davidson, 1996).

This typology describes four distinct patterns that adolescents employ as they make their transition between, and adapt to, different contexts. The first is 'congruent worlds/smooth transitions'. Here, moving from one setting to another is harmonious and uncomplicated, and commonalties override the differences between the worlds. These adolescents describe values, beliefs, expectations and normative ways of behaving as similar across their worlds. Moving from home to school, peers and society is harmonious and uncomplicated. Phelan et al. (1991) found that most of the adolescents who fell into this category were middle- to upper-middle-class European-Americans. Thus, for immigrants from European countries who feel welcome and accepted in the United States, assimilation into society and cultural integration occur with ease (Bourhis et al., 1997). The researchers also found some minority adolescents who described similarities in the sociocultural aspects of their worlds and found the transition from home to school smooth. The second pattern is 'different worlds/border crossing managed'. Here adolescents perceive differences in the values, beliefs and behaviours between contexts, but they utilize strategies that enable them to manage crossings successfully. From their ethnographic work on high-school adolescents, Phelan et al. (1998) learned that these adolescents too experience some pressures and stress that is not recognized by the adults in their school or at home. They found that high-achieving minority adolescents often fell into this category. The third pattern is 'different worlds/border crossing difficult'. Here the beliefs, values and expectations are different in the worlds that adolescents inhabit, and the latter find it difficult to reconcile the differences. Adolescents in this group are not able to master or learn or are not willing to adopt the strategies necessary for successful transition. They have trouble adjusting and reorienting as they move across the borders between the different worlds. The fourth pattern is 'different worlds/ border crossing resisted'. In this case, values, beliefs and expectations in the two worlds are so discordant that adolescents perceive the borders as insurmountable and actively or passively resist transitions. Phelan et al. (1991) found low-achieving, minority adolescents to be typical of this category. They also found some high-achieving adolescents who could not connect to their family or school falling into this category. The difference between the last two categories seems to be more a difference in the degree of difficulty in crossing and the extent of resistance to such transitions. This typology is particularly useful because it provides a broad and generic framework that encompasses societal and cultural processes, proximate social contexts and interactions therein to provide a comprehensive understanding of risk and protective factors that can aggravate or mitigate AIHA&Y's feelings of cultural dissonance to impede or help their adaptive acculturation as they traverse the boundaries between the home, societal, school and peer contexts in the United States. In short, boundary transitions and negotiations in the context of social and institutional relationships inform how AIHA&Y construct their identity (Davidson, 1996).

CONTEXTUAL RISK AND PROTECTIVE FACTORS

Bronfenbrenner (1979) proposes that the developing individual is embedded within a series of overlapping and intersecting contexts. Each context—for AIHA&Y these include the home, school/university, community and workplace—has a direct or an indirect effect on the nature and direction of development. Furthermore, the enveloping societal macrosystem exerts a profound influence on the nature of adolescents' phenomenological experiences across these multiple contexts (Bronfenbrenner, 2005). These experiences function as protective and/or risk factors to influence adolescents' developmental trajectories. In this section, therefore, we examine AIHA&Y's perceptions of specific home, school and community factors within the US societal context which function to ameliorate or exacerbate their feelings of cultural dissonance. This is important because adolescents' perceptions shape and mould their identity as they make sense of their world and whether and where they fit in, across the multiple and sometimes dissonant contexts.

THE UNITED STATES' SOCIETAL CONTEXT

It is telling that Schachter (2014) refers to Asian-Indians as 'foreigners forever'. Indeed, for the AIHA&Y, their distinctive physical features and their ethno-religious-minority status often mark them as the eternal foreigner—even when the only country they know intimately is the United States. The US mainstream society does not accord adults and youth of Asian-Indian origin the level of acceptance it extends to immigrants from European countries (Mishra, 2014). Since the events of 11 September 2001, Asian-Indians, along with immigrants from Middle Eastern nations, are viewed with suspicion, distrust and prejudice. This can take an emotional toll as AIHA&Y try to make sense of their AIH identity—with or without US citizenship. Simultaneously, Asian-Indians, along with immigrants from the Asian countries like China and Japan, are also viewed as a 'model minority'. Unrealistic expectations of academic success and having to deal with the inevitable stress associated with them, in conjunction with feelings of belonging uncertainty and devaluation, can negatively impact AIHA&Y's mental well-being. These mixed and ambivalent messages that adolescents and youth of Asian origin, including AIHA&Y, receive from mainstream society can be a potential source of stress and identity confusion. As Stonequist (1937) stated in his book *The Marginal Man*, 'It is as if he has been placed simultaneously between two looking glasses, each presenting a sharply different image of himself. The clash in the images gives rise to a mental conflict' (p. 145).

HOME AND PARENTAL FACTORS

Cross-cultural adjustment is a challenge for first-generation parents and their offspring. Exacerbating this challenge is the intergenerational acculturation gap because of asynchronous adaptation of parents and their children to the US mainstream cultural environment. This is because in many AIH families, parents are the first-generation immigrants while their children are second-generation immigrants. Indeed, even AIHA&Y who are identified as the first or the 1.5 generation spend their formative childhood years in the United States. Thus, AIHA&Y who desire to behave in accordance with US societal norms likely feel stymied because parents' behavioural expectations and their beliefs regarding normative and morally appropriate social behaviours may still be rooted in the more traditional and conservative Indian culture. As Kapadia (2008) reports, while Indian parents viewed their parenting role and the family unit from a more collectivistic perspective typical of the Eastern nations like India, their adolescent children were more likely to adopt the Western individualistic perspective to view themselves as autonomous distinct individuals, placing less emphasis on the family unit. This intergenerational acculturation gap can be grounds for misunderstanding, confusion and parent–offspring conflicts (Farver et al., 2002).

When immigrants accommodate to the host culture, they often engage in selective accommodation (Portes & Rumbaut, 2001). This is true of Asian-Indian immigrants as well. Gibson (1988) found this to be the case with Punjabi immigrants in California, where parents expected their children to do well academically but discouraged their children, particularly their daughters, from engaging in behaviours considered 'Western' or associating with their American peers. Indeed, Patel et al. (1996) found that even as fathers adopted Western cultural conventions in the public setting and work life, they continued to maintain traditional values of Indian culture at home. Furthermore, these fathers were found to demonstrate more control and authority over daughters relative to sons. Other researchers (Saraswathi et al., 2011; Segal, 1991) have also reported that Asian-Indian parents in the United States exercise their authority in deciding their offspring's career choices and marriage partner selection. Often, much to AIH adolescents' chagrin and in contrast to mainstream norms, Asian-Indian parents also believe that they have the final say regarding their adolescents' desire to date (Jensen & Dost-Gozkan, 2015).

However, Kapadia (2008) found that Asian-Indian immigrant parents were more authoritative and less authoritarian compared to Indian parents. For example, relative to Indian parents, Asian-Indian immigrant parents in the United States were more likely to use compromise as a strategy to deflect parent–adolescent conflicts. Additionally, Patel et al. (1996) reported that the length of stay in the United States was positively associated with the incorporation of US cultural values in Asian-Indian mothers' parenting styles. It is likely, therefore, that more acculturated parents are also likely to adjust their parenting and adopt a more authoritative style to meet the needs of their adolescents in the US cultural environment.

Another aspect of parenting that can potentially function as both a risk and a protective factor is the emphasis that AIH parents place on education—an important cultural value among middle-class Indians, with family honour closely intertwined with their offspring's academic success (Segal, 1991). Not surprisingly, immigrant AIH parents emphasize grades and admission into Ivy League universities, considering their offspring's achievements as a reflection of their honour and pride (Kumar & Shukla, 2019). Indeed, many AIH parents buy into the problematic model minority stereotype and place undue emphasis on their children's performance in STEM (science, technology, engineering and mathematics)-related academic domains. This places no small stress on AIHA&Y, particularly those adolescents and youth who cannot live up to the 'model minority' expectations thrust upon them by parents and society.

We propose that when AIHA&Y experience an intergenerational culture gap between themselves and their parents, and when they perceive their parents as controlling and authoritarian, they are at risk of experiencing higher levels of cultural dissonance. In contrast, absence of an intergenerational culture gap and perception of parents as authoritative would function as protective factors, lowering AIHA&Y's feelings of cultural dissonance.

THE SCHOOL CONTEXT

Adolescents and youth spend a large part of their day at either school or college, in contact with mainstream members—peers and adults. This can be dissonance-provoking, particularly when they find themselves to be a numerical minority. McGuire (McGuire et al., 1978) postulated the 'distinctiveness hypothesis' to describe conditions under which individuals' social identity becomes a very salient and distinctive feature of the self. The postulate implies that we are conscious of ourselves to the extent that we are different from others in our immediate environment, and we perceive ourselves in terms of these distinctive features. This hypothesis was supported in a recent study where Kumar and colleagues found that African-American and Chaldean adolescents were very conscious of their social identity and of their devalued status in schools, where they were a numerical minority. Indeed, even mainstream European-American students were cognizant and concerned regarding their minority status in schools where they were a numerical minority (Kumar et al., 2016, 2019). In contrast, in ethnic-enclave schools where Arab/Arab-American adolescents were a numerical majority, they felt protected from exposure to discrimination and prejudice from mainstream society and had a strong sense of belonging to the school community. These findings demonstrate that status in society interacts with the numerical-majority/-minority status within the proximal context, heightening adolescents' vulnerability to feelings of alienation in the school context (Sachdev & Bourhis, 1991). Along similar lines, we expect that AIHA&Y's numerical-minority status in the school and peer contexts is likely to precipitate feelings of dissonance, with their identity tied to feelings of being the 'Other'.

Another factor, often studied with the other minority groups like African-Americans in the US context but seldom discussed regarding Asian-Indians, is their relative invisibility in school and college curricula. There is a wealth of research demonstrating that when the school curriculum is culturally infused and teachers are culturally responsive, it creates an inclusive learning environment and fosters positive cross-cultural relationships among students and enhances their sense of belonging in the school context (e.g., Choi, 2013; Emdin et al., 2016; Gilrain, 2015; Ladson-Billings, 2014). The invisibility of Asian-Indians in school curricula conveys to adolescents and youth of Indian origin that their culture is of little value in US society and that their contributions in the areas of literature, arts and science are irrelevant. This invisibility, we argue, is a risk factor exacerbating their feelings of cultural dissonance.

THE ASIAN-INDIAN HINDU COMMUNITY CONTEXT

The AIH community in the United States is very heterogeneous; it comprises people from all parts of the Indian subcontinent who practise Hinduism in their own traditional way. Over the past two decades, Indians have built several Hindu temples in and around major cities and centres with sizeable Indian communities. These temples often function as community centres, providing physical space and social networks for families. Members of the temple congregation provide each other concrete support, particularly on how their children can achieve educational and occupational success in the United States.

AIHA&Y often participate in temple-sponsored youth groups. Thus, temples often become the anchors for inculcating Hindu values and beliefs in children from a very early age, as well as expectations of what it means to be an Indian Hindu within an American society. This feeling of solidarity and support—a consequence of being with others who share a common national heritage and a history of shared experiences—can function as a protective factor enabling youth and adolescents of Indian heritage to feel at home in a sometimes-strange land. Oftentimes, the temple and community peers attend the same school, and this is also likely to enhance their sense of belonging in the school context to mitigate feelings of cultural dissonance.

Additionally, temple community centres can be a source of stress for AIHA&Y. Participating in temple-sponsored activities can create intergenerational conflict when uninterested youth and adolescents are coerced into participating by their parents. While parents view participation as enabling their children to retain traditional values, adolescents and youth may view these efforts as interfering with their need to assimilate into mainstream US culture. Furthermore, the risk associated with the 'model minority' stereotype can be potentially exacerbated within the social comparative community context where some AIHA&Y exemplify the stereotypical expectations while others struggle to do so.

As stated earlier, we describe two phases of a study—a quantitative phase followed by a qualitative phase. For the quantitative phase, the objective was to examine risk and protective factors in the school, home and community contexts and AIH adolescents' social-identity acculturation orientations on their experiences of home–school cultural dissonance. In the qualitative study phase, we present AIHA&Y's retrospective views on their experiences in school in relation to their adjustment in institutions of higher education and workplaces as youth.

Regarding the quantitative phase, we hypothesize that perceptions of numerical-minority status in school and society and curricular invisibility will function as risk factors for AIH adolescents' experiences of dissonance (Hypothesis 1a). We also expect intergenerational cultural gap and authoritarian parenting to function as risk factors and authoritative parenting as a protective factor regarding adolescents' experiences of dissonance (Hypothesis 1b). We hypothesize that attachment to the AIH community will protect adolescents from experiencing dissonance (Hypothesis 1c). Finally, based on acculturation literature, we propose that a strong emphasis on 'only' in-group orientation or 'only' out-group orientation will be predictive of feelings of dissonance (Hypothesis 1d).

The qualitative phase included an exploratory focus-group interview with a small sub-sample of AIH youth, many of whom had participated in the first phase.

METHOD

Study Design

We used an explanatory, sequential mixed-methods research design in which we implemented the quantitative and qualitative strands in sequence. The quantitative data were collected a decade prior to qualitative data collection. The purpose of this follow-up was to examine general shifts in the AIHY's recollection of their childhood and adolescent experiences, relative to perceptions of their peers during their adolescent years. The qualitative follow-up also provided the opportunity to listen to their prospective and retrospective perspectives on the advantages and disadvantages of growing up at the intersection of cultural crossroads.

Participants

Quantitative Phase: Survey

The sample included 120 adolescents from grade 6 to grade 12 (18 sixth-graders, 28 seventh-graders, 15 eighth-graders, 22 ninth-graders,

15 tenth-graders, 10 eleventh-graders and 12 twelfth-graders) attending Balvihar (the mission forum for teaching children about different aspects of Hindu culture and philosophy) at three Chinmaya Mission centres located in Midwestern United States.[1] Two-thirds of the sample was born in the United States to immigrant parents, and the rest were born in India and immigrated with their parents to America at an early age (mean age at the time of immigration = 6 years and 4 months). Almost all the parents—mothers and fathers—were immigrants. Only three adolescents were of mixed ethnic heritage (fathers were European-American). There was an almost equal percentage (53% females) of males and females in the sample. Based on adolescents' reports, 52 per cent of mothers and 78 per cent of fathers held postgraduate degrees, and 35 per cent of mothers and 15 per cent of fathers had graduated from college. In general, one or both parents were employed in well-paying jobs. At the same time, these parents also had strong connections to their Indian Hindu roots, as demonstrated by their commitment to and participation in religious and community activities at the Chinmaya Mission centres (Kumar, 2005).

Measures

Items for all the measures on the survey were evaluated on a 5-point scale ranging from '1 = Not at all true' to '5 = Very true'.

Dependent Variable

Cultural Dissonance Between Home and School

The scale measuring feelings of dissonance between home and school was constructed for an earlier study (Arunkumar [Kumar] et al., 1999). The items in this scale were also piloted with a small sample of fifth-grader students to ensure that they were unambiguous and easily comprehended. The items assess students' discomfort or negative feelings

---

[1] Because the sample is small and includes only adolescents attending Balvihar at Chinmaya Mission centres, no attempt is made to generalize the findings to all Indian adolescents living in the United States.

resulting from differences between parents and home life, and teachers and school life. For example, 'I feel troubled because my home life and my school life are two different worlds'. The Cronbach alpha for the measure is 0.79.

Independent Variables

School Context

The two measures of AIH adolescents' experiences in the school context were numerical-minority status and curricular invisibility.

Numerical minority status. This three-item scale measures lack of a sense of belonging as a consequence of being a numerical minority in the school and peer context. Exploratory principal components analysis revealed that the three items factored as a single component. This measure has a Cronbach alpha of 0.67.

Curricular invisibility. This is a single-item measure that reads, 'I often feel that in my classes (e.g., social studies or science), the contributions made by people from my background in arts and sciences remains unrecognized'.

Home Context

Perception of parenting practices. Parental measures of authoritarian and authoritative parenting, with Cronbach alphas of 0.67 and 0.73, respectively, were developed for this study. Both authoritative and authoritarian parenting practices are four-item scales. Authoritative parenting measures adolescents' perceptions of the extent to which their parents grant them autonomy and opportunities for participating in decision-making—for example, 'My parents discuss the reasoning behind the family rules I have to follow'. Authoritarian parenting measures adolescents' perception of the need to obey and comply with standards set by parents and included items such as, 'When my parents ask me to do something, I am expected to do it without questions'.

Intergenerational conflict. This three-item measure with a Cronbach alpha of 0.80 was also developed for this study. This scale includes the items like, 'I feel upset that my parents do not understand that I need to do some of the things that my classmates do so I can fit in'.

It measures the conflict between adolescents and their parents if the former are unable to participate in social activities or engage in behaviours that would facilitate fitting in with their mainstream peers (e.g., dating).

Community Context

Attachment to the AIH community. This five-item scale (Cronbach alpha = 0.81) was adapted from the Affirmation and Belonging sub-scale of Phinney's Multigroup Ethnic Identity measure. The scale measure adolescents' feelings of belonging to the AIH community and the extent to which they participate in the community's cultural practices and customs—for example, 'I participate in cultural practices of my own religious group, such as special foods, music, or customs'.

Acculturative Orientation

Out-group and in-group orientations. Both out-group orientation and in-group orientation are four-item measures, with Cronbach alphas of 0.77 and 0.73, respectively. 'Out-group orientation' examined the extent to which adolescents were oriented towards their European-American peers and desired to spend time with them. 'In-group orientation' examined adolescents' affiliation and comfort with peers from their own cultural background. 'I enjoy being around Americans and people from groups other than my own' and 'I feel more comfortable when I am with people who share my cultural background' are sample items of 'out-group orientation' and 'in-group orientation', respectively.

QUALITATIVE PHASE: FOCUS GROUP

The focus group participants included six youths (five female and one male) and two parents (one mother and one father). One of the authors, with extensive experience in conducting focus group interviews (Kumar et al., 2019), facilitated the focus group discussion. The forum for this discussion was organized by a group of Asian-Indian immigrant youths and parents interested in understanding AIH immigrant issues. The interview was conducted in the presence of an Asian-Indian/Asian-Indian-American immigrant audience, who also had the opportunity to share their perspectives at the end of the focus group session. The atmosphere of collegiality and openness maintained during the session enabled the participants and later some members of the audience to share their personal experiences candidly.

Researcher Positionality

Rumbaut (1999) reports that many immigration scholars are themselves of immigrant stock and often studying their own ethnic immigrant communities, as was the case for this study as well. In terms of religion and nationality of origin, both authors are 'cultural insiders'. However, it is important to bear in mind that the insider–outsider dichotomy is continuously negotiated based on the research topic under consideration, data collection context and the 'status and biographical peculiarities of both researcher and participants' (Kusow, 2003, p. 598). For example, some participating youths likely viewed the interviewer as an intergenerational cultural outsider, given the interviewer's age. It was important for the interviewer to explicitly acknowledge this with the participating youths and at the same time emphasize the cultural-insider status conferred by our shared nationality. Thus, the cultural-insider status served to establish a rapport with the focus group participants and conduct the interview with sensitivity while simultaneously maintaining a vigilant, non-judgemental and neutral attitude towards our youthful participants (Ergun & Erdemir, 2010). It is also possible that while we were advantaged because of our emic position, as cultural insiders we may have lost some etic insights.

RESULTS

Quantitative Phase (Phase 1)

Bivariate correlations and regression analysis were used to test our hypotheses. Correlations between the dependent and independent variables and descriptive statistics of all the variables are presented in Table 2.1. Listwise deletion was employed when there were missing data. The distributions for all variables were approximately symmetric, except adolescents' experiences of cultural dissonance, which was moderately skewed (Brown, 2016).[2]

Race, religion and affiliation to America combined in different ways in defining these adolescents' identity. Fifty-five percent of the adolescents identified themselves as Asian-Indian-American Hindus, 20 per cent identified themselves as Asian-Indian-American, and 17.8 per cent and 6.6 per cent identified themselves as AIH and Asian Indian, respectively. Though all the adolescents did not identify themselves as 'Hindu' and about 20% of these adolescents indicated that it was hard to maintain their religious identity in the United States, the group as a whole identified strongly with their religious community (mean [M] = 4.13, standard deviation [SD] = 0.61).

Overall, the average response on the scale assessing cultural dissonance indicates that this sample of AIH adolescents reported that they experienced low levels of cultural dissonance (M = 1.93, SD = 0.78, skewness = 1.1). On average, adolescents in this sample reported that they experienced some intergenerational conflict with their parents (M = 3.52, SD = 0.88, skewness = 0.59). At the same time, the adolescents reported that, on average, their parents engaged in more authoritative (M = 3.51, SD = 0.89, skewness = −0.50) and less authoritarian (M = 2.48, SD = 1.14, skewness = −0.29) parenting practices. On average, the adolescents were more strongly oriented towards their European-American peers (M = 4.20, SD = 0.63, skewness = −0.80) than their AIH peers (M = 3.18, SD = 0.77, skewness = 0.40).

---

[2] If skewness is between −1 and −0.5 or between +0.5 and +1, the distribution is moderately skewed. If skewness is between −0.5 and +0.5, the distribution is approximately symmetric.

Table 2.1 *Zero-order Correlations and Descriptive Statistics for All Variables*

		Mean (SD)	1	2	3	4	5	6	7	8
	1. Cultural dissonance	1.93 (0.78)	1							
School context	2. Numerical-minority status	1.74 (0.73)	0.22~	1						
	3. Curricular invisibility	2.79 (1.09)	0.19	0.07	1					
Home context	4. Intergenerational cultural conflict	3.52 (0.88)	0.45***	0.16	0.22~	1				
	5. Authoritative parenting	3.51 (0.89)	−0.43***	−0.03	0.06	−0.42**	1			
	6. Authoritarian parenting	2.48 (1.14)	0.56***	0.16	0.12	0.43**	−0.35**	1		
Community context	7. Attachment to the AIH community	4.13 (0.57)	−0.42**	−0.04	0.18	0.01	0.35**	−0.24*	1	
Acculturation orientation	8. Out-group	4.20 (0.63)	0.14	−0.30*	−0.06	0.07	0.01	0.10	−0.06	1
	9. In-group	3.18 (0.77)	−0.07	0.40**	0.22~	0.05	0.16	0.02	0.42**	−0.40**

Source: Kumar and Shukla (2019).
Note: $^*p < 0.05$, $^{**}p < 0.01$ and $^{***}p < 0.001$.

Results of the multivariate regression analysis using standardized scores are presented in Table 2.2. The results provide partial support for Hypothesis 1a. In the school context, curricular invisibility was a significant risk factor ($\beta = 0.21$, $p < 0.01$) for adolescents' experiences of dissonance. Their numerical-minority status in school, though not a significant predictor of dissonance, was positively related to it. Among the home and family factors, intergenerational cultural conflict between parents and adolescents was significantly and positively ($\beta = 0.39$, $p < 0.001$) and authoritative parenting was significantly and negatively ($\beta = -0.36$, $p < 0.001$) predictive of adolescents' experiences of dissonance. However, authoritarian parenting was not a significant predictor of cultural dissonance between home and school. These

Table 2.2 *Contextual Factors and Adolescents' Acculturative Orientations Predicting Their Experiences of Cultural Dissonance*

Predictor Variables	β	95% CI
Step 1: School context		
Numerical-minority status	0.16~	[−0.015, 0.220]
Curricular invisibility	0.21**	[0.026, 0.243]
Step 2: Home context		
Intergenerational cultural conflict	0.39***	[0.145, 0.404]
Authoritative parenting	−0.36***	[−0.356, −0.107]
Authoritarian parenting	−0.06	[−0.172, 0.095]
Step 3: Community context		
Attachment to the AII community	−0.23**	[−0.274, −0.022]
Step 4: Acculturative orientation		
In-group	0.02	[−0.121, 0.152]
Out-group	0.16~	[−0.015, 0.218]

Source: Kumar and Shukla (2019).
Notes: ~$p < 0.08$, *$p < 0.05$ (This is a key but all the data are higher than −.05 significance but to cite this is common practice), **$p < 0.01$ and ***$p < 0.001$.
Adjusted R^2: .604
F change: 13.738***
*Significance Value as put in scientific papers.

results demonstrate partial support for Hypothesis 1b. Attachment to the AIH community significantly and negatively predicted dissonance ($\beta = -0.23$, $p < 0.01$), demonstrating that such attachment functions as a protective factor (Hypothesis 1c). The fourth hypothesis (Hypothesis 1d) was not supported. Neither of the acculturation orientations was significantly predictive of dissonance. However, the results suggest that trying to assimilate into the mainstream culture to the exclusion of one's own community ($\beta = 0.16$, $p < 0.08$) can be maladaptive. Overall, the predictive variables together explained 60 per cent of the variance in the adolescents' experiences of dissonance.

Qualitative Phase (Phase 2)

The two major themes that emerged from the focus group interviews included AIH youths' views on society, school and community and the multiple facets of parent–adolescent relationship. Within each of these overarching themes, the AIH youths discussed aspects that either hindered or helped their adjustment within the societal, school and professional contexts. In the sections below, we present the voices of the youth and the parent participants as they share their views on these issues.

Perceptions of Societal and Community Contexts: Acculturation, Alienation and Identity Development

Negotiating and developing an integrated identity can pose a challenge to AIHA&Y as they try to straddle their natal and US mainstream culture. There were instances when participants embraced their Americanness. As one participant stated, 'To be an American means you come from a different background, regardless. . . . Our immigration story was maybe a couple decades ago and for a lot of people it's a couple hundred years ago, but nevertheless it's an immigration story'. This is an example of the participant claiming their American identity by asserting that America is a land of immigrants. However, analysis of the discussions and interchanges among participants also demonstrated ambivalence regarding their allegiance to their various social identities, including the American, Indian and hyphenated

Asian-Indian-American identities. This is well illustrated in the following observation by the male parent participant, who stated, 'So my children are obviously Indian and American and from time to time they see themselves as one or the other. That raises some very interesting self-examination that takes place in which group they belong to, if belonging has to take place at all'. This statement not only demonstrates the dynamic and fluid nature of AIHA&Y's identity, but it also acknowledges the difficulty they experience in establishing their social identity while trying to 'fit in' in the school, peer, societal and Indian-community contexts. This may be particularly problematic during the years of youth, when AIHA&Y are trying to define their identity and their place in the different and sometimes conflicting cultural contexts of home, school, community and society. It can engender a feeling of being inauthentic and projecting a false self (Harter, 2002), both risk factors for undermining AIHA&Y's subjective well-being and healthy functioning (Bettencourt & Sheldon, 2001; Kernis & Goldman, 2006).

Numerical Minority and Cultural Invisibility

The AIH youths were aware of the phenotypic characteristics that set them apart from their peers in school and society. As they reflected on their years in middle and high school, two female participants emphasized that they were never reminded at home that they were different, that they were not 'white' or that 'you are an Indian and you are different'. These statements suggest that the two participants experienced an uncomfortable sense of distinctiveness and self-consciousness (McGuire et al., 1978), as they were very cognizant of the cultural differences that set them apart from their peers in school despite their parents' efforts to minimize these differences. Indeed, the desire to downplay their Indian identity is palpable in the following statements made by the same two participants.

Female 1 shared:

> I realized I was Indian when I was in a group of Indians. That's how I've always felt. I was so hyperaware of my ethnicity when I was around a lot of [Indian] people. I was actually more comfortable being around my daily environment.

Female 2 shared:

> I was the most self-conscious and nervous when I was in front of other Indians. That is when I felt like I was being judged the most. I got called white washed so many times when I was in high school because I didn't do anything that was Indian, really. I was pretty against it. I did Marching Band. I think there were two other people [Indian] in marching band.

An analysis of these statements suggests a desire to assimilate into the mainstream US culture. While the first participant expressed extreme discomfort in being surrounded by other Asian-Indians, the second participant engaged in extracurricular activities that she perceived as less valued by the Asian-Indian community. For the second female participant, the motivation for availing a membership in the marching band was to do things or participate in activities that supported assimilation into the mainstream culture, emphasizing her American identity while minimizing the Indian identity. One can speculate that the nervousness and 'hyperawareness' that the participants felt in the presence of other Indians may be because it heightened the saliency of their Indian background, thereby precipitating a feeling of being different from their mainstream peers. We argue that participants' efforts to decrease feelings of cultural dissonance and the associated psychological discomfort while crossing cultural borders were to distance themselves from their natal culture. As acculturation research suggests (Berry, 2005, 2008), separating and disassociating from one's natal culture is not an optimal resolution to the acculturation conflict and can potentially lead to maladaptive adjustment.

Facets of Parent–Adolescent Relationship

This theme, not surprisingly, was discussed at length by the youth and parent participants. The participating youths combined candidness and fervour when discussing various aspects of their academic, professional and social lives which had the potential for intergenerational parent–adolescent/youth conflict.

Academic Beliefs and Career Choices

There are several factors, both risk and protective, that informed the AIH youths' choice of extracurricular activities in school during adolescence and their current professional and career choices. Among the issues that emerged in the focus group interview were the risks associated with the endorsement of the model minority stereotype and the tension between AIHA&Y's desire for more autonomy while making their academic and career decisions and their parent's expectations of greater control over their offspring's decisions.

It was clear that there were occasions when the youths felt that they did not see eye to eye with their parents regarding academic and career choices. Looking back on their middle- and high-school years, participants recalled the many times when they viewed their parents as traditional, conservative and close-minded. While some of this can be attributed to parent–adolescent conflicts typical of the adolescent years, the youths' reminiscences also point to intergenerational cultural gap.

> A few years ago, when I was a freshman my parents only cared about the math and science classes. If you got an A in math and science, that is what they cared about. If I wanted to do a club, it was do math club, do science club. If I wanted to do volunteering, it was do something related to math or science. If I wanted to work with kids they were like, why are you doing that? You could be doing something better with your time.

This female youth clearly felt that her autonomy was constrained and her voice silenced when she could not pursue activities that she felt passionately about. Her parents were sending a very clear message regarding what they valued, namely success in math and science—academic domains highly valued in the Asian-Indian community. Simultaneously, the participant felt that her parents devalued her desire to volunteer her time and energy on socially relevant and important activities. These were activities encouraged by school personnel and probably valued by friends and peers. Such contrary messages from home and school regarding valued activities and experiences can leave AIHA&Y confused and conflicted.

It appears that even as AIHA&Y desired to express their more acculturated Western–independent orientation, like through self-assertion,
and the need to make their own decisions regarding life choices, parents
continued to be deeply engrained in their traditional collectivistic roots,
demanding respect and obedience for elders. The male participant's
statement below attests to this intergenerational divide.

> The point of getting a degree, which my parents kind of forced me
> to get in electrical engineering. They said, 'no son, this is what major
> you are going to take. Become an electrical engineer, that is it. No
> other choice.

Use of the authoritarian parenting practice and foreclosing of career
options are highlighted in the quote above. Both participants' statements are also illustrative of the risks associated with the model minority stereotype that Asian-Americans are intellectually gifted and high
achievers in math and the sciences. That this stereotype is enthusiastically embraced by Asian-Indian parents and is deeply embedded in the
AIH psyche is demonstrated in the unchallenged comment made in
passing by a focus group youth participant: 'of course, we all do well
in school'. However, such stereotypes can negatively affect adolescents
and youth who are not doing as well in school or are desirous of pursing
non-science careers. As one of the male participants recalled:

> I think I was 7. We were at a gas station. I ran in to get a pack of gum.
> Here is a stereotype. It was owned by an Indian person, of course. I
> am sitting there. He was like, you are Indian, you are 7 years old, what
> do you want to be when you grow up? A doctor or an engineer? I am
> sitting there freaking out because these are the only two options set
> in front of me.

It is evident that this participant felt boxed in by the model minority–stereotypic academic expectations that typify Asian-Indians regarding careers they should pursue. It is important to note that this youth
recalled with such vividness a brief interchange that occurred a decade
or so earlier. This is also indicative of how the Asian-Indian community in the United States endorses and promotes the model minority
stereotype to the younger generation. Several participants felt that the

model minority stereotype endorsed by parents sometimes constrained AIHA&Y's opportunities to pursue extracurricular activities or explore career options not aligned with these stereotypic expectations. Towards the end of the focus group session, a female participant made an impassioned plea to parents and community adults to be open-minded and to encourage and support their children to explore their academic interests and goals.

...Especially if it's something that your kid is passionate about, even as a hobby or especially if it's a career. I think what's sometimes almost more harmful than not even the opportunity to explore it, is the idea that it's not valuable because I think that leads you [the youth] to question a lot of what you are doing. Wait, is this not valuable? Am I wasting my time? Especially in some of these fields like music or humanities or social work or filmmaking, where it is a lot of emotional work, creative work. *I need my community more than I have ever needed my community ever before. My community, the community I grew up in, the Indian community, the parents.* It's a lot of emotional energy. Sometimes it's difficult to communicate. You need to still feel that you have the separate system that is rooting for you. A big part of that is in whatever shape or form you can, saying it has value and it's important.

This was a powerful plea, calling on immigrant Asian-Indian parents to listen to their children and adolescents and to value their academic and career choices, particularly when the choices were considered non-traditional and, possibly, financially risky. According to the female participant, devaluing adolescents' and youths' career choices was tantamount to devaluing their identity and integrity. As the quote above demonstrates, this participant also saw the Asian-Indian community as integral to her identity and felt a deep need for community support for herself and for adolescents and youths who, like her, desired to strike out in new and unchartered directions.

Overall, these results demonstrate that authoritarian parenting practice can result in discordant intergenerational relationships, leaving the AIH youth feeling disconnected from school and family (Patel et al., 1996; Phelan et al., 1991). In contrast, when parents engage in more authoritative and less authoritarian parenting, they are likely to create a more supportive home environment for their children. This is illustrated in the comment made by the father who participated in the focus group discussions.

> The biggest difference between growing up in India and living in the US is the fact that in India, conformity comes. The United States, individuality comes. . . .: Uniqueness counts far above sameness. Whenever that is possible, I find the American system encourages that. I love to see people strive in that sense.

This parent demonstrated an appreciation of the emphasis on individuality and personal choice typical of Western cultures, like the United States. He enthusiastically embraced the notion that American education made it possible for every individual to follow his/her unique career and professional path. Such openness to new ways of thinking and being among immigrant parents is likely to smooth the path for their adolescents, enabling the latter to develop a more integrated identity that combines the best of both cultures.

Parental Regulation of Interpersonal Relations

Deeply engrained within the Asian-Indian psyche are the rules associated with cross-gender friendships and sexual relationships. It is well documented that Indian Hindu parents feel ambivalent about the issue of dating and view it negatively because of their own conservative religious and cultural upbringing in which such practices are frowned upon (Jensen & Dost-Gözkan, 2015; Kapadia, 2008). Therefore, it was of little surprise when this issue emerged in the focus group discussions. Participants also talked about the conservativeness of the Asian-Indian community and the general negative attitude towards dating among Asian-Indian parents. More importantly, these youths were able to share their insights from their personal dating experiences or lack thereof and their parents' responses and reactions to what they perceived as dissonant cultural practices. Overall, the youths' retrospective recollections of their adolescent years and their views on dating reflected mutual accommodation and compromise with their parents. As indicated in the quote below, the participating youth demonstrated empathy towards her parents, recognizing that accepted Western social norms related to dating ran counter to her parents' closely held values and beliefs on this issue.

> I realized that it's not just that our parents don't understand dating culture, because that is true. A lot of our parents didn't go through dating culture here, did not go through relationships in adolescence the way it is here. But they have a lot of fear and uncertainty related to it too because they just don't know. You don't know how to respond to it.

Further, several youths acknowledged the difficulty and discomfort in broaching such topics with their parents, and consequently, they stated, many AIHA&Y adopted maladaptive coping strategies, like lying to their parents. As a group, the participating youth felt that 'in the Asian community, it's difficult to talk about difficult topics [such as dating]'. However, a couple of participants pointed out that frank and honest discussions on the issue of dating would be possible only if parents were empathetic and respectful of their adolescent's or youth's views on the subject. In the words of a female participant:

> So, I very much brought up the topic to break that barrier from the beginning. I always had a sense that they were probably going to be okay with talking about it, but I wasn't expecting them to have answers but the idea was that we always had that dialogue, so it becomes more and more comfortable to talk about.

Overall, the focus group discussions suggest that parents' beliefs regarding authority and the importance of parental input in all matters, including career choice and dating, can function as either a risk or a protective factor for AIHA&Ys' adjustment. The results suggest that authoritarian parenting, close-mindedness and rejection of values and behavioural norms in conflict with traditional Indian values by parents place their offspring at risk of experiencing cultural dissonance, identity confusion and associated negative psychological outcomes. On the other hand, the outcomes are likely to be more positive for AIHA&Y in terms of positive identity development and lowered cultural dissonance if their parents adopt more authoritative practices, view cultural differences through an unbiased lens and are willing to adapt and negotiate academic, social and professional decisions with their offspring.

BUILDING RESILIENCE THROUGH ENACTMENTS OF A CULTURALLY HYBRID IDENTITY

This chapter demonstrates the complexities of navigating borders across multiple cultures. It goes beyond the four ordered and systematic models outlined by Phelan and colleagues. Moreover, AIHA&Y's acculturation patterns did not fall neatly into the four acculturative patterns of marginalization, separation, assimilation and integration described by Berry (2005). Indeed, the AIHA&Y participants in both phases of the study described in the previous sections did not subscribe to a singular social identity involving a superficial mixing of US mainstream and Indian culture. Rather, their lived experiences in the diasporic context was marked by 'enactments of cultural hybridity' (Kraidy, 2002, p. 12). The participants in the focused group also described a more nuanced and multi-layered identity that included Indian, American, Indian–American, Hindu, mother tongue, gender, model–minority, career, and values both progressive and conservative. Invisibility and 'otherness' in the United States, alongside perception of oneself as an agent of emancipatory change in the community and societal context (Modood & Werbner, 2015), were also an integral part of some AIHA&Y's constructed identity.

AIHA&Y appealed for support and understanding from parents, community members, teachers and peers as they navigated their everyday lives between and betwixt cultures, enacting their intersecting cultural identities. Thus, for example, AIHA&Y reported that intergenerational conflict with parents and the associated feelings of cultural dissonance hampered their adjustment in the US context. One of the major sources of intergenerational conflict between parents and their offspring that emerged from our conversations was the extent to which parents prevented youth from exercising their autonomy and pursuing their passions. While AIHA&Y recognized personal choice, autonomy and equality in relationships as salient aspects of their hybrid identity, they perceived their parents as more discipline- and obedience-oriented and with more conservative views on the issues such as dating, sexual relationships and career. According to youth participants in the qualitative study, discomfort in discussing issues regarding sex, sexual orientation and dating was a potential barrier for honest communication between parents and youth. Against the backdrop of parents' own traditional and conservative upbringing, it is not surprising to understand why this is the case. Indeed, focus group participants were cognizant of this and even demonstrated some empathy when discussing parents' reluctance to discuss issues surrounding dating and sex. In line with earlier writings (Kapadia, 2008), parents not only need to become more open-minded and non-judgemental, but they also need to educate themselves or be educated to have these conversations with their adolescents and youth. While acknowledging that accommodating to new circumstances and environments is not easy for immigrant parents, it behoves them to be flexible for their adolescents' and youths' mental health and adjustment.

School played an important role in AIH adolescents' sense of wellbeing. In particular, perceptions of curricular invisibility heightened their cultural dissonance. Clearly, when students do not see themselves reflected in the curriculum and texts, when their cultural backgrounds are not acknowledged, the implicit message that they get is that their identities are not important and their histories are not valuable (e.g., Choi, 2013; Emdin et al., 2016; Gilrain, 2015; Kumar et al., 2019; Ladson-Billings, 2014). Such experiences of invisibility in the school context and internalization of 'otherness' in the US societal context can undermine adolescents' and youth's ability to express their authentic, culturally hybrid identity.

Some focus group participants reported vacillating between American and Indian identity in a struggle to define themselves. Such linear thinking and essentializing of one's identity can be constraining. Inability to claim both identities and feeling forced to choose one or the other identity exacerbated their feeling of dissonance. For AIHA&Y to flower and come into their own, their subjective experiences born out of their intercultural interactions need to be validated. We need to acknowledge that every context in adolescents' and youth's lives matters and that identity manifestation is dependent on their phenomenological experiences in these contexts (Bronfenbrenner, 2005). For example, being Indian, Indian-American and/or American is place- and space-dependent, and therefore, in any given cultural context, it is authentic to be one or the other or all simultaneously. However, one must wonder if AIHA&Y are destined to be marked as eternal foreigners and therefore denied access to an American identity. As we learned, the sense of being viewed as a foreigner persisted even among some focus group participants who were second-generation immigrants. For AIHA&Y born in the United States or for those who emigrate to the country as very young children, the perceived need to fully acculturate and claim their American identity to the exclusion of other identities can feel inauthentic. Paradoxically, the sense of being a perpetual foreigner and deprived of the opportunity to embrace an American identity can create feelings of rejection and alienation. This can also heighten vulnerability, where AIHA&Y feel a sense of exclusion, unable to authentically bring their intersectional identities and be part of the American mainstream.

In the final analysis, this chapter demonstrates that there are aspects to the home, school, community and societal contexts that can potentially function as risk or protective factors to exacerbate or ameliorate AIHA&Y's well-being. Rather than being essentialized to don an imposed identity, AIHA&Y deserve the opportunity to form multiple bonds of belonging across their multiple worlds and be empowered to live with a complex and multi-layered sense of self and identity. Ultimately, we argue that for AIHA&Y to thrive and establish a resilient, dynamic and pluralistic culturally hybrid identity, they deserve the liberty to develop a holistic sense of self in relation to their multiple culture contexts, including the broader US society.

REFERENCES

Arunkumar, R., Midgley, C., & Urdan, T. (1999). Perceiving high or low home-school dissonance: Longitudinal effects on adolescent emotional and academic well-being. *Journal of Research on Adolescence, 9,* 441–466.

Berry, J. W. (2005). Acculturation: Living successfully in two cultures. *International Journal of Intercultural Relations, 29,* 697–712.

Berry, J. W. (2008). Globalization and acculturation. *International Journal of Intercultural Relations, 32,* 328–336.

Bettencourt, B., & Sheldon, K. (2001). Social roles as mechanisms for psychological need satisfaction within social groups. *Journal of Personality and Social Psychology, 81,* 1131–1143.

Bourhis, R. Y., Moise, L. C., Perreault, S., & Senecal, S. (1997). Towards an interactive acculturation model: A social psychological approach. *International Journal of Psychology, 32,* 369–386.

Bronfenbrenner, U. (1979). *The ecology of human development.* Harvard University Press.

Bronfenbrenner, U. (2005). *Making human beings human: Bioecological perspectives on human development.* SAGE Publications.

Brown, S. (2016). *Measures of shape: Skewness and kurtosis.* https://brownmath.com/stat/shape.htm.

Buddington, S. (2002). Acculturation, psychological adjustment and the academic achievement of Jamaican immigrant college students. *International Social Work, 45,* 447–464.

Choi, Y. (2013). Teaching social studies for newcomer English language learners: Toward culturally relevant pedagogy. *Multicultural Perspectives, 15,* 12–18.

Davidson, A. (1996). *Making and molding identity in schools: Student narratives on race, gender, and academic engagement.* State University of New York Press.

Emdin, C., Adjapong, E., & Levy, I. (2016). Hip-hop based interventions as pedagogy/therapy in STEM. *Journal for Multicultural Education, 10,* 307–321.

Ergun, A., & Erdemir, A. (2010). Negotiating insider and outsider identities in the field: 'Insider' in a foreign land; 'Outsider' in one's own land. *Field Methods, 22,* 16–38.

Erickson, F. D. (1993). Transformation and school success: The politics and culture of educational achievement. In E. Jacob & C. Jordan (Eds.), *Minority education: Anthropological perspectives* (pp. 27–52). Ablex.

Farver, J., Narang, S., Bhadha, B., & Parke, R. D. (2002). East meets west: Ethnic identity, acculturation, and conflict in Asian Indian families. *Journal of Family Psychology, 16,* 338–350.

Garmezy, N., & Masten, A. S. (1991). The protective role of competence indicators in children at risk. In E. M. Cummings, A. L. Greene, & K. H. Karraker (Eds.), *Life-span developmental psychology: Perspectives on stress and coping* (pp. 151–174). Lawrence Erlbaum.

Gibson, M. (1988). *Punjabi orchard farmers: An immigrant enclave in rural California. The International Migration Review, 22,* 28–50.

Gilrain, J. (2015). Homer to hip-hop: Teaching writing through painting, performance, and poetry. *Language Arts, 92,* 328–342.

Harter, S. (2002). Authenticity. In C. R. Snyder & S. J. Lopez (Eds.), *Handbook of positive psychology* (pp. 382–394). Oxford University Press.

Jensen, L., & Dost-Gözkan, A. (2015). Adolescent–parent relations in Asian Indian and Salvadoran immigrant: A cultural–developmental analysis of autonomy, authority, conflict, and cohesion. *Journal of Research on Adolescence, 25,* 340–351.

Kapadia, S. (2008). Adolescent-parent relationships in Indian and Indian immigrant families in the US: Intersections and disparities. *Psychology and Developing Societies, 20,* 257–275.

Kernis, M. H., & Goldman, B. M. (2006). A multicomponent conceptualization of authenticity: Theory and research. *Advances in Experimental Social Psychology, 38,* 283–357.

Kraidy, M. (2002). Hybridity in cultural globalization. *Communication Theory, 12,* 316–339.

Kumar, R. (2005). The Asian Indian Hindu adolescent in America: Religious identity and the need to belong. In M. L. Maehr & S. Karabenick (Eds.), *Advances in motivation and achievement.* Vol. 14. Religion and Motivation (pp. 347–371). Jai Press.

Kumar, R., Karabenick, S. A., & Warnke, J. H. (2016). Role of culture and proximal minority/majority status in adolescent identity negotiations. In (Eds.), *Race and ethnicity in the study of motivation in education,* (p. 152). Routledge.

Kumar, R., Seay, N., & Warnke, J. H. (2012). Risk and resilience in adolescents' transnational school transitions: Academic motivation and psychological well-being. In Karabenick, S. A. and Urdan, T. C. (Eds.), *Transitions across schools and cultures.* Emerald Group Publishing Limited.

Kumar, R., & Shukla, S. Y. (2019). The Asian-Indian Hindu immigrant adolescents' experiences of home-school cultural dissonance and achievement motivations: Do parenting practices matter? In G. F. Liem & S. H. Tan (Eds.), *Asian education miracles: In search of sociocultural and psychological explanations.* Routledge, Taylor & Francis Group.

Kumar, R., Karabenick, S. A., Warnke, J. W., Hany, S., & Seay, N. (2019). Culturally inclusive and responsive curricular learning environments (CIRCLEs): An exploratory sequential mixed-methods approach. *Contemporary Education Psychology, 57,* 87–105. https://dx.doi.org/10.1016/j.cedpsych.2018.10.005

Kusow, A. (2003). Beyond indigenous authenticity: Reflections on the insider/outsider debate in immigration research. *Symbolic Interaction, 26,* 591–599.

Ladson-Billings, G. (2014). Culturally relevant pedagogy 2.0: a.k.a. the remix. *Harvard Educational Review, 84,* 74–84.

Mcguire, W. J., Mcguire, C. V., Child, P., Fujioka, T., & Greenwald, A. G. (1978). Salience of ethnicity in the spontaneous self-concept as a function of one's ethnic distinctiveness in the social environment. *Journal of Personality and Social Psychology, 36,* 511–520.

Mishra, P. (2014). Asian Indian immigrants. In L. H. Cousins (Ed.), *Encyclopedia of human services and diversity* (Vol. 3, pp. 110–111). SAGE Publications.

Modood, T., & Werbner, P. (2015). *Debating cultural hybridity: Multicultural identities and the politics of anti-racism*—New Edition (Vol. 9). Zed Books.

Patel, N., Power, T., & Bhavnagri, N. (1996). Socialization values and practices of Indian immigrant parents: Correlates of modernity and acculturation. *Child Development, 67,* 302–313.

Phelan, P., Davidson, A., & Cao, H. (1991). Students' multiple worlds: Negotiating the boundaries of family, peer, and school cultures. *Anthropology & Education Quarterly, 22,* 224–250.

Phelan, P., Davidson, A. L., & Yu, H. C. (1998). *Adolescents' worlds: Negotiating family, peers, and school*. Teachers College Press.

Phelan, P., Yu, H. C., & Davidson, A. L. (1994). Navigating the psychosocial pressures of adolescence: The voices and experiences of high school youth. *American Educational Research Journal, 31*, 415–447.

Portes, A., & Rumbaut, R. G. (2001). *Legacies: The story of the immigrant second generation*. University of California Press.

Rosenberg, M. (1962). The association between self-esteem and anxiety. *Journal of Psychiatric Research, 1*, 135–152.

Ruiz, N. G. (2018). *Indian migration to the United States*. https://www.brookings.edu/wp-content/uploads/2018/01/indian-migration-to-the-us.pdf

Rumbaut, R. (1999). Immigration research in the United States: Social origins and future orientations. *American Behavioral Scientist, 42*, 1285–1301.

Sachdev, I., & Bourhis, R. (1991). Power and status differentials in minority and majority group relations. *European Journal of Social Psychology, 21*, 1–24.

Saraswathi, T. S., Mistry, J., & Dutta, R. (2011). Reconceptualizing lifespan development through a Hindu perspective. In L. A. Jensen (Ed.), *Bridging cultural and developmental approaches to psychology: New syntheses in theory, research, and policy* (pp. 276–300). Oxford University Press.

Schachter, A. (2014). Finding common ground? Indian immigrants and Asian American panethnicity. *Social Forces, 92*, 1487–1512.

Schwartz, S. (2007). The structure of cultural identity in an ethnically diverse sample of emerging adults. *Basic and Applied Social Psychology, 29*, 159–173.

Segal, U. (1991). Cultural variables in Asian Indian families. *Families in Society, 72*, 233.

Sheth, M. (1995). Asian Indian Americans. In P. G. Min (Ed.). *Asian Americans: Contemporary trends and issues* (pp. 198–199). SAGE Publications.

Stonequist, E. (1937). *The marginal man; A study in personality and culture conflict*. Scribner/Simon & Schuster.

Suarez-Orozco, C., & Suarez-Orozco, M. M. (2001). *Children of immigration (Developing child)*. Harvard University Press.

Walton, G. M., & Cohen, G. L. (2007). A question of belonging. *Journal of Personality and Social Psychology, 92*, 82–96.

Ward, C. (2013). Probing identity, integration and adaptation: Big questions, little answers. *International Journal of Intercultural Relations, 37*, 391–404.

Ward, C., Bochner, S., & Furnham, A. (2001). *The psychology of culture shock* (2nd ed.). Routledge.

Chapter 3

Mental Health Vulnerabilities of the Third-Gender Community

Divyani Khurana and Ishita U. Bharadwaj

INTRODUCTION

'Transgender' and 'gender-non-confirming' are often the terms used to describe the third-gender community. In the recent past, this community has been seen approaching mental health practitioners for various reasons, including support for their transition from their assigned gender to the one they identify with or for the gender dysphoria they go through. Gender dysphoria is often encountered by most during the childhood years when they first realize or start understanding their gender as different from the one assigned to them at birth by society. However, for some, the dysphoria is encountered during the years of puberty; making sense of one's gender identity at puberty brings in a range of other psychological stressors. Puberty is not just a time when an individual goes through hormonal changes that define his/her secondary sexual characteristics but also a time when the individual makes sense of who he/she is, that is, develops the concept of self. Often, the change in understanding and seeing oneself differently during the puberty years shakes the ground of self and leads the individual to myriad disturbing emotions and diminished self-worth. Clients from the third-gender community when visiting mental health practitioners report the struggles and distressing emotions they experience. Many even report self-hatred, which increases when they face rejection from their own family and friends. Others report how they have to hide their true being every single day from their own family in order to protect themselves from rejection/humiliation from the family and also to protect their family from the shame that their being a transgender would bring. The everyday struggle of hiding their true feelings often makes them express how their soul is caged in an unwanted body. Many transgender individuals suffer from symptoms of depression and anxiety. Stressors experienced by this population lead to increased susceptibility to depression and anxiety (Budge, Adelson & Howard, 2013). As per the minority stress model, the manifestation of mental health conditions in this community could largely be the result of the oppression they experience from peers, authority figures and parents during childhood (Mallon & DeCrescenzo, 2006) in developing a positive and authentic self-presentation (Levitt & Ippolito, 2014).

THE CONCEPT OF THE THIRD GENDER

Third gender or transgender individuals are often referred to as hijra, *kinner, kothis, aravanis, jogappas, shiv-shakthis,* eunuchs, etc. The term hijra is derived from the Persian word *hiz,* which refers to an individual who is effeminate and/or ineffective or incompetent (Sawant, 2017), whereas the term *chhakka* is often used in a derogatory sense to refer to transgender people. The term eunuch is derived from the Greek word *euneukhos,* which means keeper of the bed (Michelraj, 2015).

Although the transgender population have been an integral part of Indian society, they have long been stigmatized and discriminated against for their identities. It was through a unique judgement of the Supreme Court of India in 2014 that 'transgender' acquired the status of the 'third gender' in the Indian subcontinent. The Supreme Court also stated that sexual orientation was an integral part of personality, dignity and freedom (Radhakrishnan, 2014). Much before the judgement and during the 2011 census, transgender data were collected separately and classified under the category of 'Others', thus giving some identity to transgender individuals in the binary gender system.

The census revealed the transgender population to be of approximately 4.88 lakh, and 54,854 children were identified as transgender by their parents (Census of India, 2011).

'Transgender' refers to an individual who experiences incongruence with respect to their assigned and expressed gender (Sangganjanavanich, 2016). In other words, it refers to individuals who identify with a gender different to the one assigned to them at birth, which primarily depends on their gentiles. According to The Transgender Persons (Protection of Rights) Act (2019), transgender persons are defined as those whose gender does not match with the gender assigned to them at birth, and the term includes transmen, transwomen, intersex persons, genderqueer individuals and persons having such sociocultural identities as *kinner*, hijra, *aravani* and *jota*. Therefore, hijra clans or gharanas consist of both gender-dysphoric and gender-variant individuals.

According to Mal (2018), hijras or transgender people are mainly classified into five gender identities, as given in Figure 3.1:

1. Khusra—an individual with a sexual deformity, that is, hermaphrodite or intersex;
2. Aqua—an individual who is a crossdresser, that is, transvestite and transsexual;
3. Zananay—an impotent male, homosexual or bisexual;
4. Khoja/Chhinni—a castrated hijra; and
5. Chhibri—a biologically fit female with a fake hijra identity.

In modern medical science, the earliest understanding of 'transgender' comes from the work of Harry Benjamin, who offered hormonal

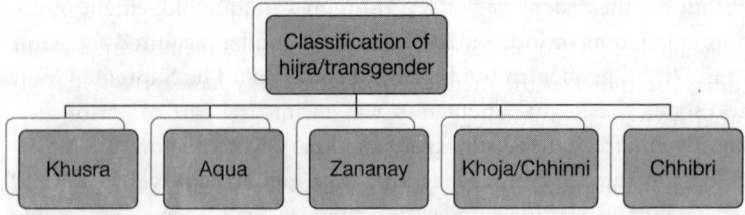

Figure 3.1 *Hijra/Transgender Classification*
Source: Mal (2018).

treatment for trans individuals, adopting the biological view and believing that transsexuals' brains were feminized in utero (Drescher, 2010). However, later, Robert Stoller saw transsexualism as a result of over-attachment with the mother and mother's body and difficulty in differentiating from the mother because of the absence of the father (Drescher, 2010). Freud then proposed the idea that during the early stages of psychosexual development humans are essentially bisexual and it is only after successful transition through the Oedipal complex that an individual gets a fully formed heterosexuality (Hansell, 2011). Despite all the work undertaken towards understanding transgender people, the community has been seen with disrespect and has long been marginalized.

THIRD GENDER AS IN THE VEDAS AND INDIAN TEXTS

Even in ancient times there were talks about the third gender. Vedic literature, dating from 1500–500 BC, has various accounts of the third gender identity. It talks about three different individuals depending on their nature or *prakriti*. For example, the *Kama Sutra* identifies the third gender as *tritiya prakriti* (Michelraj, 2015), whereas the Naradasmrti, Sushruta Samhita, Charaka Samhita, Smritiratnavali, Sabdakalpadruma, etc. describe persons of the third gender as those who do not beget offspring, being either physically impotent or devoid of desire for the opposite sex (Vasumathi & Geethanjali, 2018).

From the understanding and recognition of the third gender in Vedic literature, transgender people were also considered to be an integral part of society, with all the basic rights. They were often invited to attend occasions like birth, marriages, religious ceremonies for good luck and their auspicious presence (Vasumathi & Geethanjali, 2018).

Michelraj (2015), in his review on the transgender community in India, also indicates the mention the community has received in such other texts as the following:

- The Manusmriti (200 BC–200 AD) talks about the biological origin of the sexes, describing the third gender/sex as a result of equal male and female seeds.

- Mahabhaya (200 BC; Patanjali's work on Sanskrit grammar) states the presence of three grammatical genders resulting from the three natural genders.
- Tolkappiyam (3rd century BC; Tamil grammar work) also suggests the presence of hermaphrodites as a third, neutral gender.
- Vedic astrology talks about the third gender in terms of Mercury, Saturn and Ketu
- The Puranas also make reference to three kinds of musicians and dancers: *apsaras* (female), *gandharvas* (male) and *kinners* (neuter).

There also exist references to the third gender in Buddhism and Jainism. For example, Gyatso (2015), in the book *Being Human in a Buddhist World: An Intellectual History of Medicine*, refers to the third gender as *ma ning* and defines those belonging to the group as people without sex organs or people having both male and female sex organs and switching between them monthly. Jainism talks about psychological sex, emphasizing the psychological make-up of the individual, which is different from their sexual characteristics.

Reference to the third gender is also found in the spiritual texts like the Ramayana and the Mahabharata. There are stories in the Ramayana that hijras were sanctioned the power to bless during auspicious occasions by Lord Rama after the latter was impressed by their loyalty, as they were the only followers to stay with him. In the Mahabharata, Krishna takes the form of a beautiful woman (Mohini) to marry Aravan (the son of Arjun and Ulupi). Change of sex and cross-dressing are also mentioned in the Mahabharata, which refers to Arjuna taking on the role of a eunuch, Brihannala, during the last year of his exile.

HISTORICAL EVOLUTION OF THE THIRD GENDER

There are accounts attesting to the existence of hijra communities in India as early as 4,000 years ago (Kalra, 2012), with Vedic literature showing them to be bestowed with all the basic rights and considered as auspicious beings with the power to bless. Similarly, during the Mughal period, hijras were considered loyal, clever and trustworthy, taking esteemed positions as advisors, administrators and keepers or guardians of harems, that is, the living space of women.

However, the status of hijras was downgraded during the British rule in India, as authorities saw their existence as a breach of public decency (Kalra, 2012). Further, during the second half of the 19th century, hijras were criminalized and denied civil rights, such as right to land, right to food and right to an agricultural household. The Criminal Tribes Act, 1871 further led to marginalization and criminalization of hijras both during the British rule and post India's independence. Till date, hijras have not been fully accommodated in the country. In 2009, three hijras were denied candidature to vote unless they identified themselves as either male or female (Karim, 2013). However, things have been changing since the legislation of the Transgender Persons (Protection of Rights) Act (2019).

CHALLENGES FACED BY THE THIRD-GENDER COMMUNITY

The discrimination and disapproval of the existence of the third gender, which started in India during the British rule, still continues. The third-gender community is still treated with disrespect and disgust, despite the existence of folk theories that they bring good luck and that their curse should be avoided. One explanation for the continuous discrimination comes from the attribution theory of controllability (Weiner, 1985), which suggests that stigmatized behaviour perceived to be resulting from personal choice is perceived negatively. Often, people understand sexuality and gender identity as resulting from personal choices and preferences; since being a transgender is majorly observed as resulting from personal choice, it results in discrimination. Likewise, according to the attribution value model of prejudice (Crandall et al., 2001), it is justified to socially stigmatize undesirable traits of minorities and to make them personally responsible for the outcome of their situation. Following from this, members of the third-gender community are discriminated against and seen as responsible for their own plight. Transgender individuals, due to the incongruence between their assigned and expressed gender, experience a number of challenges throughout their life, making them a marginalized and vulnerable group in society. The very words hijras and *chhakkas* used in the Indian subcontinent to refer to transgender individuals are often used in a derogatory manner. Often not accepted and abandoned by their family, hijras face multiple adversities, ranging from a sense of loneliness and having to manage life on their own from an early stage to difficulty claiming a share in property.

Many of them, as kids, are ridiculed, scolded or threatened by their parents and siblings for cross-dressing or behaving like females. Often, family members disown their transgender child or force the latter to obey societal norms, stating the reasons like the child's behaviour bringing disgrace to the family and making them less likely to get married, thus ending the family line, etc. Similar is the attitude of others in society towards gender-variant people, thus leading to an increased risk of the latter being subjected to abuse. Apart from the oppression experienced from their family, transgender people also face social discrimination when it comes to healthcare, housing, education, employment, immigration and law.

Their challenges are not limited to external barriers or oppression experienced from the family and from society at large. Identifying oneself as different from the prevailing gender binary is also a difficult process and brings in its own challenges. The psychological impact of seeing oneself as different from the way one has been raised for years and/or different from the prevailing norm triggers myriad distressing emotions. These emotions range from sadness and guilt to hatred and anger at oneself, resulting in psychological stress and increased susceptibility to mental health conditions. Those who are even able to overcome these face discrimination at the hands of society, as mentioned earlier. Thus, the challenges faced by transgender individuals can be broadly divided in terms of social discrimination and psychological stress. However, there is another major challenge which is experienced by those born with disorder of sex development and the medical fraternity in terms of the nature and time sex reassignment surgery. Diamond and Sigmundson (1997), on the basis of their long-term research on an XY boy who underwent penis removal, who later in life rejected his sex of rearing as female and switched his identity to 'male' at puberty, concluded that in such situations the child and parents should be referred to long-term counselling rather than immediate sex correction surgery. However, much recent literature emphasizes recommendations of early surgery for relieving parental stress and to trigger the construction of the gender identity of the individual with the disorder, as well as to avoid difficulty in adulthood (Hemesath et al., 2019). Nevertheless, the controversies and challenges around the individual continue in the same manner, with the surgery simply increasing the pressure on the family and the individual themself.

SOCIAL DISCRIMINATION

Transgender individuals are at the receiving end of social ridicule, abuse and discrimination. They occupy a very low status in society, living on the margins and leading a life of non-acceptance. The gender non-conformity of transgender individuals forces them to live on the fringes of society, where they lack sexual expression, gender recognition, good education, housing facilities or decent healthcare facilities, along with being subjected to various forms of violence. Often, social discrimination for them begins in their own family and peer group. Being ridiculed for their dressing sense, gestures, behaviour, etc., transgender individuals experience bullying and harassment from an early age, often forcing them to drop out from school or even being forced by their family to leave home and start a nomadic life. This leads them to enter abusive and demanding relationships, resulting in further trauma. Violence among gender-variant individuals is common (Stotzer, 2009). Physical violence and rape are common among gender-diverse individuals, with 46 per cent *nirvana* hijras, 42 per cent *akwa* hijras and 25 per cent *kothis* reporting recent violence and 39 per cent *akwa* hijras reporting rape in previous year (2011–2012) (Thompson et al., 2019).

Discrimination by society against transgender individuals starts at a very basic level; for instance, at a hospital, the discrimination ranges from the use of male pronouns in addressing them and health workers' difficulty in understanding their sexual diversity to inadequate knowledge about their health issues. Hijras are not admitted in female wards, as females feel uncomfortable in their presence, and in male wards they face sexual abuse, leaving them with no place at a hospital for admissions. Additionally, transgender individuals have reported that the attitude and behaviour of healthcare providers show lack of respect for them (Mal, 2015). Similarly, others have reported the absence or lack of a safe healthcare environment, lack of access to health services, limited resources for their mental health concerns and lack of continuous care from their family and community (Grossman & D'Augelli, 2006). Many transgender individuals face challenges in housing, as most house owners do not rent to them, leading to their living in slums or being provided with room only if they follow restrictions set by the house owners. Many of them also shift to *gharanas*—hijra community households led by a *nayak* (head/topmost leader), followed by 'gurus' (next-level leaders) and then by the *chelas* (disciples) of the gurus. Often, these *gharanas* contain small groups, including a guru and her disciples, with a strict hierarchical structure and life governed by rules and regulations laid by one's immediate superior (Mal, 2018).

Transgender individuals often get inadequate education, and very few employment opportunities are left for them, due to discrimination. Most get an income through performing at ceremonies, like child birth, marriages, etc., begging or engaging in sex work. This adds to the economic adversity of the transgender population and also makes them susceptible to various health issues (like sexually transmitted diseases).

THE PSYCHOLOGICAL IMPACT

Often, transgender people live a double life to avoid stigma and discrimination. They wear clothes and adopt gestures according to their birth gender when visiting relatives, so as to avoid criticism and questions or discrimination or to avoid embarrassment for their family. On the other hand, they don gender-variant clothes and names and mannerisms when interacting with the general society. This often results in an identity crisis, as it remains difficult for them to cross the boundary of the male–female gender binary and find a space for themselves (Mal, 2018), thus leading them to deny and ignore their feminine emotions. This further adds to their mental stress and diminishes their mental health.

Similarly, influenced by the norms and values of society and the confusion occurring from the same, people belonging to this group often feel worthless and unfit for society at large. This results in their taking the major step of leaving home, which further brings in economic, social and psychological suffering and a sense of loneliness. Lewins (1995) identified four themes in issues faced by transsexuals: (a) long-standing tension between their biological sex and preferred gender; (b) awareness and experience of being different since childhood, along with bullying and teasing at school; (c) an inner struggle to reconcile the conflict between the biological sex and psychosexual identity; and (d) continued coping with negative response from society on disclosure of these feelings, thus impacting the psychological welling of the third gender community and leading them to undermine their self-esteem and –worth.

PHYSICAL AND MENTAL HEALTH ISSUES AMONG THE THIRD-GENDER COMMUNITY

The challenges faced by the transgender community and their psychological impact make the community highly vulnerable to mental and physical illness. Some of the reasons for their high susceptibility to illness are limited economic opportunities (Shivakumar & Yadiyurshetty, 2014), family pressures to conform to prevalent gender norms, difficulty in coming to terms with sexual identity and orientation and migration to cities (Kalra, 2012). Other reasons include poor self-acceptance and social acceptance and abuse of various kinds from family, society and law enforcement officers (Shivakumar & Yadiyurshetty, 2014). Thus, the long-standing exposure to stigma, discrimination and psychological distress, along with lack of social support and economic disadvantage, lead to mental and physical health conditions among transgender people, in line with the minority stress theory that describes that the high chronic stress experienced by members of a minority group impacts their medical and mental health (Hendricks & Testa, 2012; Meyer, 2003).

Also, rejection and discrimination from an early age leads transgender individuals to feel shame and unworthiness (Grossman & D'Augelli, 2006), thus impacting their self-esteem negatively and increasing their risk of mental health conditions, such as those due to substance use, suicidal thoughts and psychiatric conditions.

Hijras are identified to be more vulnerable to alcohol and substance abuse in comparison to the general population (Goyal et al., 2014). Anxiety symptoms are the most common complaint, reported by at least 20%–30% of those visiting a gender clinic (Budge et al., 2013; Wallien et al., 2007). In a study, in a sample of 50 self-identified hijras, 48 per cent suffered from psychiatric disorders ranging from alcohol abuse and dependence to depression with low help-seeking behaviour (Kalra & Shah, 2013). Runwal et al. (2018) identified 40 per cent of their study sample to have borderline to severe depression and about half of them to have mild depression. These hijras were also identified to have a poor quality of life.

Transgender individuals are vulnerable to sexually transmitted infections, including HIV/AIDS (human immunodeficiency virus/acquired immunodeficiency syndrome). Almost 64 per cent of a transgender sample had a HIV-positive status (Setia et al., 2006). Similarly, higher prevalence of HIV (18.1%) and syphilis (13.6%) is reported among hijras in comparison to other groups (Brahmam et al., 2008). According to Grossman and D'Augelli (2006) male to female transgender are not seen as health risk by sexual partners as they can't get pregnant along with being sexually less inhibited due to their transgender status.

The road of suffering for hijras does not end here, as seeking quality healthcare is also challenging for them due to social stigma, their lack of awareness about healthcare services and health practitioners being less aware of their struggles. In short, not only are hijras highly susceptible to mental and physical health conditions due to their life challenges and marginalized status, but the lack of a sensitive healthcare system also often adds to their sufferings.

A RAY OF HOPE: SUPREME COURT VERDICT OF GENDER BEING NON-BINARY AND THE TRANSGENDER PERSONS (PROTECTION OF RIGHTS) ACT, 2019

The long struggle and fight of the third-gender community saw a ray of hope with a landmark judgement in 2014 by the Supreme Court of India. The judgement for the first time acknowledged gender as non-binary, thus making things hopeful for the long-discriminated section of society. In the year 2019, finally, the Transgender Persons (Protection of Rights) Act, 2019 was passed by both the Lok Sabha and the Rajya Sabha. The act provides protection to transgender individuals in terms of recognition of their transgender identity, prohibition of discrimination in such areas as education, employment, healthcare, housing, etc. and mandating of welfare measures by the government for their effective participation and inclusion in society. With the commencement of the act from January 2020, things are bound to change in terms of the welfare and inclusion of transgender people into the mainstream society, thus limiting their vulnerability and disadvantages. Also, the reservation made for the hijra community is a positive step towards ending the long-standing discrimination and prejudice of years.

The recent years have marked a change in the plight of India's transgender community, with many social movements arising to take a stand for them. Indian cinema has also been talking about transgender rights, with celebrities being part of social movements and through the portrayal of transgender individuals and their rights in various films. Many television and film stars, in the past few years, have come out with their own gender identity that varies from the gender binary, thus changing the view of the society towards transgender people. Also, many transgender people now hold eminent positions in society, whether holding a bureaucratic office or a political position or working as a healthcare professional, leading to their acceptance in the mainstream society. However, a lot still needs to be done to uplift the status of transgender individuals in India. More steps at the grassroots level would lead to better inclusion of the community in mainstream society, such as taking measures to ensure that transgender kids do not drop out of the education system due to social discrimination or bullying, organizing widespread sensitization and awareness programmes towards the needs and recognition of transgender people and also conducting awareness programmes to educate the hijra community about sexual health and sexually transmitted diseases—to reduce the spread of sexual diseases and mortality because of the same. Similarly, sensitization of the healthcare fraternity towards the needs and issues of the transgender community would lead to better and timely treatment.

Also, there is a need for us to learn from more gender-tolerant and diverse countries around the world. For example, Indonesia is referred to as a highly gender-tolerant country, with five terms to refer to various combinations of gender and sexuality: *makkunrai* (female women), *oroani* (male men), *calalai* (female men), *calabai* (male women) and *bissu* (transgender priests) (Davies, 2010). Learning from Indonesia would help us be more accepting of transgender people and understand gender in its non-binary conceptualization. Attribution-based interventions at the grassroots level would also help change the perception of the larger society towards the transgender minority group and reduce discrimination.

CONCLUSION

The third-gender or transgender community has a long-standing history of discrimination in society, making them highly vulnerable to various adversities. The community has been denied means of dignified living in terms of education, employment, healthcare, etc. and has been living on the edge of society. This marginalization and discrimination have made them vulnerable to both physical and mental health issues, along with stress. However, with the recent legal changes and social movements, it is hoped that things will change for the better for this oppressed section.

REFERENCES

Brahmam, G. N. V., Venkaiah, K., Rajkumar, H., Rachakulla, H. K., Kallam, S., Myakala, S. P., Paranjape, R. S., Gupte, M. D., Ramakrishnan, L., Kohli, A., Ramesh, B. M., & IBBA Study Team. (2008). Sexual practices, HIV and sexually transmitted infections among self-identified men who have sex with men in four high HIV prevalence states of India. *AIDS, 22*(5), S45–S57.

Budge, S. L., Adelson, J. L., & Howard, K. A. (2013). Anxiety and depression in transgender individuals: The roles of transition status, loss, social support and coping. *Journal of Consulting and Clinical Psychology, 81*(3), 545–557.

Chandramouli, C., & General, R. (2011). Census of India 2011. Provisional Population Totals. Government of India, 409–413.

Crandall, C. S., D'Anello, S., Sakalli, N., Lazarus, E., Wieczorkowska, G., & Feather, N. T. (2001). An attribution-value model of prejudice: Antifat attitude in six nations. *Personality and Social Psychology Bulletin, 27*, 30–37.

Davies, S. G. (2010). *Gender diversity in Indonesia: Sexuality, Islam and Queer Selves* (1st ed.). Routledge.

Diamond, M., & Sigmundson, K. (1997). Sex reassignment at birth: Long-term review and clinical implications. *Archives of Pediatrics and Adolescent Medicine, 151,* 298–304.

Drescher, J. (2010). Transsexualims, gender identity disorder and the DSM. *Journal of Gay & Lesbian Mental Health, 14*(2), 109–122.

Goyal, S., Deb, K. S., Elawadhi, D., & Kaw, N. (2014). Substance abuse as a way of life in marginalized gender identity disorder: A case report with review of Indian literature. *Asian Journal of Psychiatry, 12,* 160–162.

Grossman, A. H., & D'Augelli, A. R. (2006). Transgender youth: Invisible and vulnerable. In J. Harcourt (Ed.), *Current issues in Lesbian, Gay, bisexual and transgender health* (pp.111–128). Harrington Park Press.

Gyatso, J. (2015). *Being human in a Buddhist world: An intellectual history of medicine in Early Modern Tibet.* Columbia University Press.

Hansell, J. (2011). Where sex was, there shall gender be? The dialectics of psycho-analytic gender theory. *The Psychoanalytic Quarterly, 80*(1), 55–71.

Hemesath, T. P., de Paula, L. C. P., Carvalho, C. G., Leite, J. C. L, Guaragna-Filho, G., & Costa, E. C. (2019). Controversies on timing of sex assignment and surgery in individuals with disorders of sex development: A perspective. *Frontiers in Pediatrics, 6,* 1–6.

Hendricks, M. L., & Testa, R. J. (2012). A conceptual framework for clinical work with transgender and gender nonconforming clients: An adaptation of the m nority stress model. *Professional Psychology Research and Practice, 43*(5), 460–467.

Kalra, G. (2012). The unique transgender culture of India. *International Journal of Culture and Mental Health, 5,* 121–126.

Kalra, G., & Shah, N. (2013). The cultural, psychiatric, and sexuality aspects of hijras in India. *International Journal of Transgenderism, 14,* 171–181.

Karim, M. (2013). Hijras now a separate gender. *Dhaka Tribune.* https://www.dhakatribune.com/uncategorized/2013/11/11/hijras-now-a-separate-gender

Levitt, H. M., & Ippolito, M. R. (2014). Being transgender: Navigating minor-ity stressors and developing authentic self-presentation. *Psychology of Women Quarterly, 38*(1), 46–64.

Lewins, F. (1995). *Transsexualitism in society: A sociology of male to female transsexuals.* Macmillan Education Australia.

Mal, S. (2015). Let us to live: Social exclusion of Hijra community. *Asian Journal of Research in Social Sciences and Humanities, 5*(4), 108–117.

Mal, S. (2018). The Hijra of India: A marginal community with paradox sexual identity. *Indian Journal of Social Psychiatry, 34,* 79–85.

Mallon, G. P., & DeCrescenzo, T. (2006). Transgender children and youth: A child welfare practice perspective. *Child Welfare, 85*(2), 215–241.

Meyer, I. H. (2003). Prejudice, social stress and mental health in lesbian, gay and bisexual populations: Conceptual issues and research evidence. *Psychology Bulletin, 129*(5), 674–697.

Michelraj, M. (2015). Historical evolution of transgender community in India. *Asian Review of Social Sciences, 4*(1), 17–19.

Radhakrishnan, K. S. (2014). In the Supreme Court of India civil original jurisdiction writ petition (civil) No. 400 of 2012 National Legal Services Authority versus Union of India and others with writ petition (civil) No. 604 of 2013 judgment. https://indiankanoon.org/doc/193543132/

Runwal, R. R., Thakur, M., Sani, S. K., Ghai, S., & Mittal, S. (2018). Physical and mental health status, life style and quality of life among Hijra/Transgender woman: An exploratory study in Chandigarh, India. *International Journal of Innovative Research in Medical Science, 3*(2), 1717–1723.

Sangganjanavanich, V. F. (2016). Trans identities, psychological perspectives. In N. A. Naples (Ed.), *The Wiley Blackwell Encyclopaedia of gender and sexuality studies* (1st ed., pp. 1–3). John Wiley & Sons, Ltd.

Sawant, N. S. (2017). Transgender: Status in India. *Annals Indian Psychiatry, 1,* 59–61.

Setia, M. S., Lindan, C., Jerajani, H. R., Kumta, S., Ekstrand, M., Mathur, M., Gogate, A., Kavi, A. R., Anand, V., & Klausner, J. D. (2006). Men who have sex with men and transgenders in Mumbai, India: An emerging risk group for STIs and HIV. *Indian Journal of Dermatology, Venereology & Leprology, 72*(6), 425–431.

Shivakumar, S. T., & Yadiyurshetty, M. M. (2014). Markers of well-being among the hijras: the male to female transsexuals. In S. Cooper & K. Ratele (Ed.), *Psychological serving humanity: Proceedings of the 30th International Congress of Psychology* (Vol. 1, pp. 218–232). Psychology Press.

Stotzer, R. L. (2009). Violence against transgender people: A review of United States data. *Aggression and Violent Behavior, 14*(3), 170–179.

The Transgender Persons (Protection of Rights) Act (2019). https://indiacode.nic.in/bitstream/123456789/13091/1/a2019-40.pdf

Thompson, L. H., Dutta, S., Bhattacharjee, P., Leung, S., Bhowmik, A., Prakash, R., Isac, S., & Lorway, R. R. (2019). Violence and mental health among gender-diverse individuals enrolled in human immunodeficiency virus program in Karnataka, South India. *Transgender Health, 4*(1), 316–325.

Transgender in India. https://www.census2011.co.in/transgender.php

Vasumathi, T., & Geethanjali, M. (2018). Transgender Identity as hidden in Vedic literature and society. *International Journal of Humanities and Social Science Invention, 7*(1), 62–65.

Wallien, M. S., Swaab, H., & Cohen-Kettenis, P. T. (2007). Psychiatric comorbidity among children with gender identity disorder. *Journal of American Academy of Child and Adolescent Psychiatry, 46*(10), 1307–1314.

Weiner, B. (1985). An attributional theory of achievement motivation and emotion. *Psychological Review, 92,* 548–573.

Chapter 4

Voicing Vulnerabilities Around 'Caste' Stigma
A Qualitative Study

Ritu Singh and Alka Bajpai

The issue of 'caste' in India is still a mainstay of many social discourses and a lived reality for everyone transacting a social–organizational life. With every reported episode of caste discrimination or debate around the reservation system, the issue stands yet again at the forefront. Jodhka (2015) opines that caste is not dead with modernity and development, nor is caste surviving because of media and government policies. According to him, caste has adapted to the fast-changing society of India; its organization is evolving, its hierarchical logic declining, but it still continues to exist in a renewed form of highly complex relational discrimination and domination.

Clearly, the above assertion hints at changes in the way caste operates in society. Owing to several legal mandates around social inclusion, there is increased participation of under-represented and marginalized groups; however there is repeated voicing of the implicit biases that still exist when it comes to social and interpersonal interactions. Vasavi (2006) highlights the issue of covert discriminatory practices and policies in higher educational institutions and also draws our attention to the issue of 'subjected personhoods' (p. 3766), which implies the effects caste-based social stratification has on identity and self-worth. More empirical studies are needed to understand the experiences around 'caste' by individuals belonging to particular social groups as they participate in different systems and organizations.

This chapter reports the findings of a qualitative study undertaken to: (a) understand the nature of stigmatization experienced around 'caste' in educational settings; and also (b) explore the meaning making of such experiences.

CASTE IN INDIAN SOCIETY: HISTORICAL ROOTS AND CONTEMPORARY SCENARIO

Caste is considered a closed system of social stratification of the Indian society and one of the key dimensions on which people are differentiated. Gorringe and Rafanell (2007) have highlighted three dimensions of caste: (a) social hierarchy; (b) endogamous separation, where inter-marriages and close social interactions are not encouraged and are mostly forbidden; and (c) interdependent division of labour. The caste system ascribes a 'pure' status to those from higher castes and a 'polluted' status to Dalits or those who are placed at the lower rung. This purity–pollution distinction is primarily based on distinction, wherein certain occupations are considered polluting (Jaspal, 2011). According to Jaspal (2011), the social stigmatization of the Scheduled Castes (SCs) is a pervasive reality, in view of the fact that caste identity is essentialized by the dominant groups and therefore construed as inherent and inescapable. The SCs are stigmatized despite their social mobility. This is a common experience of the SC people in urban India and the South Asian diaspora (Mahalingam, 2007).

'CASTE' AND INTERGROUP RELATIONS

Some social–psychological work done recently has focused on the dynamics of inter-caste relations, offering insights into how unequal relations are maintained over time. Coterill et al. (2014) explain how the concept of 'karma' in the Indian society works as a legitimizing ideology of the Indian caste system. In their study on graduate and postgraduate students of a public university, they found support that social-dominance orientation and right-wing authoritarianism had significant positive effects on the endorsement of karma, which in turn offered support for generalized social policy characterized by anti-egalitarianism and hierarchical social relations. Jaspal (2011), in his article 'Caste, Social Stigma and Identity Processes', talked about the psychological processes in caste identity. He explained that society is divided into caste groups that are allocated differential social status (positive or negative) in accordance with their position as per the social hierarchy. Therefore, the maintenance of caste-based stigma and caste segregation may entail social and spatial segregation, as well as the maintenance of particular behavioural patterns in inter-caste interactions. According to Jaspal (2011), for high-caste groups (HCGs) the self-esteem, distinctiveness and continuity principles will facilitate the perception of inter-group differentiation and a sense of temporal continuity that is implicated in the maintenance of 'tradition'. Conversely, these demeaning social practices are unlikely to benefit the self-esteem principle among the SCs, since they act as a reminder of their relatively low social status. Jaspal further opines that even among the SCs the continuity principle may remain intact, owing to the maintenance of segregation and restrictions on inter-caste social interactions—since individuals generally resist social change conducive to the restructuring of a social system to which they are accustomed. Thus, despite the potential benefits for self-esteem, the continuity principle may favour the maintenance of these demeaning social practices.

In other words, the maintenance of caste-based segregation may work positively for identity processes among the HCGs and, conversely, maintain the threatened position of the SCs. Given the social and political hegemony of the HCGs, social and spatial de-segregation will be resisted by them (for example, Jodhka, 2004; Ram, 2004).

CASTE-BASED RESERVATIONS IN INSTITUTIONS

Caste-based reservations are a tool of social inclusion through which deprived and marginalized sections of the society are given opportunities to uplift themselves (Chalam, 2007). According to Chauhan (2008), the policy of reservation for lower castes in India is similar to that of affirmative action in the United States. As per him, such affirmative action has not benefitted the lower castes due to the contextual factors like low school enrolment or education completion rates, as well as high dropout and failure rates. As more and more castes are being added to the fold of reserved categories, the positive impact of the reservation policy has been diluted. In Chauhan's view, the under-representation of any social group in educational institutions should be assessed with reference to sub-populations of secondary-school completers, and Chauhan argues that, unlike SCs and Scheduled Tribes, Other Backward Classes are not markedly under-represented. He also highlights the social, pedagogic, psychological and political issues involved in the policy of reservation and suggests that quotas should be based on economic criteria rather than on caste considerations. Many studies have argued that the consequences of caste reservation in educational institutions have also given rise to much suffering for the educated weaker sections. There are parallel views that question such quotas on the grounds of merit and efficiency. According to Chalam (2007), these arguments that the less meritorious among the reserved categories are chosen in preference to the more meritorious among the non-reserved categories are erroneous, since children from the reserved categories in general do not enjoy the advantages of educated parents, books at home and a tradition of education within the family and among the kinship groups. He says that generally we talk about efficiency, but social efficiency is more important. According to him, there are no substantial empirical grounds that reservation has compelled us to compromise merits and efficiency.

With reference to Dalits whose social economic status has improved, Jenkin (2003) opines that the issue is not about changing their financial status through the quota system in jobs and equal opportunities for entering the educational system. There is a need to look at what matters to them. For those who have entered the system, what kinds of challenges or threats does it bring? for instance concerns related to identity/image, looks, way of talking, dressing, the doubt factor on them, the attitude towards them are some of the major concerns Dalit students face on a day-to-day basis. Various studies reveal that Dalits face discrimination at multiple levels. Vasavi (2006) has drawn attention to the impact of the caste system on the personhood of such individuals at the receiving end, specifically in educational institutions. Dovidio et al. (2000) have discussed the psychological, social and even the physical well-being of the stigmatized SC groups. However, more needs to be understood about the nature of stigma faced by these groups and the nature of their interpersonal experiences with dominant groups.

The proposed study attempts to explore the experiences of caste stigma faced by Dalit students who are part of a higher-education institution, specifically: (a) the nature of stigmatization experienced; and (b) their meaning making of these experiences.

METHOD

The participants of this study were research scholars from a public university who also had taken up temporary teaching assignments in undergraduate colleges. Eight males and females were selected through convenience sampling, and all participants were from the Dalit group, with their age ranging from 26 to 30 years. Semi-structured interviews were conducted, and the areas explored were particularly related to their day-to-day life experiences at the university, their relationships with peers and their experiences with General-category individuals. Each interview was of a duration of 50–60 minutes, and with the permission of the participants the interviews were recorded on an audiotape. The recordings were later transcribed for analysis. Thematic analysis has been used for data analysis, involving multiple readings of the interview and identification of connections, patterns and themes.

THEMES

The findings presented in this section are based on themes extracted from the participant interviews and coded with respect to the nature of stigma experienced, as well as the sense making of the participants around the same. Some of the themes are as follows.

DESIRE TO PROVE COMPETENCE AND COUNTER THE 'STEREOTYPE THREAT'

Most of the participants reiterated that they face very vocal, as well as implicit, judgements around their competence. The very fact that there are certain entitlements availed by them subjects them to stigma. Participants, through their narratives, communicated their different interactions and their constant struggle to prove themselves in the academic space. One of the respondents spoke about his interaction with regard to availing fellowship, wherein the administrator at one of the offices said, your people get fellowship without any competition, you are taking it like a freebie...People with JRF have passed the competition and they are coming here and you people are getting things for free'. Similarly, a female PhD scholar recalled an incident where she was selected through an entrance examination and a fellow classmate who was not selected commented, 'it is a crime to be a Brahmin. I wish I belonged to a (lower) caste group then even I would have gotten somewhere'. Such views were reported by other respondents also, which caused much hurt among the participants. Respondents expressed facing such stigma around competence and expressed their views on confronting the 'threat' and asserting their competence.

Many participants talked about proving their competence and identity based on potential and worthiness when given an opportunity. One respondent shared an incidence:

> I told you I have always been hard working girl in studies and I got admission in Hansraj college and my own classmates said that my admission was because I belonged to the SC category. I felt really said. Also, I used to wait for them till one point and then I answered back to them that if you feel that my SC category gave me admission easily, then it is not the case. I got a gold medal and I told them that in this case my SC status does not help me and it was purely due to my academic capabilities.

The above interview excerpt suggests how the stigma around competence is being countered through an assertion of merit.

RE-ASSERTION OF IDENTITY IN ACADEMICS

Continuing from the above-stated theme, many scholars expressed the desire to assert and re-assert their identity in the public space and institutions. A participant recalled the time when he proposed a study of Dalit literature as a part of his PhD dissertation and sensed resistance on the part of a department. As per him:

> When I had to bring a research topic... I choose Dalit literature as my topic of interest, so initially I was told that you cannot work on Dalit Literature...There is not enough reference on Dalit literature. But then I told them that I have thought of the reference list but still they did not give my topic any attention and my research proposal was rejected. I felt like the department did not like researching on Dalit literature.

Some participants spoke about countering the stigma through asserting their merit and Dalit identity. In the words of one of the scholars,

> In every case I would love to represent myself I would say that I am a Dalit guy I would work hard to prove my mettle. We too have the same capability as compared to the high caste. I have never hidden my caste identity and why should I do this?

Another respondent stated:

> I never hide my Dalit identity, though I am a woman. So far my Dalit identity helped me in judging high caste people. I really feel proud of my parents who struggled a lot for upbringing me here and helping me in realizing my Dalit identity.

INTERGROUP DYNAMICS WITH THE 'OTHER' CATEGORY

Some participants spoke about the different layers of social stratification in the Indian society. One of the respondents elaborated upon it as 'Neech–Uccha kul [low caste–high caste], Shrestha–Heen [superior–inferior], Chhut–Achhut [touchable–untouchable] and Pavitra–Apavitra [pure–impure] *samaaj ka prathmik unit hai'*. With the increased representation of under-represented groups in the academic space, many participants reported feeling resistance from the high-caste others. According to them, the intergroup relations are characterized by jealousy and feelings of competition. One of the male respondents narrated two incidents that happened in the past:

> The incident that happened in Guhana was that the Dalits there were becoming prosperous and the Upper caste people weren't very happy about that Dalits were becoming prosperous so they decided to burn the houses in the Dalit Shanty and they surrounded the entire place and there was a girl named Suman, who was disabled and her father was burnt inside the house. This incident happened in 2009–2010 and this was because the uppercaste felt that how could the lower caste people live in better houses than us, and how could they wear better clothes and how could they ride 4 wheelers. It was their jealousy and their hate that came out that the sofas in the courtyard were tarnished by small screws, there was this much hate filled in their hearts which came out in that manner.

Another participant expressed: They feel that, our group should not be able to compete with them (upper caste) and should not be able to look like them. A female research student took a similar stance, saying: *'kahin na kahin wo jealousy hai kyunki unhe lagta hai ki hum log empowered ho rahe hai…. Wo log ab hume apna competition dekhne lage…'*. These excerpts hint at a perceived change in the intergroup dynamics when spaces are shared by the dominant and marginalized groups. Such experiences bring forth the nature of implicit resistances and power dimensions of unequal intergroup relationships.

CASTE STEREOTYPING IN INTERPERSONAL INTERACTIONS

There are different social perceptions held by dominant groups towards the marginalized groups, and these were highlighted by some of the participants. One participant reported:

> I was on the field work as a researcher……so we have to stay in field often for data collection. There I happen to visit one college, when

I introduced myself as a researcher and the moment I told about my SC background immediately teacher over there replied that u don't look like SCs.

Another female participant stated:

> There is a certain kind of thought process that if one belongs to a caste then they live like that, they are dirty, or they are like they are, they are dark-skinned, they will wear certain clothes which will be dirty, these are the notions, it is okay. That is what I am saying that untouchability-touchability is not only physical, you have to see how much respect you have, that matters, that means you can be from any caste and in my view, you must be entitled to some respect.

These excerpts highlight the rampant nature of caste stereotyping faced by many Dalit scholars in their day-to-day interactions.

DISCUSSION

The study attempts to explore the nature of stigmatization faced by Dalit research scholars and also their own sense making of these experiences. Most of the participants reported experiences of facing stereotypes and essentialized identity portrayals and their own rising consciousness of their Dalit identity with each successive experience. Most of them cited their interactions with their General-category colleagues or friends to be characterized by a sense of contempt by the latter towards the reserved category; General-category individuals are seen as having an air of superiority, doubting the competence of the reserved groups and being jealous of the latter's lifestyle. Tripathi (2016) has explained how, against the backdrop of different types of identity contestations, an 'other' is created, through various mechanisms of 'othering'. This 'other' is stigmatized through an attribution of various negative evaluations attached to it. It serves as an important determinant of fostering in-group distinctiveness. However, Tripathi adds that this 'other' is often constructed by the powerful to maintain the power structure and hegemony. The nature of caste stereotyping around competence and physical appearance hints at rationalization and justification by HCGs (Jaspal, 2011) and the essentialized social representations of caste (Mahalingam, 2007).

The desire for re-assertion of identity around competence and merit figures prominently in the participant interviews. This process of identity construction also marks the shift in the ideology of Dalits, from being passive victims of discrimination to becoming active advocates for their rights. Now, Dalits are finding ways to interpret their own identities differently.

Securing positive distinctiveness for one's own group can be seen as an effort at managing stigma and reclaiming the collective pride. Baumeister and Muraven (1996, p. 405) have rightly pointed out that 'people clearly do exert considerable choice and influence on their identities'.

The study attempts to highlight that rather than understanding caste only as a membership category, the subjective experience of identity, characterized by much flux, turbulence and varied experiences, must also be understood. Wallace and Tice (2012) have discussed the concept of 'meta-perceptions' that refer to the fact that people form subjective impressions of others' views of them. Such meta-perceptions can give an insight into how intergroup interactions shape up over time and the implications they might have for any intergroup interventions with General-category members.

The importance of this study lies in its field-based explorations and unravelling of certain psychological forces that do not operate in the physical space but are very active at the cognitive level. An exploration of the mutual meta-perceptions may play an important role in facilitating positive interactions between dominant and marginalized groups.

REFERENCES

Baumeister, R. F., & Muraven, M. (1996). Identity as adaptation to social, cultural, and historical context. *Journal of Adolescence*, *19*(5), 405–416.

Chalam, K. S. (2007). *Caste-based reservations and human development in India*. SAGE Publications.

Chauhan, C. P. S. (2008). Education and caste in India. *Asia Pacific Journal of Education*, *28*(3), 217–234.

Coterill, S., Sidanius, J., Bhardwaj, A., & Kumar, V. (2014). Ideological support for the Indian caste system: Social dominance orientation, right wing authoritarianism and karma. *Journal of Social and Political Psychology*, *2*(1), 98–116.

Dovidio, J. F., Major, B., & Crocker, J. (2000). Stigma: Introduction and overview. In T. F. Heatherton, R. E. Kleck, M. R. Hebl, & J. G. Hull (Eds.), *The social psychology of stigma* (pp. 1–30). Guilford Press.

Gorringe, H., & Rafanell, I. (2007). The embodiment of caste: Oppression, protest and change. *Sociology, 41*(1), 97–114.

Jaspal, R. (2011). Caste, social stigma and identity processes. *Psychology & Developing Societies, 23*(1), 27–62.

Jenkins, L. D. (2003). Race, caste and justice: Social science categories and anti-discrimination policies in India and the United States. *Connecticut Law Review, 36*(3), 747–785.

Jodhka, S. S. (2004). Sikhism and the caste question: Dalits and their politics in contemporary Punjab. *Contributions to Indian Sociology, 38*(1–2), 165–191.

Jodhka, S. S. (2015). *Caste in contemporary India.* Routledge.

Mahalingam, R. (2007). Beliefs about chastity, machismo, and caste identity: A cultural psychology of gender. *Sex Roles, 56*(3–4), 329–349.

Ram, R. (2004). Untouchability, Dalit consciousness and the Ad Dharma movement in Punjab. *Contributions to Indian Sociology, 38*(3), 323–349.

Tripathi, R. C. (2016). Violence and the other: Contestations in multicultural societies. In R. C. Tripathi & S. Purnima (Eds.), *Perspectives on violence and othering in India* (pp. 3–28). Springer.

Vasavi, A. R. (2006, September). Caste indignities and subjected personhoods. *Economic and Political Weekly, 41*(35), 3766–3771.

Wallace, H. M., & Tice, D. M. (2012). Reflected appraisal through a 21st century looking glass. In M. R. Leary & J. P. Tangney (Eds.), *Handbook of self and identity* (pp. 124–140). The Guilford Press.

Chapter 5

Psychological Trauma in Child Sexual Abuse
Withstanding Vulnerability and Nurturing Resilience

Sujata Satapathy and Rajesh Sagar

INTRODUCTION: THE CONTEXT OF CHILD SEXUAL ABUSE

Child sexual abuse (CSA), and the consequent psychological-trauma manifestation, is a complex and multi-layered individual, familial and societal issue that has several short- and long-term effects on the lives of its survivors, their families and the larger society. Because of the considerable magnitude of incidents and their profound consequences in a majority of cases, CSA has become a serious public health concern throughout the world, cutting across geographical regions, castes, classes, religions and races. Nevertheless, CSA is a mere reflection of violence against children in a society.

SCOPE OF DEFINITION

The definition of CSA includes but is not limited to a range of sexual activities, such as talking about sexual contents, caressing, luring a child to touch or be touched sexually, performing penetrative sexual acts, exhibiting sexual organs and pornography and involving a child in prostitution. In other words, it indicates the involvement of a child (below 18 years) in any sexual or related activity where the child does not fully/partially understand the adverse consequences or is not developmentally prepared for such activity or information and therefore cannot give informed consent to it, hence violating the law.

The purview of CSA's definition has evolved over the last few decades to reflect more comprehensiveness and specificity about the victim, perpetrator and description of crime and crime situation. The definition of CSA itself highlights the hidden vulnerability and resilience issues embedded within it. Four important definitions illustrate the evolution of CSA's definition (between 1999 and 2014) from being totally child-centred to being more inclusive, including child-perpetrator-specific contexts within its scope:

1. According to the World Health Organization (WHO, 1999), CSA refers to the participation of a child in any sexual activity that:
   - The child does not comprehend;
   - The child is incapable of providing informed consent to;
   - The child is not developmentally equipped to handle; and
   - Violates the laws or norms of society.
2. United Nations Children's Fund (UNICEF) operationalized the definition of CSA as contacts or interactions between a child and an older or more knowledgeable child or adult (stranger, sibling, parent or caretaker) where the child is being used as an object of gratification for the older child's or adult's sexual pleasure. Such contacts or interactions are carried out against the child using force, trickery, bribes, threats or pressure.
3. CSA is defined as the employment, persuasion, inducement, enticement, or coercion of any child to engage in any sexually explicit conduct for the purpose of producing any visual depiction of such conduct, or the rape, molestation, prostitution or other form of sexual exploitation of children or incest with children (Crosson-Tower, 2002). Estes (2001) highlights that a distinction must be made between assault and abuse, as assault is a forcible act where no consent is given, but abuse is based on a relationship of trust where the perpetrator is/may be a significant person in the child's life and

consent is often given, owing to the nature of the relationship and the age of the child.

4. Protection of Children from Sexual Offences (POCSO) Act, 2012 by Government of India provides a detailed account of activities to be considered as sexual abuse in India. It defines four types of abuse to be included when defining CSA: penetrative sexual assault (Section 3), non-penetrative sexual assault (Section 7), sexual harassment (Section 11) and use of a child for pornography (Section 13).

- 'Penetrative sexual assault' involves the use of any object or any part of the body to cause penetration into any part of the body of a child or making the child do so.
- 'Sexual assault without penetration' includes:
  o Touching the penis, vagina, anus or breast of a child with sexual intent; and
  o Making physical contact with a child with sexual intent or making the child do so.
  o 'Sexual harassment' includes:
    - Making any sound or gesture or exhibiting any object or part of the body with sexual intent, such that it would be heard or seen by the child;
    - Making a child exhibit his body or make a gesture so that the child or other person with sexual intent sees it; and
    - Constantly following or watching a child either directly or through digital or any other means with sexual intent.
  o 'Use of a child for pornography' includes:
    - Showing any object in any form to a child with sexual intent or enticing a child for pornographic purposes.

5. The most recent definition of sexual assault is:

illegal sexual contact that usually involves force upon a person without consent or is inflicted upon a person who is incapable of giving consent (as because of age or physical or mental incapacity) or who places the assailant (as a doctor) in a position of trust or authority. (Merriam-Webster online dictionary, 2014)

The definitions clearly outline the nature, content and gravity of the crime, specific conditions around the crime, condition of the victims and their vulnerabilities in such a situation and the indirect role of stakeholders. However, mentioning vulnerable conditions that make some children more susceptible to CSA or mentioning specific resilience conditions is perhaps not required or out of the purview of such definitions.

MAGNITUDE OF THE PROBLEM AND POPULATION PROFILE

According to a WHO (2002) estimation, worldwide, at least 150 million girls and 73 million boys have faced forced intercourse or some form of sexual assault. The National Incidence StudY (NIS-4; Sedlak et al., 2010) records that 180,500 children, or 2.4 per 1,000 children, had faced CSA in the United States in 2005 and 2006. CSA is thus a worldwide problem with a lifetime prevalence of 4 per 1,000 children according to informant-based and 127 per 1,000 children according to self-report-based studies (Stoltenborgh et al., 2011). The figures are not very different in other developed and developing countries though.

Children below 18 constitute 41 per cent of India's population. A significant proportion of these are predisposed to various forms of traumatic childhood experiences comprising major deprivations. The first ever prevalence study on CSA in India reported that one out in three girls and one in 10 boys were sexually abused as children and that 50 per cent of these incidents happened at home. Subsequently, Samvada Survey reported that 47 per cent of girls were molested or experienced sexual approaches, and 15 per cent had been subjected to serious sexual assault, such as rape. The study also revealed that in a third of the children the abuse occurred when they were under 10 years of age. The study 'Voices from the Silent Zone' revealed that 76 per cent of 600 middle- and upper-class women in Chennai, Mumbai, Kolkata and Goa experienced sexual abuse as children, out of which 2 per cent experienced it before age 4, 17 per cent between ages 4 and 8, 28 per cent between ages 8 and 12 and 35 per cent between ages 12 and 16 (RAHI, 1998). Another study revealed that at least one in three girls had experienced rape before the age of 10. In a similar vein, another study reported that 39 per cent of the girls faced sexual assault, compared to 48 per cent of the boys; thus, a total of 42 per cent confronted sexual assault.

A landmark survey titled 'National Study on Child Abuse' (M of WCD, 2007) covering 13 states with a sample size of 12,447 children, 2,324 young adults and 2,449 stakeholders reported that 53.18 per cent of children in a family environment not going to school and 49.92 per cent of those going to school faced sexual abuse. It also revealed that 61.61 per cent of children at workplaces (shops, factories or other places), 54.51 per cent of street children and 47.08 per cent of children in institutional care faced sexual abuse, and 20.90 per cent of the overall sample experienced severe forms of sexual abuse, including sexual assault, fondling of sex organs and forcing of children to exhibit private body parts for nude photography. The significant finding was that 50 per cent of the perpetrators were known to the child or considered as trustworthy and responsible by the child.

During 2012–2013, the National Crime Records Bureau (NCRB) reported a 52.5 per cent increase in crime against children, of which rape and sexual assault constituted a high proportion: 44.7 per cent. As per NCRB (2017) data, 106,958 cases of crimes against children, including 36,022 POCSO cases, were recorded in 2016. These figures reiterate the fact that CSA is a regular incident affecting at least 40%–50% of Indian children.

CSA victims comprise children of both sexes but more females, more children belonging to lower age groups, like 5–8 years and 9–12 years, and more children with a lower socio-economic status. Poverty and its associated vulnerabilities perhaps are considered as the strongest risk factors for CSA. Nevertheless, the truth remains that CSA cuts across all ages (0–18 years), sexes, races, castes, religions and socio-economic–cultural segments of any country.

KEY ISSUES AND CONCERNS: REPORTING, CONSENT AND DISCLOSURE

Reporting, Non-reporting and Delay in Reporting

Similar to the global trend in terms of the pattern of CSA, the Indian government's data (WCD, Govt. of India, 2007) also confirm that in more than 90 per cent of the cases, the perpetrators are known people, and in 53 per cent of these cases children are abused within the family environment. With mandatory reporting subsequent to the legislation of the strict legal framework POCSO, India also has witnessed a sharp rise in CSA reporting. However, this rise in the reporting of CSA cases is limited to reporting of penetrative–sexual abuse cases only and is higher in case of female as compared to male children. Unlike in the developed countries, in India a whole range of non-penetrative sexual activities do not even get reported or, if at all, get reported only in a negligible number of cases. The primary reasons could be lack of or inadequate knowledge about CSA's definition and people's perception of severity of other forms of sexual abuse which need legal attention or the lower social stigma associated with the perceived severity of other forms of CSA. In addition, incidences of non-reporting or negligible reporting of CSA happening within the primary or extended family, where the perpetrator is in a significant position (financial and/or social) to support the family, are high. Non-reporting or delay in reporting by caregivers could also be due to many key social–familial–financial–emotional–legal dynamic factors and therefore is a complex but sensitive social phenomenon and a hard nut to crack.

Consent Concerns

In the case of an adult perpetrator of CSA, the consent of an individual below age 18 is not valid under POCSO in India, whereas the legal consequence of consent between two children of similar ages or between individuals below 18 years of age is still a grey area and hence a point of discussion and debate. This point has the potential to lead to unnecessary delays in legal action and is conflicting for professionals working in the area of adolescence sex education, keeping the stage of inquisitiveness towards sexual exploration in adolescence in view. It is equally difficult to prove or disprove who the abuser and the abused are in such cases.

Some key provisions around minor sexual offenders include the following:

- If the offender is a minor, the matter goes before the Juvenile Justice Board (JJB).

- If the alleged offence is heinous, JJB may send it to a Children's Court after preliminary assessment.
- In the case of consenting minors, there is a possibility of a case being lodged against both.
- If the accused is an adult with a child's mental age, the court would have to examine the report of the medical board and then decide on the matter.
- If the victim is an adult with the mental age of a child, the offence would be considered out of the purview of the POCSO Act.

Delay in Disclosure

Another important point to highlight is the delay in disclosure by a child victim. Again, in this regard, there is a dynamic interplay of various sociocultural factors, such as low socio-economic status, huge social stigma and consequent expulsion of the victim as well as their family, lack of awareness, possible marriage-related difficulties after the abuse is disclosed, cumbersome legal procedures to get justice, etc.

However, from a child's perspective, non-disclosure or delay in disclosure can happen due to the following significant reasons:

1. The child's dilemma over complaining against a trusted individual in the family, or the child's perception of his/her caregiver's trust and belief in what the child says to the latter, or the child's fear of further abuse (physical, emotional or verbal—even yelling/screaming at the child) due to disbelief in what the child says, or the child's perception of the risk of being blamed for whatever has happened, may prevent the child from sharing his/her experience.
2. A child's perception of and beliefs about being alone and being different from others (as the incident has happened only with him/her and not with others) may also prohibit the child from disclosing the incident. The fear or shame of being labelled could be the sole concern for the child. Thus, non-disclosure brings down the anxiety of being targeted for being different from others.
3. Young children have limited language capacity and ability to express what has happened with them.

4. The perpetrator's position in the family and their threats or incentives (even saving the child when the latter is scolded or beaten by another family member) could restrict the child from self-reporting the crime.

5. In case of chronic sexual abuse in the family, grooming by the perpetrator and eventual habit formation (the child might have started enjoying the act after a few incidences or developed a belief that this is what happens with other children too) might also limit the scope of a spontaneous self-reported disclosure.

Thus, the onus of disclosure of sexual abuse remains on the child, and the grim silence due to one or more reasons mentioned above could be burdensome for a child, resulting in delay in disclosure and chronic abuse. Consequently, the physical and psychological agony and suffering of the child continue in silence, increasing the risk of lowering of the functionality and productivity of the child and his/her developing a mental illness.

THEORIES OF CHILD SEXUAL ABUSE

A sound etiological theory of sexual offences against children should ideally focus on the reason of onset of the offence, development of the offence mindset and the maintenance factors (which could include specific vulnerability of some children who are abused).

The key theories (Table 5.1) explaining the reasons for or pathways of CSA are biological, psychodynamic, family systems, behavioural, attachment, feminist, cognitive-behavioural and integrated theories. Following are important points to consider:

- Many theories lack sufficient empirical evidence to establish the pathways of sexual offences in general and those against children in particular. Some theories focus on a single factor (e.g., presence of empathy deficits in the attachment theory by Marshall et al. [1995] and in the organic theory by Berlin [1983]), while other focus on multiple factors accounting for sexual offence (e.g., Marshall and Barbaree [1990], the Four Preconditions Model by Finkelhor

Table 5.1 *Key Theories of Child Sexual Abuse*

Name of the Theory and Authors	Description	Expanded Description	What Is Not Explained?
Biological theory (Berlin, 1983; Marshall & Barbaree, 1990)	Organic explanations of human (male) sexual behaviour	This theory outlines the impact of physiological variables, like hormone levels and chromosomal make-up, on sexual behavior. It asserts the role of androgen and androgen-releasing hormones in promoting sexual arousal, orgasm and ejaculation, as well as regulating sexuality, aggression, cognition, emotion and personality (Marques et al., 2002; Rösler & Witztum, 2000). From a chromosomal perspective, Berlin (1983) discusses the possibility of a biological condition, like Klinefelter's syndrome, predisposing a male towards sexually abusive behaviour.	1. The theory does not give an organic explanation of female sexual offenders. 2. It does not explain why only some males are prone to it. 3. There is insufficient evidence to date to support concerns about exceptional risk of sex offering among men with Klinefelter's syndrome (Donovan & Vollm, 2018).
Psychodynamic theory (Freud, 1953)	Psychosexual development stages: oral, anal, phallic and genital	The theory explains sexual deviance as a result of the unresolved conflicts experienced during the stages of development. It shows these unresolved problems bringing about fixations or hindrances during stages of development, with consequent distortion of a sexual object or a sexual aim (Schwartz, 1995). The theory portrays the human psyche to be in a constant struggle to fulfil the primal desires of the id and the moral strength of the superego. According to it, sexual offenders lack a strong superego and therefore can become overwhelmed by primal id (pleasure principle).	1. The theory lacks empirical evidences. 2. It does not discriminate between a male and a female perpetrator's psychological make-up.

Theory		Description	Critique
Family systems theory (Carper, 1979; Machotka et al, 1967)	Child sexual abuse (CSA) blame is directed towards the victim.	The systems theory emphasizes the relationship dynamics among members of the system and the entire family to be the unit of interaction analysis (Bertalanffy, 1968). Therefore, all behaviour must be considered within the context of the larger system (Davidson, 1983). Sexual abuse happening in a family is a betrayal of relational ties and family roles. It damages a survivor's capacity to trust and comfortably interact with others (Haugaard, 2000). This theory of CSA, which was derived from the general systems theory, posits a systemic approach to father–daughter incest. All members of the family, including the mother and victim, are hypothesized not only to be responsible for the initiation of the incest but also to abet in its maintenance (Kadushin & Martin, 1988).	1. While the thrust of the original systems theory is on breach of trust in the relationship within a family as a unit, this family systems theory is applied primarily to father–daughter incest and so does not explain incest beyond this relationship. 2. It also removes blame from the offender but puts it on the victim and the mother.
Behavioural theory (Laws & Marshall, 1990)	Deviant sexual behaviour is a learned condition.	The model addresses the acquisition processes and maintenance processes of abuse. The role of six basic conditioning principles (Pavlovian conditioning, operant conditioning, extinction, punishment, differential consequences and chaining of behaviour), two social learning influences (general social learning influences and self-labelling influences) and three maintenance processes (specific influences, specific social learning influences and intermittent reinforcement) are explained. The model adopts the position that maladaptive behaviour can result from quantitative and qualitative combinations of processes that are intrinsically orderly, strictly determined and normal in origin. Thus, deviant sexual preferences and cognition are hypothesized to be acquired by the same mechanisms through which other individuals learn more conventionally accepted modes of sexual expression.	1. The theory sounds reasonable to a large extent but still does not explain the mechanism of why some people with similar conditioning and influences still do not commit sexual offences, in general, and those against children, in particular.

(Continued)

Table 5.1 (Continued)

Name of the Theory and Authors	Description	Expanded Description	What Is Not Explained?
Attachment theory (Alexander, 1992; Marshall, 1989; Marshall et al., 1993; Mulloy & Marshall, 1999)	Lack of adequate parenting fosters poor quality of attachment and inappropriate social skills in children and facilitates imbalanced development, resulting in sexual offending.	The attachment theory asserts that men who sexually abuse children often have not developed the social skills and self-confidence necessary for them to form effective intimate relations with peers. This failure causes frustration in these men which may cause them to continue to seek intimacy with underage partners. Sex offenders have deficiencies in social skills (i.e., problems in accurately perceiving social cues, problems in deciding on appropriate behaviour and deficiencies in the skills essential to enact effective behaviour) which seriously restrict their possibility of attaining intimacy. The evidence suggests that deficiencies in intimacy (loneliness) are a distinctive and important feature of sex offenders (Seidman et al., 1994). Marshall and Marshall (2002) emphasize that sexual offenders, who have a preoccupied 'insecure attachment style', characteristically 'court' the child and treat him/her as a lover.	1. Emotional distress, or loneliness/isolation, as a key reason for sexual offences directed towards children is not self-explained, as not all perpetrators develop intimacy with and court children. The theory does not explain CSA committed by strangers. 2. Also, insecure attachment style does not explain all the people involved in gang-rapes. 3. In many of the cases where the perpetrator has very close attachment and reputation in his family, CSA is committed against children outside the family. The theory does not explain this.

Attachment theory (Bowlby, 1973)

Early affectional bond between caregiver and infant

Infants hold an 'attachment behavioural system' that functions to elicit comfort from and maintain proximity to the caregiver, leading to a consistent sense of security and healthy development in a child (Bowlby, 1973). A secure base can be identified as a caregiver to whom the child turns whenever protection is needed (Mikulincer & Shaver, 2007). Through the secure base, the child aims to maintain a balance between exploration and proximity-seeking behaviours. Through repeated interaction, infants learn what to expect and adjust their behaviour accordingly.

There are four categories of infant attachment style, including one secure-attachment category and three categories of insecure attachment. Insecure attachment styles are avoidant, resistance ambivalent and disorganized–disoriented (Mikulincer & Shaver, 2007). Among abused and neglected children, insecure attachments are commonly found (Alexander, 1992), and secure attachment in infancy yields greater competence and functioning later in childhood (Mikulincer & Shaver, 2007). Secure attachment has buffering impacts on psychological distress in adolescent survivors of CSA (Shapiro & Levendosky, 2009).

1. The original attachment theory outlines both vulnerability and resilience factors in a child. How secure attachment leads to resilience and how an insecure attachment style results in increasing vulnerability is not explained.

(Continued)

Table 5.1 *(Continued)*

Name of the Theory and Authors	Description	Expanded Description	What Is Not Explained?
Feminist theory (Herman, 1990)	Patriarchy and abuse of power by men	The overall make-up of the feminist theory emphasizes why certain children are at greater risk of abuse than others (Herman, 1981; Rush, 1980). This perspective considers that patriarchy provides males with the social opportunity to commit CSA. It is argued that the social construction of masculinity provides the motivation for abuse, and male sexual socialization provides the direction for expression of the motivation. It has to be understood in the context of a society with structured inequalities of class, gender and race, not as the symptom of malfunctioning relationships. Crucially, the understanding in the context of power—the power of men and of adults used against children is: men learn and are allowed to express their power through sex; women, without having the power, are expected to take responsibility both for men's sexuality and for their children's safety. The feminist perspective sees the abuser, not the family or the child, as totally responsible for the abuse. CSA is an abuse of power that men (individually and collectively) could change if they intend to do so (MacLeod & Saraga, 1988).	1. The theory does not talk about CSA committed by female perpetrators. 2. It does not talk about societies where matriarchy is prevalent but males still commit CSA. 3. It fails to adequately explain what motivates some males to take advantage of patriarchy.

| Cognitive-behaviour theory (Abel et al., 1984) | Thinking errors result in offence behaviours | The theory postulates that cognitive distortions (CDs), or distorted thinking patterns, allow the offenders to remove from themselves any responsibility, shame or guilt for their actions (Abel et al., 1984). These rationalizations protect the offenders from self-blame and allow them to validate their behaviour through cognitive defences. Cognitive-behaviourists explore how offenders' thoughts affect their offending behaviour. Some researchers suggest that CDs are self-serving, and thus the offender consciously distorts thoughts initially (Abel et al., 1984). Regardless, CDs are considered crucial to the maintenance of offending behaviour for both rapists and child molesters, because they serve the needs of the offenders to continue their behaviour without feeling guilt for their actions. Researchers also label sexual entitlement as a specific CD resulting from the narcissistic attitudes of offenders who seek only to fulfil their own desires (Hanson et al., 1998, p. 197). However, these distorted thoughts are conducive to the maintenance of deviant sexual practices.

The theory postulates that all sex offenders have a tendency to misread social cues by others and are poor at identifying the emotions like anger or fear in their victims. Both rapists and child molesters often perceive their victims as initiating sexual contact and see their victims' actions as sexually provocative. | 1. The theory does not explain why at all some people have such kinds of thoughts and what the source of these thoughts is. It also does not explain how the beliefs and schemas are created, whether under specific vulnerable conditions of life or otherwise. |

(Continued)

Table 5.1 (Continued)

Name of the Theory and Authors	Description	Expanded Description	What Is Not Explained?
		Child molesters misread cues from children in several ways, and the better they know the victim the more is this likely to happen. Children are naturally affectionate towards adults, particularly those whom they know well. Child molesters view these naturally affectionate actions—such as sitting on an adult's lap—as sexual in nature and perceive the children as initiating sexual contact. They also perceive any sexual curiosity displayed by the child as a desire to know about sex, and they want to 'teach' the child through sexual experiences.

These misperceptions reinforce the offenders' narcissistic beliefs and remove their ability to feel any empathy for the victim. | |

| Integrated theory (Finkelhor, 1984) | Sexual offence against children is multifaceted and is related to a variety of the perpetrator's needs, as well as important situational and contextual variables. | The theory focuses on the inhibitions of the offenders (internal barriers) and how these barriers are diminished during the act of sexual abuse; it hypothesizes these to be the underlying factors of CSA. The primary focus of Finkelhor's model is on the internal barriers, or the 'self-talk', comments and observations of sex offenders about the world around them. This self-talk allows offenders to break through the barriers that, until then, had prevented them from acting out their feelings about perceptions of injustice, loneliness and other such stressors.

The process of internal barriers influencing deviant sexual behaviour is further explained by Finkelhor's (1984) organizational framework consisting of four separate underlying factors that explain not only why offenders abuse but also why the abuse continues. These factors are: (a) sex with children is emotionally satisfying to the offender (emotional congruence); (b) men who offend are sexually aroused by a child (sexual arousal); (c) men have sex with children because they are unable (blockage) to meet their sexual needs in more socially appropriate ways; and finally (d) these men become | 1. Finkelhor's precondition model contains a mixture of psychological theories from markedly different traditions, for example, psychoanalytic, attributional and learning theories (Howells, 1994). While this strategy has the advantages of flexibility and inclusiveness, it runs the risk of inconsistency and incoherency. To speak of castration anxiety alongside skill deficits and classical conditioning is to engage very different theories and competing causal mechanisms.
2. Why intimacy or emotional-congruence needs (non-sexual motives) are expressed sexually by some people is not explained. |

(Continued)

Table 5.1 (Continued)

Name of the Theory and Authors	Description	Expanded Description	What Is Not Explained?
		disinhibited and behave in ways in which they would not normally behave (disinhibition). Finkelhor suggests that the first three factors explain why some individuals develop sexual interest in children and the fourth why this interest is manifested in sexually abusive behaviour. These factors may be complementary or work antagonistically or even synergistically.	
		The framework precisely describes the high-risk group of individuals (e.g., those dealing with substance abuse or stress) who are more vulnerable to indulging in a sexual offence. According to this framework, a combination of coping problems and the stress exerted by these problems on the coping system of the individual contribute towards the development of an attitude favourable to sexual abuse. This high-risk or vulnerable nature of the individual in turn increases the probability that the individual often engages in sexually deviant behaviour, because his belief system filters out the normal inhibitions that prevent him from sexually offending a child.	

Source: Choudhary et al. (2019).

[1984]), and yet other theories outline micro-level factors or offence process models (e.g., Pithers, 1990; Ward et al., 1995) predicting the role of cognitive, behavioural, motivational and social factors in the commission of a sexual offence.

- A few theories address distal factors that constitute causal factors relating to predisposition or vulnerability emerging from both developmental experiences and genetic inheritance. These predisposing factors make a person vulnerable to offending sexually if triggering or precipitating and situational factors are present. Similarly, some theories include proximal factors or triggering processes or events that emerge from the functioning of vulnerability factors. Proximal factors function to disinhibit the self-regulation of behaviour and thereby erode an individual's capacity to control strong internal states, such as deviant sexual fantasies, strong affect or negative cognition. The failure to adequately deal with these states elevates the likelihood of a sexual offence, particularly once the opportunity arises.
- All key theories, except the feminist theory, explain CSA largely from a perpetrator's perspective, that is, why somebody commits a sexual offence against children.
- Perhaps due to the fact that a disproportionately high number of the sexual offences against children that get reported are committed by males, not a single theory explains the sexual offences against children committed by female perpetrators.
- Neither specific vulnerability nor specific resilience factors contributing to a particular child becoming the prey of a perpetrator's sexual offence are explained by any theory.

Therefore, embracing theoretical pluralism, which means focusing on different factors highlighted in different kinds of theories, seems a rational strategy to adopt. The process that CSA perpetrators adopt has been discussed over the past few years to prevent CSA. The grooming model seems to make a plausible argument to start with for empowering children and adults in the community and educating them regarding the obvious warning signs of a probable CSA incident.

THE GROOMING MODEL OF CHILD SEXUAL ABUSE

While theories of CSA explain the perspectives of a sexual offender (why a sexual offender commits CSA), models of CSA explain more about how CSA can occur in different methods and in different circumstances.

Grooming Model

Fear of being caught or seen by someone or fear of disclosure by the child forces a sexual offender to carefully plan the offence in a certain way or to create the opportunity to offend. This phase of planning, known as 'grooming', is thus a careful process that aims to control/lure/convince/attract a child, to ensure that the child does exactly what the perpetrator wants him/her to do. Grooming is also an action deliberately undertaken to befriend and establish an emotional association with a child, to reduce the child's inhibition, to create an opportunity to sexually abuse the child. Grooming has two quite distinct functions that a perpetrator would seek to complete before progressing to the abuse.

- Creating the opportunity to abuse; and
- Preventing disclosure or detection of the abuse.

In order to commit a sexual offence, and get away with it, a prospective perpetrator generally prepares or 'grooms' two groups:

- The victim(s); and
- Others who can play a role in protecting the victim or preventing the incident from happening.

Perpetrators of CSA feel power—real or perceived—over the children they abuse. This felt power could be due to their age, their social or financial position in the family/school/neighbourhood, their intellect/cleverness or their physical strength. This felt power helps them manipulate, convince, force and control the children they victimize. The initial soft expression of power in terms of gifting and showering a child with attention and affection may later turn into blackmail, threats of violence or actual violence.

- **The relationship grooming model:** A perpetrator befriends a child and then coerces/convinces the latter to engage in sex/sex-related activities. Many a time, they also convince the child that such relationship is natural between two people (e.g., father–daughter) and exists everywhere. Sometimes, the perpetrator favouring the child in the family, when the latter is at fault or has displayed some less accepted behaviour or done something wrong or has not finished a normal task, also makes the child feel good and believe that the perpetrator really cares for him/her. Favouring the child over another, distributing stuff partially, playing/talking with the child, taking the child's side always, etc. are also used as grooming methods by perpetrators.

- **Organized/network model and trafficking model:** Sex trafficking of children in and out of a country or 'purchase and sale' of the sexual services of children by perpetrators usually happens as part of an organized network. Children and adolescents involved in this may also be used to bring other children into the network. This model usually involves numerous victims and perpetrators, including the nexus of service personnel too.

- **Inappropriate–relationship model:** This usually involves one perpetrator who has inappropriate power or control over a child— one indicator could be a significant age gap or a person in a position of authority exploiting a young person for sex (e.g., intra-familial abuse or abuse by a teacher). Entering a house when a child is alone/sleeping and picking up and carrying the child forcefully to some place is also part of this model.

Grooming in the Cycle of Sexual Abuse and the Abuser's Behaviour

As part of a complex and widely heterogeneous group, a combination of internal and external psychological processes and their interaction with the interpersonal and environmental contexts may motivate individuals to commit a sexual offence against children. The static risk factors are the characteristics of the offenders which do not change (such as their sexual abuse history, failure to establish sexual relationship with age-mates, antisocial personality traits, intelligence level, etc.) (Startzyk & Marshall, 2003). The dynamic factors may include changing course of a psychiatric disorder. Irrespective of the static or dynamic risk factors predisposing an individual to committing a sexual offence, the actions/planning in various phases of the sexual abuse act almost occur in a sequential or cyclic manner.

1. **Deviant arousal factors:** These factors include any reason acknowledged/experienced by the offender to get attracted to the offence—for example, failure to have an intimate/sexual relationship.

2. **Seemingly unimportant decisions:** These decisions involve events that the offender strings together which when mutually exclusive of each other may not be important but when woven together somehow always place the offender in a position to offend. A cognitive distortion (or a series of automatic thoughts) may be present in the backdrop of these decisions.

3. **High-risk factors:** High-risk factors include the occupation of the offender that places a child at risk or which makes the child more accessible to the offender (i.e., school bus driver, sports coach, immediate neighbour, babysitter, teacher, etc.). These factors vary among offenders.

4. **Target selection:** The offender identifies the most vulnerable child to victimize (i.e., selecting a child who possesses specific physical characteristics or belongs to a particular gender, or selecting a certain 'type' of child on the basis of the child's vulnerability).

5. **Planning and deviant fantasy:** The offender fantasizes about the deviant offending behaviour. The use of pornography is often noticed before, during or after the sexual abuse.

6. **Grooming or force:** The offender grooms the child in such a way that the child is available for repeat offence.

7. **Conduct of offence:** The offender carries out the physical act of sexually abusing a child.

8. **Maintenance of secrecy and fake normalcy:** The offender maintains secrecy around the sexual abuse and acts as normal as

possible—as his/her previous self. The offender also ensures that the child maintains secrecy about the act as part of the grooming or coercion. This lack of or delay in disclosure by the child results in continuation of the sexual abuse.

9. **Remorse or fear:** Offenders may feel different levels of remorse or guilt, or may not feel either at all, over their behaviour. However, even if there is remorse at some point, it is not an effective inhibitor to guard against future offending behaviour.

EFFECTS OF CHILD SEXUAL ABUSE: VULNERABILITY AND RESILIENCE FACTORS

The relationship among CSA, vulnerability and resilience may be linked to the pathogenic paradigm (why do people get ill?) or the salutogenic paradigm (why, when people are exposed to the same stress that causes some to become ill, do some remain healthy?) of health and well-being (Antonovsky, 1979, p. 56; Antonovsky, 1984, p. 117; Strümpfer, 1990, p. 267). How does the same traumatic incident or stressor result in different consequences even after controlling confounding factors? What moderates the effects of vulnerabilities in a child and what makes the child resilient to the effects of vulnerabilities? A discussion on individual differences in vulnerability and resilience would throw more light on understanding individual differences in CSA effects.

BIO-PSYCHOSOCIAL FRAMEWORK: MULTIDIMENSIONAL EFFECTS OF CHILD SEXUAL ABUSE

Children survivors of sexual abuse (particularly penetrative sexual abuse) undergo a squeal of adverse physical, behavioural and mental health consequences hampering their overall development and having further ramifications in their adulthood depending upon the type and severity of abuse and availability of support. Further, in the absence of other visible physical signs, CSA's impacts on a child often remain hidden, misunderstood by most as absence of impact or naturally healed impact. Not acknowledging of its grave impacts can also happen due to the caregivers' strong perception that children forget such incidents with time, hence effects multiplies to be noticed by the caregivers to seek help. Thus, due to delay in reporting or non-reporting and non-seeking/non-availability of professional treatment, the risk of development of psychosocial–behavioural and neuro-developmental problems and subsequent serious psychopathology in such children increases. The evidence-based research in this area has reached a global consensus regarding CSA's multidimensional effects on the victims, their families and society at large.

Physical Effects

Apart from the immediate risk to life, grave genital injuries (particularly in the case of very young children) and unwanted pregnancies, the visible physical impacts CSA can include intense and persistent pain due to tissue injury or bleeding, anal/vaginal itching, reddening of the skin caused by rubbing for hours until the skin is excoriated and minor scratches. CSA can have delayed physical impacts in the form of difficulty in controlling the bladder and stool, reduced appetite, sleep disturbances, headache, vague body pain, temporary muteness, amnesia and pseudo seizures/loss of consciousness or dissociative spells. Deterioration in sleep and appetite is also very common.

Neuro-psychological Effects

A series of scientific studies have proved that a traumatic life event like CSA at an early age can result in a smaller hippocampus, increased amygdala functioning and decreased prefrontal cortex functioning. CSA can also lead to chronic changes in specific brain regions. Further, since the central nervous system and cognitive functions are not fully matured in childhood, trauma can adversely affect brain development, cognitive and academic skills and language acquisition.

Risk of Psychiatric Illness due to Child Sexual Abuse

Due to a delay in identification and or absence of adequate and appropriate treatment seeking, the child victim's treatment needs get compromised. Further, in the presence of other adversities and risk factors, the risk of development of psychiatric illness is elevated. The common psychiatric illnesses in such cases are acute stress disorder, somatization, dissociative spells, post-traumatic stress disorder (PTSD), obsessive–compulsive disorder, adjustment disorder, delusional disorder, social phobia, trance and possession disorder, eating disorder and even psychosis.

Behavioural Effects

Children's external behaviours are a reflection of their internal mental state. CSA can result in susceptibility for substance addiction and suicide, anger, irritation and mood swings, self-abuse/self-destruction/self-harm, hurting of others, non-compliant and disruptive behaviours, conduct issues (such as running away), particularly in boys, increased hyperactivity/passivity, over-protectiveness of younger siblings/known children, avoidance of a particular set of people, places and objects, regressive behaviours and socially unaccepted and age-inappropriate sexual behaviour.

Traumatic sexualization: The child may exhibit the behaviours such as sexual preoccupations, repeated sexual behaviours (masturbation or touching of others inappropriately), sexual aggression and victimization of peers, aversion to sex in adult life, negative attitudes towards the body, difficulty in sexual arousal, confused sexual identity, homosexual tendencies and difficulties/dysfunctions in adult sexual life.

Social Effects

Many studies have identified that refusing to attend school or dropping out is the commonest social effect of CSA. Along with this, poor interpersonal and peer relationships, poor social competence, rejection by peers, abrupt diminished peer attachment, running away from home; delinquent/antisocial criminal activities and increased risk of trafficking are the key bunch of social consequences of CSA.

Effects on Academics

CSA may take its immediate toll on children's academic behaviour and competencies. Some of the significant impacts of CSA are decreased interest in studies, increased mistakes/incompletion in work, sudden deterioration of academic performance, language difficulties, sudden stammering while reading aloud, blanking of mind, tendency to get stuck at a particular point, inability to recall things or poor memory and complaints of difficulties in attention/concentration.

Effects on Emotions

Children who experience CSA generally report considerable guilt, shame and self-blame. Along with this, they develop a poor self-image and low self-esteem, relationship difficulties and a feeling of sadness or hopelessness. They also report fear of being abused again, resulting in their social withdrawal or feeling of disconnection from near and dear ones.

Effects on Self-efficacy

The traumatic experience of CSA leaves deleterious effects on a child's self-efficacy, which is defined as the belief in one's own ability to effectively function and exercise internal control of perceptions across specific situations (Bandura, 1982; Benight & Bandura, 2004; Finkelhor & Browne, 1986; Lamoureaux et al., 2011). Significant decreases in self-esteem and mastery following CSA result in a reduced sense of self-efficacy (Finkelhor & Browne, 1986; Cecil & Matson, 2001; Cieslak et al., 2008; Foster & Hagedorn, 2014; Lamoureaux et al., 2011). The gravity of CSA's impacts on a child's overall development is largely mediated by the child's lowered sense of self-efficacy follow-ing the abuse (Benight & Bandura, 2004; Finkelhor & Browne, 1986; Lamoureaux et al., 2011). In particular, self-efficacy predicts the amount of effort a child is able to make in persevering through adverse experi-ences, as well as levels of vulnerability to stress and mental illness, self-motivation, resilience and the nature of the victim's decision-making and outlook on life (Bandura, 1982; Benight & Bandura, 2004; Cieslak et al., 2008). Decreased self-efficacy also increases the risk of negative mental health and behavioural outcomes, such as PTSD, symptoms of dissociation, re-victimization, self-devaluation and maladaptive coping mechanisms, like self-harm and suicidal ideation (Bagley et al., 1995; Benight & Bandura, 2004; Briere & Elliot, 2003; Cecil & Matson, 2001; Cieslak et al., 2008; Coohey, 2010; Lamoureaux et al., 2011; Lev-Wiesel, 2000; Reese-Weber & Smith, 2011; Stern et al., 1995; Swanston et al., 2003). Furthermore, some studies found the association of CSA with ineffective interpersonal skills in the child victim, leading to greater conflicts, risky sexual behaviours and re-victimization (Hovsepian et al., 2010; Kearns & Calhoun, 2010; Lamoureaux et al., 2011; Swanston et al., 2003). However, these detrimental effects do not develop in all victims of CSA, and the intensity and duration of the symptoms vary between individuals (Briere & Elliot, 2003).

This synthesis of research on how CSA may impact a child (Figure 5.1) indicates that the higher the impact of CSA on a child, the more vulnerable would the child become in any/few/all aspects of his/her development/functionality/productivity. However, certainly a child who has a traumatic CSA experience somewhere gets derailed from his/her normal predictable life within the existing familiar vulnerabilities such as poverty, homeless, shelter homes, etc.

A child's reactions to sexual abuse trauma are wide-ranging—from normal, positive functioning in everyday life without any warning signals to slightly distinctive signals to obvious and extremely negative signals. The child may not show any sign even during ongoing abuse, and the trauma reactions may surface only in late adolescence or in

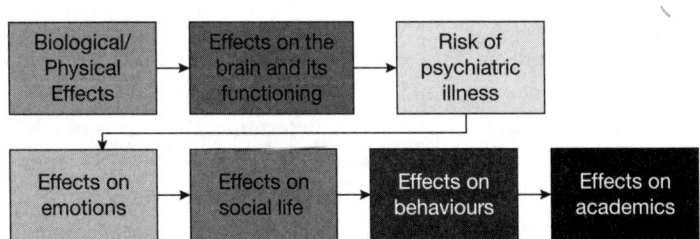

Figure 5.1 *Multidimensional Effects of Child Sexual Abuse*
Source: Choudhary et al. (2019).

adulthood; these are known as sleeping trauma consequences (Briere, 1992).

This phenomenon of delayed onset of trauma or sleeping trauma consequences may be explained by the fact that the inflicted scar would be fully displayed only after the critical period of personality development, due to active defence mechanisms during the said period. These defence mechanisms allow the child to function normally for some time, during which the damage caused by the trauma is disguised and lies in the subconscious, in order to ensure the organism's survival.

The absence of noticeable expected trauma reactions may result in the premature conclusion that the child suffered no harm. Paradoxically, the non-existence of symptoms can also be used to undermine the victim's credibility. Sometimes, those assessing the evidence deliberately create their own categories of trauma symptoms—eligible/ineligible symptoms, tolerable/unacceptable symptoms and symptoms raising sympathy/antipathy. As a result, a boy who acts aggressively among his peers is not considered a credible victim.

Interestingly, 'Spaccarelli's (1994) model of the mental health effects of CSA' considers CSA as a stressor consisting of a 'series of abuse events, abuse-related events and disclosure-related events' where each contributes to increasing the risk of maladaptive outcomes. The model proposes that coping responses and cognitive appraisals mediate the effects of these events, developmental and environmental factors moderate the relationships between events and victim responses, and the victims' initial responses may affect subsequent levels of abuse-related stress.

Nevertheless, concern about the deleterious effects of CSA trauma exposure goes hand in hand with the unprecedented interest in resilience research. Not every child who experiences sexual abuse would go through all these effects; indeed, what determines the effects of CSA in a particular child is interesting to know. The impacts of CSA connect the string between vulnerability and resilience. However, according to O'Dougherty-Wright and Masten (2006), deeper understanding of the context highlights risk factors that predict negative outcomes (e.g., h/o mental illness in parent/s, parental divorce), cumulative risks (e.g., combination of multiple risk factors, like exposure to domestic violence and sexual and physical abuse) and vulnerability, meaning individual susceptibility to traumatic events with pathological outcomes (e.g., detached children with increased anxiety traits) and protective factors, referring to environmental components in resilience—an interaction between individual attributes and contextual buffering with positive outcomes in an adverse situation (e.g., secure attachment, continuity and predictability of child care-giving situations).

INDIVIDUAL DIFFERENCES IN VULNERABILITY

Derived from the Latin word *vulnerare*, vulnerability means exposure to being wounded, by anything (within the individual or in the environment) that has the potential to harm a person in any way. Although the short- and long-term impacts of CSA appear to be scary and grave, every CSA victim suffers in a different way depending on his/her unique life conditions and vulnerability–resilience factors. Although vulnerability and resilience are not exactly inverse or opposite to each other, one of them would be less meaningful if the other does not exist. The effects of CSA may be graver in the presence of a wide spectrum of vulnerability factors. such as low age, female gender, poor income status, penetrative sexual abuse, multiple/chronic sexual abuse, long duration of abuse, severe form of abuse, existence of other forms of maltreatment, unavailability of timely assistance, etc (Figure 5.1). Again, the risk of a CSA victim developing a mental illness is moderate to high in the absence of treatment. Further, the effects of CSA and their ramifications can seep into adulthood. The effects of CSA have the potentiality to multiply in the presence of other forms of abuse and adversity. They would largely depend on the other vulnerabilities the child victim is already exposed to, especially biological and family-related vulnerabilities, as depicted in Figure 5.2.

RISK VULNERABILITY FACTORS AND EFFECTS OF CHILD SEXUAL ABUSE

Exposure to Other Forms of Maltreatment

Experiencing various coinciding and compounding abuses and instances of maltreatment is defined as 'polyvictimization' (Boney-McCoy &

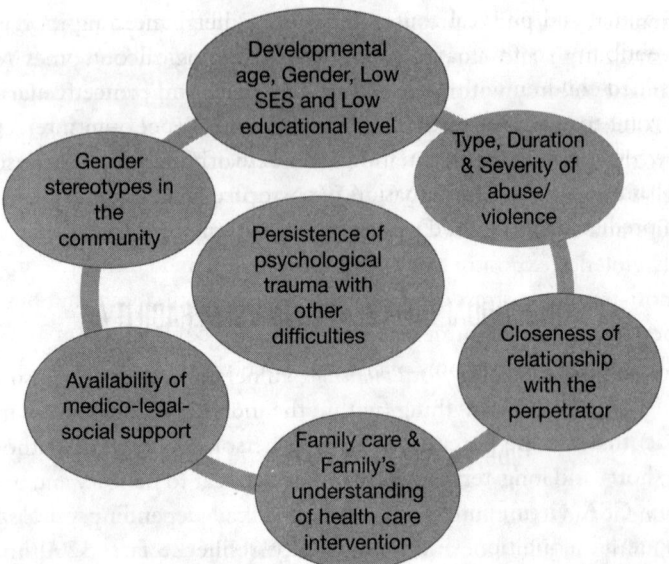

Figure 5.2 *Vulnerability Factors for Determining the Effects of Child Sexual Abuse*

Source: Choudhary et al. (2019).

Finkelhor, 1995). In a key study, CSA was found to have significant associations with nine other forms of childhood adversity (emotional and physical abuse, emotional and physical neglect, battery of mother, substance abuse in the household, parental mental illness, separation of parents and sharing of household with a criminal member) (Dong et al., 2003). In addition, a connection was found between bullying and CSA, with bully-victims (those youth who bully their peers and have also been bullied) being particularly at risk of CSA (Holt et al., 2007).

All forms of maltreatment (sexual abuse, physical abuse, neglect and witnessing of domestic violence between parents/family members) and the experiencing of more than one form of maltreatment may increase the proneness to high-risk sexual behaviours, such as having a high number of sexual partners, engaging in casual sex and experiencing first consensual sexual intercourse at a young age (Thibodeaua et al., 2017). As compared to the presence of only one type of maltreatment, the presence of multiple types of maltreatment results in more adjustment difficulties, elevated depression and anxiety, heightened anger, greater internalization and externalization of symptoms, more severe post-traumatic stress symptoms and lowered social competence (English et al., 2005; Lau et al., 2005; Naar-King et al., 2002). Longitudinal data from three waves of the National Survey of Child and Adolescent Well-Being (1999–2007) (NSCAW; National Data Archive on Child Abuse and Neglect, 2002) revealed an underlying process that links early violence exposure to the co-development and cumulative impact of post-traumatic stress on externalizing behaviour above and beyond experiences of maltreatment and the effect of complex trauma on the growth of these symptoms over time (Barboza et al., 2017).

Type, Duration and Severity of Abuse

Frequent and long duration of abuse are linked to greater psychological difficulties in adulthood (English et al., 2005; Steel et al., 2004). The presence of coercion or violence, severity of abuse (e.g., rape), young age at the time of abuse and family member being the perpetrator are associated with the most debilitating effects (Wyatt et al., 2002). Sexually abused children exhibit more depressive symptomatology and destructive behaviours in the presence of increased frequency of abuse and a high degree of physical force (Trickett et al., 2011).

Developmental Age

Scientific studies agree that children are most vulnerable to abuse between the ages of 7 and 12 (Fanslow, 2007; Finkelhor, 1994; Romano & De Luca, 2001; Smallbone & Wortley, 2000). While the median age for reported abuse is 9 (Putnam, 2003), 20%–39% of children are sexually abused before the age of 8 (Putnam, 2003; Snyder, 2000). Characteristics of sexual activities may vary with age. Studies report that children below 15 years encounter more genital touching, attempted penile–vaginal intercourse and completed penile–vaginal intercourse by the perpetrator, while adolescent victims above 15 years experience a greater range of abuse types, such as genital touching, oral sex, vaginal penetration with an object or finger, vaginal intercourse, anal penetration with a finger and anal intercourse

(Gibson & Leitnenberg, 2001). Additionally, Modelli et al. (2012) reported that boys are at a higher risk of sexual abuse when they are below the age of 6.5 years.

Gender

Girls are more likely than boys to face sexual abuse and to experience rape (NSCAW study: Maikovich-Fong & Jaffee, 2010). A multi-generational, 23-year-long longitudinal study revealed that sexually abused females (on average) show deleterious effects across a host of bio-psychosocial domains, including earlier onset of puberty, cognitive deficits, depression, dissociative symptoms, maladaptive sexual development, hypothalamic–pituitary–adrenal attenuation, asymmetrical stress responses, high rates of obesity, more major illnesses and higher healthcare utilization, dropping out of high school, persistent PTSD, self-mutilation, physical and sexual re-victimization, premature deliveries, teen motherhood, drug and alcohol abuse and domestic violence. Offspring born to abused mothers are shown to be at increased risk of child maltreatment and overall maldevelopment (Trickett et al., 2011).

Disability, Low Intelligence Quotient and Low Educational Level

Depending upon the risks associated with different types of disability, children with disabilities are more likely to experience sexual abuse than those without disability. The prevalence of CSA was reported to be 9 per cent among non-disabled children, whereas it was 15 per cent among children with mental or intellectual disabilities and 11 per cent among children with physical disabilities (Jones' et al., 2012). Again, children with speech and language impediments were three times more likely, those with intellectual disability four times more likely and those with behavioural disorders five–six times more likely to be sexually abused than children without disabilities (Sullivan & Knutson, 2012). Kvam (2004) reported that deaf children were more at risk of sexual abuse but that the level of abuse was more serious than for the general population. Also, children with communication impairments, behavioural disorders, learning disabilities and sensory impairments are likely to experience higher levels of abuse, including sexual abuse, in comparison to children without disabilities (Stalker & McArthur, 2012).

Parent-Child Interaction and Relationship Dynamics

Parents believing in CSA disclosure and supporting the child thereafter help in lowering the child's psychological and emotional trauma (Colton et al., 2010) and maintaining the child's sense of trust (OgÅodek & Araszkiewicz, 2011). The probability of unsupportive parental reactions upon disclosure is 89 per cent in case the perpetrator is known to the child or family, whereas children abused by strangers face inadequate parental reactions only in 25 per cent of cases (Lamb et al., 2008). In turn, the relationship of the family and the child with the perpetrator can heavily influence the disclosure of sexual abuse by young children (Jonzon & Lindblad, 2004; London et al., 2008). For instance, a child's fear, guilt and shame may prevent him/her from reporting the sexual assault (McNally, 2007). Furthermore, in cases of intra-familial sexual abuse, the child experiences negative caregiver reactions, such as being deprived of the physical and emotional care that he/she has become accustomed to receiving, when he/she discloses the sexual abuse activities of a family member. In addition, many times, family members may reprimand the abused child, protect the perpetrator and position the abused child as a family scapegoat for other members. These responses often hinder the child from reporting the abuse (Sinanan, 2011), and the child continues to experience sexual abuse for a longer duration and suffers more severe physical and mental damage (Gilbert et al., 2009).

Family Socio-demographic Profile

Many studies have reported that sexually abused children belong to a low socio-economic status, have parents with low levels of education (Bernard-Bonnin et al., 2008; Finkelhor et al., 2010; Priebe & Svedin, 2009; Ramírez et al., 2011) and have poor communication with their parents, resulting in late disclosure of sexual abuse incidents (Ramírez et al., 2011). Laaksonen et al. (2011) suggested that family problems, such as biological parents' alcohol abuse, substance abuse and lack of supervision, increase the risk of CSA. Finkelhor et al. (2010) added that such socio-demographic profile of parents negatively influences the parents' ability to protect and care for their children, which in turn results in passive and negative child rearing and increases the likelihood of psychological damage from CSA. Intra-familial sexual abuse results in more aggressive delinquency, sexual acting out and disruptive behaviour than sexual abuse perpetrated by non–family members (Trickett et al., 2011).

While it is true that CSA increases the likelihood of psychopathology and other vulnerabilities in later life (Cederblad et al., 1995, p. 322), such adversities are also moderated by a set of identifiable protective or resilient factors.

INDIVIDUAL DIFFERENCES IN RESILIENCE

Derived from the Latin words *re* and *salir*, resilience means bouncing back. Thus, resilience can be defined as a dynamic and multidimensional developmental process of positive adaptation in the context of adverse and traumatic life events or vulnerabilities. Resilience in children is defined as the capacity of those of who are exposed to identifiable risk factors to overcome those risks and avoid negative outcomes, such as delinquency and behavioural problems, psychological maladjustment, academic difficulties and physical complications (Rak & Patterson, 1996, p. 368). Children who are able to overcome or withstand these odds are called resilient. Resilience can be seen as a ratio of the number of protective factors to the number of vulnerable circumstances. A resilience trajectory is characterized by a relatively brief period of disequilibrium but otherwise continued health (Bonanno, 2004; Bonanno et al., 2011). The trajectory (path) of resilience is very common, that it is not simply the absence of psychopathology, and that it is distinct from other patterns of response to potentially traumatic events, some of which are neither pathological nor resilient (Bonanno, 2004, 2012). Important components of resilience, however, are the hazardous, adverse and threatening life circumstances that result in individual vulnerability. Resilience involves an active decision to keep moving forward in an insightful and integrative manner, and biological underpinnings (stable traits) determine resilience (Yehuda & Flory, 2007; Yehuda et al., 2010; Yehuda et al., 2013). Resilience refers to the capacity of a dynamic system to adapt successfully to disturbances that threaten the viability, functioning or development of that system, and the capacity for resilience in humans is distributed across many interacting systems (Masten, 2014). Resilience is a process to harness resources to sustain well-being (Panter-Brick & Leckman, 2013).

A child's attempts to manage extreme anxiety and strong impulses may lead to the child developing primitive defences. Early traumatic experiences can affect this process and decrease the child's ability to regulate affect and increase the likelihood of persisting negative effects, like anger and aggression. Perhaps, the early experience of trauma decreases the child's capacity to understand and interpret other people's behaviour and emotions, and this becomes the genesis of the child's developmental psychopathology. Again, attachment type, which reflects the child's cumulative experience, remains the central coordinator of interpersonal behaviour throughout the course of life (Bowlby, 1973).

Despite the increased risk of psychopathology, a substantial percentage of young adults exhibit resilient functioning following a history of childhood violence. Liu et al. (2017) presented a multi-system model (intra-individual, interpersonal, and socio-ecological) to explain the dynamic and multidimensional nature of the resilience process, describing it as an interaction between individuals and their larger socio-ecological context. Studies investigating the impact of these three groups of resilience factors on CSA's effects have looked at the factors in a combined way; therefore, they remain inconclusive about which factor contributes the most and when combined with which other resilience/vulnerability factors.

Intra-individual Factors

Studies also indicate that maintenance of age-normative levels of social competence and manifestation of clinically significant levels of symptoms subsequent to CSA can go hand in hand. In another systematic review of 37 studies, the percentage of CSA survivors who were found to be functioning normally despite a history of sexual abuse ranged from 10 per cent to 53 per cent. The protective factors that had the best empirical support were found to be 'education', 'interpersonal and emotional competence', 'control beliefs', 'active coping', 'optimism', 'social attachment', 'external attribution of blame' and, most importantly, 'support from the family and the wider social environment' (Domhardt et al., 2014). Pérez-Gonzálezab et al. (2017) found that all forms of sexual victimization were associated with higher levels of emotional and behavioural problems, but the presence of a low negative cognition, high social skills and high confidence could buffer internalization of problems and empathy/tolerance, connectedness to school and connectedness to the family, and low negative cognition acted as a promoting factor in relation to externalization of symptoms. The individual-level factors significantly associated with increased odds of good mental health included 'being physically active in the winter', 'utilizing positive coping strategies' and 'having positive self-esteem and an internal locus of control' (Cheung et al., 2018). With a highly victimized sample (aged 18–24 years and with an average of nine violent experiences reported during childhood), Howell and Miller-Graffb (2014) found that the potency of the protective factors such as greater spirituality, greater emotional intelligence and support from friends (but not from family) outweighed that of adversity and psychopathology when predicting resilient functioning. Ben-David and Jonson-Reid (2017) found that the vast majority of quantitative ($n = 41$) and qualitative ($n = 45$) studies on resilience among adult survivors focused on survivors of sexual and physical abuse rather than survivors of neglect. Further, these studies reached the consensus that 'resiliency prior to age 18 was strongly associated with continued resiliency and positive relationships' and that 'coping skills and optimism were protective factors'. Tianqiang et al. (2015) found 'trait resilience' to be positively correlated to positive indicators of mental health. Adversity moderated the relationship between trait resilience and mental health. The effects were significantly stronger for people in adversity than for those not in adversity. Schultz et al. (2009) reported that a strong relationship exists between a child's social competence, adaptive functioning skills and positive peer relationships and select outcomes 3 years after being investigated for maltreatment, thus 'highlighting the importance of individual-level protective factors for clinical intervention'.

Interpersonal, Familial, Social Support Network Factors

'A warm and supportive relationship with a non-offending parent and lower level of abuse stress, fewer negative cognitive appraisals of the abusive relationship, and less reliance on aggressive coping behaviors were strong correlates of resilience' (Spaccarelli & Soni, 1995). A study reviewing 50 research papers investigating resilient outcomes for people with a history of CSA during 1991–2010 suggested that 'inner resources (e.g., coping skills, interpretation of experiences and self-esteem), family relationships, friendships, community resources (e.g., church or school), as well as some abuse-related factors (e.g., older age at onset)' (Marriot et al., 2014).

Socio-ecological Factors

Using Bronfenbrenner's process–person–context–time (PPCT) ecological model, Williams and Nelson-Gardell (2012) (NSCAW, Dowd et al., 2002) found that school engagement, caregiver social support, hope and expectancy, caregiver education and Socio-economic Status (SES) predicted resilience in adolescent sexual victimization, thus advocating placing greater emphasis on the contextual environment for adolescent resilience. Cheung et al. (2017), in a large, cross-sectional, nationally representative sample of US National Comorbidity Survey: Adolescent Supplement (NCS-A; $n = 10,148$; data collection 2001–2004) adolescents aged 13–17 years and with a history of maltreatment, found that supportive parent and family relationships and positive community and school experiences were significantly associated with good mental health. Resilience studies have identified a broad range of individual and contextual (e.g., in families, communities, services) protective factors associated with buffering, restorative and growth-promoting processes (e.g., see Masten, 2014; Noltemeyer & Bush, 2013). Figure 5.3 presents a summary of the dimensionality of trauma resilience factors in the case of CSA victims.

The academic community, especially professionals studying human development under conditions of psychosocial risk, including sexual violence, has extensively discussed the concept of resilience. Despite

Intra-individual	Interpersonal	Socio-ecological/Context
• IQ, especially emotional IQ • Personality traits • Internal locus of control • Adaptive coping skills • Optimism • Physical activeness • External attribution of blame • Lower level of abuse stress • Fewer negative cognitive appraisals of abuse incident • Older age at onset of abuse • Resilience prior to 18 years	• Secure and supportive family relationships • Trusting peer group • Supportive teachers • Positive parenting and secure parent–child attachment • Stable family • Family practices	• Positive community experiences (including faster legal provisions) • Positive school experiences • Good socio-economic condition • Absence of other forms of maltreatment • Supportive healthcare systems with a robust referral mechanism to expedite healing and recovery and reduce mental health risks

Figure 5.3 *Multidimensional Resilience against Child Sexual Abuse*
Source: Choudhary et al. (2019).

epistemological differences in the theoretical approaches to resilience, a common focus has been the quest for understanding the psychological resources that ensure positive trajectories of well-being for individuals and groups, even when they face significant adversity that is commonly associated with trajectories of vulnerability (Harvey, 1996).

While addressing risk factors is often the focus of prevention activities, building protective factors is also important. To some extent, protective factors are the inverse of risk factors: in the absence of risks, like those discussed earlier, children are much more likely to thrive.

DYNAMICS OF VULNERABILITY RESILIENCE IN CHILD SEXUAL ABUSE: SOME DEBATES

Interestingly, the inherent dependency of children upon the care of others creates in them heightened vulnerability to child abuse. Further, child abuse is rather a socially constructed phenomenon that is shaped by values and beliefs regarding children, child development, child rearing and rights of adults/caregivers over children. Whether a child's vulnerability would continue or resilience would increase is largely dependent upon these socially constructed phenomena. Although theoretically every child may be at a similar risk of CSA, increased vulnerability of a child to CSA is more an indication of particular familial or sociocultural contexts in which the child grows up than an indication of the individual resilience factors within the child.

DOES A VULNERABLE CHILD BECOME A CHILD SEXUAL ABUSE VICTIM OR DOES A CHILD SEXUAL ABUSE VICTIM BECOME MORE VULNERABLE?

The answer to the question of whether a child becomes vulnerable before or after CSA hardly benefits the victim. If CSA was committed because the child was vulnerable to becoming a prey of the offender, then the multidimensional impacts of the incident multiply that child's vulnerability, even for generations. The child has absolutely no control over his/her vulnerable life conditions. He/she may have a wide range and different levels of vulnerabilities that the child has to live with because of his/her multidimensional dependency on the people around him/her. Examining a few specific contexts prevalent in India would help elaborate on the question.

1. 'Vulnerabilities due to economic reasons' include:
   - Parents putting their children into child labour;
   - Financial dependence on the perpetrator within the family;
   - Unsafe location of the residence; and
   - Unsafe neighbourhood (community with high levels of unemployment, poverty, population turnover, inadequate housing).
2. 'Vulnerabilities due to sociocultural practices' include:
   - Loss of parents or a single parent;
   - Presence of step-parents;
   - Lack of a safety network when parents are at work;
   - Large nuclear family size;
   - Low level of education of parents;
   - Child marriage;
   - Cultural beliefs on male potency; and

- CSA-induced migration of parents to other cities or to a different location within the same city, but often without any psycho-education of parents or children on the child's safety. Thus, the vulnerability of the child and parents again continues in the new place.
3. 'Victim-related risk factors' include:
- Disability;
- Poor IQ (intelligence quotient);
- Friendliness and obedience or shyness and fearfulness;
- Substance use/abuse among family member/s;
- Mental illness in parent/s; and
- Interpersonal violence between parents.

Growing up, a child has no control or choice over his/her physical environments or family environment (including child rearing practices, parents' expressed emotions and beliefs, parents' behaviour, parental socio-demographic characteristics or household characteristics). The combination of any two or more vulnerabilities may be toxic for the child in terms of his/her safety and protection. Child development is a complex process involving multiple domains of competency (physical and mental health, cognition, socialization and behaviour). Vulnerability may change over time as children's environments and needs change. Moreover, vulnerability is often accumulative; therefore, multiple vulnerability factors before and after the abuse incident only elevate the chance of intense multidimensional CSA impacts in the absence of any psychological treatment.

WHAT IS ASSESSED IN A CASE OF CHILD SEXUAL ABUSE DURING PSYCHOLOGICAL TREATMENT—RESILIENCE OR VULNERABILITY?

CSA is a serious socio-legal–psychological–pathological phenomenon. It is a social and public health problem. CSA results in a specific trauma, where the process of the victim's psychosocial recovery is demanding for both the victim and the clinician who provides psychological treatment. The manner in which both laypersons and professionals handle CSA cases oftentimes amounts to 'secondary victimization'. Resilient functioning in a child/adolescent/youth with a history of CSA may be measured in terms of different outcome variables. It may be measured in terms of absence of multidimensional impacts of CSA or presence of age-appropriate, expected adaptive functioning in multiple domains of life or presence of success/achievement traits. It may also be measured in terms of the outcomes a clinician looks for, for example, whether to reduce the individual/familial/contextual vulnerability of the child or to strengthen the existing resilience factors in the child. Although commonly well-structured history taking that includes most of the vulnerability and resilience factors helps the therapist formulate a case of treatment, customization of history and treatment protocols is not an exception.

One assessment tool in this regard is the Multidimensional Trauma Recovery and Resiliency Interview (MTRR-I), which assesses strengths and weaknesses across multiple domains of the functioning of a child. It is a semi-structured interview that elicits information concerning a trauma survivor's psychological functioning (Diagneault et al., 2007) and gathers qualitative data of the eight recovery domains (Harvey, 1996; Radan, 2007), including affect regulation and positive coping. It assesses trauma impact, resilience and recovery through open-ended questions regarding an individual's life history, including the trauma history (Radan, 2007). MTRR-I has been combined with other quantitative instruments to answer specific research questions (Diagneault et al., 2007; Radan, 2007).

A wide range of tools/scales to measure specific psychopathology/impact of a CSA incident on a child (e.g., depression, PTSD, anxiety, dissociation, behavioural problems, etc.) are available. The majority of mental health professional focus on the various facets of vulnerability and hardly make efforts to work on the child's resilience.

Along with the impact of the trauma, the level of self-efficacy and resilience of the victim may be predictive of the recovery period for the latter. More specifically, self-efficacy is thought to influence important steps of recovery, such as help-seeking behaviour, resource utilization, disclosure of abuse and reporting of the offence (Finkelhor & Browne, 1986; Foster & Hagedorn, 2014; Lev-Wiesel, 2000). Thus, self-efficacy in a child, measured early, could be a good outcome indicator later on.

FOCUS OF PSYCHOLOGICAL INTERVENTION FOR CHILD SEXUAL ABUSE: IS IT A CHALLENGE?

In cognizance of the fact that the impact of CSA trauma on a child may be moderated by several different risk, vulnerability, and resilience factors, a therapist needs to customize the existing psychotherapy models (for example, cognitive behavioral theory [CBT] or trauma-focused CBT [TF-CBT]) to the individual's needs and context.

However, one also needs to understand that cognitive appraisals and attributions of responsibility mediate the effects of CSA on psychosocial adjustment (Spaccarelli, 1994). After psycho-education, the therapist should look into the child's attribution of responsibility, which might be highly linked to blaming the self or the perpetrator and thus might affect the self-efficacy of the child. The age and gender dynamics of self-blame suggest to a clinician that females are more likely to blame themselves than males (Hunter et al., 1992), and younger females are more likely to blame themselves for CSA incidents than older females. Also, children who blame themselves for the abuse may take longer to disclose (Goodman-Brown et al., 2003). Therapeutic interventions for CSA survivors typically involve helping them recount the sexual abuse while simultaneously attempting to train them to reprocess or restructure beliefs related to the experience(s) and decrease self-blame (Whiffen & Macintosh, 2005).

DOES RESILIENCE HAVE A PREVENTIVE OR CURATIVE ROLE IN CHILD SEXUAL ABUSE?

If disclosure of CSA is considered as an active form of coping (problem-focused) and non-disclosure as avoidant coping (emotion-focused), which is associated with more negative outcomes (Whiffen & Macintosh, 2005), then disclosure itself is part of resilience. Also, children's appraisals of how other people may react to the disclosure, along with their perceptions of responsibility for the abuse, have been associated with the likelihood of disclosure (Goodman-Brown et al., 2003). Wyatt and Mickey (1988) reported that children were less likely to disclose when they attributed the cause of the incident to internal, as opposed to external, events. In the case of CSA victims, the resilience process might have started before the disclosure, but the point of disclosure perhaps can be considered as an active resilience indicator that theoretically and empirically has a primarily preventive role in terms of early diagnosis of signs and symptoms of any abnormality (e.g., onset of pregnancy or mental or behavioural problems). Defining the magnitude and severity of CSA impacts, as well as has a curative role in, early treatment seeking, early reporting and legal processing, etc.

PROMOTING AND NURTURING RESILIENCE DURING CHILDHOOD

Do the Legal Frameworks Focus on Vulnerability or Resilience?

The primary purposes of all legal frameworks in terms of acts and bills are perhaps to highlight issues, to identify the vulnerable and to deter the behaviours that cause vulnerability. Thus, the core focus of the legal frameworks on CSA is on prevention of crime and protection of the vulnerable. Whereas some may perceive the legal frameworks as more vulnerability-focused, others might perceive them as building a resilient socio-ecological environment through deterring criminal behaviour. The cumbersome process of justice delivery and recovery of the family to normalcy mediate whether the legal process increases the vulnerability of the child or increases the resilience of the child. Nevertheless, resilience in terms of CSA has never been spelt out so overtly in any legal framework as it has been in the POCSO Act; the very name of the act contains the word 'Protection' in it. Perhaps, this inbuilt resilience has seen resulting in the increased number of formal reports of CSA cases in India, but there is a long way to go to actually prevent or deter the criminal behaviour and reduce the actual vulnerability of the children, which calls for massive community awareness and prevention programmes.

Models of Child Sexual Abuse: Role of Society/Culture as a Whole in Preventing Vulnerabilities and Promoting and Nurturing Resilience

Two predominantly referenced models that explain CSA are the public health model and the socio-ecological model (Esposito & Field, 2016).

1. The primary goal of the 'public health model' is prevention of any event that has potential health risks. In the case of CSA, it does emphasize primary (preventing abuse before it occurs), secondary (reducing the risk of sexual abuse occurring in vulnerable populations) and tertiary prevention (minimizing the impact of CSA once it has occurred) of CSA. It includes a four-stage approach to defining and responding to CSA:
   - Surveillance—identifying the extent of the problem and also specific vulnerable areas;
   - Risk and protective factors—identifying the causes and correlates of violence, victim or offender (like alcohol and drug abuse by the offender) factors that increase the risk of CSA taking place and factors that can be modified through interventions, particular large-scale community-based interventions;
   - Evaluation of interventions—establishing what works for whom, when and where in preventing violence through the design, monitoring and evaluation of interventions; and
   - Scaling up of promising interventions and monitoring of their economic and policy impacts.
2. The 'socio-ecological model' is often applied in conjunction with the public health model. Although the model examines the complexity of relationships between individuals, families, communities and the wider social environment which either put people at risk of CSA or protect them from experiencing or perpetrating violence, it is primarily based on the resilience theory. The four key elements in the model are:
   - Microsystems—individual-level factors that increase the likelihood of a person becoming a victim or offender of CSA (earlier discussed in vulnerability and resilience factors). Microsystems are generally a product of interaction among the ecosystem, mesosystem and macrosystem.
   - Ecosystems—interpersonal relationships (friends, extended family, school peers) that may increase the risk of perpetration/experience of CSA by offenders/victims;
   - Mesosystems—community-level influences (school, workplace, neighbourhoods) that increase the risk of or protect against experience by victims or offenders of CSA, for example,

reduction in social isolation, support for housing or employment and policies within schools and workplaces;

- Macrosystems—societal values or norms that support or inhibit sexual abuse against children.

While implementation of the public health model appears difficult, it could still be feasible if states take the matter seriously, at least the vulnerable pockets of the states, to start with. CSA as a public health issue does not even come under the purview of the National Health Policy in India. On the other hand, the socio-ecological model is more complex and its implementation less feasible, due to the diversities presence in India. Although efforts can start from the meso-systems of the socio-ecological model, that is from school where prevention of CSA offending and building resilience both are still feasible but again depends on the priority of the CSA to be considered as a serious social or public health issue by the state/society. Ensuring the safety and protection of a child is an adult responsibility and also is fundamental for building resilience and nurturing it in the child. In this line, educating a child about his/her safety although futuristic and preventive in perspective there are many other measures that should start simultaneously to build a resilient society.

CONCLUSION

Child abuse is a complex phenomenon, with multidimensional effects and multiple causes explaining its occurrence, development and sustenance of deleterious effects and recovery to normalcy. It is important to know that each child reacts to and copes with CSA in a different way, depending on his/her specific risk and resilience factors. Therefore, each child victim needs psychiatric and psychological assessments to expedite the process of treatment and recovery. However, comprehensive protective, preventive and curative services are still a dream, and currently the service provision following CSA reporting is limited to essential legal, medical and lay counselling services in India. Preventive and clinical interventions for survivors of CSA should focus on both behavioural and cognitive strategies that are adapted to the developmental level of the victim and which seek to enhance social support from significant others. Longitudinal research examining multiple dimensions of resilience as a dynamic process in both socio-ecological and child-developmental contexts should be promoted.

REFERENCES

Alexander, P. C. (1992). Application of attachment theory to the study of sexual abuse. *Journal of Consulting & Clinical Psychology, 60*(2), 185–195.

Alexander, C. (1993). The differential effects of abuse characteristics and attachment in the prediction of longterm effects of sexual abuse. *Journal of Interpersonal Violence, 8,* 346–362.

Antonovsky, A. (1979). Health, stress, and coping. New perspectives on mental and physical well-being, 12–37.

Antonovsky, A. (1984). Health, stress and coping. Family Systems Medicine, 2(1), 94–98.

Bagley, C., Bolitho, F., & Bertrand, L. (1995). Mental health profiles, suicidal behavior, and community sexual assault in 2112 Canadian adolescents. Crisis, 16(3), 126–131.

Bandura, A. (1982). The assessment and predictive generality of self-percepts of efficacy. Journal of behavior therapy and experimental psychiatry, 13(3), 195–199.

Barboza, G. E., Dominguez, S., & Pinder, J. (2017). Trajectories of post-traumatic stress and externalizing psychopathology among maltreated foster care youth: A parallel process latent growth curve model. *Child Abuse & Neglect, 72,* 370–382.

Ben-David, V., & Jonson-Reid, M. (2017, July). Resilience among adult survivors of childhood neglect: A missing piece in the resilience literature. *Children and Youth Services Review, 78,* 93–103.

Benight, C. C., & Bandura, A. (2004). Social cognitive theory of posttraumatic recovery: The role of perceived self-efficacy. Behaviour research and Therapy, 42(10), 1129–1148.

Bernard-Bonnin, A., Hébert, M., Daignault, I., & Allard-Dansereau, C. (2008). Disclosure of sexual abuse, and personal and familial factors as predictors of post-traumatic stress disorder symptoms in school-aged girls. *Pediatrics and Child Health, 13,* 479–486.

Bonanno, G. A. (2004). Loss, trauma, and human resilience: Have we underestimated the human capacity to thrive after extremely adverse events? *American Psychologist, 59,* 20–28.

Bonanno, G. A. (2012). Uses and abuses of the resilience construct: Loss, trauma, and health-related adversities. *Social Science and Medicine, 74,* 753–756.

Boney-McCoy, S., & Finkelhor, D. (1995). Prior victimization: A risk factor for child sexual abuse and for PTSD-related symptomatology among sexually abused youth. *Child Abuse & Neglect, 19*(12), 1401–1421.

Bowlby, J. (1973). *Attachment and loss: Vol. 2. Separation.* Basic Books.

Briere, J., & Elliott, D. M. (2003). Prevalence and psychological sequelae of self-reported childhood physical and sexual abuse in a general population sample of men and women. Child abuse & neglect, 27(10), 1205–1222.

Cecil, H., & Matson, S. C. (2001). Psychological functioning and family discord among African-American adolescent females with and without a history of childhood sexual abuse. Child Abuse & Neglect, 25(7), 973–988.

Cheung, K., Taillieu, T., Turner, S., Fortier, J., Sareen, J., MacMillan, L. H., Boyle, H., & Afifi, O. T. (2017, August). Relationship and community factors related to better mental health following child maltreatment among adolescents. Child Abuse & Neglect, 70, 377–387.

Cheung, K., Taillieu, T., Turner, S., Fortier, J., Sareen, J., MacMillan, L. H., Boyle, M. H., & Afifi, O. T. (2018, May). Individual-level factors related to better mental health outcomes following child maltreatment among adolescents. Child Abuse & Neglect, 79, 192–202.

Choudhary, V., Satapathy, S., & Sagar, R. (2019). Qualitative study on the impact of child sexual abuse: Perspectives of children, caregivers, and professionals in Indian context. Journal of Child Sexual Abuse, 28(4), 489–510.

Cieslak, R., Benight, C. C., & Lehman, V. C. (2008). Coping self-efficacy mediates the effects of negative cognitions on posttraumatic distress. Behaviour research and therapy, 46(7), 788–798.

Colton, M., Roberts, S., & Vanstone, M. (2010). Sexual abuse by men who work with children. Journal of Child Sexual Abuse, 19, 345–364.

Coohey, C. (2010). Gender differences in internalizing problems among sexually abused early adolescents. Child Abuse & Neglect, 34(11), 856–862.

Crosson-Tower, C. (2002). When Children Are Abused: An Educator's Guide to Intervention. College Division, Allyn & Bacon, Inc., 75 Arlington Street, Suite 300, Boston, MA 02116. http://www. ablongman.com.

Domhardt, M., Münzer, A., Fegert, J. M., & Goldbeck, L. (2015, October). Resilience in survivors of child sexual abuse: A systematic review of the literature. Trauma Violence Abuse, 16(4), 476–493. https://dx.doi.org/10.1177/1524838014557288

Dong, M., Anda, R. F., Dube, S. R., Giles, W. H., & Felitti, V. J. (2003). The relationship of exposure to childhood sexual abuse to other forms of abuse, neglect, and household dysfunction during childhood. Child Abuse & Neglect, 27(6), 625–639.

Dubey, V., Prakash, S., & Gupta, A. (1998). Voices from the silent zone-Women's experiences of Incest and Childhood Sexual Abuse'. Recovering and Healing from Incest (RAHI), New Delhi.

English, D. J., Upadhyaya, M. P., Litrownik, A. J., Marshall, J. M., Runyan, D. K., Graham, J. C., & Dubowitz, H. (2005). Maltreatment's wake: The relationship of maltreatment dimensions to child outcomes. Child Abuse & Neglect, 29, 597–619.

Estes, R. J. (2001). The sexual exploitation of children: A guide to the empirical literature.

Fanslow, J. (2007). Urgent need for child abuse prevention. *Women's Studies Association (NZ) Newsletter, 28*(2), 11.

Finkelhor, D. (1984). *Child sexual abuse; New theory and research.* The Free Press.

Finkelhor, D. (1994). The international epidemiology of child sexual abuse. *Child Abuse & Neglect, 18*(5), 409–417.

Finkelhor, D., & Browne, A. (1986). Impact of child sexual abuse: A review of the research. *Psychological Bulletin, 99,* 66–77.

Finkelhor, D., Turner, H., Ormrod, R., & Hamby, S. L. (2010). Trends in childhood violence and abuse exposure: Evidence from 2 national surveys. *Archives of Pediatrics and Adolescent Medicine, 164,* 238–242.

Foster, J. M., & Hagedorn, W. B. (2014). Through the eyes of the wounded: A narrative analysis of children's sexual abuse experiences and recovery process. Journal of child sexual abuse, 23(5), 538–557.

Gibson, L. E., & Leitenberg, H. (2001). The impact of child sexual abuse and stigma on methods of coping with sexual assault among undergraduate women. *Child Abuse & Neglect, 25,* 1343–1361.

Gilbert, R., Widom, C. S., Browne, K., Fergusson, D., Webb, E., & Janson, S. (2009). Burden and consequences of child maltreatment in high-income countries. *Lancet, 373,* 68–81.

Holt, M. K., Finkelhor, D., & Kantor, G. K. (2007). Multiple victimization experiences of urban elementary school students: Associations with psychosocial functioning and academic performance. *Child Abuse & Neglect, 31*(5), 503–515.

Howell, K. H., & Miller-Graffb, L. E. (2014, December). Protective factors associated with resilient functioning in young adulthood after childhood exposure to violence. *Child Abuse & Neglect, 38*(12), 1985–1994.

Jonzon, E., & Lindblad, F. (2004). Disclosure, reactions, and social support: Findings from a sample of adult victims of child sexual abuse. *Child Maltreatment, 9,* 190–200.

Laaksonen, T., Sariola, H., Johansson, A., Jern, P., Varjonen, M., von der Pahlen, B., Kenneth Sandnabba, N., & Santtila, P. (2011). Changes in the prevalence of child sexual abuse, its risk factors, and their associations as a function of age cohort in a Finnish population sample. *Child Abuse & Neglect, 35,* 480–490.

Lamb, M. E., Hershkowitz, I., Orbach, Y., & Esplin, P. W. (2008). *Tell me what happened: Structured investigative interviews of child victims and witnesses* (p. 201). Wiley.

Lamoureux, B. E., Palmieri, P. A., Jackson, A. P., & Hobfoll, S. E. (2012). Child sexual abuse and adulthood-interpersonal outcomes: Examining pathways for intervention. Psychological Trauma: Theory, Research, Practice, and Policy, 4(6), 605.

Lev-Wiesel, R. (2000). Quality of life in adult survivors of childhood sexual abuse who have undergone therapy. Journal of Child Sexual Abuse, 9(1), 1–13.

Liu, J. J. W., Reed, M., & Girard, T. A. (2017, June). Advancing resilience: An integrative, multi-system model of resilience. *Personality and Individual Differences, 111,* 111–118.

London, K., Bruck, M., Wright, D., & Ceci, S. (2008). Review of the contemporary literature on how children report sexual abuse to others: Findings, methodological issues, and implications for forensic interviewers. *Memory, 16*, 29–47.

MacLeod, M., & Saraga, E. (1988). *Child sexual abuse: Towards a feminist professional practice.* Report of the conference held by The Child Abuse Studies Unit, Department of Applied Social Studies. The Polytechnic of North London.

Maikovich-Fong, A. K., & Jaffee, S. R. (2010). Sex differences in childhood sexual abuse characteristics and victims' emotional and behavioral problems: Findings from a national sample of youth. *Child Abuse & Neglect, 34*, 429–437.

Marriot, C., Hamilton-Giachritsis, C., & Harrop, C. (2014, January/February). Factors promoting resilience following childhood sexual abuse: A structured, narrative review of the literature. *Child Abuse Review, 23*(1), 17–34.

Marshall, W. L., & Barbaree, H. E. (1990). An integrated theory of the etiology of sexual offending. In Handbook of sexual assault (pp. 257–275). Springer.

Masten, A. S. (2011). Resilience in children threatened by extreme adversity: Frameworks for research, practice, and translational synergy. *Development and Psychopathology, 23*(2), 141–154.

Masten, A. S. (2014). Global perspectives on resilience in children and youth. *Child Development, 85*(1), 6–20. https://dx.doi.org/10.1111/cdev. 12205

McNally, R. J. (2007). Betrayal trauma theory: A critical appraisal. *Memory, 15*, 280–294.

Mikulincer, M., & Shaver, P. P. (2007). *Attachment in adulthood: Structure, dynamics, and change.* Guildford.

Modelli, M. E., Galvão, M. F., & Pratesi, R. (2012). Child sexual abuse. *Forensic Science International, 217*, 1–4.

Naar-King, S., Silvern, L., Ryan, V., & Serbring, D. (2002). Type and severity of abuse as predictors of psychiatric symptoms in adolescence. *Journal of Family Violence, 17*(2), 133–149.

OgÅodek, E., & Araszkiewicz, A. (2011). The Jung model of active style of schema. *Pol MerkurLekarski, 31*, 378–380.

Panter-Brick, C., & Eggerman, M. (2012). Understanding culture, resilience, and mental health: The production of hope. In M. Ungar (Ed.), *The social ecology of resilience: A handbook of theory and practice* (pp. 369–386). Springer.

Panter-Brick, C., & Leckman, J. F. (2013). Editorial commentary: Resilience in child development—Interconnected pathways to wellbeing. *The Journal of Child Psychology and Psychiatry, 54*, 333–336. https://dx.doi.org/10.1111/jcpp.12057

Panter-Brick, C., Grimon, M.-P., & Eggerman, M. (2014). Caregiverchild mental health: A prospective study in conflict and refugee settings. *Journal of Child Psychology and Psychiatry, 55*(4), 313–337. https://dx.doi.org/10.1111/jcpp.12167

Panter-Brick, C., Goodman, A., Tol, W., & Eggerman, M. (2011). Mental health and childhood adversities: A longitudinal study in Kabul, Afghanistan. *Journal of the American Academy of Child & Adolescent Psychiatry, 50*(4), 349–363.

Pérez-Gonzálezab, A., Georgina, G., Noemí, P., & Adolfo, J. (2017). Protective factors promoting resilience in the relation between child sexual victimization and internalizing and externalizing symptoms. *Child Abuse & Neglect, 72*, 393–403.

Pithers, W. D. (1990). Relapse prevention with sexual aggressors. In Handbook of sexual assault (pp. 343–361). Springer.

Priebe, G., & Svedin, C. G. (2009). Prevalence, characteristics, and associations of sexual abuse with sociodemographics and consensual sex in a population-based sample of Swedish adolescents. Journal of Child Sexual Abuse, 18, 19–39.

Priest, R., & Smith, A. (1992). Counseling adult sexual offenders: Unique challenges and treatment paradigms. *Journal of Counseling & Development, 71*, 27–32.

Putnam, F. W. (2003). Ten-year research update review: Child sexual abuse. *Journal of the American Academy of Child & Adolescent Psychiatry, 42*(3), 269–278.

Putnam, F. W. (2003). Ten-year research update review: Child sexual abuse. *Journal of the American Academy of Child & Adolescent Psychiatry, 42*(3), 269–278.

Ramírez, C., Pinzón-Rondón, A. M., & Botero, J. C. (2011). Contextual predictive factors of child sexual abuse: The role of parent-child interaction. *Child Abuse & Neglect, 35*, 1022–1031.

Reese-Weber, M., & Smith, D. M. (2011). Outcomes of child sexual abuse as predictors of later sexual victimization. Journal of Interpersonal Violence, 26(9), 1884–1905.

Romano, E., & De Luca, R. V. (2001). Male sexual abuse: A review of effects, abuse characteristics, and links with later psychological functioning. *Aggression and Violent Behavior, 6*(1), 55–78.

Schultz, D., Tharp-Taylor, S., Haviland, A., & Jaycox, L. (2009, October). The relationship between protective factors and outcomes for children investigated for maltreatment. *Child Abuse & Neglect, 33*(10), 684–698.

Sedlak, A. J., Mettenburg, J., Basena, M., Peta, I., McPherson, K., & Greene, A. (2010). Fourth national incidence study of child abuse and neglect (NIS-4). Washington, DC: US Department of Health and Human Services, 9, 2010.

Sinanan, A. N. (2011). The impact of child, family, and child perspective services factors on reports of child sexual abuse recurrence. *Journal of Child Sexual Abuse, 20*, 657–676.

Smallbone, S., & Wortley, R. K. (2000). *Child sexual abuse in Queensland: Offender characteristics and modus operandi.* Queensland Crime Commission and Queensland Police Service.

Snyder, H. N. (2000). *Sexual assault of young children as reported to law enforcement: Victim, incident, and offender characteristics.* A NIBRS Statistical Report.

Spaccarelli, S. (1994). Stress, appraisal, and coping in child sexual abuse: A theoretical and empirical review. *Psychological Bulletin, 116*(2), 340–362.

Spaccarelli, S., & Soni, K. (1995, September). Resilience criteria and factors associated with resilience in sexually abused girls. *Child Abuse & Neglect, 19*(9), 1171–1182.

Startzyk, K. B., & Marshall, W. L. (2003). Childhood family and personological risk factors for sexual offending. *Aggression and Violent Behaviour, 8*, 93–105.

Steel, J., Sanna, L., Hammond, J., Whipple, J., & Cross, H. (2004). Psychological sequelae of child sexual abuse: Abuse-related characteristics, coping strategies, and attributional style. *Child Abuse & Neglect, 28*, 785–801.

Stern, A. E., Lynch, D. L., Oates, R. K., O'Toole, B. I., & Cooney, G. (1995). Self esteem, depression, behaviour and family functioning in sexually abused children. Journal of Child Psychology and Psychiatry, 36(6), 1077–1089.

Stoltenborgh, M., Van Ijzendoorn, M. H., Euser, E. M., & Bakermans-Kranenburg, M. J. (2011). A global perspective on child sexual abuse: Meta-analysis of prevalence around the world. Child maltreatment, 16(2), 79–101.

Strümpfer, D. J. W. (1990). Salutogenesis: A new paradigm. South African Journal of Psychology, 20(4), 265–276.

Swanston, H. Y., Plunkett, A. M., O'Toole, B. I., Shrimpton, S., Parkinson, P. N., & Oates, R. K. (2003). Nine years after child sexual abuse. Child abuse & neglect, 27(8), 967–984.

Thibodeaua, M., Lavoiea, F., Hébert, M., & Blais, M. (2017). Childhood maltreatment and adolescent sexual risk behaviors: Unique, cumulative and interactive effects. *Child Abuse & Neglect, 72*, 411–420.

Tianqiang, H., Zhang, D., & Wang, J. (2015, April). A meta-analysis of the trait resilience and mental health. *Personality and Individual Differences, 76*, 18–27.

Trickett, P. K., Noll, J. G., & Putnam, W. F. (2011, May). The impact of sexual abuse on female development: Lessons from a multigenerational, longitudinal research study. *Developmental Psychopathology, 23*(2), 453–476. https://dx.doi.org/10.1017/S0954579411000174

Ward, T., Hudson, S. M., Marshall, W. L., & Siegert, R. (1995). Attachment style and intimacy deficits in sexual offenders: A theoretical framework. Sexual Abuse, 7(4), 317–335.

Ward, T., Louden, K., Hudson, S. M., & Marshall, W. L. (1995). A descriptive model of the offense chain for child molesters. Journal of Interpersonal Violence, 10(4), 452–472.

Whiffen, V. E., & Macintosh, H. B. (2005). Mediators of the link between childhood sexual abuse and emotional distress: A critical review. *Trauma Violence Abuse, 6*(1), 24–39.

Williams, J., & Nelson-Gardell, D. (2012, January). Predicting resilience in sexually abused adolescents. *Child Abuse & Neglect, 36*(1), 53–63.

World Health Organization. (1999). Report of the consultation on child abuse prevention, 29–31 March 1999, WHO, Geneva (No. WHO/HSC/PVI/99.1). World Health Organization.

World Health Organization. (2002). World health organization says violence against children can and must be prevented. In World Health Organization says violence against children can and must be prevented (pp. 2–2).

Yehuda, R., & Flory, J. D. (2007). Differentiating biological correlates of risk, PTSD, and resilience following trauma exposure. *Journal of Traumatic Stress, 20*(4), 435–447.

Yehuda, R., Bierer, L. M., Pratchett, L. C., & Pelcovitz, M. (2010). Using biological markers to inform a clinically meaningful treatment response. *Annals of the New York Academy of Sciences, 1208,* 158–163. https://dx.doi.org/10.11 11/j.1749-6632.2010.05698

Yehuda, R., Daskalakis, N. P., Desarnaud, F., Makotkine, I., Lehrner, A. L., Koch, E., Flory, J. D., Buxbaum, J. D., Meaney, M. J., & Bierer, L. M. (2013). Epigenetic biomarkers as predictors and correlates of symptom improvement following psychotherapy in combat veterans with PTSD. *Frontiers in Psychiatry, 4,* 118. https://dx.doi.org/10.3389/fpsyt.2013.00118

Chapter 6

Invulnerable Parkinson's Caregivers
An Existential Phenomenological Perspective

Supreet Kaur Bhasin and Ishita U. Bharadwaj

CAREGIVING AND VULNERABILITY

Being able to care for one's loved ones can be a rewarding experience, but such experiences, expecting one to lean into possibilities and capacities, which were never known, come with their own share of obstacles. Individuals and families living with chronic neurodegenerative diseases are often required to deal with several kinds of care responsibilities and needs, which are not only unanticipated but also need to be endured for years and decades into the future. With the countless tasks that need to be shouldered and increasing responsibility, a caregiver undergoes a turbulent journey of exhaustion, fatigue and upheaval. However, in the light of the patient's hardships and difficulties, the sufferings of the caregivers are often neglected. Does not witnessing the decline in the well-being of one's loved ones, experiencing the most treasured relationships of one's life becoming obscure and undergoing depletion of salient aspects of one's own personhood, due to the endless sacrifices, make also the caregivers a group of vulnerable individuals? Through this chapter, we hope to re-examine the journey of caregiving for persons with Parkinson's disease (PD) and thereby explain the shades of vulnerability in the context of caregivers. It is critical to acknowledge how the repetition of servitude, neglecting oneself in the process of donning the caregiver identity and silently, without any surety, persistently working to improve the ailing health of a loved one, for a long-standing period, without any closure, can make caregiving an arduous reality to live with. This chapter highlights the vulnerability experienced by caregivers of Parkinson's-afflicted patients as they battled through the disease, through discussing a phenomenological study performed to understand the lived experience of being a Parkinson's caregiver in the sociocultural context of India.

OVERVIEW OF NEURODEGENERATIVE DISORDERS AND CAREGIVING

I can't control my body the way I want to, I can't control when I feel good or when I don't, and I can't control how clear my mind is…with Parkinson's your body has a mind of its own….

Michael J. Fox (2007)

The Face of Parkinson's Disease: A Neurodegenerative Disorder

Neurological disorders are becoming increasingly prevalent all over the world, and it is with profound ruthlessness that a neurodegenerative disease strikes the life of an individual. From experiencing immobilization of voluntary muscles, to experiencing frequent falls due to inadequate control over one's reflexes, to living with the terror of losing one's mind and cherished self, a neurodegenerative disease slowly weighs upon each and every aspect of an individual's life. Neurodegenerative diseases are chronic diseases, caused due to damage to the neurons in the brain and spinal cord, which makes them immedicable and debilitating in nature. One such disease is PD, which with its exigent yet indeterminate characteristics is likely to take a toll on any person. PD is an age-related illness and usually arises around the age of 50–65 years (Abbas et al., 2017). It impacts various systems of an individual's body and causes both motor (tremors, rigidity, bradykinesia, akinesia and balance impairment) and non-motor impairments (depression, sleep disturbances and pain) (National Institute of Neurological Disorders and Stroke, 2013). On an everyday basis, it usually entails battling with frozen limbs, hampered speech and swallowing, distorted gait, frustratingly long time for performing basic, ordinary movements and a decline in memory (Sveinbjornsdottir, 2016). What makes it all the more problematic is that the range of symptoms in PD can constantly fluctuate on a daily or even hourly basis within the individual (Zhao et al., 2010). Consequently, sufferers live with this disease for the rest of their lives and, as the disease advances, patients increasingly become disabled, until eventually their movement and functioning becomes vastly limited (Hammarlund et al., 2018).

Parkinson's and Caregiving: Family Members as Agents of Informal Care

Nabokov had once written in his novel *Pale Fire*: 'Neurodegenerative diseases do not just "happen" to a single individual, they affect the individual's spouse, children, grandchildren, friends, neighbours and colleagues'. Apart from an insight into the severity of the symptoms prevalent in PD, this contains an inference about how PD does not just affect the person living with it but also affects the entire family and an extended community of friends, since the burden of caring for the person with PD is largely borne by his/her loved ones. In literature, a caregiver has been defined as an individual who helps with physical and psychological care for a person in need (Abendroth et al., 2012). The role of a caregiver involves different kinds of tasks. The term 'instrumental caregiving' includes the responsibilities like providing personal care and helping with daily household chores, whereas 'expressive caregiving' is used to refer to providing aid in social activities and emotional support (Sherman et al., 1988; Smith et al., 2019).

Studies have shown that individuals caring for family members with PD, referred to as informal caregivers, often face numerous challenges and have to constantly adapt themselves to the unpredictable nature of the disease and consequent demands of the patient. This often results in an experience of caregiver burden (Abendroth et al., 2012; Leiknes et al., 2015; Martínez-Martin et al., 2008). Caregiver burden had been recognized as early as in the 1960s, and a lot of research has since focused on the burnout experience of caregivers, as well as their deteriorating quality of life (Croog et al., 2006; Leiknes et al., 2015; Takai et al., 2009). Literature on caregiving consistently documents high psychological costs (Kim et al., 2010; Lee & Kim, 2009; Lee et al., 2019), with an escalated risk for developing health problems, sadness and anxiety and for facing social isolation (Joling et al., 2010; Richardson et al., 2013; Salvatore et al., 2015). In addition, caregiving has also been found to contribute to psychiatric morbidity, as well as functioning as an independent risk factor for mortality (Schulz & Beach, 2009).

Prevailing Models of Caregiving

One of the earliest models for the burden experienced by families who care for the elderly was proposed by Poulshock and Deimling (1984)—the analytic model. This model assumed that the burden experienced by caregivers is dependent on their personal response to specific caregiving contexts. As per the researchers, the caregiver's own mental and physical well-being influences their capacity to engage in caregiving responsibilities. Consequently, those with lower levels of well-being experience higher burden.

Braithwaite (1986, 1987) was also one of the prominent scholars to propose a model to account for the frustrations around basic needs of caregivers leading to caregiver burden among them. He identified the following five characteristics of family care for elderly people: awareness of generation; unpredictability; time constraints; the caregiver–receiver relationship; and lack of choice in ways of caring for the ill relative.

Rew et al. (1987) also developed a nursing intervention model, AFFIRM, for caregiving of elderly patients. This model emphasizes five steps that aim to promote mastery among family caregivers: availability, formulation, factual information, referrals and monitoring (AFFIRM).

Despite adding significant knowledge to the understanding of caregiver strain, these caregiving models have been known to suffer from certain limitations (Lawton et al., 1991; Pearlin et al., 1990). For instance, they under-emphasize the complexity of relationships between stressors, protective factors and appraisal variables (Spruytte et al., 2002). In addition, while many of these models have been validated and been applicable in cases of varied caregiving populations (e.g., persons with dementia, elderly persons), rarely has any study focused on the association between burden and well-being, specifically in PD caregivers. Since, with every disorder, the impacts and needs of the caregiver are likely to vary, understanding the concerns and challenges associated with PD, specifically, becomes crucial.

The noteworthiest and most significant contribution to the caregiving paradigm, annulling the limitations of various models, was that by Goldsworthy and Knowles (2008), who proposed the path model. This model investigated the interrelationships between the caregiver, various stressors and their impact on the burden of the caregiver. In addition, it also explored the role of protective factors, such as perceived social support, self-esteem, frequency of breaks and quality of the caregiver–care recipient relationship, on caregiver burden.

Caregiving in India: Acknowledging Culture in the Provision of Care

With a dramatic increase in the ageing population of India, the incidence of neurodegenerative diseases like PD is also rising and subsequently contributing to a greater number of individuals having to assume the caregiver role (Radhakrishnan & Goyal, 2018). To date, however, the nature, variations and epidemiology of PD, as experienced by individuals residing in regions outside of the United States, Canada and Europe, have been rarely examined (Pringsheim et al., 2014). Furthermore, over the years, literature has demonstrated, though not conclusively, that there is a plausibility that in the context of epidemiology, genetics or response to treatment of PD, the Indian population may be at variance with the rest of the world (Radhakrishnan & Goyal, 2018). When the experience of disease varies, the consequent role, demands and hassles thrust upon the family caregivers are also likely to vary.

Additionally, the social–cultural–psychological scenario and the family structures and dynamics are also specific and unique in our country. The context and experience of informal caregiving are shaped differently in a country like India, since the allocentric and collectivistic values and norms place greater emphasis on the well-being of the family over the self (Kadoya & Khan, 2015). Moreover, the moral, emotional and religious values influence the kind of engagement and responsibility deemed as necessary by the family members of an ailing person, making caregiving an indelible part of any family relations in our culture. In addition, the gendered expectations of care and social sanctions ensure that most of the caregiving responsibilities are undertaken by women in the family (Ugargol & Ajay Bailey, 2018). However, there is a paucity of explanatory models accounting for the subjective experiences of PD caregivers in the current sociocultural milieu of India (Sanyal et al., 2015).

INTERSUBJECTIVITIES OF CARE

Re-examining the Concept of Caregiving: Identifying Lacunas

Even though the established models of caregiving are of assistance, as stepping stones for moving closer to the experience of burden borne by the caregivers, they majorly offer correlates of caregiver stress and shed little light on the experiential understanding of the caregiving phenomenon.

Furthermore, despite the objective indicators of stress faced by caregivers, there is considerable variability in terms of the reactions that each caregiver displays to the demands of caregiving. It is, hence, necessary to intimately understand the life of these individuals existing as a 'being-for' other, finding coherence in their lives while dealing with uncertain roles, pressures and challenges. Individuals providing care to their family members afflicted with PD are embedded in such realities and are coerced to re-position themselves with the insidious nature of the disease, and its encumbering impact on their loved ones.

Keeping this in mind, it becomes critical to broaden the understanding of caregiving as lived and endured by an individual, and be encompassing of the varied arrays of experiences encountered by the person while donning the caregiver role. Thus, the following section elaborates on the experiences of being a PD caregiver, through accounting for the caregiver narratives as another equally valid perspective of living with PD. Taking an idiographic approach to family members' experiences of living with PD, it makes sense of their subjective experiences while dealing with the challenging complications of the disease, in the course of daily life, within their relational realms. Additionally, it sheds light on the meaning making indulged in by the caregivers while negotiating a spacio-temporal realm with a timeless, irreversible disease.

Admixing Narratives and Caregiving

As a caregiver, what is one's personal meaning of giving care? What form of commitment did I perceive and expect of myself while investing in the caregiver role? How did that shape my life, my frustrations and my moments of hope and contentment? It is through such reflections about one's life events, developing personal narrative accounts to integrate and retain countless emotions and thoughts encountered on a daily basis, that an individual finds coherence in his/her life events. As proposed by Reissman (2008), narratives, being constructive in nature, present an individual with the opportunity to weave their experiences into stories and thereby form the foundation to give meaning to one's life. Narratives have usually been defined as means of communication which bespeak of change and permanence simultaneously, by allowing an individual to reflect on the spatial, temporal, mental and cultural meanings of their life experiences. This helps form a coherent whole for a better understanding of the self and the other (Ricoeur, 2003; Ryan, 2007).

The core essence of narratives is thus to share power through conversations and enable a participant to share their story in their own way, to move closer to their lived experiences. Furthermore, narratives allow for complexities, such as negotiations, problems, dilemmas and contradictions, to exist, both in the exchange of the conversation and in a subjective sense, within the researcher and the researched. Consequently, the authors like Bury (1982) and Hyden (1997) have often stressed, over the years, the significance of using narratives with individuals suffering from challenging life situations, like chronic illnesses. This is because, they believe, an illness constitutes a disruption and discontinuance in one's ongoing life. As a result, in cases when a person faces a prolonged illness, the need to reconstruct one's life story by linking the past life with the present state of illness is strong.

Analogically, even caregivers are coerced to confront a non-normative transitory phase in their lives, by virtue of being the nearest member in the vicinity of an ailed individual. As a result, these individuals living with those inflicted with chronic illnesses also seek an opportunity to re-position themselves and communicate their subjective experiences. In this particular context, narrative becomes an opportunity for the caregivers to give voice to the disruption and to do so within a time framework not separated from the other life events that form part of their autobiographical story.

Author's Positionality: Exploring One's Subjective Grounds in the Course of Research

In 1934, T. S. Eliot had suggested that one of the key purposes of our life is to matter to others. However, I wondered, can mattering too much also create paradoxes within and impact the mental health of an individual? As a child I had seen my father take care of my grandfather who was suffering from cancer, and it was while observing him that I discovered how excessive responsibilities and role strain impacted his sense of mattering and, instead, often clouded his daily life with contradictory emotions. I had witnessed him needing assistance in dutifully performing the additional responsibilities, feeling emotionally drained, evaluating himself over the quality of care he could provide and, in between those stressful moments, waiting and silently appreciating the 'good days' as well. However, the meaning and experience of good days and moments altered with the severity of my grandfather's illness.

As a researcher who aligns with the interpretive paradigm, I feel that my own experience as a witness to a caregiver's life influenced my values and my subjective understanding of my participants' experiences. While moving closer to the lived and embodied meaning of caregiving for these individuals, I also found myself time and again re-examining the fundamental meaning and facets of care itself. As they shared their daily struggles around routine, exhaustion, a questionable sense of agency and the accompanying frustration of being overburdened, they also shared the fear and guilt of not being enough, the sadness of losing an integral family member and a persistent desire to improve their reciprocal commitment of care for the other. Hence, through a narrative inquiry, I wished to understand if our shared space of expression of vulnerability could also serve as an opportunity for the caregivers to acknowledge and nurture their resilience through their moments of vulnerability. At the same time, I wanted to move close to their lived and felt experiences, so as to understand the meaning of being an embodied caregiver, having to find coherence in conflicted emotional and physical states while continuously reshaping the arduous yet dreary cycle of caregiving.

Considering this background, the next segment describes a study that was done with an aim to understand the lived experience of caring for a family member suffering from PD, and to unravel the meaning making of the caregivers' experience.

Study: Exploring the Lived Experience of Caregivers of Parkinson's-Afflicted Patients

The current study is based on the dissertation done by Ms Bhasin, under the supervision of Dr Bharadwaj (2017), in Delhi with PD caregivers. It aimed to understand the experiential reality and journey of embodying the caregiver identity. During this, narrative accounts of eight females from middle-class families (with 65% of them of age 58 years and above) were gathered. These women had been engaged in the role of caregiving for male patients in their family, for a minimum of 5 years.

The decision of how to gather data is a critical one for any researcher, because, as Charmaz (2006) asserted, '*how* you collect data affects *which* phenomena you will see, *how, where,* and *when* you will view them, and *what* sense you will make of them'.

Considering this carefully, an in-depth narrative inquiry, delving into the routine of caregivers, their journey of acquiring the caregiving role, the barriers experienced in embodying the same and their relationships, as well as the change experienced in engagement with life on a daily basis while continuing the role, was performed.

Furthermore, the caregiver experiences were understood through a phenomenological lens. Adopting a phenomenological lens was critical, since it aids in understanding the caregiving experience, while accounting for the cultural embeddedness and determinants responsible for shaping one's experiences, as well as the subjective positions borne by the caregivers. Phenomenology acknowledges that every individual ascribes a personal meaning to oneself, one's actions, to the actions of others around them and to the various events, episodes and happenings that affect their lives. Since caregiving takes place in a particular context, it is important to account for how the intersubjective experiences of caregivers' daily lives impact their world view and their association with the caregiving role, which a phenomenological approach allows for. This philosophy further strengthened the purpose of using narratives in generating a more holistic understanding of the lived experiences of the participants. It also allowed space for the researcher to not be separated from the inquiry, through focusing on the interactive space created during the inquiry. Gaining a more comprehensive understanding of caregiving experiences could thus provide insights into how to support PD caregivers, when to intervene with them and how to be of aid to them, while re-engaging with their innermost self, so as to enhance their quality of life and therefore that of their care recipients.

UNVEILING THE EXPERIENCE OF BECOMING A 'BEING-IN-CAREGIVING'

Coalescing Caregiving and Existential Phenomenology

Existential phenomenology as a term refers to various philosophical approaches shared by such philosophers as Heidegger, Jaspers, Sartre, Binswanger, Merleau-Ponty and Yalom. In this chapter, we focus on the basic tenets of Yalom and Heidegger. Existential phenomenology is fundamentally interested in understanding 'What is it to be a person?' and the particular problem of 'As a person, who am I?' This is because it primarily focuses on the experience of 'being-in-the-world' by understanding human existence through the existential givens of temporality, spatiality, historicity, coexistence, mood, bodyhood and mortality.

As per Yalom's (1980) philosophy, every individual's self-identity develops while existing in spiral dynamics. Spiral dynamics comprises both the 'I' as in the self-expressive side of the spiral and the 'We' that is the self-sacrificial side of the spiral. The spiral is therefore a reflection of life as defined by both parties (the individual and the others) involved in creating this world. Existential phenomenologists believe that people are actively involved in their everyday dealings with the world, and it is through an agentic movement on the spiral that an individual attains meaning of the self and the world. Furthermore, existential phenomenology looks into the concepts of death, freedom, isolation and meaninglessness. Yalom (1980, 2008) has emphasized that any individual, when faced with the unconscious fears of inevitability of death, a sense of meaninglessness in life, ultimate loneliness and a fear of loss of freedom, is bound to experience conflict, anxiety and emotional turmoil.

In terms of caregiving, an individual, by virtue of sharing the same physical space with the patient, construes his/her life and experiences in conjunction with the limiting realities of the latter. As caregivers witness the decline in the health of their family member, they are confronted with existential conflicts, and these anxiety-provoking concerns, coupled with the additional physical and emotional demands thrust upon them, impact their meaning making of life as a caregiver.

At the same time, existential phenomenology also places importance on the context and how the context and the individual co-constitute one another. Through presenting a detailed account of human existence, where the individual is understood as an embodied and socially and culturally embedded being-in-the-world, existential phenomenology provides a guiding ground to understand caregiving as a process and the existential–psychosocial facets of life as a caregiver.

Basing on the principles of existential phenomenology, caregiver experiences could be illuminated and understood through the following meaning units: (a) shouldering responsibilities—an imperative, vigorous and insistent addition to the life as a caregiver; (b) juxtaposed identity of the patient—failing to lend congruency to the caregiver; (c) encountering meaninglessness in life—pain in witnessing the fallacy of the karmic attribution of well-being; (d) experience of timelessness—living in pain with the uncertainty and duration of the disease; and lastly (e) personal modes of respite in continuing with caregiving.

Shouldering Responsibilities—An Imperative, Vigorous and Insistent Addition to the Life as a Caregiver

This theme looks at the sudden yet persistent and choiceless increase in the responsibilities borne as a caregiver, and its impact on their personal and relational matrices.

PD leads to a decline in the functional abilities of an individual. The caregivers in the study shared how the functional disabilities varied in severity, from the patient's incapability of maintaining stability of limbs at a given point of time to their inability to control their bowel movements. These inabilities placed additional demands on the caregiver to extend help in ways more than they could anticipate.

In concordance with previous studies (Abendroth et al., 2012; Martínez-Martin et al., 2012), it was found that the participants were burdened with the demands of providing instrumental caregiving to the ailed while being sensitive to not emphasize the patient's incompetence. The instrumental caregiving included assisting with basic activities of daily living (e.g., bathing, feeding, driving, shopping), as well as mental activities, such as making decisions on behalf of the person with PD. The participants were able to rationalize the development of the illness as a consequence of old age, but it was due to the additional workload and the hassles in meeting with the fluctuating needs of the patient that they experienced strain and a compromised sense of well-being.

For instance, one of the participants shared her own disgust at and tiredness in having to clean her husband's soiled clothes, as well as his dump:

I have cleaned his poop, what else can we do…. I have done it!! I am constantly working round the clock in managing the household chores, his medicines, mobility routine but in between, such moments also occur and I hate doing it…. I hate having to look after his toilet needs, but I have to…if I won't who else will, as a dutiful wife…. I have to do it come what may…. (62-year-old spouse)

On the one hand, their narratives highlighted the challenging nature of the responsibilities to be shouldered by them, but on the other hand, they reverberated the struggle of lack of choice felt by these caregivers. Similarly, narratives of women positioned as a daughter or daughter-in-law to the patient shed light on their difficulties, like experiencing unease and extreme discomfiture due to the relational matrix while engaging in similar tasks of bathing, toileting or putting their father or father-in-law to sleep. Nonetheless, all the participants believed it was imperative for them to fulfil these uncomfortable demands of the patient. The participants also confessed that the monotony of repeating the same chores time and again, despite finding them aversive, while being mindful of the patient's self-esteem, caused tremendous mental fatigue. Yet, the caregivers struggled to admit the unpleasant nature of the demands placed on them and imputed to their own shortcomings whenever they were not able to endure the caregiving responsibilities tirelessly. This is reflective of the cultural schemas attached with the process of caregiving (Gupta, 2009; McDermott & Mendez-Luck, 2018; Meyer et al., 2015). It appeared that the women implicitly agreed that being a good carer is indistinguishable from being a good woman and that both these labels are non-negotiable. Research has shown that moral aspects often remain central in the formation of personal narratives (Bury, 2001; Kleinman, 2006). Consequently, following a disruption in their life narrative, occasioned by the onset of caring responsibilities, it became salient for the caregivers to maintain their identity closely bound with their orientation of the 'good'. As a result, it became critical for them to assume all the responsibilities necessary for being a good carer and thereby maintain their identity of being a good woman as well.

The participants, however, expressed that the exhaustion and burden intensified to a much greater extent when their position, and the expectations associated with their role as a woman, precipitously altered. Conventionally, these women were accustomed to being subservient in monetary matters or in the affairs of vital family decisions, but the declining health of the prominent male family member in the house drastically changed the dynamics of functionality of their relationship as well. Due to the male member's status of patienthood, the reins of maintaining the efficiency of the family fully shifted into the hands of the participants, and the entire responsibility of compensating for the absence of operationality of the patient, undertaking unfamiliar duties and bearing the risks, as well as consequences, of critical decisions was to be borne solely by the caregiver.

For instance, one of the participants shared that it was due to a complete decay of her husband's executive capacity that she faced the difficulty of handling aspects of functionality, which she had been unversed in for 38 years of their marriage:

> I used to depend on him before for a lot of things, but I have had to take on all those roles, am managing and planning the finances. Though it was not really my domain but I have had to learn it…it was a necessity, I didn't have a choice or else how would we survive. (60-year-old spouse)

This sudden shift from being a team to being compelled to become the sole person in charge was found to be burdening and difficult to manage by most of the participants. This was more so because their situatedness imposed on them innumerable responsibilities and expectations of acting with coherence and tolerance, while restricting their choice and agency to mould these accountabilities in their own unique manner. Moreover, the sociocultural norms subliminally contributed to the increased pressure to perform their caregiving duties impeccably, so much so that the feelings of weariness were accompanied with mixed emotions, like dismay and importunate moral accountability.

This is reflective of how as caregivers these women had to navigate through uncertainties and, in doing so, sustain the vulnerabilities and apprehensions while stepping into newer, untested grounds. As I became part of their lived experience, I could not help but feel that this entire process of becoming a caregiver would also induce bewilderment and loneliness, since not only were they undertaking responsibilities single-handedly, but they were also standing alone at a critical stage of their life, without their familiar anchors to seek support or share their difficulties and dilemmas with.

Parallel to my thoughts exists a vast literature of qualitative studies that illuminate a potential connection between lack of preparedness and uncertainty towards the innumerable duties, with caregiver reports of fear, anxiety, stress and feelings of insufficiency, and a consequent battle with loneliness as well (Bužgová et al., 2019; Funk et al., 2010; McLaughlin et al., 2011).

Juxtaposed Identity of the Patient: Failing to Lend Congruency to the Caregiver

This theme looks at the incongruence felt by the caregiver while understanding and supporting their family member, due to their inability to reconcile their past with their present. Since PD is an irreversible disease, with time it seeps into all the spheres of an individual's life, through gradually causing complete degeneration of motor abilities, executive functioning and social faculties (Abendroth, 2012; Haar et al., 2011). In other words, it can incapacitate an individual and can therefore be detrimental to the personhood and identity of the patient suffering from it. For the caregivers, this often meant a sudden disruption in the given patterns of living and a need to learn new ways of living together as a family (Smith, 2016).

Narratives of various caregivers shed light on the loss, bewilderment and pain experienced as they cohabitated with a family member, but the cohabitation had transformed into sharing space with an unfamiliar person, since the identifiable markers of that person, which made him salient, had faded away. This was illustrated by one of the participants, who acted as the primary caregiver for her father:

> Since my childhood and throughout my life, he has been the strong-est, most responsible, proactive man I have ever known. If I were to ever describe him, I would think of calling him as a happy, disciplined man, who was always eager to go an extra mile for the people he cared for. I have seen him being active, being that person you would come to for advice, but its like today, its him but not him…there is nothing left of any of that…and it is so hurtful to see him like this, and to be honest, how do you deal with him now, when all your life you have understood him differently? (48-year-old daughter)

Based on the interaction with the participants, I could gauge that the disease not only robs the functional abilities of the individual inflicted with the disease, but it also robs the caregiver off a sense of congruency in their life. Since the caregivers felt cornered to forego the known patterns of identification and association with the patient, established after years of togetherness, it was with a huge sense of dejection that they unwillingly accepted a distorted and altered being of their family member. This was also because distancing oneself and differentiating between what that family member had been and what he had become placed an additional demand of erasing the memories of the past and beginning from scratch in understanding the individual.

The internal agony of the caregivers, however, rose not just from being hampered from experiencing fluidity in their interface with the patient; instead, it stemmed more from having to live with a physi-cally present yet mentally absent loved one. As highlighted in other studies as well (Hurt et al., 2017; Tan et al., 2012), caregivers often bore emotional downfalls, neglect and loneliness, because they missed the companionship and the familiarity of their family member in the patient. One of the participants who lived with her husband and was the sole caretaker, for instance, reiterated:

> I am with him physically and mentally even when I am drained out because otherwise I cannot take care of him, but I find that he is men-tally absent sometimes and that in itself is upsetting, because he used to look after me, he took care of everything for me. I miss him…some-times I still want to talk to him, sometimes practical things…sometimes emotionally but there is nothing much I can discuss because he is in such a condition…. (65-year-old wife)

Accordingly, many of the caregivers expressed feeling alienation, grief and discontentment, as their close family member was neither able to participate in their everyday life nor able to communicate with them, invariably breeding a sense of distance and disconnect within the caregivers. The deterioration in the quality of relationship was all the more chaos-inducing, because it generated a feeling of being neglected among the caregivers, making them feel worthless and hollow inside. There has been enough research showing that due to feeling lonely or neglected the possibility of depression, anxiety and caregiver stress increases among caregivers (Birgersson, 2004). However, these negative emotions in the caregivers could also emerge since the disregard and remoteness of the patient subsequently impact their ability to affiliate and emotionally engage with the patient, which further invokes in them guilt and unease with themselves.

The caregivers shared how the absence of closeness and familiarity with their family members unknowingly drove them to deal with the patient in an impassive and mechanistic manner. The caregivers felt that they often reduced the personhood of their family member to an illness, by lending saliency to their patienthood. Repeatedly having to do this caused emotional turmoil within them which dangled over them as a moral dilemma.

As highlighted by the phenomenologist Karl Jaspers (1969), the possibility of existence of an 'I' germinates from interaction, engagement and co-construction with the other. It appeared as if the anguish experienced at dehumanizing a person created an emotional upheaval among the caregivers, because it was perceived as a reflection of diminishing humanity within. For instance, one of the participants attending to her father-in-law disclosed:

> We used to look up to him as our elder, we still do, but earlier he was a good decision maker, very well-organized, co-operative man and a huge support system to all of us…but over the years, due to the illness, he has completely transformed. He is lost in his own world, unaccommodating, he is always irritable and has abrupt endless list of continuous demands, which are not just difficult to meet but sometimes also injurious to himself. We try but we can't connect with him in the same manner, especially when he becomes uncooperative for treatment. We even have to tie him to bed at times. Initially, I used to feel ashamed

for doing that, but now I am habitual to it...otherwise he gets way too much to handle at times. Though, it sometimes makes me wonder how indifferent I have become, after all he is my father in law and me...doing all this...I don't know.... (43-year-old daughter-in-law)

As she shared her challenge of facing and managing a completely contrasting state of her father-in-law, I could perceive her own difficulty in locating herself and her doubts and anxiety over her own lack of morality and humanness in dealing with a human. She felt extremely uncomfortable with the experience of being enslaved to the symptom management of the patient, as opposed to experiencing the helplessness and impact of her actions on the sense of the self of a valuable individual in her life.

Her thoughts were echoed by other participants as well. As the familiar spaces and known grounds of relationships, participation and interaction between the caregivers and their family members collapsed, they also fractured the sense of wholeness experienced as individuals, and as embodied caregivers, within the participants.

Furthermore, this fluctuating engagement with the caregiver role and moral ambiguity over the quality of involvement created a sense of dissonance within the participants regarding their own conscientiousness and ideologies. They experienced a distinct conflict, due to the dichotomy of, at one end, being a caregiver and lending beneficence to the patient and, at the other end, becoming oblivious to the person in the patient. Consequently, the caregivers daily battled in making sense of the situation, of themselves as a person and their moral grounds and values. Hence, to sustain the caregiver role and the burdens created by it, it was critical for the caregivers to feel connected with their family members; however, they had to bear the complexity of finding coherence and living with contentment even in the absence of such a relationship.

Encountering Meaninglessness in Life: Pain in Witnessing the Fallacy of the Karmic Attribution of Well-being

Meaning in life is an important construct in psychology (Debats, 2000; Heisel et al., 2016). Nonetheless, existentialists, like Yalom (1980), have proposed that life is inherently meaningless but every individual desires for a sense of coherence and purpose in life, and therefore most individuals connote the greater meaning of existence to cosmic meaning. Yalom proposed that the cosmic meaning aids in dealing with the existential anxiety, by further providing comfort in the belief that there is some superordinate and coherent pattern to life. This theme refers to the disenchantment in the cosmic patterns and meaning systems experienced by the participants while witnessing the unpleasant nature of the disease and the inevitable degeneration of their family member.

Although the caregivers themselves believed that death was inescapable and bound to strike in one form or the other, it was the sudden shattering of the just-world belief that created discontent and a sense of injustice within them. This is in congruence with studies that show that illness and death are considered part of life in Eastern cultures, like India (Nelson, 2015; Salagame, 2015), but it is the unwavering faith in karmic beliefs that forms a strong ground for engaging in prosocial behaviour and experiencing safety from being thrown into a harrowing life situation (Mata & Simão, 2019).

A participant catering to her husband felt a lack of comprehensibility in the unbalanced equation of life, since as per her he had committed himself to the service of others and had been an uncomplaining individual throughout. For her it was perturbing to discover the imbalance and difficult to accept it as a fact of life. She shared:

> I feel that it just unfair...throughout his life he has never done even a single deed where he could have harmed or hurt anyone, but such a terrible disease has hit him...there is nothing much left of him...for such a thing to happen to a good soul!! It's heart-breaking...and to be honest it makes you re-question the values in your life in itself! (60-year-old spouse)

Another participant echoed her thoughts and shared that an emotionally heart-wrenching and unacceptable part of the process of caregiving was to watch the suffering of a good person. She felt agitation towards God and a betrayal of her trust in her basic beliefs of life. The participant was a caregiver to her father-in-law, and she had observed his interaction with the family and his contribution to the greater good of humanity through associating himself with a cause; yet, due to the disease, he was now bedridden and in suffering. She shared:

> He has always been one of the purest souls I have known, the most helpful person you would ever know of and to see him in such a rotten state. You know how it is said that if you do, good happens unto you…looking at him, I have lost complete faith in this!! I don't see that happening to him and I can't have faith on it any longer…and that just makes you feel all the more demotivated…I also feel angry at God…had he known the plans of god better, at least he won't have exhausted himself so much in service of others…he devoted himself for others at that time and now…it is as if it is hard for him to even be alive…honestly, after all this, life, values, goodness all of it just seems meaningless to me!! (43-year-old daughter-in-law)

As I interacted with the participants, I understood better that caregivers often came in contact with uncertainty, but the faith in the greater scheme of things acted as a support mechanism. However, with the advent of the disease, the plight of witnessing the gradual deterioration of a loved one often filled them with dismay and created a void within them. The disappointment stemmed not just from their decline but also from the safety net of the cosmic principles being no longer available to them, creating a sense of purposelessness and loss of meaning. Research has acknowledged that humankind faces difficulty in its attempt to find meaning in the absence of comforting external structures, like religion, etc. (Yalom, 2000).

This is also because situational meaning and global meaning are interdependent (Reker & Wong, 2012; Schnell et al., 2013). As their global ultimate beliefs and worldview about life collapsed among the caregivers, their ability to find meaning in day-to-day situations, their current engagement with their caregiver role and the vision for their own future became devoid of any meaning or worth. Hence, by virtue of being a constant observer of a patient of Parkinson's, their ability to find purpose in the daily undertakings of life was completely lost, which became evident in their expression of feeling an existential vacuum, characterized by a state of emptiness, lack of direction and questions about the point of life. Despite feeling unanchored, there was no respite for them from their caregiving role, and it was in a lot of anguish that the caregivers daily impelled themselves to still continue with their duties, as well as searching for a better meaning to their life circumstances.

Experience of Non-timeliness: Living in Pain with the Uncertainty and Duration of the Disease

This theme focuses on the transforming meaning of time structures for the caregivers. Due to the disruptive nature of the disease and discontinuity in their routine, events and life situations becoming a bitter truth of their life, time becomes one of the most salient themes for the informal caregiver. The temporality while caring for another is experienced as unending, repetitive and not enough.

In general, caregiving is a full-time job, regardless of the caregiver's other responsibilities (McLaughlin, 2010; Tan et al., 2012). Even when not specifically performing caregiver functions, due to the uncertainty associated with the caregiver role, there is a sense of always being on call and needing to be vigilant about the unexpected (Greenwell et al., 2014; Hurt et al., 2017). As the participants explained the unremitting nature of the caregiver role, they shared feeling a huge lack of sufficient time on their hands. Irrespective of their professional statuses, the caregiving responsibilities expected them to don multiple roles, due to which disengaging with the role of a caregiver became impossible. Even if there was additional help available, the caregiver was depended upon to do nearly everything.

For most of the caregivers, their errands were unending and extremely time-consuming. As a result, time was experienced as ruptured yet rushing, since their present centredness required focused commitment to their role, which came at the cost of restricted autonomy and social exclusion, but at the same time their thoughts were clouded by the fear of financial strain, uncertain prognosis of the illness and their own exhaustion due to the draining nature of involvement. This became more a pressing concern in cases where the caregiver had to recurrently engage in nocturnal duties for the patient (Grun et al., 2016; Viwattanakulvanid et al., 2014).

In some instances, time was also sensed as repetitive, especially in the case of participants engaged in the caregiver role for a long period of time. The caregivers shared that the same routine was often to be repeated day in and day out. Consequently, it brought within them a sense of monotony, isolation and disengagement with the patient and his needs. For example, one of the participants shared that she had to continuously perform the same actions for her father throughout the day, and instead of being able to connect with him or feel her own emotional vulnerability, on witnessing her father being dependent for even the basic needs, she ended up developing numbness and non-reactivity towards his condition:

> He calls out to me in every two minutes…whether it is night or day, he keeps calling out to me persistently, if I make him sit, he would instruct me to help him lie down, when I do that in the next two minutes he will call that now he wants to sit upright…sometimes it gets too much…initially I used to still feel bad…but time and again doing the same thing for years at a stretch, I just feel mechanical and sometimes just emotionally blunted. (48-year-old daughter)

In addition, the disease brings about a change in the concept of time for the care receiver. Since the meaning of time understood by the patient changes, the demands generated for the caregivers also alter the notion of time and autonomy experienced in establishing a well-timed routine for oneself. A few of the narratives highlighting this element of life disclosed how the patient's notion of change in time resulted in, at one end, wakefulness at night but, on the other, an excessive slowing of time for the everyday self-management activities, coercing the caregiver to follow the same timeline as that of the patient:

> If he calls me at night, I have to get up, or else he would be angry. There are times when he will sleep for 3 hours at night and feel that it was noon and he needs his evening tea, and I can't argue beyond a point, I need to get up, so I am so tired with the work that I actually lose track of time, his time line is what becomes my timeline too…when does

the night end and the day begins, I often don't understand. (43-year-old daughter-in-law)

Earlier we still had some routine, but since his diagnosis, he is indoors and the entire routine goes for a toss, the world operates on a different timeline and we operate on his timeline!! It gets very frustrating, the timings at our home are modified as per his schedule, which can be abrupt at times and extremely prolonged at other times. (58-year-old spouse)

Yet another tangent of the fragmented sense of time originated from the inability to experience time as moving. In concurrence with other studies (Smith, 2016), the caregivers also experienced an excessive slowing of time. One of the participants shared how the nature of the disease had impacted her husband's motility in his everyday routine and disrupted his discipline and how, thereby, she had to spend her entire day hovering around him:

It seems my entire day is centered around him. Simple activity like getting up from his bed, or consuming a meal, takes him 2 hours...every second feels never ending, and I am relentlessly absorbed in ensuring that despite the delay all his needs are met, it seems an entire day stretches into eternity. (63-year-old spouse)

This feeling also heightened in the case of participants who had been embodying the status of caregiver for years, and the uncertainty of the nature of the disease furthered the sense of being stuck for an indefinite time period and an incessant slowing down of the time on an everyday basis, as also found by previous studies (Bradley, 2014).

Caregivers are thus often inevitably caught in the care receiver's sense of time. For the caregiver, this leads to an inability to move on when desired. Thus, the experience of time continuously fluctuates, and the caregivers experience their past, present and future as disjointed. As per phenomenologists, the inhibition of temporal fluidity also impacts the manner in which the subjective body is experienced by an individual (Tatossian, 1983).

The time and effort involved in caregiving were also found to take a physical toll on the body of the caregiver, increasing the possibility of the caregiver experiencing fragmentation of the body as well. The role of a caregiver is a long one, not limited to a particular point in time but rather drawn out over months or years. The physical toll could greatly affect what he/she is able to do and how he/she is able to thrust his/her body forth in the world.

As confessed by the caregivers, the responsibility for all the household chores, increased workload and reduced ability to sleep, due to the demands of the patient, as well as the constant uncertainty around the illness, exhausted the physically felt body and the subjective experience of well-being, as encountered through one's lived body, among them. A participant caring for her husband echoed these concerns and loss of bodyhood:

> My life took a full 360degree change! I have lost weight, I have lost my hair, I have lost my strength and at one time I had lost my appetite as well…I have lost my sense of well-being…I was initially very fond of dressing up, how I look, my presentation, my food…but this is so physically draining that I do not bother much now, I do not have the energy to look at all this, nor do I get any sense of pleasure from anything at all. (62-year-old spouse)

As emphasized by Husserl (1973) and Legrand (2006), with an alteration in the experienced temporality, the lived body also experiences a reduction in the fundamental form of receptivity and expansive ability while connecting with the world. As a result, the caregivers often felt tattered and incapacitated to engage with themselves and the world as a whole while dealing with the residues of caregiving, even as they were persistently confronted with the unsettling uncertainty of the duration of the patient's illness.

Personal Modes of Respite in Continuing with Caregiving

As the participants tried accounting for the expressive and instrumental needs of their family members, they also had to relentlessly strive for safeguarding their vulnerable selves, so as to prevent themselves from reaching the verge of collapse. This final theme focuses on the mechanisms chosen by the caregivers to seek some respite from the unending role and strain of caregiving and thereby preserve their self-identity.

As emphasized in various studies previously, seeking of support from one's friends, family and medical professionals is a strategy often employed by caregivers to deal with the physical, emotional and mental stress of caregiving (Abendroth et al., 2012; Goldsworthy, 2008). Similarly, some of the participants revealed that attaining physical support from their family members, be it via diffusing responsibilities or through finding cathartic help, offered them some respite in their daily lives. One of the participants, for instance, shared that she depended on her daughters for the rudimentary work in caregiving, while another participant adopted a managerial position, by allocating self-management responsibilities to her house help staff, as illustrated in her narrative:

Actually, we have a lot of help, my husband is extremely helpful, I have a full-time maid who has been with me for 21 years, and I have the caretaker boy, so we all help each other and it makes managing things a lot easier.... I definitely need to be vigilant and manage all of them, but it doesn't burn me out with excessive load. (54-year-old daughter-in-law)

In cases where distributing responsibilities was not an option, the participants attempted to step out of the physical and embodied spaces of the caregiver role, by manifesting their energy into other activities of distraction and social interaction. Research has shown that communal interactions and gatherings often act as a buffer for caregivers. Although most of the caregivers felt a lack of time and had to withdraw from such interactions yet being able to maintain connectivity and emotional release over telephonic communication was also enough to find slight alleviation of the draining aspect of their role. People who were not used to being social preferred reading books, listening to religious hymns or finding an escape in the fictional characters on television. These activities aided in replenishing their reserve and improved their mental well-being and engagement in looking at the positive part of their experience, through helping them somewhere find an escape in fictional narratives or rationalize their circumstances and find a middle ground.

However, an overarching mechanism that most of the participants engaged in was finding meaning in spirituality and fate.

> I feel that God is the supreme power, it is tough not to, but still better not question him…because we don't know of his plans and even when I feel weak, I know that in those moments, when I ask for help, he always looks out for me and my family. (65-year-old spouse)

> When you have faith on God, you gradually realise that everything falls in place. There are some grander reasons for things to happen the way they happen and for you being in that situation in a particular time period…this thought gives me a lot of strength and purpose in continuing with my caregiver roles and responsibilities. (63-year-old spouse)

Research (Matusek & Knudson, 2009; Tan et al., 2012) has shown that believing in cosmic meanings of life provides the caregivers an opportunity to acknowledge the existence of an all-encompassing design outside of one's control and seek consolation in a magical or spiritual order of the universe. This is primarily helpful in coping with the uncertainty and meaninglessness encountered by the caregivers over the prolonged course of the disease. Moreover, as per existentialists, realizing one's potential and fulfilling it provides meaning to an individual's life (Farran & Kuhn, 1998). Through selflessly devoting themselves to caregiving, most of the caregivers felt that they were able to connect with their higher purpose. It not only enabled them to find meaning in their suffering but also enhanced the acceptance of illness in their family member, as well as offering an antidote to the uncertainty of the future. Hence, spirituality played a key role in their acceptance of the disease, as well as their role of a caretaker. In conclusion, these strategies were observed as critical in easing the challenges and complications of caregiving.

CONCLUSION

This chapter provides an insight into what it means to live as a caregiver engaging in the everyday care of a person with PD. It elucidates the radical changes an individual has to go through while transitioning from being only a family member to becoming a caregiver. Through their narratives, this chapter sheds light on their vulnerabilities as these individuals grappled with adapting to their role while accepting the irreversible nature of the illness and the ailing status of their loved one. Due to the chronic nature of PD, the caregivers not only had to confront uncertainty, chaos and perplexity because of their responsibilities and duties critical to providing adequate care to their family member, but they also had to unwillingly cope with a rupture in their understanding of good health or recovery.

Since Parkinson's is a progressive disease, impacting the functionality of the affected individual, upon the caregivers are thrust unending chores, as well as the immense responsibility of compensating for the lost operationality of their family member. This not only places additional demands on them but also pushes them into unfamiliar and abstruse circumstances. However, the caregivers have to persevere and persist with their duties, despite feeling unconfident and directionless.

In addition to the difficulty of dealing with uncertainty, the timelessness and infinite progression of the disease furthers a perception of anguish, anxiety and despondency among the caregivers. This is because navigating through the disease also involves losing aspects of personhood of their family member, on a day-to-day basis, and the caregivers are therefore often unable to reconcile the past with the present state of their loved one. As they struggle to search for the person in the patient, they invariably experience dissonance while engaging in the caregiving role.

Through this chapter, an effort has been made to capture the essence of living and embodying the caregiver identity, by acknowledging that although these individuals do not display the symptomatology of Parkinson's as a disease, in their journey of navigating through it, they too live with the disease and bear its complexities. It was through the voicing of their raw, vulnerable emotions towards the altered meaning of life since the onset of the disease, through their expression of emotional turmoil and conflicts, as well as the faint acknowledgements of feeling alienated and isolated, that the intricacies, exhaustion and struggle of being a caregiver could be apprehended.

This chapter also highlights how caregiving, with its numerous sacrifices, difficult choices and vulnerable moments, was often perceived as a constant act of balancing, where these individuals centred their lives around the patient, readily foregoing parts of their self to give for and uplift the quality of life of their loved one, yet cherished the desire to and attempted to find an equilibrium, so as to preserve their own selves as well. Nevertheless, this raises the question: is it not the need of the hour for these individuals to acknowledge and insist on reciprocity during this journey of their life, to transition from being a caregiver to becoming a care partner and, for their struggles and toils, to not only be appreciated by others, as well as their own selves, but also be alleviated through support? However, it also brings to light that it was in the expression and acceptance of their vulnerabilities that these individuals found their resilience and hope. Thus, by attending to their veiled vulnerabilities and personal narratives, healthcare professionals can not only aid in enabling these individuals to find meaning in their caregiving journey but also promote healthier emotional expression and acceptance of oneself while working through the caregiving challenges.

REFERENCES

Abbas, M. M., Xu, Z., & Tan, L. (2017). Epidemiology of Parkinson's Disease-East versus west. *Movement Disorders Clinical Practice, 5*(1), 14–28. https://doi.org/10.1002/mdc3.12568

Abendroth, M., Lutz, B. J., & Young, M. E. (2012). Family caregivers' decision process to institutionalize persons with Parkinson's disease: A grounded theory study. *International Journal of Nursing Studies, 49*, 445–454.

Bhasin, S. K., & Bharadwaj, I. (2017). *Exploring the lived experience of caregivers of parkinson's-afflicted patients* [Unpublished Dissertation]. University of Delhi, Delhi.

Birgersson, A. (2004). Being in the light or in the shade: Persons with Parkinson's disease and their partners' experience of support. *International Journal of Nursing Studies, 41*(6), 621–630.

Bradley, H. M. (2014). *Parkinson's diagnosis from the caregiver's perspective*. http://ro.ecu.edu.au/theses_hons/123

Braithwaite, V. (1986). The burden of home care: How is it shared. *Community Health Studies, 3*, 7–11.

Braithwaite, V. (1987). Coming to terms with burden in home care. *Australian Journal on Ageing, 6*, 20–23.

Bury, M. R. (1982). Chronic illness as biographical disruption. *Sociology of Health and Illness, 4*(2), 167–182.

Bury, M. R. (2001). Illness narratives: Fact or fiction? *Sociology of Health and Illness, 23*(3), 263–285.

Bužgová, R., Kozáková, R., & Juríčková, L. (2019). The unmet needs of family members of patients with progressive neurological disease in the Czech Republic. *PLoS ONE, 14*(3), 38–46.

Charmaz, K. (2006). *Constructing grounded theory: A practical guide through qualitative analysis.* SAGE Publications.

Croog, S. H., Burleson, J. A., Sudilovsky, A., & Baume, R. M. (2006). Spouse caregivers of Alzheimer patients: Problem responses to caregiver burden. *Ageing Mental Health, 10*(2), 87–100.

Debats, D. L. (2000). An inquiry into existential meaning: Theoretical, clinical, and phenomenal perspectives. In G. T. Reker & K. Chamberlain (Eds.), *Exploring existential meaning: Optimizing human development across the life span* (pp. 93–106). SAGE Publications.

Eliot, T. S. (1934). *After strange gods—A primer of modern heresy.* Faber & Faber Ltd.

Farran C. J., & Kuhn, D. R. (1998). Finding meaning through caring for an elderly person with Alzheimer's disease: Assessment and intervention. In P. T. P. Wong & P. S. Fry (Eds.), *Handbook of personal meaning: Theory, research, and applications* (pp. 335–358). Lawrence Erlbaum Associates.

Funk, L., Stajduhar, K. I., Toye, C., & Aoun, S. (2010). Home-based family caregiving at the end of life: A comprehensive review of published qualitative research. *Palliative Medicine, 24*(6), 594–607.

Greenwell, K., Van Wersch, A., & Walker, R. (2013). Determinants of psychosocial impact of being a carer of people living with Parkinson's Disease: A systematic review. *Journal of Parkinson's Disease, 3*, 173.

Grun, D., Pieri, V., Valiant, M., & Diederich, N. J. (2016). Contributory factors to caregiver burden in Parkinson Disease. *Journal of the American Medical Directors Association, 17*(7), 623–632.

Goldsworthy, B. K. (2008). Caregiving for parkinson's disease patients: An exploration of a stress-appraisal model for quality of life and burden. *The Journals of Gerontology Series B, 63*(6), 372–376.

Gupta, R., Rowe, N., & Pillai, V. K. (2009). Perceived caregiver burden in India: Implications for social services. *Affilia, 24*(1), 69–79.

Haar, A., Kirkevold, M., Hall, E. O. C., & Ostergaard, K. (2011). Living with advanced Parkinson's disease: A constant struggle with unpredictability. *Journal of Advanced Nursing, 67*(2), 408–417.

Hammarlund, C. J., Westergren, A., Astrom, I., Edberg, A.-K., & Hagell, P. (2018). The Impact of living with Parkinson's Disease: Balancing within a web of needs and demands. *Parkinson's Disease, 2018*(10), 1–8.

Heisel, M. J., Neufeld, E., & Flett, G. L. (2016). Reasons for living, meaning in life, and suicide ideation: Investigating the roles of key positive psychological factors in reducing suicide risk in community-residing older adults. *Aging and Mental Health, 20*(2), 195–207.

Hurt, C. S., Cleanthous, S., & Newman, S. P. (2017). Further explorations of illness uncertainty: Carers' experiences of Parkinson's disease. *Psychology & Health*, 1–18. https://dx.doi.org/10.1080/08870446.2017.1283041

Husserl, E. (1973a). *Experience and judgment* (Trans. J. Churchill & K. Ameriks). Routledge & Kegan Paul.

Hyden, L. C. (1997). Illness and narrative. *Sociology of Health & Illness, 19*, 48–69. https://dx.doi.org/10.1111/j.1467-9566.1997.tb00015.x

Jaspers, K. (1969). *Philosophy*.

Joling, K. J., van Hout, H. P. J., Schellevis, F. G., van der Horst, H. E., Scheltens, P., Knol, D. L., & van Marwijk, H. W. J. (2010). Incidence of depression and anxiety in the spouses of patients with dementia: A naturalistic cohort study of recorded morbidity with a 6-year follow-up. *American Journal of Geriatric Psychiatry, 18*, 146–153.

Kadoya, Y., & Khan, M. (2015). *The role of gender in long-term care for older parents: Evidence from India* (Economic Research Center Discussion Paper: E-Series, E14–E15). https://doi.org/10.1080/13229400.2017.1279561

Kim, Y., Kashy, D. A., Spillers, R. L., & Evans, T. V. (2010). Needs assessment of family caregivers of cancer survivors: Three cohorts comparison. *Psycho-Oncology: Journal of the Psychological, Social and Behavioral Dimensions of Cancer, 19*(6), 573–582.

Kleinman, A. (2006). *What really matters*. Oxford University Press.

Lawton, M. P., Moss, M., Kleban, M. H., Glicksman, A., & Rovine, M. (1991). A two-factor model of caregiving appraisal and psychological well-being. *Journal of Gerontology, 46*(4), 181–189.

Lee, S. M., & Kim, H. K. (2009). 'Elderly husbands' caregiving for their sick wives: Narratives of husbands and wives. *Family and Culture, 21*(4), 63–94.

Lee, G.-B., Woo, H., Lee, S.-Y., Cheon, S.-M., & Kim, J. W. (2019). The burden of care and the understanding of disease in Parkinson's disease. *PLoS ONE, 14*(5), e0217581. https://doi.org/10.1371/journal.pone.0217581

Legrand, D. (2006). The bodily self: The sensori-motor roots of pre-reflective self-consciousness. *Phenomenology and the Cognitive Sciences, 5*, 89–118.

Leiknes, I., Unn-Tone, L., & Elisabeth, S. (2015). The relationship among caregiver burden, demographic variables, and the clinical characteristics of patients with Parkinson's disease—A systematic review of studies using various caregiver burden instruments. *Open Journal of Nursing, 5*, 855–877. https://doi.org/10.4236/ojn.2015.510091

Martínez-Martín, P., Rodriguez-Blazquez, C., & Forjaz, M. J. (2012). Quality of life and burden in caregivers for patients with Parkinson's Disease: Concepts, assessments and related factors. *Expert Review of Pharmacoeconomics and Outcomes Research, 12*, 221–230.

Martínez-Martín, P., Arroyo, S., Rojo-Abuin, J. M., Rodriguez-Blazquez, C., Frades, B., de Pedro Cuesta, J., & Longitudinal Parkinson's Disease Patient Study Group. (2008). Burden, perceived health status and mood among caregivers of Parkinson's Disease patients. *Movement Disorders, 23*, 1673–1680.

Mata, A., & Simão, C. (2019). Karmic forecasts: The role of justice in forecasts about self and others. *Motivation Science*. Advance online publication. https://doi.org/10.1037/mot0000162

Matusek, J. A., & Knudson, R. M. (2009). Rethinking recovery from eating disorders: Spiritual and political dimensions. *Qualitative Health Research, 19*(5), 697–707.

McDermott, E., & Mendez-Luck, C. A. (2018). The process of becoming a caregiver among Mexican origin women: A cultural psychological perspective. *Sociology of Health and Illness, 8*(2). https://doi.org/10.1177/2158244018771733

McLaughlin, D., Hasson, F., Kernohan, W. G., Waldron, M., McLaughlin, M., Cochrane, B., & Chambers, H. (2011). Living and coping with Parkinson's disease: Perceptions of informal carers. *Palliative Medicine, 25*(2), 177–182.

McLaughlin, T., Feldman, H., Fillit, H., Sano, M., Schmitt, F., Aisen, P., Leibman, C., Mucha, L., Ryan, M. J., Sullivan, S. D., Spackman, E. D., Neumann, P. J., Cohen, J., & Stern, Y. (2010). Dependence as a unifying construct in defining Alzheimer's disease severity. *Alzheimer's & Dementia, 6*(6), 482–493.

Meyer, O. L., Nguyen, K. H., Dao, T. N., Vu, P., Arean, P., & Hinton, L. (2015). The sociocultural context of caregiving experiences for Vietnamese dementia family caregivers. *Asian American Journal of Psychology, 6*(3), 263–272.

National Institute of Neurological Disorders and Stroke. (2013). *Stroke progress review group*. http://www.ninds.nih.gov/strokeprg

Nelson, T. D. (2015). Ageism. In T. D. Nelson (Ed.), *Handbook of prejudice, stereotyping, and discrimination* (2nd ed., pp. 337–354). http://ebookcentral.proquest.com/lib/MASSEY/reader.action?docID=3570438&ppg=330

Pearlin, L. I., Mullan, J. T., Semple, S. J., & Skaff, M. M. (1990). Caregiving and the stress process: An overview of concepts and their measures. *Gerontologist, 30*(5), 583–594.

Poulshock, S. W., & Deimling, G. T. (1984) Families caring for elders in residence: Issues in the measurement of burden. *Journal of Gerontology, 2*, 230–239.

Pringsheim, T., Jette, N., Frolkis, A., & Steeves, T. D. L. (2014). The prevalence of Parkinson's disease: A systematic review and meta-analysis. *Movement Disorders, 29*(13), 1583–1590.

Radhakrishnan, D. M., & Goyal, V. (2018). Parkinson's Disease: A review. *Neurology India, 66*(Suppl, S1), 26–35.

Reissman, C. K. (2008). *Narrative methods for the human sciences*. SAGE Publications.

Reker, G. T., & Wong, P. T. P. (2012). Personal meaning in life and psychosocial adaptation in the later years. In P. T. P. Wong (Ed.), *The human quest for meaning: Theories, research, and applications* (pp. 433–456). Routledge.

Rew, L., Fields, S., Levee, L., Russell, M., & Leake, P. (1987). AFFIRM: A nursing model to promote role mastery in family caregivers. *Family and Community Health, 9*, 52–54.

Richardson, T. J., Lee, S. J., Berg-Weger, M., & Grossberg, G. T. (2013). Caregiver health: Health of caregivers of alzheimer's and other dementia patients. *Current Psychiatry Reports, 15*(7), 367.

Ricoeur, P. (2003). *The rule of metaphor: The creation of meaning in language.* Routledge Publications.

Ryan, M.-L. (2007). Toward a definition of narrative. In D. Herman (Ed.), *The Cambridge companion to narrative* (pp. 22–35). Cambridge University Press.

Salagame, K. K. (2015). Meaning and well-being: Indian perspectives. *Journal of Constructivist Psychology, 30*(1), 63–68.

Salvatore, R., Cianciulli, A., Calvello, R., & Panaro, M. A. (2015). Family caregivers of patients with neurodegenerative diseases: Life challenge. *Journal of Family Medicine, 2*(4), 1032.

Sanyal, J., Das, S., Ghosh, E., Banerjee, T. K., Bhaskar, L. V., & Rao, V. R. (2015). Burden among Parkinson's disease care givers for a community-based study from India. *Journal of the Neurological Sciences, 358*(1–2), 276–281. https://doi.org/10.1016/j.jns.2015.09.009

Schnell, T., Höge, T., & Pollet, E. (2013). Predicting meaning in work: Theory, data, implications. *Journal of Positive Psychology, 8*(6), 543–554.

Schulz, R., Beach, S. R., Hebert, R. S., Martire, L. M., Monin, J. K., Tompkins, C. A., & Albert, S. M. (2009). Spousal suffering and partner's depression and cardiovascular disease: The cardiovascular health study. *The American Journal of Geriatric Psychiatry, 17*(3), 246–254.

Sherman, S. R., Ward, R. A., & LaGory, M. (1988). Women as caregivers of the elderly: Instrumental and expressive support. *Social Work, 33*(2), 164–167.

Smith, L. (2016). Learning to live with Parkinson's disease in the family unit: An interpretative phenomenological analysis of well-being. *Medical Health Care and Philosophy, 20*(1), 13–21.

Smith, E. R., Perrin, P. B., Tyler, C. M., Lageman, S. K., & Villasenor, T. (2019). Parkinson's symptoms and caregiver burden and mental health: A cross cultural mediational model. *Behavioural Neurology, 2019*(4), 1–10.

Spruytte, N., Audenhove, C., Lammertyn, F., & Storm, G. (2002). The quality of the caregiving relationship in informal care for older adults with dementia and chronic psychiatric patients. *Psychology and Psychotherapy, 75*, 295–311.

Sveinbjornsdottir, S. (2016). The clinical symptoms of Parkinson's Disease. *Journal of Neurochemistry, 139*(Suppl. 1), 318–324.

Takai, M., Takahashi, M., Iwamitsu, M., Ando, N., Okazaki, S., Nakajima, K., Oishi, S., & Miyaoka, H. (2009). The experience of burnout among home caregivers of patients with dementia: Relations to depression and quality of life. *Archives of Gerontology and Geriatrics, 49*(1), e1–5.

Tan, S. B., Williams, A. F., & Morris, M. E. (2012). Experiences of caregivers of people with Parkinson's disease in Singapore: A qualitative analysis. *Journal of Clinical Nursing, 21,* 2235–2246.

Tatossian, A. (1983). Dépression, vécudépressif et orientation thérapeutique. In Collectif (Ed.), *La maladie dépressive* (pp. 277–293). Ciba.

Ugargol, A. P., & Ajay Bailey, A. (2018). Family caregiving for older adults: Gendered roles and caregiver burden in emigrant households of Kerala, India. *Asian Population Studies, 14*(2), 194–210.

Viwattanakulvanid, P., Kaewwilai, L., Jitkritsadakul, O., Brenden, N. R., Setthawatcharawanich, S., Boonrod, N., Mekawichai, P., & Bhidayasiri, R. (2014). The Impact of the nocturnal disabilities of Parkinson's disease on caregivers' burden implications for interventions. *Journal of Neural Transmissions, 121,* S15–S24.

Yalom, I. D. (1980). *Existential psychotherapy.* Basic Books.

Yalom, I. D. (2008). Staring at the sun: Overcoming the terror of death. *The Humanistic Psychologist, 36*(3-4), 283–297.

Zhao, Y. J., Wee, H. L., Chan, Y.-H., Seah, S. H., Au, W. L., Lau, P. N., Pica, E. C., Li, S. C., Luo, N., & Tan, L. C. S. (2010). Progression of Parkinson's Disease as evaluated by Hoehn and Yahr stage transition times. *Movement Disorders, 25,* 702–708.

Chapter 7

Positive Deviance
Use of Phenomenon in Vulnerability to Depression

Rajbir Singh, Lokesh Gupta and Dinesh Chhabra

VULNERABILITY

Vulnerability and risk both seem similar. Is there a real difference between being vulnerable and being at risk, or is it merely an issue of semantics? Is 'vulnerability' the state of being vulnerable, or is it something else, something more? Psychological vulnerability can be defined as a 'pattern of cognitive beliefs reflecting a dependence on achievement or external sources of affirmation for one's sense of self-worth' (Sinclair & Wallston, 1999, p. 120), related to maladaptive functioning. Maladaptive cognitive reactions to interpersonal events can affect coping behaviours, interpersonal relationships and psychological and physical well-being.

Vulnerability is difficult to define, because it means different things to different people, at different times, even to different organizations that are engaged in some intervention for the vulnerable sections of the society. Clarity on this concept is very critical for those who wish to mitigate vulnerabilities or their negative outcomes. It is useful for evaluating and redefining their goals or programmes. Graz (1997) asserts that a standardized definition is required for vulnerability, because it could become a criterion for setting priorities at the time of emergency situations, for example, the International Committee of the Red Cross.

Vulnerability can be understood as the diminished capacity of an individual or group to anticipate, cope with, resist and recover from the impact of a natural or man-made hazard. This concept is both relative and dynamic in its nature. Vulnerability emerged as an almost independent concept for rethinking and revaluation to provide relief.

Vulnerability is a negatively toned word within a social context, where one is 'vulnerable' to certain damage, loss or degeneration or degradation owing to certain agents or forces present in the environment (physical or social). It would result into poor growth and decline in self-worth. Many of them who are vulnerable thrive, overcome the impediments and live life above zero, though no one is immune to suffering from vulnerabilities on account of psychosocial threats. It is otherwise well documented that socio-economic deprivations have a long-lasting effect on behaviour (Sinha et al., 1995). In developing countries, owing to socio-demographic disparities and scarce economic resources, there is an abundance of vulnerabilities. The effects are so widespread that individualistic strategies shall be outmatched by the requirements. Most of the interventions furthered by psychologists are very time-consuming (one-to-one delivery model) and do not target (big) groups or sections of the community. These often fail to meet contextual, developmental and cultural expectations for a particular individual, group or social structure and, therefore, are not effective.

It would also be pertinent to simultaneously consider the vulnerabilities and strengths that change the seeming impact and valence of the vulnerability. If the strengths outweigh vulnerabilities, the outcome shall not be adverse. It is also relevant to understand the attributes of the perceived vulnerability of the vulnerable. Many in India shall interpret and ascribe their conditions to 'karma of their previous lives', while many others shall ascribe them to other reasons.

Studies on higher-education students show that psychological vulnerability is negatively correlated with adaptive constructs and positively correlated with negative health outcomes (Akin, 2014; Satici, 2016; Satici & Uysal, 2016; Satici et al., 2014; Satici et al., 2015; Uysal, 2015).

Vulnerability is the antithesis to equality, where all sections of society perceive fair treatment and opportunity to growth with minimal risk factors. Vulnerability is likely to be associated with perceived unfairness and lack of trust. It leads to greater health and social problems, mental illness and depression. On the other hand, we find people who emerge from vulnerabilities becoming models. They are the resilient ones and represent positive deviance (i.e., positive exception to the norm). Ingram and Price (2001) argue that vulnerability refers to the relatively stable causal mechanisms of psychopathology which are endogenous. For individuals, they put vulnerability and resilience at different ends of the vulnerability continuum. However, they stress that resilience implies resistance but not immunity to a disorder. It is therefore suggested that better understanding of vulnerability will help in preventing the onset of psychopathology.

Vulnerability and resilience both can be explained with the help of similar factors, such as personal traits, interpretation of events, brain structure, genetic factors, family interactions, community factors, etc. Lack of these adequate sources make a person more vulnerable. On the other hand, these adequate sources help individuals build resilience. The terms 'vulnerability' and 'resilience' should be thought to exist in a continuum; thus, it is possible to both proceed from vulnerability to resilience and regress from resilience to vulnerability (Sevi, 2018).

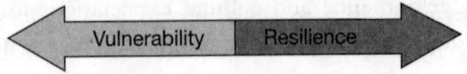

Resilience is an individual's ability to bounce back in the face of adversity (Gilligan, 2009)—successful negotiation of a challenge or a risk (Walsh, 2006). It includes growth, not mere survival. Is it invulnerability which is applicable only to specific situations that does not have to extend to all difficult situations? It is a strong buffer to stress. It can explain variation in psychological vulnerability. Six dimensions of psychological vulnerability are mental health, addictions, social support, use of external services, family stability through couple satisfaction and resilience (Mangeard-Lourme & Brunsden, 2014).

Daskalakis et al. (2013) presented an interwoven conceptualization of genetic predisposition, early-life environment and later-life environment, three hit concepts to describe the relationship between vulnerability and resilience. Stressful experiences in early life modulate the brain circuits of emotional and cognitive behaviour. Such neural bases determine the adaptation and coping in later life. Though early exposure to stress increases vulnerability, it also increases the adaptive capacity leading to resilience, both of which determine mental health.

Vulnerability can be better understood through three coordinates, namely exposure, capacity and potentiality (Delor & Hubert, 2000). 'Exposure' can be understood in terms of one's risk of being exposed to stressful situations and inability to cope with them (Chambers, 1983), whereas 'capacity' implies the availability of resources to cope with them; non-availability of resources (physical and individual) then is a risk for vulnerability. Being subjected to stress situations increases the *potentiality* of a person being rendered vulnerable.

Vulnerability is part of the human condition, a kind of existential point of view. Brown (n.d.) believes that one can experience the vulnerability emotion fully and that it signifies courage and strength rather than weakness.

DEPRESSION

A state of depression may be characterized by mood-congruent attentional bias, leading to such information processing at later stages that decrease activities in the prefrontal cortex, moderated by serotonin metabolism and prolonged activation of the 'amygdala'. Consequently, 'depressogenic' schemas lead to impaired ability to exert attention-inhibitory control over negative schemas (Disner et al., 2011). Vulnerability emerges early in life and increases the risk for later development of depression affecting the positive valence system, as it blunts the activation in the striatum during reward anticipation. On the other hand, negative valence of depression taps the neural processioning of sadness, loss and threat social feedback; exclusion and blunted response to reward.

Ferrari et al. (2013a) estimated that in 2010, worldwide, there were over 298 million cases of depression; thus, depression can be considered as a global health priority. Depression is reported to be the second global leading cause of years lived with disability.

A recent survey conducted by Sagar et al. (2020) found that in India there are more than 9 crore people suffering from anxiety and depression alone, besides other mental disorders. The survey also revealed that this figure has doubled since 1990. Further, it was also pointed out these people are going to live long years with disability. This situation warrants immediate attention of mental health professionals to make a paradigm shift in their modus operandi; otherwise, it shall not be possible to arrest this fast-rising psychological vulnerability.

Marchetti et al. (2016) explored whether dysfunctional attitudes representing the cognitive aspect, hopelessness representing internal attribution of an individual to negative events and individual reaction to distress, as response styles, together determine depressive symptoms specifically or merely overlap. They employed commonality analysis (CA) by comparing a large sample of undergraduate with a sizable sample of clinically depressed. They found considerable overlapping of cognitive factors between the healthy and clinical depressed samples but also the specificity of 'hopelessness' accompanying depressive symptoms. Further, among the individual reactions to distress are rumination and brooding.

Large-scale evidence indicates that cognitive factors play an etiological role in contributing to the continuation of depression (Beck & Haigh, 2014). Individuals make global, stable and internal attributions to their experiences of negative outcomes. Further, such thinking takes them to the state of clinical depression, amounting to the severity of the state, chance of relapse, etc.

ASSESSMENT OF PSYCHOLOGICAL VULNERABILITY

It is necessary to know who are in fact vulnerable, so that some attention can be given to them, not letting their risk turn into mental health problems. Besides demographic indicators (such as lack of material and/or social support, exclusion from social participation, habitation in areas marked by high levels of deprivation—inner cities, former industrial areas and isolated rural communities), it is important to measure psychological vulnerability through a psychometric tool. The tool most popularly and widely used is the Psychological Vulnerability Scale (Sinclair & Wallston, 1999). It is a short and easy-to-administer measure of six items covering maladaptive cognitive patterns or cognitions that promote harmful reactions to stress, specifically reflecting perceptions related to social dependence, self-oriented perfectionism, criticism, negative attributions and reliance on external sources of approval (Sinclair & Wallston, 1999). This tool has been validated and adapted in Portuguese by Nogueira et al. (2017) and is reported to have sound psychometric properties for higher-education students. The tool has been found to be reliable and valid in Turkey by Akin (2011, 2014), as well as by Satici et al. (2015), for students. There seems to be a need for such a tool, or an adaptive version of the Psychological Vulnerability Scale, for Indian samples, which may help identify the cluster or group of vulnerable people for interventions, as well as assess the outcomes of the interventions.

POSITIVE DEVIANCE

'Positive deviance' (PD) can be extremely helpful in discovering the handful of vital behaviours that would help solve a problem one is attacking. The PD approach can become very useful in solving large-scale problems, like depression in Indian youth. It is built upon a discussion between the youth (sufferer) and the practitioner. The practitioner is able to suggest how a depressive state can be handled within the living conditions the youth is experiencing. Further, other youths experiencing similar problems are encouraged to volunteer how they manage these challenges. PD is widely used in nutrition education for children, pregnant women and diabetics, food safety education and public health communication. It effectively addresses barriers and encourages behavioural change among target audiences, like rural families from low-income countries and communities with a low socio-economic status (Feng et al., 2016a; 2016b; Guldan et al., 1993; Zeitlin et al., 1993).

The PD approach functions on the fact that in every society and community there are certain individuals, small groups or large groups whose unique behaviours and innovative strategies help them find solutions to societal issues and problems, as compared to other members of the community, while facing worse challenges and having access to the same resources.

Dr Hopkins, an epidemiologist at the Centers for Disease Control and Prevention (CDC), using this technique has been able to cure Guinea worm disease in African and West Asian countries. He focused on developing water drinking behaviour using filters and solidarity at the village level. The use of influence and the involvement of local people helped billions become free from the largest human parasite without medicine.

Dr Wiwat Rojanapithayakorn of Thailand has been able to use behavioural principles to control HIV/AIDS (human immunodeficiency virus/acquired immunodeficiency syndrome) through training sex workers to follow the 'no condom no sex' compliance rule. It has helped control millions of HIV cases and stopped Thailand from becoming the AIDS capital of the world. Through the use of solidarity among sex workers across regions, the programme was willingly expanded across the entire country.

PD is one of the socio-behavioural approaches and has also been used prominently in infection prevention and control.

METHODOLOGY OF POSITIVE DEVIANCE

The PD methodology can be understood through hypothetical case examples, such as the following.

HYPOTHETICAL CASE OF DEPRESSION IN INDIA: PROPOSED POSITIVE DEVIANCE PROGRAMME

Selecting a Large-scale Problem:

As mentioned earlier, it has been found that there are more than 9 crore people in India suffering from anxiety and depression alone, beside other mental disorders. As part of a PD programme to address this, the following steps can be taken.

Going to the Field Where the Problem Exists

PD, in the context of action research, can be understood as an attempt made to arrive at solutions to problems faced by people with their involvement. It requires going to the centre, the community where the problem exists. However, first, the researcher would do an extensive survey to identify a group, a village, an institution, a hamlet or even a town where the problem does not exist. Such a unit is called a positively deviant unit. Once such unit is found, it is intensively and extensively observed using focal observation methods.

Finding a Positively Deviant Unit in the Midst of Problem Units

In the present case, the researcher would find a unit where no case of suicide has taken place in the recent past and no person has been diagnosed with clinical depression or undergone treatment under a psychiatrist or a clinical psychologist. The level of general well-being and happiness in the unit would be high, even as other communities around the unit have abundant cases of anxiety and depression. It may take quite a long time to find such a unit. The researcher interested in this methodology travels widely to attain information directly after gathering all the means of information available.

Observing Behaviours Related to the Problem

Second, the researcher would conduct a comprehensive assessment using different tools of measurement, including non-participative observation, going through the data already recorded or collecting data from the unit (randomly drawn) showing PD and the unit infested with the problem.

Establishing Contrast Behaviour to Select Vital Behaviour(s)

Third, the contrasted-group design may be used to identify the vital and unique behaviours or practices that are directly relevant to the problem at hand, that is, depression in the present case.

Taking the Vital Behaviour to the Problem Unit and Assessing Its Impact on the Problem

The researchers should focus on the behaviours or practices that had mitigated the influence of risk behaviours and vulnerabilities, there may be much such behaviour however the researcher needs to focus on 'the critical behaviour'/the vital behaviour, then after, replicating the vital behaviour experimentally (field trials) and assessing the impact. This requires longitudinal monitoring in the problem-infested community. Once the intervention seems to be working, it needs to be standardized and can be replicated in other pockets with high incidence of depression.

Replicating the Process in Other Problem Units

Large-scale problems cannot be solved solely by the social scientist but require full participation of the local people. The latter can be trained to propagate 'the vital behaviours' in their locality. The researcher would later continue to support and monitor the progress of the intervention programmes.

REFERENCES

Akin, A. (2011). Self-compassion and self-deception. *The International Journal of Educational Researchers, 2*(3), 25–33.

Akin, U. (2014). The predictive role of the self-compassion on psychological vulnerability in Turkish university students. *International Journal of Social Science & Education, 4*, 693–701.

Beck, A. T., & Haigh, E. A. (2014). Advances in cognitive theory and therapy: The generic cognitive model. *Annual Review of Clinical Psychology, 10*(1), 1–24. https://.doi.org/10.1146/annurev-clinpsy-032813-153734

Brown, B. (n.d.). *The power of vulnerability.* https://www.ted.com/talks/brene_brown_the_power_of_vulnerability?language=en

Chambers, R. (1983). *Rural development: Putting the last first.* Prentice Hall.

Daskalakis, N. P., Bagot, R. C., Parker, K. J., Vinkers, C. H., & de Kloet, E. R. (2013). The three-hit concept of vulnerability and resilience: Toward understanding adaptation to early-life adversity outcome. *Psychoneuroendocrinology, 38*(9), 1858–1873.

Delor, F., & Hubert, M. (2000). Revisiting the concept of 'vulnerability'. *Social Science & Medicine, 50*(11), 1557–1570.

Disner, S. G., Beevers, C. G., Haigh, E. A., & Beck, A. T. (2011). Neural mechanisms of the cognitive model of depression. *Nature Reviews Neuroscience, 12*(8), 467–477. https://dx.doi.org/10.1038/nrn3027.

Feng, Y., Bruhn, C. M., & Health Management and Education. (2016a). Food safety education for people with diabetes and pregnant women: A positive deviance approach. *Food Control, 6*, 107–115.

Feng, Y., Bruhn, C., & Marx, D. (2016b). Evaluation of different food safety education interventions. *British Food Journal, 118*(4), 762–776.

Ferrari, A. J., Charlson, F. J., Norman, R. E., Flaxman, A. D., Patten, S. B., Vos, T., & Whiteford, H. A. (2013a). The epidemiological modelling of major depressive disorder: Application for the Global Burden of Disease Study 2010. *PloS one, 8*(7), e69637. https://doi.org/10.1371/journal.pone.0069637

Gilligan, R. (2009). *Promoting resilience, supporting children and young people who are in care, adopted or in need.* British Association for Adoption & Fostering (BAAF).

Graz, L. (1997). A question of vulnerability. *Red Cross, Red Crescent, 3*, 2–7.

Guldan, G., Zhang, M.-Y., Zhang, Y.-P., Hong, J.-R., Zhang, H.-X., Fu, S.-Y., & Fu, N. S. (1993). Weaning practices and growth in rural Sichuan infants: A positive deviance study. *Journal of Tropical Pediatrics, 39*(3), 168–175.

Ingram, R. E., & Price, J. M. (2001). The role of vulnerability in understanding psychopathology. In R. E. Ingram & J. M. Price (Eds.), *Vulnerability to psychopathology: Risk across the lifespan* (pp. 3–19). The Guilford Press.

Mangeard-Lourme, J., & Brunsden, V. (2014). Measuring psychological vulnerability in the shanty towns of Manila: The challenges of research within a different cultural context. *SAGE Research Methods Cases.* https://doi.org/10.4135/978144627305014529497

Marchetti, I., Loeys, T., Alloy, L. B., & Koster, E. H. (2016). Unveiling the structure of cognitive vulnerability for depression. *Plos One, 11*(12), e0168612.

Nogueira, M. J., Barros, L., & Sequeira, C. (2017). Psychometric properties of the psychological vulnerability scale in higher education students. *Journal of the American Psychiatric Nurses Association, 23*(3), 215–222. https://doi.org/10.1177/1078390317695261.

Sagar, R., Dandona, R., Gururaj, G., Dhaliwal, R. S., Singh, A., Ferrari, A., & Dandona, L. (2020). The burden of mental disorders across the states of India: The global burden of disease study 1990–2017. *The Lancet Psychiatry, 7*(2), 148–161. https://doi.org/10.1016/s2215-0366(19)30475-4

Satici, S. A. (2016). Psychological vulnerability, resilience, and subjective well-being: The mediating role of hope. *Personality and Individual Differences, 102*, 68–73. https://doi.org/10.1016/j.paid.2016.06.057

Satici, S. A., & Uysal, R. (2016). Psychological vulnerability and subjective happiness: The mediating role of hopelessness. *Stress and Health, 33*(2), 111–118. https://doi.org/10.1002/smi.2685

Satici, B., Saricali, M., Satici, S. A., & Eraslan Çapan, B. (2014). Social competence and psychological vulnerability as predictors of Facebook addiction. *Studia Psychologica, 56*(4), 301–308. https://doi.org/10.21909/sp.2014.04.738

Satici, S. A., Uysal, R., Yilmaz, M. F., & Deniz, M. E. (2015). Social safeness and psychological vulnerability in Turkish Youth: The mediating role of life satisfaction. *Current Psychology, 35*(1), 22–28. https://doi.org/10.1007/s12144-015-9359-1

Sevi, O. M. (2018). From vulnerability to resilience: A coping related approach to psychosis. *Psychosis—Biopsychosocial and Relational Perspectives.* https://doi.org/10.5772/intechopen.78385

Sinclair, V. G., & Wallston, K. A. (1999). The development and validation of the Psychological Vulnerability Scale. *Cognitive Therapy and Research, 23*(2), 119–129. https://doi.org/10.1023/A:1018770926615

Sinha, D., Tripathi, R. C., & Misra, G. (1995). *Deprivation, its social roots and psychological consequences.* Concept Pub.

Uysal, R. (2015). Social competence and psychological vulnerability: The mediating role of flourishing. *Psychological Reports, 117*(2), 554–565. https://doi.org/10.2466/21.pr0.117c18z2

Walsh, F. (2006). *Strengthening family resilience* (2nd ed.). The Guilford Press.

Zeitlin, M., Ghassemi, H., & Mansour, M. (1993). Positive deviance in child nutrition: A discussion. *Ecology of Food and Nutrition, 30*(2), 79–87.

Chapter 8

Women and Work in Post-reform India
Reality of Vulnerability and Exclusion

Padmini Ravindra Nath and Chandrika Soni

Employment has been widely accepted as a crucial pathway for the economic empowerment of women all over the world, in general, and in developing countries, in particular. Thus, expansion of employment opportunities for women has been the main focus of development planning in India. It was realized by policy planners that larger and more efficient use of available human resources is the most effective way to reduce poverty and inequality, as well as ensure rapid, inclusive and equitable economic growth. However, in spite of repeated emphasis in state policy on this aspect, economic gender gap runs deep in Indian society, rendering women vulnerable and voiceless.

This has happened largely because gendered division of work in the family has culminated in gender-based division of labour in the society. The Global Gender Gap Index of World Economic Forum, which is a composite of gender-based gaps in certain dimensions, namely participation in economic life, educational achievement, health and survival and political empowerment, places India at the 112th place in 2019–2020, actually a drop of four places from 2018. A cursory look at the sub-indices reveal the actual extent of inequity prevalent in the work sphere. India performs dismally, ranking 149th in economic participation and opportunity and 117th in wage equality between the sexes for the same work. India is the only country in the world which is performing worse on indicators of economic participation as compared to political participation. Women in India are not only pushed into low-paying jobs in the informal sector, but also their contributions to domestic work and care work, which take up many hours of their productive life, go unacknowledged.

EMPLOYMENT AND WOMEN EMPOWERMENT

In many Asian and African countries women are excluded from full participation in economic life. This has unfortunate consequences not only for the welfare of individual families but also for the economy as a whole. An increase in employment opportunities for women is a precondition for improving women's lives and accelerating economic growth and development. The International Labour Organization (ILO, 2012) has reiterated that access to resources, availability of opportunities and equal participation in economic life enable women to take advantage of sustainable and inclusive growth.

Employment has a positive effect on women empowerment at both the individual and societal levels. It has a deep-seated impact on women's economic status, health choices and participation in the decision-making process within the family. A clear difference can be seen in the relative status of employed women vis-à-vis their unemployed counterparts. Jobs that enhance women's agency increase the spectrum of available choices and their capacity to act on those choices. Paid employment frequently leads to greater investments in the health and well-being of themselves, their families and their communities. Employed women tend to have fewer children, and the income earned by women invariably contributes to the household budget. In other words, a regular income translates into sexual and reproductive autonomy. The own income of a woman reduces her dependence on others within the patriarchal power structures, placing her in a stronger negotiating position within the family and allowing her to exercise greater control over her own life. In fact, studies in developing countries have shown a clear decrease in the incidence of domestic violence too against employed women. Gainful employment may reduce women's vulnerability and contribute to empowerment by allowing their participation in the public sphere. This would facilitate their interaction with a wide network of individuals, which would have positive implications for their self-esteem and self-worth (Banu et al., 2001; Bi, 2016; Hancock, 2001; Heyzer, 1985; Hossain & Jaim, 2011; Khan, 2006; Levine et al., 2009; Moghadam, 2003; Nakkeeran, 2003; Norton & Haan, 2013; Odutola et al., 2003; Papanek & Schwede, 1988; Schular et al., 1996; Speer et al., 2001; Sultana & Hossein, 2013; Tibandebage, 1995; West, 2006).

The nature of employment, it has been observed, plays a crucial role in the workings of this mechanism. Women's economic empowerment (or at the very least their right to co-determine familial resource distribution) is greater when they are employers, or in formal wage work that is protected through legislation that guarantees their rights. Full-time wage employment has emerged in empirical studies as a significant predictor of subjective well-being. Formal work that provides higher earnings, benefits, rights and opportunities for skill development is more likely to expand women's agency. Informal work, while providing much-needed income, is inherently more exposed to risks, as the safeguards like organized collective action or labour legislation are absent. Work that offers regular and relatively independent income has greater transformative potential for women. The key here is to realize that simply access to employment does not reduce the vulnerabilities of women. This can occur only if they have bargaining power, control over resources and realization of their own identity (Bose et al., 2009; Dixon-Muller, 1993; Goetz & Gupta, 1996; Kabeer et al., 2011; Kishor & Gupta, 2004; World Development Report [WDR], 2012).

Traditionally, in both developed and developing countries, women are found clustered in certain occupations to a large extent. According to estimates by ILO (2012), women's employment is concentrated in certain occupational pockets, like clerical and services and retail sales work, in developed countries. In contrast, female work participation is heavily skewed towards the informal sector or part-time work in developing countries. This could be due to the women's perceptions about safety while travelling to the workplace which make them prefer home-based work, their inability to spare the time for work, due to lack of an adequate support system to help meet their domestic care work obligations or simply the absence of skill set and training needed to enter the formal sector. In turn, this deprives them of the benefits that formal employment would grant them.

UNPAID WORK OF WOMEN: THE LOST EFFORT

Women's unpaid care work leads to both economic poverty and time poverty for them, because it is usually overlooked by the mainstream conception of labour (that focuses on paid employment). Unpaid female contribution is invisible in national accounts and subsequently in economic and social policies, although women perform the bulk of unpaid work across the world.

The term 'unpaid care work' has a specific connotation here. It refers to the services rendered or 'given within households for other household and community members' for which the person does not receive a wage. However, the performed activities have a time and energy cost and are undertaken due to social relationships, like marriage (UNIFEM, 2000, 2005).

According to the United Nations System of National Accounts (1993), unpaid work refers to household maintenance, cleaning, washing, cooking and shopping, as well as care for infants and relatives. In short, unpaid care work includes all the work that is carried out at homes and not counted as national income.

Studies across the world have shown that men are more likely to engage in System of National Accounts (SNA) (market-based) work and also for a longer time as compared to women, while women are more likely to engage in unpaid care work for a longer time as compared to men. The work is almost always unequally distributed between men and women; this in turn means that women carry more burden as compared to men. Women do not have the luxury of enjoying ample discretionary time, as they perform multiple activities simultaneously, such as childcare, housework and maintenance of stocks. As women's increased participation in the labour market is not always accompanied by an increase in men's share of unpaid domestic labour, it does not necessarily improve the non-economic well-being of the family. Poor working women who cannot afford domestic help have to cope with the double burden of household tasks and employment due to the indifference of men towards sharing the household burden. Women therefore have to sacrifice their working hours to take over care work (Bhatia, 2002; Blackden & Wodon, 2006; Budlender, 2008; Corner, 2002; Fleming & Spellerberg, 1999; Gibb et al., 2013; Hirway, 2015; Ironmonger & Hill, 1999; Medeiros et al., 2007; UNRISD, 2010).

Thus, there is a fundamental vicious cycle in which women are caught. First, women's primary responsibility for unpaid care work, such as child rearing, handling of children's education and basic family services, seems to channel them into similar working areas in the labour market. Second, time poverty means that they are forced to accept low-paying, part-time or informal-sector employment that may offer them greater flexibility. Third, their unpaid work, although taxing in terms of effort and time, is not visible in economic terms. It is unfortunate that in spite of the numerous time-use surveys being carried out all over the world, including in India, there has been no concrete attempt so far to develop a comprehensive methodological framework to evaluate the unpaid–care work economy.

DETERMINANTS OF WOMEN'S WORKFORCE PARTICIPATION

Identification of the factors that determine the participation of women in the workforce is crucial to determine the correct policy responses. Studies conducted in developing countries of Asia and Africa have observed that in rural areas, marital status, religion, poverty rate and per capita income have emerged as significant determinants, whereas in the case of the urban sector, age and literacy rate play a dominant role. In the case of married women, education, number of children, number of dependents, family size, income of husband, monthly expenditures of the family, positive attitude of the husband, as well as his family, towards the job of women and job satisfaction have a positive impact on their labour force participation. Non-work determinants, especially pressures from the matrimonial home, emerged as one of the strongest factors responsible for female labour turnover in the developing countries. Similarly, in the context of all women, their education, as well as ethnicity or caste, seems to play a very important role in shaping their decision to enter the labour market. In countries like India, marriage migration, particularly rural-to-urban migration, impacts female workforce participation. Some studies have also pointed to the U-shaped relation between female labour participation and development, wherein the former first declines and then increases with the latter (Bhalla & Kaur, 2011; Bibi & Afzal, 2012; Faridi et al., 2011b; Iweagu et al., 2015; Lisaniler & Bhatti, 2005; Mammen & Paxson, 2000; Pastore & Verashchagina, 2008; Umar & Karofi, 2007).

Any policy aimed at increasing the workforce participation of women would have to not only address these amorphous determinants but also be tailored around the needs of specific socio-economic groups. It has to be kept in mind that a common thread that runs across countries is the positive role that can be played by education and upskilling in increasing the employability of female workers.

WOMEN AND GLOBALIZATION

In 1991, India initiated the structural adjustment programme (SAP), which is referred to in common parlance as LPG on the basis of its three major components: liberalization, privatization and globalization. This policy, which was initially introduced to meet the conditionalities of an International Monetary Fund (IMF) loan sought by Government of India, had far-reaching consequences for the way India worked. The reforms, especially privatization and globalization, that were ushered in without an adequate safety net led to increased unemployment and informalization of the labour market. The impact was particularly hard on vulnerable groups, like women.

Various studies have confirmed that globalization is not an inclusive process, at least as far as women are concerned. It confines women to poorly paid, low-status part-time jobs that perpetuate their subordination and devalue their contributions (Enloe, 1990, 2014; Mason, 1986). In the countries like India, in spite of globalization, women still remain marginalized in the informal sector, with poor access to land, credit, education and health facilities. They are often exploited through being made to work long hours and being paid low wages, and they also lack voice and participation (Pande, 2007). The roots of this could lie deep in the agrarian structure of employment not only in India but also in other developing countries. The change in the production structure, especially the shift to manufacturing, has been shown to impact gender equity positively (Seguino, 2006).

At the global level, over the recent years, the informal sector has risen as a greater source of employment for men (63.0%) than for women (58.1%). In fact, out of the 2 billion workers in informal employment worldwide, just above 740 million are women. This overall picture however hides important regional disparities. If we consider only low-income and lower-middle-income countries, a higher proportion of women are in informal employment than men. Women are more exposed to informal employment in more than 90 per cent of sub-Saharan African countries, 89 per cent of countries in South Asia and almost 75 per cent of Latin American countries. A major difference between women and men in informal employment is in the proportion of women contributing to family work, which is more than three times higher than that of men (ILO, 2018).

However, this should not be taken to mean that globalization has been wholly detrimental for women's work. If the policies of globalization are pursued with proper safeguards, they may lead to certain improvements in the status of women. The economic aspects of globalization can bring new opportunities, efficient resource allocation and diffusion of equality norms for women. Increased economic growth and per capita income can also lead to reduction in the occupational wage gap (Gray et al., 2006; Oostendorp, 2004). The subsequent sections explore whether globalization has indeed succeeded in pulling women into the mainstream of economic development.

GENDER DISPARITY IN UNEMPLOYMENT: A POST-REFORM SCENARIO

In the post-globalization landscape, female unemployment has increased, raising concerns that women are either being pushed out of the workforce or being denied entry into the formal workspace.

In India, there are three commonly followed estimates of unemployment, which are based on different approaches or reference periods, used to classify an individual's activity status.

1. Usual Status (US) approach, with a reference period of 365 days preceding the date of survey, is also known by the names open unemployment and chronic unemployment. This measure estimates the number of persons who remained unemployed for a major part of the year. It is also defined as 'ps + ss'—principal status plus subsidiary status.

2. Current Weekly Status (CWS) approach, with a reference period of 1 week preceding the date of survey, is that in which a person is said to be unemployed if he/she was not able to work even for 1 hour during the date of survey.

3. Current Daily Status (CDS) approach is based on the daily activity pursued by individuals on each day of the reference week preceding the date of survey. If a person did not find work on a day or some days during the survey week, he/she is regarded as unemployed.

The labour force is measured in terms of persons under the first two approaches and in person days under the last approach.

In Figure 8.1, if we compare the estimates of the unemployed in absolute numbers corresponding to NSSO's (National Sample Survey Office) 66th Round (blue bars) and 68th Round (red bars) in different broad activity statuses, we find that the absolute number of the unemployed among males is more as compared to that among females in both rural and urban sectors. However, a disturbing pattern that is emerging is that the absolute number of unemployed urban females has increased in all three statuses during this period, whereas the absolute number of unemployed females in rural areas has decreased in the same period. This could indicate a feminization of workforce in agricultural

Figure 8.1(a): Usual Status (ps+ss)

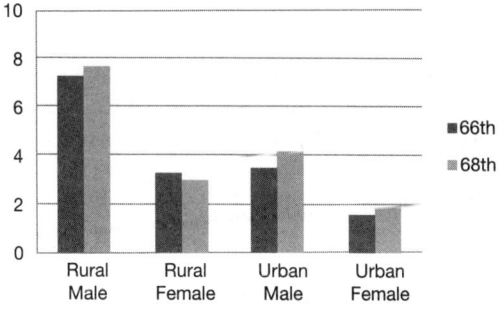

Figure 8.1(b): Current Weekly Status (CDS)

Figure 8.1(c): Current Daily Status

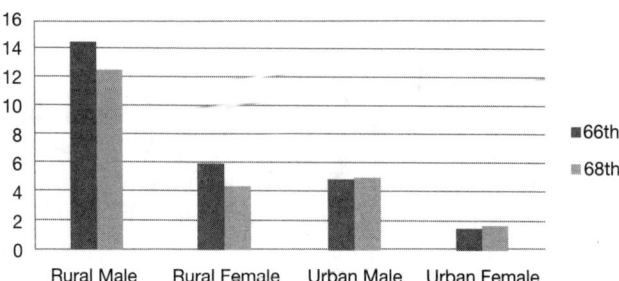

Figure 8.1 *Overview of Unemployment in India (in millions)*
Source: NSS 66th Round (July 2009–June 2010) and NSS 68th Round (July 2011–June 2012).

activities, which by their very nature are low-skilled, back-breaking and low-paid.

GENDER DISPARITY IN WORKFORCE PARTICIPATION IN THE POST-REFORM PERIOD

Female workforce participation is the other side of the coin for female unemployment. The census of India uses the concept of WPR (work participation ratio) to measure the extent of participation in labour force. It is commonly defined as follows:

$$WPR = \frac{\text{Total workers (main+marginal)}}{\text{Total population}} \times 100$$

where, main workers are those who worked for more than 6 months (180 days) in the reference period and marginal workers are those who worked for less than 6 months (180 days) in the reference period.

A cursory look at the data in Figure 8.2 brings three significant trends to mind:

1. The WPR of both males and females has increased, but female WPR still lags behind male WPR.

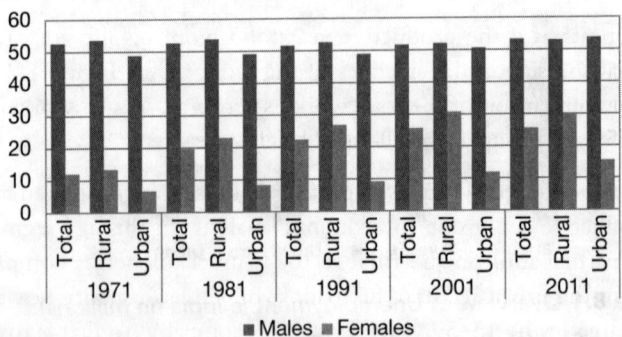

Figure 8.2 *Work Participation Rate in India (%)*
Source: Census data (relevant years).

2. Till 2001, the rural female WPR had increased by more than the urban female WPR, although a marginal decrease is seen in 2011.

3. The gap between urban male and urban female WPRs has remained almost constant, which indicates that economic reforms have not resulted in any significant improvement in women's employment status vis-à-vis their male counterparts.

This feminization of the rural workforce can be understood better when we observe the breakup of total workers into main and marginal workers in the male–female and rural–urban categories.

It is clearly noticeable from Table 8.1 that women's participation in the rural sector is much higher as compared to that in urban areas. This may be because rural women prefer to be engaged in agricultural or household industries that allow them to manage their domestic duties easily along with the paid economic activity. Further, female workers in rural areas do not require any special training that may be required for female workers in urban areas.

If we look at main workers, we find that male WPRs are higher than female WPRs at all levels—total, rural and urban. However, in the category of marginal workers, we find that rural and total female WPRs are more than rural and total male WPRs, respectively. This can be seen as a proof of our earlier contention that women are giving time to unpaid domestic and care work and can participate only partly in economic activity.

It appears as if the productive years of a woman's life are largely wasted as she sits on the sidelines of the work arena. Figure 8.3 is a pictorial comparison of the total workers across all ages to workers in the 15–59 age group at the all-India level.

The age group of 15–59 is important, because it is considered to be the productive age group in economic analysis. In this age segment, female participation in the rural sector is much higher as compared to that in the urban sector. The shadow of gender disparity however looms large in the 15–59 years segment as compared to that across all ages. This is seen in both urban and rural areas, dispelling the myth that urbanization leads to greater inclusion for women. They seem to

Table 8.1 *Percentage of Workers to Total Population in 2011, All India (All Age Groups): Main and Marginal Workers*

	Total Workers			Main Workers			Marginal Workers		
	Persons	Males	Females	Persons	Males	Females	Persons	Males	Females
Total	39.80	53.26	25.52	29.94	43.83	15.21	9.85	9.42	10.31
Rural	41.83	53.03	30.03	29.49	41.63	16.69	12.34	11.39	13.33
Urban	35.31	53.76	15.44	30.95	48.65	11.88	4.36	5.11	3.56

Source: Calculated by the authors from Census of India (2011), Economic table: B-1 series.

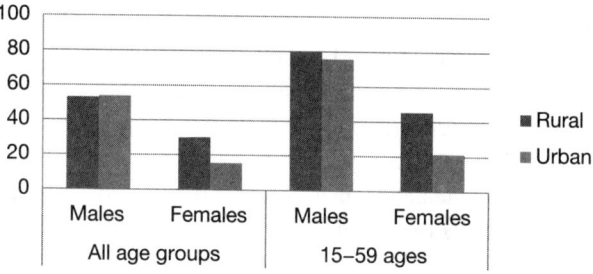

Figure 8.3 *Total Workers of All Age Groups Compared with Workers in the 15–59 Age Group*
Source: Census of India (2011).

be staying at home more in their productive work years, which incidentally also happens to be the time when their childbearing and child rearing responsibilities peak.

Two clear trends are emerging here in this age group, namely disparity between males and females and disparity within females (between urban and rural women). This intra-female disparity is often overlooked by policymakers, who treat all women as one block, which reduces the efficacy of the state's efforts targeted at women.

INTERSTATE DISPARITY IN FEMALE WORK PARTICIPATION RATES IN POST-REFORM INDIA

Any macro analysis should guard against treating this country as a homogeneous whole. Often, the all-India trends do not reflect the ground realities of many states, particularly those that are less developed. This is the reason for undertaking an interstate evaluation of female WPRs in this section. The census years of 2001 and 2011 have been chosen to ensure comparability of data, because the three states of Uttarakhand, Chhattisgarh and Jharkhand were formed in the year 2000.

The female WPRs are abysmally low in both 2001 and 2011. This is very surprising when we consider the commonly believed media discourse around economic reforms and their supposed socially liberating and economically empowering impact on women. The larger picture clearly shows that women have been out of the labour force in the years following the reforms in India. The female WPRs are higher in the hilly, tribal or north-eastern states that traditionally have female-centric social systems. There does not seem to have been much change over the span of the decade between 2001 and 2011, and the chief takeaway from Table 8.2 seems to be that the role of sociocultural factors cannot be underestimated as a determinant of female work participation.

Table 8.2 Female Work Participation Rate: 2001 and 2011 (States and Union Territories)

S. No.	State/Union Territory	Female Work Participation Rate 2001	2011
1.	Himachal Pradesh	43.7	44.8
2.	Nagaland	38.1	44.7
3.	Chhattisgarh	40	39.7
4.	Sikkim	38.6	39.6
5.	Mizoram	47.5	36.2
6.	Andhra Pradesh	35.1	36.2
7.	Arunachal Pradesh	36.5	35.4
8.	Rajasthan	33.5	35.1
9.	Meghalaya	35.1	32.7
10.	Madhya Pradesh	33.2	32.6
11.	Karnataka	32	31.9
12.	Tamil Nadu	31.5	31.8
13.	Maharashtra	30.8	31.1
14.	Jharkhand	26.4	29.1
15.	Orissa	24.7	27.2
16.	Uttarakhand	27.3	26.7
17.	Dadra and Nagar Haveli	38.7	25.3
18.	Tripura	21.1	23.6
19.	Gujarat	27.9	23.4

S. No.	State/Union Territory	Female Work Participation Rate	
		2001	2011
20.	Assam	20.7	22.5
21.	Goa	22.4	21.9
22.	Jammu and Kashmir	22.5	19.1
23.	Bihar	18.8	19.1
24.	Kerala	15.4	18.2
25.	West Bengal	18.3	18.1
26.	Haryana	27.2	17.8
27.	Andaman and Nicobar Islands	16.6	17.8
28.	Puducherry	17.2	17.6
29.	Uttar Pradesh	16.5	16.7
30.	Chandigarh	14.2	16
31.	Daman and Diu	18.6	14.9
32.	Punjab	19.1	13.9
33.	Lakshadweep	7.3	11
34.	Delhi	9.4	10.6

Source: Office of the Registrar General and Census Commissioner, Ministry of Home Affairs, Government of India.

SAGA OF SELF-EMPLOYMENT: AN OVERVIEW OF FEMALE ENTREPRENEURSHIP IN INDIA

Self-employment is often seen as a remedy for unemployment, harassment and marginalization of women. It is looked upon as a tool to convert women into job creators, thereby providing them with an economic identity and enabling the actualization of self.

In India, a women-owned enterprise is defined as a small-scale industrial unit or industry-related service or business enterprise 'which is managed by a woman or group of women entrepreneurs as proprietary concerns or in which she or they individually or jointly have a minimum share capital of not less than 51% as partners or shareholders' (MSME, Government of India). Similarly, a female entrepreneur is defined as a woman or group of women who initiate, organize and combine factors of production, as well as running a business enterprise (Suganthi, 2009).

Female entrepreneurship in India is mostly concentrated in the informal or unorganized sector. The female labour force participation rate, affordable credit and women's participation in decision-making are significant factors that enhance female entrepreneurship. An increase in female entrepreneurship can also be seen due to a lack of other employment opportunities available for women. However, in India, it remains mostly a necessity-driven activity with limited scope for innovation (Daymard, 2015; Khokhar, 2019; Khokhar & Singh, 2016; Samantroy & Tomar, 2018).

The total number of agricultural establishments under female entrepreneurship was 2.76 million, which constituted 34.3 per cent of the total establishments owned by women, whereas about 5.29 million establishments (65.7%) were involved in non–agricultural activities, as given in Figure 8.4. It is interesting to note that while female workers are concentrated in agricultural activities, female entrepreneurs are clustered in non-agricultural activities.

As far as the nature of women-owned enterprises' operations is concerned, a large part (89%) of the establishments were perennial,

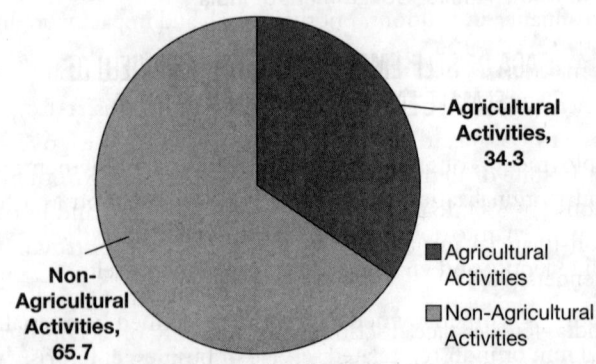

Figure 8.4 *Share in Total Establishments Under Female Entrepreneurship*
Source: Sixth Economic Census (2013–2014), Ministry of Statistics and Programme Implementation, Government of India.

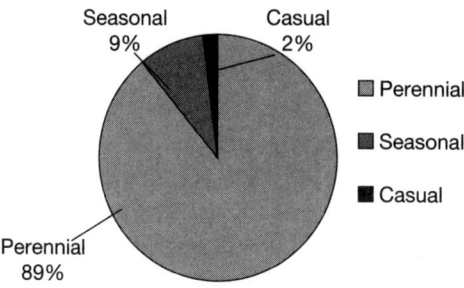

Figure 8.5 *Nature of Operations (%)*
Source: Sixth Economic Census (2013–2014), Ministry of Statistics and Programme Implementation, Government of India.

9.03 per cent were seasonal and the remaining 1.97 per cent were casual establishments, as depicted in Figure 8.5. Fortunately, this shows that the majority of women-owned enterprises are perennial in nature, indicating a regular stream of income from entrepreneurial activity.

Figure 8.6 gives a bird's-eye view of access to credit, which is an important determinant of female entrepreneurship. Credit lines were limited for women till recently. It is only over the past few years that a focused effort has been made to help women access much-needed finance. At a policy level, the public sector banks were supposed to lend to women even before 1991 through the self-help group model and microfinance institutions, but their reach and impact were limited.

The major source of finance in women-owned establishments is self-finance (79.07%), followed by donation or transfer from other agencies (14.65%) and financial assistance from the government (3.37%). In spite of all the different schemes, borrowing from financial institutions (1.08%), loans from self-help groups (1%) and borrowing from non-financial institutions are negligible, as is borrowing from moneylenders (0.84%).

In India, females face discrimination not only on account of their gender but also on account of their socio-religious group. Thus, being part of a particular religious or social group renders them doubly vulnerable. The data available in the public domain point towards the marginalization of certain subsects even within the broad sector of

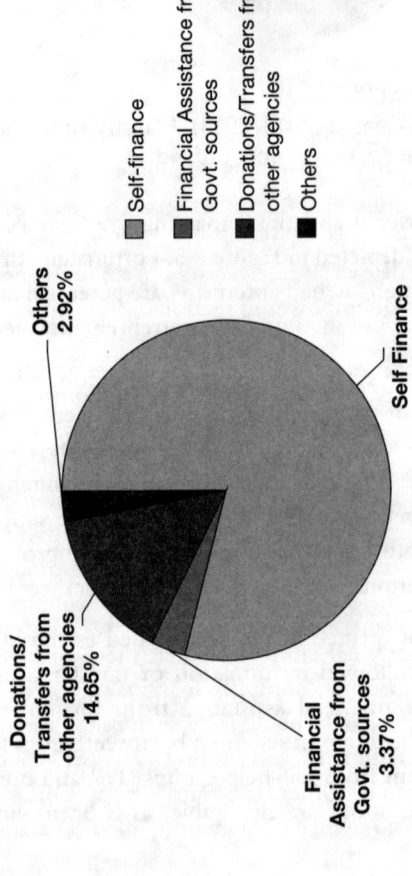

Figure 8.6 *Source of Finance (%)*

Source: Sixth Economic Census (2013–2014), Ministry of Statistics and Programme Implementation, Government of India.

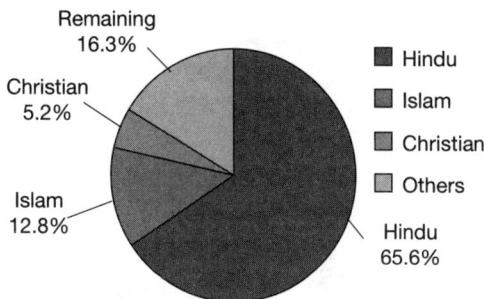

Figure 8.7 *Religion of Owner (%)*

Source: Sixth Economic Census (2013–2014), Ministry of Statistics and Programme Implementation, Government of India.

Note: 'Remaining' includes Sikh, Buddhist, Parsi, Jain and Others.

female entrepreneurs. It can be referred to as a subset that is the most vulnerable among the disempowered sections.

As shown in Figure 8.7, most of the female-owned establishments (65.6%) were owned by Hindu entrepreneurs, followed by Muslims (12.8%) and Christians (5.2%). The remaining enterprises were owned by Sikhs (0.9%), Jains (0.5%), Buddhists (0.5%) and women belonging to other religious communities (14.4%). This could be explained on the basis of certain communities being more conservative than others in allowing public interaction of women and some minority groups having a low share in the overall population of the country.

In line with our original contention that there is discrimination nested within discrimination, a complete marginalization of Scheduled Castes (SCs) and Scheduled Tribes (STs) is seen in the ownership pattern; 3.27 million establishments, constituting 40.65 per cent of the total enterprises, were owned by Other Backward Classes (OBCs), followed by others (General), who owned 3.23 million (40.20%) establishments. SCs owned 0.98 million (12.18%) and STs 0.56 million (6.97%) of the total enterprises, which has been shown in Figure 8.8.

It is unfortunate that even after the inception of reforms, various barriers are being faced by female entrepreneurs in starting their business, including lack of access to formal finance facility, limited

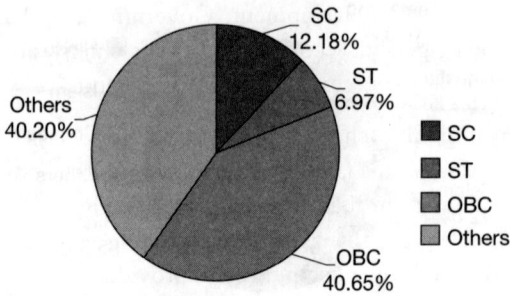

Figure 8.8 *Distribution of Establishments under Female Entrepreneurs by Social Group of Owner*

Source: Sixth Economic Census (2013–2014), Ministry of Statistics and Programme Implementation, Government of India.

mobility, lack of education, low risk-taking ability and marketing problems. Female entrepreneurs also suffer because they do not have the access to the business information and knowledge networks that males have.

POLICY PRESCRIPTIONS FOR INCREASING WOMEN'S PARTICIPATION IN THE WORKFORCE IN POST-REFORM INDIA

As mentioned earlier, gainful employment is a key driver in reducing the vulnerability of women to exploitation by patriarchal power structures in the family and community. However, any study of gender disparity would be meaningful only if situated in its cultural, geographical and historical context. Post 1991, Government of India has implemented a plethora of schemes and programmes in order to enhance employment and empower women. Yet, numerous well thought out schemes have failed in the past to increase significantly the participation of women in the workforce either as workers or as entrepreneurs. Effective implementation of the policy interventions too is needed to make women key stakeholders in the development process. Lack of effective implementation leads to the potential of women remaining untapped and underutilized.

The major schemes mentioned below have a common thread running through them. First, they are mostly administered by the Ministry of Women and Child Development, Government of India, which works as a nodal agency. Second, the focus is chiefly on improving access to economic resources, especially microcredit.

The Swayamsiddha scheme (2001), Swadhar scheme (2001) and Mahila Samriddhi Yojana (1993) all revolve around the core theme of empowering women through education and livelihood. For the same purpose, the public sector banks have been making a concerted effort to develop female entrepreneurship through providing women easy lines of credit for establishment of new businesses, as well as for upgradation and expansion of existing enterprises.

In recent years, the spotlight has been on upskilling rather than on giving out almost-free handouts in the form of cheap loans. This idea has been echoed by the National Policy for Skill Development and Entrepreneurship, 2015, which envisions skill development as a vehicle for women's empowerment. The policy outlines three main strategies: setting up of additional training and apprenticeship seats exclusively for women, incorporation of women-related issues in the guidelines for skill training procedures and promotion of an Internet- or mobile-based platform for women's employment. The Deen Dayal Upadhyaya Deen Dayal Upadhyaya Grameen Kaushalya Yojana mandates that one-third of the seats be reserved for women, and the gram panchayats are expected to make special efforts in this direction.

In addition to the above general schemes aimed at all women, there are eight specific schemes targeted at would-be female entrepreneurs, whose implementation is mainly in the domain of public sector banks: Annapurna Scheme (Bank of Mysore and now-defunct Bharatiya Mahila Bank); Stree Shakti Package (State Bank of India); Cent Kalyani Scheme (Central Bank of India); Mahila Udyam Nidhi Yojana (Punjab National Bank and Small Industries Development Bank of India); Dena Shakti Scheme (Dena Bank, now merged with Bank of Baroda); Orient Mahila Vikas Yojana (Oriental Bank of Commerce, now merged with Punjab National Bank) and of course the flagship Pradhan Mantri MUDRA Yojana, which gives a no-collateral, no-guarantee loan up to ₹10 lakh for female entrepreneurs.

However, if an honest answer is sought by women themselves, it is obvious that in many cases the real beneficiaries have been the male members of their family. The enterprise, although owned in the name of the female beneficiary, is actually controlled and run by the male relatives.

COVID-19 AND THE FUTURE OF FEMALE WORK

The recent pandemic has left women even more exposed and vulnerable, if that were possible. However, it has also succeeded in bringing the issues of female workers to the forefront, not least because they are concentrated in the informal sector.

The WIEGO (Women in Informal Employment: Globalizing and Organizing) framework of three V's—visibility, validity and voice—can be extended by adding a fourth V, namely 'vulnerability', and it can be expanded to include all women, whether employed in the formal sector, working in the informal sector or providing unpaid care work at home. This pandemic has provided validity to female workers, especially those in the informal sector, because it has brought them mainstream recognition as legitimate economic agents. Their contributions are being increasingly quantified, and women's work is moving into the centre of the discourse, thus conferring greater visibility on them. There has also been greater realization over the past few months that any policymaking exercise would be incomplete without listening to the voice of the stakeholders. This pandemic has also exposed the vulnerability of women in both the domestic and public spaces. At one end of the spectrum, they are struggling to retain their livelihoods, while on the other end they are facing increased violence at home, particularly that perpetrated by intimate partners.

The economic crisis induced by COVID-19 is different because it is an employment crisis more than a financial crisis. If in future businesses decide to change the way they transact, then jobs, especially female jobs, would be the first causality. There is already a distinct shift taking place towards artificial intelligence and automation across industries, even in a labour-intensive country like India, coupled with increased informalization of labour markets. If women have to retain their place in the emerging scenario and perhaps increase their participation, then specific women-centric measures consisting of reskilling and multiple entry–exit points into the employment stream would have to be put in place by the state.

CONCLUSION

The policy of economic reforms introduced in 1991 was based on the three pillars of liberalization, privatization and globalization, which led to basic structural changes in the industrial landscape of India and transformed modes of production. The increased integration of India with the global economy was supposed to confer economic gains on all sections of the society, including the vulnerable and marginalized sections, but that was not how the story played out.

India is a textbook example of gender disparity in the arena of work, with most females being pushed to the informal sector, to low-skilled, low-paid, temporary jobs, as compared to their male counterparts. The linkage between formal employment and female empowerment is clear and well established, but the same benefits do not accrue to women who are informally employed in other activities as domestic workers, vendors, ragpickers or home-based workers. In spite of widespread realization that gainful employment is the only way to provide a voice to the voiceless, women have remained largely excluded from the formal workplace in India.

Self-employment for women is emerging as a viable alternative, but an analysis of female-owned enterprises shows disparity nested within disparity. Women belonging to religious minorities or weaker social groups do not have a significant presence among female entrepreneurs.

The government policies treat women as one homogeneous block, which needs to be changed if women are not to slip in through the cracks of the development process. This has already been experienced once in India, with the comparatively richer states and union territories (UTs) such as Punjab, Haryana and Delhi figuring in the bottom five states/UTs in female WPR and with the all-India female WPR stagnating at half the level of the male WPR.

The policies for inclusion and empowerment should be concrete and practicable rather than mere academic exercises. All efforts should be made to ensure that women are able to enter and then continue in the work sphere, through adopting the measures like provision of flexible working hours, a safe working environment, quality childcare and subsidized transport. The ultimate change however has to be in the perception and mindset, which would lead to more equal sharing of the unpaid care burden at home, leaving women free to enter the labour force. The state can at best be only a facilitator, and the onus of transformation would ultimately rest on women themselves.

The combined efforts of all the stakeholders, that is, the state, researchers and, of course, women themselves, can truly empower the women of India and unlock their full potential. This would be the ultimate 'smart economics' that would benefit not only the women but also their family, community and country.

REFERENCES

Banu, D., Farashuddin, F., Hossain, A., & Akter, S. (2001). Empowering women in rural Bangladesh: Impact of Bangladesh Rural Advancement Committee's (BRAC's) Programme. *Journal of International Women's Studies, 2*(3), 30–53.

Bhalla, S. S., & Kaur, R. (2011). *Labour force participation of women in India: Some facts, some queries* (Working Paper 40). Asia Research Center. http://eprints.lse.ac.uk/38367/1/ARCWP40-BhallaKaur.pdf

Bhatia, R. (2002). Measuring gender disparity using time use statistics. *Economic and Political Weekly, 37*(33), 3464–3469.

Bi, F. (2016). Women empowerment through employment opportunity in India. *The Rights, 2*(1), 1–7.

Bibi, A., & Afzal, A. (2012). Determinants of married women labour force participation in Wah Cantt: A descriptive analysis. *Academic Research International, 2*(1), 599–622.

Blackden, C. M., & Wodon, Q. (2006). *Gender, time use, and poverty in Sub-Saharan Africa.* The International Bank for Reconstruction and Development/World Bank. http://siteresources.worldbank.org/INTAFRREGTOP GENDER/Resources/gender_time_use_pov.pdf

Bose, M. L., Ahmad, A., & Hossain, M. (2009). The role of gender in economic activities with special references to women's participation and empowerment in Rural Bangladesh. *Gender, Technology and Development, 13*(1), 69–102.

Budlender, D. (2008). *The statistical evidence on care and non-care work across six countries* (Gender and Development Programme Paper Number 4). United Nations Research Institute for Social Development.

Corner, L. (2002, October 8–9). *Time use data for policy advocacy and analysis: A gender perspective and some international examples.* Paper presented at the National Seminar on Applications of Time Use Statistics, UNIFEM Asia-Pacific and Arab States, Regional Programme for Engendering Economic Governance,

UNDP Conference Hall. http://www.unifem-ecogov-apas/ecogovapas/EEGProjects Activities/TimeUseMeeting

Daymard, A. (2015). *Determinants of female entrepreneurship in India* (OECD Economics Department Working Paper No. 1191). OECD Publishing.

Dixon-Mueller, R. (1993). *Population policy and women's rights: Transforming reproductive choice.* Praeger.

Enloe, C. (1990). *Bananas, beaches & bases: Making feminist sense of international politics.* University of California Press.

Enloe, C. (2014). *Bananas, beaches & bases: Making feminist sense of international politics* (2nd ed.). University of California Press.

Faridi, M. Z., Chaudhry, I. S., & Malik, M. S. (2011b). Why women are self-employed? Empirical evidence from Pakistan. *International Journal of Economics and Finance, 3*(1), 198–207.

Fleming, R., & Spellerberg, A. (1999). *Using time use data: A history of time use surveys and uses of time use data.* Statistics New Zealand.

Gibb, S. J., Fergusson, D. M., & Boden, J. M. (2013). Gender differences in paid and unpaid work: Findings from a New Zealand birth cohort. *Policy Quarterly, 9*(3), 65–71.

Goetz, A. M., & Gupta, R. S. (1996). Who takes the credit? Gender, power and control over loan use in rural credit programmes in Bangladesh. *World Development, 24*(1), 45–63.

Government of India. (2001). Census of India (2001) by Office of Registrar General & Census Commissioner, Ministry of Home Affairs.

Government of India. (2011). Census of India (2011) by Office of Registrar General & Census Commissioner, Ministry of Home Affairs.

Government of India. (2011). Selected socio-economic statistics India (2011) by Central Statistics Office, Social Statistics Office, Ministry of Statistics and Programme Implementation.

Government of India. (2014). *Employment and unemployment situation in India* (NSS 68th Round July 2011–June, 2012). NSS Report No. 554 (68/10/1) by National Sample Survey Office, Ministry of Statistics & Programme Implementation. http://mospi.nic.in/sites/default/files/publication_reports/nss_report_554_31jan14.pdf

Government of India. (2014). Statistical profile on women labour (2012–2013) by Labour Bureau, Ministry of Labour & Employment.

Government of India. (2014–2015). Annual report (2014–2015) by Ministry of Women and Child Development.

Government of India. (2016). All India Report of Sixth Economic Census (2013–2014) by Central Statistics Office, Ministry of Statistics and Programme Implementation.

Gray, M. M., Kittilson, M. C., & Sandholtz, W. (2006). Women and globalization: A study of 180 countries, 1975–2000. *International Organization, 60*(2), 293–333.

Hancock, P. (2001). Rural women earning income in Indonesian Factories: The impact of gender relations. *Gender & Development, 9*(1), 18–24.

Heyzer, N. (Ed.). (1985). *Missing women: Development planning in Asia and the Pacific.* Asian and Pacific Development Centre.

Hirway, I. (2015). *Unpaid work and the economy: Linkages and their implications* (Working Paper, No. 838). Levy Economics Institute.

Hossain, M., & Jaim, W. M. H. (2011). *Empowering women to become farmer entrepreneur: Case study of a NGOs supported programme in Bangladesh.* International Fund for Agricultural Development (IFAD).

International Labour Organization (ILO). (2012). *ILO global estimate of forced labour: Results and methodology.* International Labour Office (ILO) and Special Action Programme to Combat Forced Labour (SAP-FL).

Ironmonger, D. S., & Hill, H. (1999). *Women's economic participation in five Pacific Island Countries.* International Development Issues No. 50 AusAID—Australian Agency for International Development.

Iweagu. H., Yuni, D. N., Chukwudi, N., & Andenyangtso, B. (2015). Determinants of female labour force participation in Nigeria: The rural/urban dichotomy. *Journal of Economics and Sustainable Development, 6*(10), 212–219.

Kabeer, N., Mahmud, S., & Tasneem, S. (2011). *Does paid work provide a pathway to women's empowerment? Empirical findings from Bangladesh* (Working Paper, 2011(375), pp. 1–42). IDS.

Khan, H. (2006). NGOs and gender development, the case of AKRSP in district Chitral, NWFP, Pakistan. *Lahore Journal of Economics, 11*(1), 81–98.

Khokhar, A. S. (2019). What decides women entrepreneurship in India? *Journal of Entrepreneurship and Innovation in Emerging Economies, 5*(2), 1–18.

Khokhar, A. S., & Singh, D. B. (2016). Role of women entrepreneurship in inclusive growth. *South Asia, 11*(9.6), 18–3.

Kishor, S., & Gupta, K. (2004). Women empowerment in India and its states: Evidence from the NFHS. *Economic & Political Weekly, 39*(7), 697–712.

Kuhn, S., Milasi, S., & Yoon, S. (2018). World employment social outlook: Trends 2018. International Labour Office.

Levine, R., Lloyd, C. B., Greene, M., & Grown, C. (2009). *Girls count: A global investment & action agenda (A Girls Count Report on Adolescent Girls).* Centre for Global Development.

Lisaniler, F. G., & Bhatti, F. (2005). Determinants of female labour force participation: A study of North Cyprus. *Review of Social, Economics & Business Studies, 5*(6), 209–226.

Mammen, K., & Paxson, C. (2000). Women's work and economic development. *The Journal of Economic Perspectives, 14*(4), 141–164.

Mason, K. O. (1986). The status of women: Conceptual and methodological issues in demographic studies. *Sociological Forum, 1*(2), 284–300.

Medeiros, M., Osório, R. G., & Costa, J. (2007). *Gender inequalities in allocating time to paid and unpaid work: Evidence from Bolivia* (Working Paper No. 495). The Levy Economics Institute.

Moghadam, V. M. (2003). Engendering citizenship, feminizing civil society: The case of the Middle East and North Africa. *Journal of Women Politics & Policy, 25*(1), 63–87.

Nakkeeran, N. (2003). Women's work, status and fertility: Land, caste and gender in a South Indian Village. *Economic and Political Weekly, 38*(37), 3931–3939.

Norton, A., & Haan, A. de. (2013). *Social cohesion: Theoretical debates and practical applications with respects to job* (Background Paper for the World Development Report 2013). OKR.

Odutola, O., Adedimeji, A., Odutolou, O., Baruwa, O., & Olatidoye, F. (2003). Economic empowerment and reproductive behaviour of young women in Osun state, Nigeria. *African Journal of Reproductive Health, 7*(3), 92–100.

Oostendorp, R. H. (2004). *Globalization and the gender wage gap* (World Bank Policy Research Working Paper No. 3256). World Bank. http://documents.worldbank.org/curated/en/609671468778198853/ Globalization-and-the-gender-wage-gap

Pande, R. (2007). Gender, poverty and globalization in India. *Development, 50*(2), 134–140.

Papanek, H., & Schwede, L. (1988). Women are good with money: Earning and managing in an Indonesian City. *Economic and Political Weekly, 23*(44), WS73–WS84.

Pastore, F., & Verashchagina, A. (2008). *The determinants of female labour supply in Belarus* (IZA Discussion paper No. 3457). https://papers.ssrn.com/sol3/papers. cfm?abstract_id=1136178

Samantroy, E., & Tomar, J. S. (2018). Women entrepreneurship in India: Evidence from economic censuses. *Social Change, 48*(2), 188–207. https:// doi.org/10.1177/0049085718768898

Schular, S. R., Hashemi, S. M., Riley, A. P., & Akhter, S. (1996). Credit programs, patriarchy and men's violence against women in rural Bangladesh. *Social Science and Medicine, 43*(12), 1729–1742.

Seguino, S. (2006). *The great equalizer? Globalization effects on gender equality in Latin America and the Caribbean* (MPRA Paper No. 6509). http://mpra.ub.uni-muenchen.de/6509/

Speer, P. W., Jackson, C. B., Peterson, N. A. (2001). The relationship between social cohesion and empowerment: Support and new implications for theory. *Health Education & Behavior, 28*(6), 716–732.

Suganthi, J. (2009). Influence of motivational factors on women entrepreneurs in SMEs. *Asia-Pacific Business Review, 5*(1), 95–114.

Sultana, A., & Hossen, S. S. (2013). Role of employment in women empowerment: Evidence from Khulna City of Bangladesh. *International Journal of Social Science & Interdisplinary Research, 2*(7), 117–125.

Tibandebage, P. A. (1995). *In search of improved women's status in Tanzania: determinants at the household Level.* University Microfilms International.

Umar, M. S., & Karofi, U. A. (2007). Non-work factors and labour turnover among female employees in Kebbi State Civil Service. *Bangladesh e-Journal of Sociology, 4*(2), 1–7. http://www.bangladeshsociology.org/BEJS%204.2.%20 Karofi.pdf

UNIFEM. (2000). *Progress of the world's women 2000 (UNIFEM Biennial Report).* United Nations Development Fund Organization. http://iknowpolitics.org/ sites/default/files/progress_of_the_world_s_women_2000.pdf

UNIFEM. (2005). *Progress of the world's women 2005: Women's work & poverty.* United Nations Development Fund Organization.

United Nations Statistical Commission. (1993). *System of national accounts 1993.* United Nations Statistical Division, 152–154.

UNRISD. (2010). *Why care matter for social development* (UNRISD Research and Policy Brief 9). Gender and Development (2000–2009). http://www.unrisd. org/80256B3C0 05BCCF9/(LookupAllDocumentsByUNID)/25697FE238 192066C12576D4004CFE50?OpenDocument

West, B. S. (2006). *Does employment empower women? An analysis of employment and women's empowerment in India.* https://ecommons.cornell.edu/bitstream/ handle/1813/3360/West-Thesis%20Final.pdf;sequence=1

World Development Report. (2012). *World development report-2013 on jobs.* International Bank for Reconstruction and Development/The World Bank. http://econ.worldbank.org/external/default/main?contentMDK=23044836 &theSitePK=8258025&piPK=8258412&pagePK=8258258

Chapter 9

Vulnerabilities of Desire
A Qualitative Study with Indian Housewives

Annie Baxi

This chapter, using a focus group discussion, illustrates how four female friends individually and collectively encounter the desire of other women or another woman. The group was shown the film *Parama*, which depicts the multiple inner turbulences of an Indian housewife as she revisits her lost, silent and silenced desires. The film raises questions around legitimized notions of Indian womanhood and its psychological complexities. The analysis reveals the psychological processes of identification, othering and resistance as the participants reflect and relate to the protagonist's silence and her desirous assertions. The chapter explores the conceptualization of female desire in modern times among Indian housewives and how it continues to be a site of both intimacy and vulnerability.

What does it mean to be a desirous woman? Which desires find legitimacy in the dominant discourse of womanhood? Where and how are the illegitimate desires packaged and lived? How do women view the desire of another woman or other women?

REVISITING DESIRE

In a recent book titled *Infinite Variety: A Brief History of Desire in India* (2018), author Madhavi Menon explores the diverse, nuanced and storied manifestations of desire as seen, heard and lived by the inhabitants of the subcontinent. She states that desire cannot be neatly defined in its act and experience but almost always includes pleasure, pain and recognition. It spells out the impossibility of a neat narrative of female desire and encourages readers to contest consensual imaginations of female sexuality that tend to depict the desire of women often through the prism of patriarchal oppression. Thus, what might be popularly considered as 'sin' or simply 'wrong' is a relatively recent colonial construction that prompts one to catalogue desires within the domains of morality.

With the coming of British rule, the British Raj, attempts were made to bring a sense of uniformity in ways and forms of living through institutions of education and law. The late 20th century saw the conceptualization of laws around obscenity and the importance of 'sanitizing' art, literature and even private spaces around the dictates of English morality (Gupta, 2008). These definitions have had their strongest impact on the activities of women, their spaces, their songs and their rituals. Some of the earlier expressions of desire and intimacy were reframed as obscene, offensive and foul acts. The erotic *nayika* forms of Radha were replaced by poetry describing a 'chaste and virtuous Hindu wife' (Gupta, 2008). Following this, during the freedom struggle the discourse of the 'nation' took prominence, and sexual behaviour for pleasure and non-reproductive reasons was nearly excluded from literature.

The post-colonial hybrid India made sexuality and desires a convoluted space for women. The 19th century, propelled by both Western feminism and Christian missionaries, constructed women as 'victims' of tradition and insinuated movements against child marriage, Sati, early widowhood and, most importantly, the Hindu male (Gupta, 2008; Khanna & Price, 1994). The Bollywood films of the 1990s often had the 'other' to the main heroine, often called the 'vamp', cast opposite the *pativrata* (righteous) wife (Tere, 2012). The 'vamp' was often 'Western', sexually promiscuous and displaced from her roots (Gangoli, 2005). The vamp almost always had a tragic end, either realizing her 'wrongdoing' or succumbing to a life of suffering. This growing sense of binariness was beautifully articulated in the novel *Tat Ki Khoj* by Harishankar Parsai (1985), where the female protagonist describes her dilemma over having to choose between being *Abla* (the helpless or disempowered woman) or *Kulta* (the immoral and socially transgressive woman). In a study on perceptions of single women in Kangra district by Berry (2008), it was noted that single women were constructed as 'bad' and 'deviant', as they are outsiders to the sanctioned and revered institution of marriage. The single women, however, negotiate with these 'deviant' identities not through alternative constructions but through actions that echo the discourse of 'good women', through leading a life of a celibate and effectively silencing or invisibilizing sexual desire. Kakar (1982) states that the sanctity of the *pativrata* imagery of the wife glosses over the hostility and rage in the lived experience of desire. Hence, cultures must produce narratives that aid social reproduction and tame desires that serve to threaten it.

This split sees an interesting manifestation in urban India, as, on the one hand, we have writers and thinkers aggressively asserting a 'reclamation' over women's bodies and pleasures and, on the other, an ever-increasing number of hymenoplasty surgeries that declare the woman's virginity and hence her purity (Desai & Dixit, 2018). In a study analysing the failure of SlutWalk in Delhi, Borah and Nandi (2012) illustrated how the campaign was more about creating awareness regarding dangers of victim blaming than about embracing a sexual woman against the negative label of 'slut'. Psychiatrists too have been known to diagnose women with 'abnormal' sensual behaviour like prostitutes or delinquents as psychopaths for their departure from conventional morality (Lunbeck, 1987). It leaves one to wonder whether the inability to disengage with the word 'slut' and the feminist assertion to replace it with a positive and acceptable assertion of sexuality would in any way be representative of female desire in its experiential essence.

MAKING OF THE MODERN INDIAN HOUSEWIFE

Women in India have traditionally enjoyed an exclusive sphere of domesticity that gave them an opportunity to experience autonomy and power. Modern women are now facing a challenging situation where, on the one hand, society encourages them to believe that they are in every respect equal to men and should think of themselves as such, while, on the other, it systematically denies them the opportunity to compete on equal terms (Taylor, 1988). With the neoliberal reforms, the idea of womanhood went through rapid changes, more so in the visible sphere. These changing social structures brought in newer definitions of 'agency' characterized by women working outside the home (Waldrop, 2012). The global forces permeated the domestic space in a manner that women in 'outer' spaces have gained privileges over other women, and norms originally more Western have been adopted and internalized, creating a hybrid identity in the name of global India (Thapan, 2004). However, in its lived form, beyond the glamourized ideal of this woman, accompanying is also a sense of turbulence, loss and self-doubt. Despite the thrust of the working-woman imagery, taking care of the house continues to be the desired role for women in many middle-class households (Mitra & Knottnerus, 2008; Rai, 2002). The revered imagery of a *grehani* who skilfully manoeuvres through her many physical and emotional roles often becomes the dictate of deciding her functionality.

INVISIBLE VULNERABILITIES OF MODERN INDIAN WOMEN

The prospect of a woman being 'dangerously different' poses a threat to the orderly functioning of the family (Addlakha, 2005, p., 256). And while difference is disregarded, housewives and similar groups with normatively feminine positions are often evaluated negatively, similar to persons with disabilities (Garland-Thomson, 2017). These findings indicate to a gap in psychological research where while women are increasingly taking leadership positions, housewives account for the highest suicide deaths in the country (Dandona et al., 2016). In the Indian context, it is seen that with the absence of an employment structure, combined with the responsibilities and burdens of domestic work and caregiving activities, housewives are more susceptible to mental illness (Vindhya et al., 2001).

At a more interpersonal level, while sensual adornment at the time of marriage is a sanctioned experience of desire, there is little reflexive exploration of the individual meaning making around bodies and desire. Rituals attempt to package desire for women in a uniform manner, conveying to them the 'shoulds' and 'musts' of feminine life, and little is said about 'ifs', especially when the woman does not see herself aligning to the rituals. In contemporary India, women's bodies are rarely experienced as pleasurable and are mostly defined in terms of 'daily requirements' and 'symbolic aspects of marriage, auspiciousness and fulfillment' (Thapan, 2009, p. 157).

THE CURRENT STUDY

The chapter attempts to study the psychosocial matrix of desire through a focus group discussion with four female friends using the film *Parama*. The film served as both a text and a vignette, prompting the participants to explore and discuss their roles as housewives, their sexuality, individual desires and how they all come together to frame ideals of womanhood in contemporary times. This collective sense making of desire offers an insight into how patterns of condemnation and approval facilitate the experience of desire for women.

PARTICIPANT DETAILS

The participants were four intimate female friends who identified themselves as housewives. They attribute their friendship to 'common background, upbringing and current family life'. They frequently meet over dinner parties and kitty lunches and also take vacations together. They have a WhatsApp group titled 'Friends Forever', where they exchange jokes, quotes and experiences. They view monthly 'kitty' as a space for intimate sharing and cathartic and mutual support. The researcher was perceived as a daughter by all the participants, and they have on a few occasions discussed their personal conflicts with her.

Following is a brief biographical sketch of the participants.

Meenakshi, 56 years
Often described as an 'ideal woman' in family conversations, she is appreciated for having built a home in tough circumstances and handling the difficult temperaments of her family members. She stays with her husband, two sons and a daughter-in-law. She also contributes to the family business and divides her time between household responsibilities and the family store. Domestic duties, however, still continue to be the dominant responsibility upon her.

Divya, 57 years
She stays with her husband, younger son and mother-in-law. Her eldest son is married and lives in Dubai with his wife. Her husband has recently quit his job and wishes to stay at home, a cause of major distress for her. She often hopes that he would join some work again. She tried to fulfil the demands at home while also trying to be a companion to her husband for the new endeavours he wishes to indulge in. This places her in a difficult position, and she is made to juggle between the needs of others.

Tanya, 48 years
She is the youngest of the four and stays with her in-laws, husband and son. She is part of many kitties and has many groups of friends. Within the group, she is known to share the most 'non-veg' (sexual) jokes. She loves to shop and try on new outfits. She often expresses her regret at having married early and hopes she had a career. She is very attached to her son and worries about him.

Urvashi, 53 years
She is playing the host and is the only one in the group who has a daughter. She is known for her candid remarks and is the most 'outspoken' among them. During the focus group discussion, she took the role of a co-researcher and often probed her friends to go beyond the obvious.

FOCUS GROUP DISCUSSION

The group was shown the film *Parama*, directed by Aparna Sen and released in the year 1985. The film opens with the festivities of

Durga Puja being organized by Parama, daughter-in-law of a joint Brahmin Bengali family. During these festivities, Rahul, an internationally recognized photographer, visits the family. He is a friend of Parama's brother-in-law and expresses his wish to take photos of Parama for his project on Indian housewives. She is reluctant but is pushed by her family members, as they wish to help their son-in-law's friend. As she moves 'outside' the home with Rahul, she encounters situations that are unusual and challenging and finds in Rahul a listener to share stories of her childhood, natal family and hobbies and how she seems to have lost them after marriage. Through this sharing, Parama is able to revive her interest in playing the sitar. She also experiences moments of extreme discomfort and worry and resists further meetings; however, she is too emotionally involved for distance. The relationship deepens and they become sexually intimate with each other on several occasions. Outside her house, she explores the city with Rahul and on an occasion is described as his wife. They often spend time finding the name of the plant that Parama remembers from her childhood days. After Rahul leaves the country, they continue their interaction in a secret manner. One day, a semi-nude photo of Parama gets published in a magazine, and this discloses her relationship with Rahul for the entire family. She is rejected, ridiculed and isolated by all of them. She is considered impure, and her husband calls her a 'whore'. To add to her misery, Rahul also becomes inaccessible. In the following scene, while taking a bath, she looks at a shaving blade. The maid finds blood coming from the bathroom. Parama is taken to the hospital, and the family and doctors conclude that she attempted suicide; hence, she is declared 'depressed' by the psychiatrist. As part of the operation, her hair is cut short. This change in her appearance is combined with her silence to make her family members assume her 'guilty' position. They try to make her feel included and accepted, but she seems distant and aloof. In the last scene, she expresses her decision to work as a saleswoman and is finally able to recollect the name of the plant she had been searching for with Rahul.

The film, though located in a Bengali household, echoes concerns similar to those voiced by the participants during the interviews. The experienced loss of 'I' and the sublimation of personhood in duties is a site of both emancipation and oppression. The film verbalized and visualized concerns felt but not spoken by the participants. It evoked discussion on topics around functionality in domestic spaces and how women engaged in joint sense making to both reaffirm and resist dominant notions of womanhood.

Women's conversation in their intimate circles is a crucial site to understand how they frame their agency and contest the normative understanding of their sexuality (Thompson, 2011). Kitty parties are collectives of women in urban India belonging mostly to middle-class and upper-middle-class families, who meet for lunch and also generate financial savings through rotations (Waldrop, 2012). Analyses of women's friendship and their talks reveal that the solidarity and mutual support experienced by female friends through their friend circles help them mediate their circumscribed life (Coates, 1997). The popularity of women's clubs and groups facilitated spaces that enabled merging between the private and public spheres of women's lives (Cohen, 2009). Even in the seemingly restricted atmosphere of a religious gathering, female collectives contest and assert themselves, thus simultaneously aligning to and resisting desired images of a woman (Torab, 1996).

The focus group approach in feminist research helps articulate larger social processes in which the individual is embedded and highlights the discursive nature of knowledge production (Wilkinson, 1997). The explicit use of group interaction in understanding psychological processes make this tool an efficient choice when one wishes to understand the ways in which norms and discourses around womanhood translate into lived experiences. The aim of using the focus group approach in this research was to unravel the ways in which consensual reality and normalization of experiences around female desire are created. For this, characteristics of speech, pauses, silence and laughter were noted and analysed for their role in building a collective and shared argument of the participants' experiences as housewives.

ANALYTICAL APPROACH

The data gathered were analysed using a dual-focus approach, combining tenets of interpretative phenomenological analysis (IPA) and critical discourse analysis (CDA). IPA facilitates an insight into internal life worlds and focuses on subjective experience as a unit of inquiry (Smith et al., 2009), while CDA maps the ways in which discursive resources are mobilized by the participants to justify their individual positions and in turn warrant certain social positions over others. Thus, individual subjectivity is asserted and made visible by social vantage points, called subject positions, that make available the resources the speaker can avail in a particular discourse (Burr, 2003). Also, the repertoires of a discourse influence the way subjectivity is packaged for an individual in their relatively private worlds. While CDA enables an imagination of the defining contours in which an experience is embedded, it rarely articulates the felt actuality of the phenomenon. For instance, an understanding of silence as experienced by the researcher and participants, though a depiction of shared social locations, needs a closer examination of the felt mutuality in the context.

While complimenting a psychosocial inquiry, the two approaches are also contradictory in some aspects. IPA empowers the speakers with hermeneutic agency in ascribing meaning and form to their psychological worlds, which may or may not align with consensual reality. CDA represents the ways in which dominant patterns of a society become shared meanings that are retained in individual narratives to feel affiliations with local cultures. Thus, the dual-focus analysis is a coming together of 'hermeneutics of empathy and suspicion' (Colahan et al., 2012). In other words, during analysis the focus is on the content of the talk and ways in which experience is reconstructed and simultaneous critical engagement with the structure of talk as drawn from the linguistic depository of the culture.

RESEARCHER'S POSITION

I had first seen the film *Parama* during my postgraduate course, and over the years, as I have grappled with my understanding of womanhood, my impressions and understanding of *Parama* have evolved. In a way, the film also marked my changing association with desire, body and sexuality. After my first watch, I found myself feeling helpless, upset and angry at Parama's state. However, over the years, I have found a greater appreciation for her silence, her longings and her relationship with Rahul. Her engagement with Rahul was not in the style of 'assertion' typical of contemporary cinema; it was more a portrayal of a woman grappling with her desire, some lost and some silenced, which finds a sudden articulation through a relationship. It was her non-assertiveness yet strong acknowledgement of her desire which enabled me to understand the psychosocial complexities of being a 'good' woman in India.

During the focus group interview, I was mostly silent, as there existed a stark difference in my reading of *Parama* and their comments. The female participants were much older than me and spoke from being married for over 20 years. As a young, unmarried, daughter-like researcher, I felt I had little to contribute to the discussion. The silence from my end was also appreciated by them, as it allowed an undeterred and free-flowing discussion. They also felt 'in charge' as they asked me to stop the film for discussions, questioned each other for their views, probed for clarifications and expanded with their own life experiences.

THEMES AND FINDINGS

This section includes themes that were narrowed down after the dual-focus analysis (Colahan et al., 2012) which were both reflective of the participants' inner world evoked through Parama and larger discursive constructs of womanhood manifested in their overt linguistic expressions to describe Parama. The analysis is representative of the participant's lifeworld, the beingness of a married woman and experiential nuances, as they encounter the desire of other women or another woman. This was inferred and made visible through their relational sense making and perceptions of Parama's desire and, through it, how they framed their own lived and unlived desires. The themes include macro analyses of the linguistic repertoires of the participants as indicative of larger constituting discursive structures that govern notions of legitimized desires for a married woman. In other words, key phrases used by the participants were seen to be illustrative of subject positions (Donaghue, 2018) that enable the making and articulation of a desire as sanctioned, liveable and perhaps morally attainable. Thus, the analysis presents a negotiation between 'hermeneutics of empathy' and 'hermeneutics of suspicion' (Colahan et al., 2012) as the participants attempt a seemingly coherent narrative of desire.

Coates (1997), in her chapter 'Women's Friendships, Women's Talk', provides a comprehensive linguistic analysis of women's conversations and states their primary goal as construction and maintenance of connection and minimization of social distance. In conversations with same-sex friends, women mirror each other through shared stories, revisit existing knowledge and establish a shared reality through linguistic competence. Women's interactional spaces do not merely provide emotional support but are also sites of resistance which challenge given gender structures. An identifying aspect of the focus group data is the creation of a collaborative floor, where through group voice consensual reality is constructed. Thus, as the female participants were voicing the desire of Parama and, through her, their own, they were signalling the need to build a familiar and shared perspective.

SOLIDARITY THROUGH THE SILENT SELF: IDENTIFYING WITH PARAMA

Silencing, in the present context, can be defined as a psychological process that female participants undergo to unhear, unvoice and unregister aspects of their experiences in lieu of sustaining a consensually validated normative reality. Self-silencing can be defined as one's ability to inhibit their thoughts, emotions and expressions in view of larger harmony and capacity to retain compliance even while feeling resentful (Jack, 1991). Though a culturally validated experience, the unhearing can also bring a state of internal chaos that could take the shape of low confidence, fatigue, withdrawal, aggression and, in some cases, forms of diagnosable psychopathology.

Metaphor of 'Doll'

The beginning of the focus group discussion saw Parama as a 'typical housewife' who worked extensively and exclusively in the household, taking care of the many needs of her family members. Her presence and position in the household were familiar and relatable to the participants, and this was inferred through their minimal responses and joint laughter (Coates, 1997). In a scene, Parama resists Rahul's suggestions to climb a steep slope, and he remarks, '*Har waqt saaje sajaye flat mein gudiya ki tarah bethi rehti hain* (All the time, you are sitting like a doll in your well-decorated house)'. The women together broke into laughter after listening to this dialogue. They looked at each other, expressing a feeling of being shared. Linguistic analysis suggests that sarcasm is both funny and hurtful, intended as a negative evaluation (Partington, 2006). The act of laughing suggests at one level solidarity to the metaphor (Bell, 2007; Hay, 2000; Kalcik, 1975) and works towards warding away psychological tensions the moment evokes (Politi, 2009). The metaphor of a 'doll' shows the woman as a passive, decorative, mute, aesthetically pleasing object and as having childlike qualities. It also depicts someone living in a protected, insulated and 'make-believe' world. In the following scene, Urvashi repeated Rahul's dialogue to Parama, '*Kabhi khatra mor kar bhi jeena seekhiye* (Learn to live in unsafe spaces as well)'. The use of repetition as a linguistic strategy signals solidarity with Parama (Coates, 1997). The statement speaks to the protected world the participants have lived in and how it works to isolate them from possible adventures and avenues of discovery.

Dominance of 'Duties'

While attempting to understand the attributions of this silence, Meenakshi stated, '*Humne apne "mein" ko daba diya* (I had to kill my "self" in being a wife)'. Similarly, while explaining Parama's relationship with Rahul, Urvashi shared, '*Apni duties mein na apne shauk ko maar diya usne* (To fulfil her duties, she killed her interests/passions/desires)'. Here, the lifeworld of the women is seen as a split between their desire and their 'duties'. The 'duties' come at the cost of their desires. This represents a unique paradox faced by contemporary Indian women wherein in their quest for personal autonomy they continue to be governed and self-evaluated by socially sanctioned markers of care and selflessness, packaged as 'duties' and 'sacrifice' (Burn, 2000; Karlekar, 1988; Mitra & Knottnerus, 2008).

To further explain this silent sacrifice, Urvashi noted,

'*Mein' kahin nahi hai. Aur mein ko kahin baari bahut buri tarah daba bhi diya jaata hai, mein ki baat karte hain to humara husband khud hi barre disrespectfully kahin baar usko karta hai, jaane unjaane mein. Aur hum koi aadat bhi par gayi hai, hum isko kahin bari, ignore bhi karte hain.* (The 'I' or individual self is not there for us and Parama. And often, we have to bury the 'I'. If we talk too much about 'I', knowingly or unknowingly the husbands become disrespectful to us and then we have to ignore the 'I'. Now we have grown accustomed to ignoring the 'I'.)

This difficulty in the assertion of the 'I', the fear of being rebuked and the consequent feeling of being 'accustomed' signify this process of identification through which alignment with prescribed roles maintains structural harmony (Althusser, 1991/1997). The structural harmony also comes to be psychic harmony, where to avoid dissonance the individual overtly continues to align with the consensual ideas of their identity and roles. Applying the structural ritualization theory by Knottnerus (1997), the action repertoire of a housewife signals the purity, sacredness and harmony of her household. Her actions, aided by her roles, rituals and relationships, work to consolidate her identity, linking it to the sanctity of the household. The woman in such a matrix through her embodiment negotiates with these givens, often through silencing her desires and legitimizing her silenced desires.

One notices the salience of duty in various mythologies and folklores as a defining attribute of the marital bond, often placed higher than romantic passion (Channa, 2014). This sense of duty is mostly defined in terms of domestic obligations of care and nurturance towards family members. In the execution of these duties, women become carriers or bearers of implicit social norms that are rarely overtly stated as expectations but continue to be conveyed through metaphors, folk tales and rituals (Moghaddam et al., 2000). This socialization of the individual to be responsive to the other through the fulfilment of duties has further given birth to the moral order in societies (Shweder, 1996). Domesticity defines the identity of Indian women, and its failure is attributed to the 'incapacities' of women.

'Duties' are constructed to be the opposite of their individual desires. Furthermore, the effectiveness of their execution is contingent on the extent of silence around desires. Participants are seen negotiating and sublimating their desires by constructing them as duties, and vice versa. Hence, an interesting mechanism plays out in the conceptualization of duties and desire, as their separation ensures the functionality of the family system. Desires that question concerns of domesticity are shunned, systematically excluded and discouraged by women. These desires often have to be secretly lived, dreamt about or repressed. Hence, the embodiment of duties accompanies a self-silencing schema where the 'good woman' regulates her desire and expresses it 'for others' (Jack, 1991).

ENCOUNTERING DESIROUS ASSERTIONS: OTHERING OF PARAMA

The goodness of one is often established through claiming the inferiority and failure of the other. In order to establish and retain goodness, women engage in the construction of the immoral 'other'. This relative positioning is a critical feature of women's conversations as they engage in the construction of the 'other' though gossip. Often termed as 'bitching', the discursive function of this behaviour is to mark a boundary between the self and wrong others. The dichotomies and mechanisms of othering work to label social deviance as 'bad' (Chesler, 2005).

Deviancy of a desire is marked by its difference, unacceptable nature, 'unknownness' and sanctioned condemnation, which collectively work to strengthen the domain of 'normalized' desires (Pickering, 2001). The desires viewed as problematic, conflicting and deviant by the participants were those of sexual urges, expressions and relatedness 'outside' the contours of the conjugal bond. Thus, sexual norms and the regulation of desire for women were linked to the idea of the household. Transgressing these notions is strongly condemned, and women are continued to be constructed as upholders of the family, community and state.

Through the process of othering, the participants adopted an onlooker position, becoming less participative towards Parama's feelings. They distanced themselves from Parama and described her in a subtle yet strong tone penalizing her.

The Other 'Bold' Woman

The sense of othering is seen evidently in their adjectives used for Parama as she initiates sexual intimacy with Rahul. These included 'superfast', 'too bold', 'adventurous' and 'fearless'. During this reflexive engagement with Parama, the participants embodied the 'regular' or standard view and evaluated her 'fastness', 'boldness', sense of 'adventure' and 'fearlessness'. The nomenclature of 'bold' women in India signifies women who are identifiably outspoken and uninhibited and often in contrast to the cherished docility of 'wifely modesty' (Gold, 1997). The vulnerability of Parama manifested in the metaphor of *gudiya* (doll) was hence relatable; however, her attempts to claim a desire in flesh evoked a penalizing streak in the voice of the participants.

Reinstating normative morality through echoing a relationship between chastity and morality, the act of interpreting her as a wrongdoer helped the participants position their superiority. Analyses of women's conversations suggest that women achieve symbolic capital by establishing moral work in their intimate circles (Eckert, 1992). Women's gossip functions to reinforce group membership through creation of the moral character of the 'other' (Guendouzi, 2001).

'Feeling Guilty' as an Accomplice of Desire

In a scene, Parama cries after kissing Rahul, to which Meenakshi remarked, '*Regret ho raha hai bahut* (She is deeply regretting her act)', and Divya extended, 'This means she has also come back to her senses now'. This display of grief and guilt aligned with their framings of her desire and brought a sense of relief. However, as the movie progressed and Parama's overt display of guilt reduced, the participants expressed wonder, confusion, dismay and rejection at the 'absence' of guilt. As Meenakshi commented: 'Earlier she was feeling guilty for seeing him and now all that guilt has gone'. Attempts were now made to find suitable attributions for her behaviour, attempting to make legit claims for her overt deviations. The discomfort felt at the 'absence' of guilt was stated by Tanya as '*Usse pehle kuch aur bhi dikhana chahiye tha…kuch aur bhi scenes hone chahiye the before getting involved aise* (Before her growing intimacy to Rahul, they should have shown some more scenes)'. Tanya felt that Parama's actions lacked enough support from her lived reality. She continued to verbalize this confusion by stating, '*Ek baat samajh nahi aa rahi. Sab kuch hote hue bhi, happy family, devoted husband, why has she been attracted to Rahul?* (I do not understand that despite having everything, a happy family and devoted husband, why has she been attracted to Rahul?)'. The lack of an 'obvious' reason baffled the participants. The felt affinity was considered important, as they were now condemning Parama's actions. Questions, remarks and arguments were rhetorical in nature and established a sense of unity among the participants.

Hamer et al. (2014) explored the dual purposes of othering: exclusion and inclusion. Othering, on the one hand, works to identify the rejected and marginalized and, on the other, establishes a coherent and stable identity through the felt difference. The participants, while witnessing Parama and making sense of their reactions, engage in this back and forth movement, where they position themselves within the contours of legitimized morality and grapple with Parama's seemingly outsider position. Women feel a sense of 'empowerment' while establishing difference with and moral superiority over another woman or other women (Scharff, 2011). From a systemic functional linguistics point of view, arguments that evoke fear and construct the social actor as the 'other' to the speaker legitimize the inferences of the speaker about the phenomenon and the social actor (Reyes, 2011).

POCKETS OF RESISTANCE: CREATING SPACE FOR DESIRE

While the participants largely oscillated between the earlier two positions, there were small but significant pockets where they held space for Parama's desire without cataloguing it along moral codes. While reflecting on why she and her friends were not able to relate to Parama's relationship with Rahul, Urvashi stated,

Asal mein, kya hai ki humne na shaadi ke baad aisi koi cheez experience nahi ki like koi independent cheez pe gaye hon…abhi tak wohi routine mein hum chalte aa rahein hain, waise hi idealism ki tarah…right wrong ke chakar mein. (Actually, we have never experienced anything independent after marriage...we are confined to our routine and stuck in an idealism around right and wrong.)

Hence, while being distant, Urvashi attempted to initiate a dialogue to understand the inner turmoil and desire of Parama. However, it must be noticed that there is little ownership of desire and instead an attempt to locate attributions that for her justify Parama's actions. Stanko (1997) argues that women's thrust on the importance of 'safekeeping' is one way of reinforcing their 'respectable femininities' (Stanko, 1997, p. 489).

Urvashi's holding was followed by humour that allowed a deviance from holding Parama's desire. Meenakshi responded laughingly,

Tumhare kehne ka matlab hai ki abhi tak photographer koi nahi aaya humari zindagi me.... Yeh picture basically husbands ko dikhani chahiye so that they take more interests in their wife (You mean to say that this has not happened to us because no photographer has come in our life.... This film needs to be shown to our husbands so that they take more interest in us).

Divya extended the joke by saying, '*Taaki unki biwiyaan hay-wire na jayein* (So that we don't get haywire)'. Often, women's resistance is challenged, ignored and trivialized, reinstating the dominant narrative of female vulnerability (Hollander, 2002).

Urvashi re-attempted to understand desire by responding,

Nahi yeh unavoidable cheez hai, aap deliberate nahi parte ho isme.... Woh kya hai stereotype life ho jaati hai na, kahin baar aap yeh, human ek taken for granted, emotional touch na ek doosre se na sideline ho jaata hai, hum woh hi yaar usko khaana dena hai, usko yeh dena hai, usko woh dena hai, kahin bare hum ek doosre ki expressions bhi nahi read kar paate hai, ki woh humse kya kaehna chahte hai. (No, this is unavoidable, one doesn't enter this thing deliberately, it just happens.... We often live in a stereotypical manner and take each other for granted. We lose the emotional touch and sideline each other, we keep focusing on what is to be cooked, who needs what, we sometimes even overlook the expressions of each other, not knowing what they want from us.)

Thus, Parama's assertion of her desire evoked a reflection of the narratives of marriage and womanhood the participants had come to accept as 'givens'. The participants revisited their dominant female scripts and wondered whether in pursuit of being functional they were ignorant of desires, both their own and those of others.

DISCUSSION

Brown (2006), in her theory on shame resilience, proposes the awareness and acceptance of personal vulnerabilities are key to dealing with shame as experienced by women. Continued non-acknowledgment of vulnerability and desire leads to states of inner confusion, chaos, fear, blame and judgement (Brown, 2006). Perceived invulnerability is linked to barriers in preventive health work (Aiken et al., 2001) and psychopathology (Ingram & Price, 2010).

The negotiation of desire with the dominant discourses of self-sacrifice could lead to burnout, exhaustion and psychological fatigue among women. Burnout can be defined as psychological exhaustion resulting from excessive demands and lack of corresponding resources or strength (Shukla & Trivedi, 2008). Frustration and alienation are two key components of burnout (Whitaker, 1982). As seen in the focus group discussion, witnessing Parama's emotional labour, the participants voiced their similar experiences and expressed how systematically domestic work and associated social roles create a distance from their loved ones, even though the work is done 'for them'. This points to the structural making of this alienation that works to sanction the overlooking of desires of the self and of others. The established sense of mutuality diluted their emotional pain, as while comforting each other, they sketched their experience as typical of womanhood.

It is through othering that the participants situated their personal, moral and social stand around being a woman. The inability to perceive the emotional self of the other is the mechanism through which the participants built their gender citizenship of an imagined mutuality. Hence, what has been narrated as 'hidden benefits of mutualism' among women through the establishment of commonness and generalizability to their experiences could also be masked parasitism resulting in a slow psychological decay. Thus, what appears to be mutualism on the surface holds within it a deep sense of estrangement from the self and the other, and these lacunae are systematically sustained through dominant discourses around normalcy for women. The study offers a shift in the understanding of the gendered psyche, as it departs from the standard man-versus-woman viewpoint and speaks of the interpersonal and intrapersonal psychological dynamics of gendering among, within and by women.

The above analysis suggests that vulnerability, though commonly associated with risk, resilience and psychopathology (Ingram & Price, 2010), is intrinsically linked to the ability to imagine and live one's desires. To desire it is to lay bare one's very personal needs in pursuit of enhancing one's emotional and psychological repertoire. Narratives of identity frame individuals as and predispose them to living and containing desires in a manner that retains the status quo and hence ensure a functional social system. Desire can offer a breakthrough to this regimented living and offer alternatives that align more with the human condition of existence.

CONCLUSION

The chapter, through a qualitative analysis, speaks of the relational sense making of female desire and provides an insight into ways dominant narratives infiltrate the very personal and intimate terrain of sexual desire. A closer look at lived vulnerabilities and unarticulated desires offers possibilities of reframing these narratives to make them more responsive to and representative of the inner world of Indian women.

REFERENCES

Addlakha, R. (2005). Ethical quandaries in anthropological fieldwork in psychiatric settings. *Indian Journal of Medical Ethics, 2.* https://doi.org/10.20529/ijme.2005.027

Aiken, L., Gerend, M., & Jackson, K. (2001). Subjective risk and health protective behavior: Cancer screening and cancer prevention. In A. Baum, T. Revenson, & J. Singer (Eds.), *Handbook of health psychology* (pp. 727–746). Erlbaum.

Althusser, L. (1971/1977). Ideology and ideological state apparatuses (Notes towards investigation). In L. Althusser (Ed.), *Lenin and philosophy and other essays* (pp. 142–147, 166–176). New Left Books.

Bell, N. D. (2007). Safe territory? The humorous narratives of bilingual women. *Research on Language and Social Interaction, 40*(2–3), 199–225.

Berry, K. (2008). Good women, bad women and the dynamics of oppression and resistance in Kangra, India. *Humboldt Journal of Social Relations, 31*(1/2), 4–38.

Borah, R., & Nandi, S. (2012). Reclaiming the feminist politics of 'SlutWalk'. *International Feminist Journal of Politics, 14*(3), 415–421.

Brown, B. (2006). Shame resilience theory: A grounded theory study on women and shame. *Families in Society, 87*(1), 43–52.

Burn, S. M. (2000). *Women across cultures: A global perspective.* Mayfield Publishing.

Channa, S. M. (2014). *Gender in South Asia: Social imagination and constructed realities.* Cambridge University Press.

Chesler, P. (2005). *Women and madness.* Palgrave Macmillan.

Coates, J. (1997). Women's friendships, women's talk. In R. Wodak (Ed.), *Gender and discourse* (pp. 245–262). SAGE Publications.

Cohen, B. B. (2009). Networks of sociability: Women's clubs in colonial and postcolonial India. *Frontiers: A Journal of Women Studies, 30*(3), 169–195.

Colahan, M., Tunariu, A. D., & Dell, P. (2012). Understanding lived experience and the structure of its discursive context. *Qualitative Methods in Psychology Bulletin, 13*(1) 48–57.

Dandona, R., Bertozzi-Villa, A., Kumar, G. A., & Dandona, L. (2016). Lessons from a decade of suicide surveillance in India: Who, why and how? *International Journal of Epidemiology, 46*(3), 983–993.

Desai, S. A., & Dixit, V. V. (2018). Audit of female genital aesthetic surgery: Changing trends in India. *The Journal of Obstetrics and Gynecology of India, 68*(3), 214–220.

Donaghue, N. (2018). Discursive psychological approaches to the (un) making of sex/gender. In N. K. Dess, Marecek, & L. C. Bell (Eds.), Gender, sex, and sexualities: Psychological perspectives, (pp.127–146). Oxford University Press.

Eckert, P. (1992). Think practically and look locally: Language and gender as community based practice. *Annual Review of Anthropology, 21*(1), 461–490. https://doi.org/10.1146/annurev.anthro.21.1.461

Gangoli, G. (2005). Sexuality, sensuality and belonging: Representations of the 'Anglo-Indian' and the 'Western woman in Hindi cinema. In R. Kaur & A. J. Simha (Eds.), *Bollyworld: Popular Indian cinema through a transnational lens* (pp. 143–162). SAGE Publications.

Garland-Thomson, R. (2017). Integrating disability, transforming feminist theory. In L. J. Davis (Ed.), *The disability studies reader* (pp. 1–16). Routledge, an imprint of the Taylor & Francis Group.

Gold, A. G. (1997). Outspoken women: Representation of female voices in a Rajasthani folklore community. *Oral Tradition, 12*(1), 103–133.

Guendouzi, J. (2001). You'll think were always bitching: The functions of cooperativity and competition in women's gossip. *Discourse Studies, 3*(1), 29–51. https://doi.org/10.1177/1461445601003001002

Gupta, C. (2008). *Sexuality, obscenity, community: Women, Muslims, and the Hindu public in colonial India.* Orient BlackSwan.

Hamer, H. P., Finlayson, M., & Warren, H. (2014). Insiders or outsiders? Mental health service users' journeys towards full citizenship. *International Journal of Mental Health Nursing, 23*(3), 203–211.

Hay, J. (2000). Functions of humor in the conversations of men and women. *Journal of Pragmatics, 32*(6), 709–742.

Harishankar, P. (1985). *Tat Ki Khoj.* Vani Prakashan.

Hollander, J. A. (2002). Resisting vulnerability: The social reconstruction of gender in interaction. *Social Problems, 49*(4), 474–496.

Ingram, R. E., & Price, J. M. (Eds.). (2010). *Vulnerability to psychopathology: Risk across the lifespan.* Guilford Press.

Jack, D. C. (1991). *Silencing the self: Women and depression.* Harvard University Press.

Kakar, S. (1982). *The inner world.* Oxford University Press.

Kalcik, S. (1975). "... like Ann's gynecologist or the time I was almost raped": Personal narratives in women's rap groups. *The Journal of American Folklore, 88*(347), 3–11.

Karlekar, M. (1988). Women's nature and education. In K. Chanana (Ed.), *Socialization, education, and women: Explorations in gender identity* (pp. 129–165). Orient Longman.

Khanna, R., & Price, J. (1994). Female sexuality, regulation and resistance. *Gender & Development, 2*(2), 29–34.

Knottnerus, J. D. (1997). The theory of structural ritualization. In B. Markovsky, M. J. Lovaglia, & L. Troyer (Eds.), *Advances in group processes* (Vol. 14, pp. 257–279). JAI Press.

Lunbeck, E. (1987). "A new generation of women": Progressive psychiatrists and the hypersexual female. *Feminist Studies, 13*(3), 513–543. https://doi.org/10.2307/3177879

Mitra, A., & Knottnerus, J. D. (2008). Sacrificing women: A study of ritualized practices among women volunteers in India. *Voluntas: International Journal of Voluntary and Nonprofit Organizations, 19*(3), 242.

Moghaddam, F. M., Slocum, N. R., Finkel, N., Mor, T., & Harrè, R. (2000). Toward a cultural theory of duties. *Culture & Psychology, 6*(3), 275–302. https://doi.org/10.1177/1354067x0063001

Partington, A. (2006). *The linguistics of laughter: A corpus-assisted study of laughter-talk.* Routledge.

Pickering, S. (2001). Common sense and original deviancy: News discourses and asylum seekers in Australia. *Journal of Refugee Studies, 14*(2), 169–186.

Politi, P. (2009). One-sided laughter in academic presentations: A small-scale investigation. *Discourse Studies, 11*(5), 561–584.

Rai, S. M. (2002). *Gender and the political economy of development.* Polity Press.

Reyes, A. (2011). Strategies of legitimization in political discourse: From words to actions. *Discourse & Society, 22*(6), 781–807.

Scharff, C. (2011). Disarticulating feminism: Individualization, neoliberalism and the othering of 'Muslim women'. *European Journal of Women's Studies, 18*(2), 119–134.

Shukla, A., & Trivedi, T. (2008). Burnout in Indian teachers. *Asia Pacific Education Review, 9*(3), 320–334. https://doi.org/10.1007/bf03026720

Shweder, R. (1996). True ethnography: The lore, the law and the lure. In R. Jessor, A. Colby, & R. Shweder (Eds.), *Ethnography and human development* (pp. 15–52). University of Chicago Press.

Smith, J. A., Flowers, P., & Larkin, M. (2009). *Interpretative phenomenological analysis: Theory, method and research.* SAGE Publications.

Stanko, E. A. (1997). Safety talk: Conceptualizing women's risk assessment as a technology of the soul. *Theoretical Criminology, 1*(4), 479–499.

Burr, V. (2003). *Social constructionism* (2nd ed.). Routledge.

Taylor, S. E. (1988). Illusion and well-being: A social psychological perspective on mental health. *Psychological Bulletin, 103*(2), 193–210.

Tere, N. S. (2012). Gender reflections in mainstream Hindi Cinema. *Global Media Journal: Indian Edition, 3*(1), 1–9.

Thapan, M. (2004). Embodiment and identity in contemporary society: Femina and the 'new' Indian woman. *Contributions to Indian Sociology, 38*(3), 411–444.

Thapan, M. (2009). *Living the body: Embodiment, womanhood and identity in contemporary India.* SAGE Publications.

Thompson, K. D. (2011). Zanzibari women's discursive and sexual agency: Violating gendered speech prohibitions through talk about supernatural sex. *Discourse & Society, 22*(1), 3–20.

Torab, A. (1996). Piety as gendered agency: A study of Jalaseh ritual discourse in an urban neighbourhood in Iran. *Journal of the Royal Anthropological Institute, 2*(2), 235–252.

Vindhya, U., Kiranmayi, A., & Vijayalakshmi, V. (2001). Women in psychological distress: Evidence from a hospital-based study. *Economic and Political Weekly, 36*, 4081–4087. https://doi.org/10.2307/4411294

Waldrop, A. (2012). Grandmother, mother and daughter: Changing agency of Indian, middle-class women, 1908–2008. *Modern Asian Studies, 46*(3), 601–638.

Whitaker, K. S. (1982). *An exploratory study to identify and describe the nature of burnout among secondary teachers.* https://elibrary.ru/item.asp?id=7345373

Wilkinson, S. (1997). Feminist psychology. In D. Fox & I. Prilleltensky (Eds.), *Critical psychology: An introduction* (pp. 247–264). SAGE Publications.

Chapter 10

Reflections on Psychic Pain Around (In)Fertility and 'Being' of a Woman

Ishita U. Bharadwaj

To begin with, while deciding the very title of this chapter, several contradictory yet prevailing academic debates crossed my mind as to how to treat the conception of being a 'woman'. Initially, the term womanliness (Nandy, 1980) was used. This led to the question of how to understand the issues of (in)fertility in women without addressing her 'being'. Often, discourses around this simmering issue regarding women are marked by existential apathy—emphasizing the paradoxical notions of one's perception of 'womanhood' through the explicit markers of being 'fertile' and 'reproductive'. Hence, in the contemporary gender discourses, there is emphasis on bodies for conceptualizing the category of woman as a gender. Almost like a standard error, the societal constraints around womanhood did influence the academic debates on gender discourses, blinding them from addressing the 'beyond-ness' of bodies.

One of the reasons for writing this chapter is derived from the existing prevailing gap. Being a woman myself and undergoing my own challenges around infertility made me look deeper to discover the how and what of its psychic textures. This chapter should be read as an honest inquiry towards a 'much-lived' yet 'less spoken' 'pain' around the experience of being an infertile woman. This chapter intends to bring on board some centric issues that call for closer inquiry into what seeps into the making of a woman's psyche.

The chapter entails three segments. The first segment revisits the historical build of the feminist lens, acting as a catalyst for exploring the concepts of sexualities, (em)bodied self and reproductivities. The second segment attempts to unveil the spaces between the 'felt' and 'said' embeddings of (meta)narratives of the women who have experienced infertility. This segment also facilitates an insight into the nuances of phenomenological methods from a clinical perspective. The third segment intends to raise a few epistemological questions around the relationship between women and sexualities and how it reverberates in the psyche of a woman while dealing with her infertile body.

RE-EXAMINING THE PERCEPTIONS AND MEANINGS OF CHILDBEARING AND CHILDLESSNESS

Women and Motherhood

The attainment of motherhood has been considered a choiceless decision, around which there is universal consensus. On the contrary, most of the psycho-feminist studies have focused on the absence of this decision/choice. Becoming a mother has been considered as an important decision in a woman's life and been shown to have a long-term longitudinal impact on various parameters of her being (Meyers, 2001). Motherhood has been pitched as the ultimate fulfilment for women as part of 'hegemonic femininity' (Gillespie, 2003). Womanhood and motherhood intersect to such an extent that when some women fail or decline to attain the latter status, they are challenged, questioned and often robbed off the consideration as 'real women' (Peterson & Engwall, 2013). The irony of this staunch position on motherhood led to another polarized series of studies on motherless-ness, leaving scarce space for the multiplicity of the experience of 'not being a mother' felt by different women at different times. Charlotte Perkins Gilman, an American feminist, advocated a woman-centred, and further a mother-centred, world (Bagchi, 2017). In the early stage of feminism, especially in North America, patriarchy defined power, while matriarchy defined inner strength. Female reproductive powers have also been seen as the genesis of feminist reproductive consciousness.

Cultural Metanarratives Around Becoming a 'Mother': A Slice of Hegemonic Femininity

Maa banna bahut badi baat hoti hai. Maa hogi tab samjhogi, bacche ka dard kya hota hai. Who aurat hi kya jo maa nahi bani. Maa banne ke liye bahut kuch tyaagna hota hai. Bina bacchhe ke aurat kabhi poori aurat nahi banti. Bina bacche ke pati patni ka rishta adhoora hi rahata hai. Bachche ghar ki raunak hai. Bachhe ke sahare zindagi kat jaati hai. Kaisi aurat hai jo bachha nahi janamna chaahti hai!

(It's a big thing to become a mother. You would understand the pain of it only once you become one. There are lots of sacrifices you need to make for becoming a mother. Without having a child, a woman is never a complete woman. The relationship between husband and wife is incomplete without a child. Child is the delight of a home. One gets the hope of spending an entire life with a child. (Verbatim)

Familiarity with the above phrases or similar others is almost mandated by virtue of being reared in an Indian society. Proclaiming one's reproductivity through bearing a child is all that can ensure a woman's relational/structural position in her social context. Despite being informed (and influenced) by the global wave of empowerment, we still breathe in a society where *Beti Bachao, Beti Padhao* is the need of the hour. A close observation of the larger social discourse seems to indicate a deep-seated psychic struggle 'within' and 'outside' a woman in search of her own existence. This psychic struggle resonates with questions like: is a woman less herself in her experience of infertility; is her status of being a woman only attained through explicit markers of fertility; can womanliness be about more than just reproductive power; can womanhood as a desired status be only preceded by the expressions of fertility; and most importantly, can fertility be understood beyond its reproductive location?

Motherhood, a complex ambivalent phenomenon, is central to a woman's lived reality that is often seen as oscillating between power-lessness and power (Krishnaraj, 2012), highlighting the potent contra-diction between the ideological glorification of motherhood as *shakti* (power) and the powerlessness faced by mothers in their everyday life (Bagchi, 2017). Through the lens of feminism, Catherine Mackinnon suggests motherhood to be that 'which is most her own and most easily taken away'. Hence, the power to reproduce is then used against a woman for her enslavement, as argued by Sojourner Truth. Bagchi (2017) further hints at the convergence of traditional and modern societies on the issue of motherhood for boosting patriarchal control through the body over the mind of women. Culture, which provides a means of organizing experiences through a framework of values and beliefs, determines the lens through which interpersonal encounters are to be experienced. The interpersonal encounters deeply embedded within the intrapsychic aspect of experiences thus call for exploring the processes of gendering. In Indian feminist literature on motherhood, there have been series of writings, including personal narratives (by 12 Indian feminists) serving as an intergenerational testimony. It is also strongly asserted that the impulse behind recording of one's experience, voice, space of mothering by Indian feminist scholars interspersed with nation building process as well.

Most of the academic literature on infertility is silent on the 'desired and desirous' facets of womanhood. There seem to be two dominant tropes around women's sexualities. One tries to understand the issues of sexuality through their reproductive location. The other engages with the 'desired' and 'desirous' women expressing their sexual liberation. Hence, the question that still remains unexplained is what happens to the very 'desire' and essence of that woman who experiences infertility.

Motherhood: Bodies and Beyond

Pathology of the female body covers great volumes in the history of psychiatry (Sáenz-Herrero & Díez-Alegria, 2015) and has remained constant across time and culture. It is argued that one of the signifi-cant ways in which the body is evident in medical sociology today is through the more fully embodied perspective on matters of heath and illness. Young (2005) subscribed to the notion of the 'lived body', suggesting a unified idea of a physical body enacted and experienced in a unique sociocultural context. Studies by Peterson and Engwall (2013) on Swedish childless women highlight the concept of 'silent bodies' (bodies without the biological urge of reproducing). The reproductive capacity of the female body has always been considered as an ontological basis for defining the distinguishing features of a 'woman' different from those of a man (Malson & Swann, 2003). The idea of exploring motherhood from the physical site of the body calls for a better understanding of the psychological impact one experiences in motherhood's absence. With regard to the body, it has been contested that the way one experiences one category depends on how one inhabits the other, that is, the body and the embodiment of subjectivity that makes the body a site of politics (Penttinen & Kynsilehto, 2017).

Cultural imagery surrounding the term 'motherhood' is also often located at the site of the female physical body, which plays a crucial role in essentializing motherhood at an intrapsychic level. The history of Western culture's preoccupation with motherhood as a central aspect of female identity could be traced to Greek mythological texts (Herrero & Algeria, 2015).

With such lineage, a natural phenomenon like motherhood undergoes a processing of its position, at both the interpersonal and intrapsychic levels, altering the psychosocial aspects around it. Badinter (2012) and others (McMahon, 1995; Ruddick, 1982) refute the concept of maternal instinct. Badinter further contends that the politics of ecology (desire to return to simpler times), behavioural science based on ethology and essentialist feminism glorifying breastfeeding and natural childbirth have severely impacted women's independence and their conception of motherhood (Sáenz-Herrero & Díez-Algeria, 2015).

Feminist thought too could not refrain from essentializing the female identity, positing an essential womanliness to all women, irrespective of their class, caste, race, sexual orientation, cultural differences, etc. (Spelman, 1988). Later, postmodernists argued against this line of thinking. They delved into the dimensions of female oppression other than male dominance, that by other women. Many women share narratives of their experience of infertility in this light, which is a complex process to be unearthed.

Feminism from the start has been deeply concerned with the body, which is seen as a standard, something to be reclaimed as the very essence of the feminine. A third alternative is largely associated with feminist postmodernism, which emphasizes that embodiment needs to be looked at with a more fluid lens than as a construct limited to the givens of the society at large. For instance, Atwal (2016), through a feminist analysis of the book *Vidhwa ki Aatmkatha* by Priyamvada Devi, makes note of the fact that the use of women's bodies and in turn formation of their identities around their bodies was a persistent phenomenon even in the pre-independence era. Hence, in the case of women, 'body identity' has been a crucial factor in shaping their 'self-reflexive' position. It is here that Ponty's argument of the human body being an expressive space contributing to the significance of personal action gains importance. Ponty mentions that the body is both the origin of expressive movements and a medium for perception of the world. Therefore, bodily experience gives perception a meaning that is beyond the meaning established simply by thought. There is a body of work challenging the mind–body dualism while trying to gather an embodied perspective on the conceptualization of pain. Bagchi (2017) notes the utility of mothers of the pre-independence era (in the Indian context) as a hegemonic instrument in keeping the binaries intact.

It has also been pointed out how in postmodernist societies identities are fragmented and seem to fail to match with the individual experiences at a subliminal level. In this light, it could be seen how the Indian society, experiencing modernity after post traditional transition, seems to be in a phase of flux, trying to reconcile the transition into modernity, with its deep-rooted subconscious adherence to traditionalism. Though the dominant slogan of 'being modern' is prevalent, one's attitudes, actions and institutions seem to be influenced by one's tradition. This explains the overemphasis on In vitro fertilization (IVF) clinics and treatment, whereby the social scripts have been able to claim that the only salvageable portion from the lost tradition is that of motherhood. In the absence of motherhood, a woman's womanhood is not only doubtful but also incomplete. The need for creating an alternative powerful narrative that could give a more accurate account of one's experience is both felt and shared, but such creation has rarely been attempted in the context of women vis-à-vis their (in)fertility concerns. IVF centres have become one of the promising catchment sites for accentuating the sense of womanliness, irrespective of education, class, caste and social affluence in Indian society. Gidden's view on pride and shame holds merit in this context. He hints at pride and self-esteem being based on confidence in the integrity and value of a narrative of self-identity. Shame, on the other hand, grows from anxiety about the inadequacy of the narrative on which self-identity is based. It is basically a fear that the story one has is not good enough. Similar phenomena can be witnessed with the growing importance of medicalization of motherhood, which leaves little or no space for the experience of pride/integrity by a woman living with her infertile body.

Gendering of Motherhood

Studies on Egyptian families (Hatem, 1987) throw light on the conception of mothering in Western societies. It was argued that because female workers earned lower wages in workplaces during industrial times, they served as a threat to male employment positions; hence mass resistance against the female workforce was perceived. As a result, women were exclusively pushed to be identified with the family context, which was also undergoing a transition from the joint to the nuclear system.

The major change perceived with this transition was the onus on the mother of taking sole responsibility for child rearing, which in the previous joint-family set-up was taken care of by the extended family as well. This is how the role of the mother became exclusive and intensive, making the mother central to determining the social and emotional development of the child. While in the West infertility is politically veiled, in non-Western societies, it becomes a source of pain, open discussions, comments and social gossip. Scholars have grappled to mark the boundary where the purely biological role of a woman as a child bearer stopped and her roles as a mother, wife, trader and farmer began. It becomes imperative to discover the point at which the woman's responsibility to bear and raise children came into the picture.

Studies in different cultures reflect interesting patterns around mothering. Oyewumi (2000) highlights that in some parts of Africa, the term 'wife' was not gender- or sex-specific but symbolized the subordinate one in any couple. It was used more as a role for strategic deployment than as an identity. Oyewumi (2000) also points out that wifehood was a functional necessity for the transitional phase to motherhood. Promiscuous women were associated with the use of contraception, multiple abortions, diseases and infection in African culture. Infertility is a ground for divorce among the Bangangte tribe in Cameroon, leading to the woman losing her land (Feldman-Savelsberg, 1994). In Ekiti, South West Nigeria, infertile women are buried on the outskirts of the town alongside the graves of demented persons (Ademola, 1982). In fact, in South West Nigeria, there are social meanings associated with infertility. The people differentiate between women facing 'primary' and those facing 'secondary' infertility—*yoruba* and *idaduro*, respectively. Yoruba is that person who has never been pregnant despite being married for some time, whereas *idaduro* is a person who has difficulty in achieving another pregnancy after having one or two babies, which could be a serious issue if none of the existing children is male. Common *yoruba* custom expects a woman to get pregnant before marriage and considers it as a good sign.

Contemporary feminists theorized motherhood as a historical and social construct, failing to question the major assumption around the physical presence of the mother. The dominant literature on motherhood describes the phenomenon through the close proximity of mothers living with their children. This has been reiterated by psychological studies on the mother–child relationship, which have often positioned the mother as the 'sacred–selfless' one. Numerous studies have highlighted the importance of the physical presence of mothers in the overall well-being of their children, further creating an evident distinction between 'good mothers' and 'bad mothers'.

Psychosocial Politics in the Name of Infertility

McLeod and Ponesse's work (2008) sheds light on the issue of self-blame of women who undergo infertility-related concerns. According to them, women attribute 'many bad reproductive experiences such as unwanted pregnancy and infertility wholly or partly to their bad luck'.

Researchers have identified lifestyle factors, stress level, depression and anxiety to be some of the prominent causes of infertility in women (Domar, 2004). It is said that infertility as a biological phenomenon is on the rise. Biomedical models have been working towards finding solutions for inflicted infertility.

Apparently, scientific solutions are being developed to address the issue of infertility, yet there is cause for concern about this from a psychological perspective. In the attempt to make 'motherhood a reality for all', motherhood becomes an espoused aspiration for all, leaving an unbridgeable chasm if it is not met. This chapter intends to bring to light some such issues that call for closer inquiry into what seeps into the making of a woman's psyche.

Publicity of Modern Techniques Around Becoming a 'Mother'

The notion of 'womanhood' has been prevalently entwined with 'motherhood', to an extent that the image/idea of a complete woman seems to join the circle only through the latter following the former. Several said and unsaid phrases have been precipitators shaping the female psyche vis-à-vis how and what meaning a woman ascribes to her 'being'. One cannot be an inhabitant of Delhi and pass through different areas of the city without witnessing the presence of fertility clinics/hospitals. Besides, the mass propaganda around achieving successful parenting, without which happiness is often at stake, has been a serious cause of distress/depression for many women across cultures, with 8–12 per cent of the couples worldwide experiencing involuntary infertility (Ryan et al., 2017).

To begin with, a woman's capacity to produce offspring is termed fertility, whereas her biological potential to produce a child based on the monthly probability of conception is called fecundity (Wood, 1989). Evidence of primary and secondary infertility is estimated to be 25 per cent women (Larsen, 2003; Van Balen & Bos, 2009). Even with advancement in reproductive technology, the incidence of infertility is set to rise by 7.7 per cent by 2025. The prevalence of infertility is highest in those areas of the world which otherwise have good rates of fertility, which seems to be a major paradox. Studies have also stated lifestyle issues to be contributing factors in subfertility (Norman, 2007).

Rhetoric of Fertility in Commercial Media

Maa maa hi hoti hai; aurat maa ban kaar hi sampoorn stree ban paati hai; maa banna aurat ha doosra janam hota hai.... (A mother is not just any other woman, she is only a mother; it's only after attaining motherhood that a woman becomes complete; otherwise she remains incomplete; becoming a mother is like getting another birth in a woman's life....)

Studies on the issue of infertility have focused on the impact of its medicalization and the psychological stigma and social marginalities associated with it. Medicalization in infertility often comes at the cost of not regarding the feelings in being infertile, such as depression, anger, emotional distress, anxiety, shame, loss of control, sense of isolation and stigmatization. Whatever be the cause of infertility, the burden of invasive procedures related to its diagnosis and management has to be borne by women. Right from the discovery of *one's inability to 're-produce'*, living the panic assertions and attempts to be able to 'reproduce', and then the angst of undergoing the treatment for her/his infertility 'is a complex state of being for a woman. Infertility not only changes her life situation but also shakes her anchors of identity and world view. It almost takes her to the zone of questioning her very femininity, which for years has been shaped around the notions of sexuality and motherhood. Gender politics around motherhood often seem to end in the self-blame of women who experience infertility (McLeod & Ponesse, 2008).

On the other hand, fertility is growing into a big business. Entrepreneurs both within and outside of what was once seen as a developing world are mushrooming as a promising market for ART (assisted reproductive technology). However, interestingly, issues of infertility prevailing in lower socio-economic strata have not been accounted for in the existing literature. Sandelowski and De Lacey (2002) termed infertility as a 'cultural disorder' mirroring the cultural norms and cultural change. Hence, in explaining the social construction of infertility, the politico-institutional power determining the business of reproductivity could also be mapped (Ginsburg & Rapp, 1991).

OUTLINING THE FRAMES AND RESEARCH CONTEXTS

Methodological Lens and Framework

Against this backdrop, the current study was undertaken. The inception of this section emerged from my encounters (as a therapist) during some clinical sessions. The data discussed in this section were collected from intensive narratives of nine infertile women, out of which five, due to clinical concerns, were referred for therapeutic intervention. These latter women, during their time of referral, were not undergoing their IVF treatment. However, it was later discovered that two of them were in the gap phase, between two cycles of their IVF, while one of them was in her first cycle of treatment. The other two women, both aged 42, had been through two consecutive unsuccessful trials of IVF treatment. The important point to be noted here is that these women had been referred for therapeutic intervention due to clinical concerns that apparently had not been associated with their infertility-related experiences.

The other four narratives were gathered from the counselling centre of an infertility clinic where the researcher volunteered to provide her assistance in engaging with women who felt uneasiness, discomfort or mental blocks while initiating/undergoing IVF treatment (owing to confidentiality concerns, the name of the clinic cannot be disclosed). The ethnographic mode of inquiry became a reliable and trustworthy tool for building the relational bond between the researcher and the client in this setting. The ease of living with their discomfort without being called for articulation was a crucial 'felt' by these clients which further triggered a deep sense of dissonance in them. They admitted to feeling shared through expressing their unheard pain; however, the very awareness of this pain pushed them into guilt manifested through absences from their clinical sessions.

The narratives were captured through a mix of the 'existential' and 'phenomenological' approaches. For some clinical sessions, participants were engaged in 'relational therapy' as a suggestive tool for psychic exploration. However, the potential of 'encountering' as a 'tool' created a movement from dialectic to dialogue, which is further explained in the following section. The high points in eliciting the narratives were the employment of 'introception' (Merleau-Ponty, 1982) and Hubert Hermans and Dimaggio (2004) suggestive notions of the 'dialogical self'.

The gathered narratives were further analysed using the phenomenological approach, with emphasis on the dialogical self as a tool of inquiry. Insights that emerged from the analyses dealt with the intrapsychic conflicts between 'ought to be' and 'being' dominant in the experience of void. The analysis unveiled the psychic processes witnessed in the absence of meaning, which, through deeper probing, highlighted the prevalence of 'consensual being'.

About Them: Who, What and Why of the Clients

Savita: A 45-year-old businesswoman (dress designer) from the elite strata of South Delhi, Savita was living with her husband (who was in the defence services), mother and mother-in-law. She was undergoing medical treatment for her clinical depression 'diagnosed' by her psychiatrist, who referred her for therapy.

Saheli: A 42-year-old school teacher working in a government organization, Saheli was living with her husband and his brother's family. Insomnia and phases of withdrawal were the clinical concerns for which she underwent psychiatric treatment and therapy.

Maadhavi: A 34-year-old corporate woman married and working in a multinational corporation (MNC) in Gurgaon, Maadhavi was diagnosed with panic disorder (psychiatric medication) under therapy.

Sulbha: A young journalist of 30, Sulbha had a complex sexual history. She was referred by a psychiatrist but was not on medication.

Naina: The 38-year-old housewife of a businessman (financially affluent), Naina had given birth to twins through IVF 3 years back. She had been diagnosed with depression for the last 1 year and was under medication.

Jaanvi: A 25-year-old law graduate, Jaanvi was the housewife of a corporate lawyer. She had been undergoing IVF treatment for infertility for the last 2 years.

Anshula: A 35-year-old university teacher, Anshula had been undergoing IUI (intrauterine insemination) and IVF treatment for the last 4 years with no accomplishment.

Baani: A 29-year-old businesswoman from a high-class business family, Baani had been undergoing treatment for the last 6 months.

Chaand: A 37-year-old creative designer in the advertising world, Chaand had gone through six failed cycles of IUI and one failed cycle of IVF. She was under consideration for another one.

Myself: A 40-year-old university teacher, married for the last 10 years, I live with my in-laws. Owing to relational circumstances, I attempted to get pregnant for 6 years since the marriage. After one unsuccessful attempt of IUI, I decided to withdraw from medical treatment for family planning.

Reflections/Observations/Insights on/Around the 'Said' Narratives: 'Felt' in the Researcher's Experience

Handling the intense sessions of 'listening' was one of the most vulnerable experiences while being with the clients. This 'listening' during the course of elicitation transcended from the known 'pain' to a state of 'apathy' towards the 'unknown' yet 'shared', 'told' and 'reinforced' in the cultural scripts given to both the 'researcher' and the 'client'.

Often, during the course of sharing, the clients' emotional spectrum oscillated from a 'painfully helpless state' towards a 'deep angst' wherein the 'individual' within the client sought to search for their 'own body' and its 'desires'. There were also moments of deep remorse felt by these women, sometimes expressed through contempt towards me, while at other times they pitied my own childless state. Hence, in documenting these narratives and making sense of them, examining my own inner state was imperative.

Our 'shared barrenness' unfolded in myriad shades, which was both overwhelming and had deep roots. The natural urge in me to sustain their 'angst' was often coupled with emotional bruises reflexively encountered (coupled with pain).

The emphasis on the given heading to this section is not to create a jargon of a new kind. It is also to flag caution towards the assumption that a researcher can attune oneself to flawlessly capture each and every element of the complexities and intricacies lived and shared by the participants. What is left 'unsaid and unheard' may lie beyond the dichotomy of 'silence' and 'voice'. As a therapist and researcher, I have often stumbled upon the thought of how voicing could perhaps be another shade of silence and, hence, been left with the daunting question of how to create accountability for either. Most researchers import a sense of awe to silence. Instead of the sacred and profound silence, consistently during the course of this research, I found myself to be in a state of perpetual dilemma (conjoined with a deep sense of void) about the 'how' and 'why' of the said and the unsaid.

EMERGENT THEMES

Encountering Re-appropriation Between Me and Them

The alienating loneliness in their pain was a dominant expression shared by these women. Their reflections highlighted a jarring psychological dissonance, originating from trying to internalize the ordinariness of their efforts to become a mother and keeping up with the structural/ collective norm of not being allowed to express their pain at the same time.

aap toh samajh hi rahi hongi...doc bhi kehete hain there is some problem in my way of understanding my problem...lekin...khair...kya kahoon...par aisa nahi hai. Ek ajeeb se band hone ki feeling jaise kuch dabaa hua hai...doctor isko depression keh rahe ha.... (You must be understanding...even the doctors say that there is some problem in my way of understanding my problem...but...still...well, what can I say, but just that this is not the case. It's a strange feeling of being trapped, as if something is being suppressed...the doctors call it depression....) (Naina)

Har baar...bas mein hi kyon samjhu...galat hi sahi...mera kuch to hai.... (Every time, why does it need to be who understands? Though wrong...but at least something is mine....) (Naina)

Trust me there are times when I do wish...desire...not that I am always seeking being hooked.... Like you, them I too have desires in me for moments.... (Sulbha)

They say all weird stuff about me...my mother is worried...friends find me manipulative...but how to explain them I am not so.... I wish to experience myself fully...completely...but I end up.... (Naina)

You see...I don't know why they feel there is some problem to the way I feel and how I feel...well I know they are concerned about me, they all are...they should be....

My mother says its because I don't have a sense of responsibility.... Even sometimes my husband says had I been a mother, I would have been more careful with myself.... (Savita)

The second layer of data gathering from the sessions engaged introception and the dialogical self as techniques to 'explore the experience of experiencing embodied disengagement'.

During the course of the sessions, with the space to live outside of the bodies and given identities, the narrators expressed relief from the burden of being in the bodies. The wish to be out and away was strongly sensed in them. In some very vulnerable moments, they also wished to feel themselves without being driven by the notions of the 'ideal woman', who could only be a mother.

Yes I really struggled to become a mother...you can't imagine the pain I went...but now I feel my body was used. Am I only this body?? I love my children, who wouldn't…but I feel burdened mothering…i used to think that once i become a mother, i might feel more of me…its not that…I feel drained…sometimes I wish to run away, not from place but from this body who is only seen as a mother. I am relieved in being like this now (laughs). (Naina)

…you asked me to see this as a body away from me…I am trying to…I think maybe I trying outliving my womanhood through these…they say I am attractive…. Many appreciates my style…even he does…but I dislike my body…no…honestly I do…there is nothing I see good in it. (Sulbha)

…kabhi mujhe bhi man hota tha…ab nahi…isliye nahi ki mein nahi ban paayi…banti to kaisa lagta iska bhi ab ehsaas nahi hota…. Mummy aur maa ko dekh lagta shaayad acha hi hua nahi bani…. They really fail to understand my feelings.

(…sometimes I too desired it…but not now…not because I couldn't be one…I don't even has the urge to explore how i would have felt if i been a mother…. After seeing my mother and mother in law, I feel glad I didn't become one…. They really fail to understand my feelings. (Savita)

During the course of the session it was discovered that Savita's experiences were unlike what her psychiatrist and family felt about her 'illness'. For instance, she shared, 'Aksar mujhe sab bahut door lagte hain… bahut door…kai baar main khud bahut door hoti hoon…khud se bhi. (Often I find everyone very distanced from me…very much distant…there are times when I feel estranged and far from my own self….)' She also revealed, 'I feel better now…after being diagnosed'. With further sessions, she revealed, 'It has given me a sense of body…'.

Feeling of Imposture: Making It Up Behind the Mask of Competency

During the course of the sessions, there was this dominant feeling encapsulating the narrators' sense of loss around mothering. Yet, there was also a shared sense of incompetency thrusted by them. Thus, on the one hand, the desire to outgrow the weight of mothering was shared, and on the other, the pain of not being the mother was also expressed but consciously denied. These modern women do not wish to see infertility as their failure, yet, deep within, they are breaking in resistance to the shared archetypes of the collective psyche.

...metro mein...road pe...clinic ke waiting room mein...sabko dekhte hain sabke ke paas bachha hai...sab khush hian.... Kya hum khush hone laayak nahi? Aap toh samajhti hongi, bin bachhe ke, kaisa lagta hai...hai na? Itne samay se try kar rahe hain...bas ho jaye...phir to sab theek ho jayega.

(...in metro...on road...in the waiting room of the clinic...everyone just seems to staring at me...everyone had children.... They all appeared happy.... Don't we deserve to be happy? I hope you can understand this feeling, how it feels to be without a child...isn't it? We are trying for such a long time now.... We just hope for it to happen...just happen. I know after that everything is going to be alright.) (Jaanvi)

Ghar mein bahut alag dynamics hoti hai, kabhi lagta hai agar pataa hota ki nahi kar sakte hai ohir shaayad kisi aur ki zindagi nahi kharaab karte. I feel this all the time. *Kya jawaab de ki kyon nahi kar paaye.... Bas nahi hua...par sab nahi samajhte is cheez ko....*

(The dynamics in the home are different, sometimes I wonder if I knew I couldn't do it I would not have ruined somcone else's life.... I feel this all the time. What answer do I give to the question 'why couldn't we do it'.... It just didn't happen...but everyone does not understand this....) (Anshula)

...I am trying...and will keep trying...my friend has finally succeeded... I am sure I too would...like her I would also go that Dr (taking the name) I feel at loss...but I don't allow it to get in my work. Last week I came back from a big assignment, and I am trying to give my best to. But with family people I now feel like avoiding. Except for children they have nothing else to speak about...I too feel the loss. But what to do...don't you? (Chaand)

Dissociation with the Body: Complexity Towards Their Sexualities

This was a difficult turn to navigate with the clients and to some extent with my own self. The root of one's felt state was inevitably entwined with the existence of one's body both consciously and unconsciously.

The task during such sessions was to feel oneself as someone from the outside, so as to begin with a sense of 'encountering' oneself. This was needed for creating a space for witnessing the shared and unshared experiences as much as possible. However, often, emotional resistance, overwhelming turbulence and stirring of memories were witnessed during the course of these sessions. These emotional trails called for a subtle yet intense engagement even after the closure of sessions both for the therapist and for the client.

> I also know if I had been a mother, I would have been more responsible.... Is becoming a mother everything? Sister-in-law, mother-in-law, everyone is already a mother. What could happen if only I don't become one? It's my body, true. Am I wrong in feeling this? It's my body who feels it.... (Sulbha)

Encountering her inner struggle with her reality enabled Sulbha to discover her own silent fight with it, which held a core position as 'inevitable'. As long as Sulbha perceived it as a loss against the inevitable, her struggle put her in a double bind. A great part of her pain came from feeling at war with a loss, without getting any space to discover her own wound. Jaanvi shared, '...*pattaa nahi aap kaise ab rahati hongi*....my body cries for bearing.... (...I don't know how are you managing to live without this...I feel my body cries...it just cries out for bearing...my body cries for bearing....)'

Jaanvi's position was slightly different from Sulbha's, as discovered while engaging in this part of the session. There was a constant pressure felt by Jaanvi to get validation from me for failing to bear her pain. This calls for close examination. Getting close to 'her' pain required Jaanvi to move beyond the social self, which was emotionally draining for her. However, it was only in those moments when she felt that movement that she felt some release oozing out with her pain. This was only possible when she felt shared with her body at one level and yet, at another, could see herself beyond the body as well. This led to another complex terrain of the women's sexuality when unmasking their sexual frigidity. Having reached this point, they could feel their silenced emotional blocks entangled in their sexual experience.

'Am I at fault if my body fails to produce a baby?' rued Anshula. She reflected a deep sense of guilt for her infertility. Often, as a woman, one is rarely aware of carrying the guilt, especially that at a subconscious level. It took a while for her to discover the roots of her sexual frigidity, which predominantly emerged from her moralized position towards motherhood. This was a common problem encountered in many female clients for whom, owing to their traditional and cultural systems, sexuality and motherhood were pitted against each other, leading to strange kinds of 'complexities towards their sexuality'.

Chaand shared, 'My husband is a nice man. Well, he has been very kind to me. But I no longer wish to be intimate with him. ...I don't know...or maybe I do know'. When asked whether he still wishes to get intimate with her, she responded, '...oh he does, I think men are like that, but now I don't feel like it...sometimes without being into it I still do it...i feel very emotionally heavy while being in this process...'.

Further, Sulbha shared, '...*shareer ki apni needs hoti hai...my body is not meant for mothering maybe...I don't desire in that way....* (...body has its own needs...my body is not meant for mothering maybe...I don't desire in that way....)'

Both the above excerpts depict a sense of sexual frigidity due to the psychological construct of motherhood. Though their sexual experiences were taken as a matter of concern by their partners and clinicians, they were often left 'unseen beyond their bodies', or in better words, were located just 'within their bodies'.

Unbecoming the Mother: A Possibility Within/Outside the Body

Engaging with the clients throughout the course of our sessions with a sense of meaning derived uniquely by them was possible only through entering into a dialogical journey with them. The burden of not bearing physically while desiring to nourish the 'motherly instinct' without reflection left them in a complete psychic dissonance. This psychic dissonance built an unmotherly position in them, leaving them more scarred and unshared. This part of their session flow attempted to enable a kind of exploration into the unlived space of their experiential world where they could feel a sense of movement beyond the explicit motherhood position. The phase of going 'beyond motherhood' was attempted through bringing them closer to their experience of 'non-consensual pain'.

'...I really don't know whether I would have been happy being a mother or not...how would I? I am not very happy now...but is it only because of me not being a mother?', Baani rued.

Itni to maaye hain...kya sab khush hai? ...main bhi khush nahi hoon...maa banne ya na banne se...pataa nahi.

(There are so many mothers all around...are they all very happy in being so? ...even I am not happy...don't know is it because of my inability to bear a child...really don't know. (Maadhavi)

Resonating self-doubt towards the unlived came across as a challenge for some of the clients, as reflected in the above statements of Maadhavi and Bani. Delving into their self-doubts brought them closer to the larger consensual templates through which they tend to perceive their life scripts. This phase enabled them to move towards exploring the ideas of happiness, loss and being and nothingness while trying to understand their lived experiences.

...I am ok with my life.... Its ok if i am unable to bear a child...but trust me I am not unhappy kinds...however, wherever you go, this is what people make you feel...that i should be unhappy and try harder... why did you stopped trying? Are you really, really happy? (Chaand)

...I wish I was a mother. When I see women mothering their children, I do long for that. As if I shall never know what this feeling is. So yes, when I see that I feel vacuumed. It pains too. ...but more than that, the rhetoric of negating the motherly instinct for infertile women is what pains me the most. ...so more than anything, my own desire to bear a child is often to socially validate my own maternal instinct.... *Mujh mein bhi maatritva hai.* (There is motherhood in me as well.) I wish I could explain this.... (Jaanvi)

In the case of Jaanvi and Chaand, one can see them juggling the void of motherhood and the desire for mothering. While Chaand's statement reflects exploring social validation through the therapist's experience of being childless, Jaanvi's narrative clearly touches upon her awareness that she could differentiate between her non-motherhood position and her desire for mothering. This awareness further helped in giving them a sense of unburdening sense of movement in revisiting their 'untold' narratives even to understand their 'told' ones.

Being an infertile woman myself, often I had to listen to women sharing the phenomenal pain they suffered in bearing and rearing their children. The experience of not being included in these metanarratives of 'despites and besides' pained the clients the most. The aspect of being reduced to 'nothing' as compared to the other's volume of pain made them feel not cared for. Hence, the reason they felt pushed into aligning with the conception of biological mothering also served to lend legitimacy to their existing pain.

> *...maa keheti thi aurat hona dard se bharaa hua hai. Bas dard hi mila hume-sha.... Bin bacche ki aurat hone ka dard koi kya samjhega...lekin bachhe karne ka jo dard hai who kaise kahe?...last cycle of treatment was terrible. But maa keheti hai yeh dard kuch nahi hai. Jab bachha hoga to sab achha lagega... shaayad...let me hope aisa hi ho....*

(...my mother says being the process of becoming a mother is full of pain. I have always found pain....One fails to understand the pain of being a childless woman...people pretend to know what it feels... the worst part is...how to share the pain of undergoing the process of very bearing? ...last cycle of treatment was terrible. But my mother says this pain is pittance to the grand one. Once I succeed in bearing a child, things will fall in place...maybe...let me hope It happens in this way...'.) (Jaanvi)

...during the course of this treatment, there has been several nights which I spent just not being able to sleep...he thinks I am thinking too much...but how to tell him what it is...the futility of the cycle, you won't believe every time when I bleed, I cry aloud in the bathroom... how to tell all this.... You think I don't wish to...but I also don't wish to go through this pain...please help me...please. (Anshula)

Who says it doesn't pain.... It pains...it does...but they say...everyone says its important...why?? But now...let us take it. I dread going for sessions...trust me.... (Chaand)

Children as Masks for One's Marriage

This aspect found profound expression in most of the women. This feeling had a lot to do with the gap/unlived space/unfelt aspects with their partner. Being infertile appeared to them as being naked with their partnership failures in the eyes of society. Most of them felt that having children had little to do with a successful marriage partnership, quoting from their surroundings. However, not having children did work as an inability to mask their distanced/dysfunctional married space, which to them was a bigger concern.

> As a young woman I believed having children was only possible when two people are connected and feel for each other...*lekin aisa kahan hota hai? Sarla* (her friend) *keheti hain* I am too idealistic.... *Satish* (her husband) *se bahut kuch mera nahi milta, par sabke rishte mein yehi mein dekhti hoon. Pehele lagta tha, jab hum dono mein sab settle ho jayega, then we would start a family...ab nahi.* I wish I had started then.... *Aise rishtey bhi ek samay ke baad aapke bhaar ko nahi le paate.*

> (As a young woman I believed having children was only possible when two people are connected and feel for each other...but where does this happens? Sarla (her friend) says i am too idealistic.... Satish (her husband) and me don't match at many levels, but i get to see this in every second marital relationships around me. Initially I thought, once we both strive a chord of compatibility, then we would start a family... but I decline from this thought now. I wish I had started then.... Such relations after a point fail to take the weight of yours.) (Saheli)

When probed further on her understanding of weight, Saheli elaborated:

> *aapke hone na hone ka;* your being and not being in a relationship; *agar bacche ho to na hona dikhta nahi utna...aur hone ki alternatives mil jaate hain.*

> (of being and unbeing yourself; your being and not being in a relationship; if we had children, this unbeing wouldn't have been visible...we might have found alternatives of being as well...who knows.)

Often it was evident during the IVF counselling process that clients felt relieved to be accompanied by their partners. Further probing however, revealed a sense of burden in them while living with the impression of 'all is well between us'. Therefore, the legitimacy of seeking medical intervention outweighed their cognizance of interpersonal gaps.

Sab kehete hain...ek bachha ho jayega to sab theek ho jayega.... Meine bhi yehi soch ke bachhe kiye. But the relational pain remained dear.... I still feel the pain of our partnership. *Ab kaise chode? Bachhe ke liye hum saath hain.* Where do I go and really free myself from this guilt.... I am sure Sandeep might be feeling the same....

(Everyone is absolutely right in saying...once there is a child, everything falls in place.... I too adhered to this thought for myself. But the relational pain remained dear.... I still feel the pain of our partnership. Now how do I quit from this relationship? We both are together just for the sake of the child. Where do I go and really free myself from this guilt.... I am sure Sandeep might be feeling the same....) (Naina)

WEAVING THE NARRATIVES: DISCUSSION

The narratives reveal the lived and unlived paradoxes within the female sample which resonate with the deeper impacts of the contemporary discourses around being fertile. The emotional fatigue in trying and failing to attain motherhood had been a journey of complex experiences for the participants, who often felt their pain remain unheard and silenced themselves on realizing it. The hardship of the process of attaining motherhood is rarely seen as an individual journey; rather, perceived more as a collective effort with 'oughts' and 'shoulds'. The multiple attempts made by some of the participants unfold a story that goes beyond their individual choice of attaining motherhood. These stories of despair, loss, pain, apathy and dissociation culminate in shaping the individual and collective subconscious beliefs around women and motherhood.

This piece of research was almost a personal journey for me. I was dealing with my own issues of infertility and searching to express the 'mother' in me. This research provided me with an extensive existential space to be sceptical of my own understanding of the phenomenon in question. As an insider in the field of counseling, I could access the receptivity to witness the pain; however, there were times when I did distance the academic 'me' to capture and perhaps live the emotions stirred in the course of listening to shared narratives. Going back to the gathered stories was a difficult prospect. Yet, one question that kept echoing within me was: what is it that I seek to understand through their stories? At other times, I asked myself: am I really able to understand what it means? These dominant paradoxes were like guideposts for me in shaping the psychological perspective around this work.

(Un)Mothering and Affective Solidarity

I encountered a paradoxical experience around affective solidarity as I went deeper into the therapeutic process with my clients. Their meeting with me and revealing themselves to me was facilitated by their sense of trust that I would understand—a seeking of confidentiality. However, the idea of my intentionally not getting medical aid for my infertility triggered emotional dissonance in them. It pushed them to the extent where they felt at ease venting out their discontent over my peculiarity and doubting my womanhood. However, it was often this cathartic expression of theirs which sometimes enabled them to be themselves in my presence. There was a stark reaction among all the participants (my clients) towards other women, including myself, who they felt chose to abstain from sharing the burden of bearing a child. Reactions were also displayed towards their own significant other, who they felt failed to identify with their pain. Ironically, these emotions were accompanied by a sense of envy as well, towards those women who were unlike them and were successful in their endeavour of child-bearing. Hence, the possibility of coexistence with other women only happened through complex pain. The difficulty with these clients lay in their failure to acknowledge the pain of other women who they felt were not in a similar state as them.

Ideation of Pain in Being a Woman

This was an important aspect processed in the narratives. Much of the guilt suffered by the clients was rooted in their *own* imagined pain, assumed as a significant milestone towards womanhood. The assumptive notions of womanhood often led to negation of their felt state and emotional anguish. When probed on why they felt like this, there was an absolute consensus echoed: *'Aisa hi hota hai. Aurat banna itna asaan nahi hai.* (It is always like this. It's not easy being a woman.)' The urge to be acknowledged as a woman was felt much deeper by them than their infertile state. Becoming fertile was often expressed as their claim for redeeming their womanhood, which could validate their suffering. Hence, much of their own guilt emerged from the meta-belief that 'only the mother goes through "that" pain'. As a woman and a researcher, this left me with a question: how often are we in need of a fertility tag for validating our existence in the eyes of other women?

The Paradox Between 'Becoming' a 'Mother' and 'Being' Maternal

Association of maternal instinct with the female gender is perhaps common across all the cultures in the world. In fact, when a woman fails to feel the motherly instinct, she is condemned and treated as an atypical exemplar of the population. Thus, the seeking of corrective measures for one's infertility often is driven by the deep-seated urge to legitimize one's womanhood. As a woman I could relate with this urge and desire for legitimacy. However, the cause of concern among this study's participants was more complex and alarming. It seemed that often this need for validating their womanhood through the identity of becoming a mother, took the participants towards the medical facilitation of their infertile state. However, at the same time, it was only addressed as a medical phenomena, not allowing them the chance to be in touch with their emotional state at all. Often, their own family structures, partner and parents, while sustaining the anxiety and uncertainty of the process, failed to experience the motherly instinct within them. This was the case during their medical procedures. As a result, maternal instinct, claimed to be natural, not only got trivialized in the process but also faced inhibitions curbing it. It appeared as a crucial marker in their inability to explore their mine-ness in ways that could enable them to express their urge. As a therapist, I discovered this damage to be integral to their clinical manifestation unknowingly. The pain of addressing this damage was profound and thus negated, defended and sometimes denied. But eventually, some of them did witness it during the therapeutic session which led us to explore the psychic matrix in this light.

Corporeal Experience Around (Un)Mothering

Women's disowning of the body and deliberate or otherwise abstinence from pleasure or overindulgence in sexual pleasure seem to suggest the difficulties of these women in breaking through the situatedness of the barrenness within their body. Sexual distancing between the couple owing to the infertility concerns of the woman was a common pattern perceived in the group. Issues around sexuality were rarely spoken about for quite some time by the clients, as they perceived them to be unrelated to their medical condition. Yet through deeper exploration of their being, it was discovered that sexual frigidity was a significant expression in their sexual equation. Many of them accepted this as an extension of their disinterest in sexual encounters. Two of them unknowingly challenged this through indulging in sexual promiscuity. The explicit sexual frigidity seemed to be an extension of their emotional frigidity. Their unconscious disownment of their sexual bodies precipitated from the shared cultural archetype that a good woman's sexuality is to be reserved for only reproduction. Hence, the predicament between the lived and the told churned the emotional dissonance to a level where it could only be stabilized through sexual frigidity. Ironically, some of them even mentioned how their partners, in approaching them sexually, failed to touch upon this emotional bruise that called for deep healing in the process of experiencing the touch. Eventually, with unhealed emotions and a curbed sense of expansion, the resultant feature of sexual frigidity seemed to be a common and explicit yet unexplained manifestation.

Disembodying the 'Mother'

Almost all the women shared their failure to experience joy around mothering, to such an extent that their own relationship with their mothers (some of them) had turned difficult. The guilt of non-mothering was echoed in their narrative of relationalities not just due to their infertile state; it was also a subconscious reaction to the medical trivialization of an instinct that eventually lost the charm of its celebrated existence. This was witnessed in a few intense, overwhelming moments with the clients. For instance, Naina said: '*man hota hai...bahut man hota hai...par himmat nahi hoti...darr sa ab lagta...* ('I do yearn for it...really I do...just that don't have the courage for it...I fear now... what if something doesn't go well...).'

TOWARDS A CLOSURE: WHERE AM I IN THIS RESEARCH?

Despite being grounded in qualitative and clinical approaches to understanding psychological processes, one does face difficulty in observing oneself and mapping out the process of how one builds a perspective for a given situation.

As mentioned earlier, my interest in the area of infertility arose precisely after I experienced emotional turmoil within my own self owing to my prevailing infertile state. Social remarks, curiosities and subtle yet deep dismissals of my 'existence devoid of a child' reverberated intense pain. Often I would wonder: if I being an academician and a therapist could feel this, how about those women who undergo the same situation but probably have no aid in making sense of the 'why' and 'how' of this pain? Social atrocities do not always involve physical or explicit abuses. The glamorization of motherhood, and motherhood's positioning as a great (and often the only) source of joy in urban spaces, makes it difficult to live and explore an alternative narrative for oneself. Realizing the intense struggle within, internalized and silenced, I felt some amount of exploration needed to be done. Hence, this research is perhaps a culmination of my personal quest to get into the psychic terrain for the unexplained yet lived and untold pain of infertility.

My reaching out to the clients was not through planned steps or a method but through my becoming aware of my own inner state while being with them, which was of help in building a sense of connection with them. Revisiting their stories in a manner such that I could listen to them without my own baggage was the self-work I undertook.

Therefore, I made sure to read their narratives and re-read them after some time gap. For some stories, the gap stretched for months, as unblocking the emotional knots felt during the emergence of the sessions seemed to be a requisite in making sense of their stories.

THE DISGUISED VULNERABILITY

Despite the upsurge in psychological studies on issues pertaining to infertility, most of the time, they end up echoing the deep consensual validation of social givens around infertility. It is strange how being unable to experience the socially sanctioned normative life event of childbearing often marginalizes a woman and casts her out from the collective feminine identity. The experience of being misunderstood and having to endure a feeling of immense unrecognized grief both by oneself and others—a grief which if acknowledged, furthers a greater sense of isolation, abandonment, and unending loss. Such reductive understanding of oneself not only paints a dismal static picture of inability to materialize an inherent, socio-culturally inculcated dream of motherhood, but it also reinforces a sense of inadequacy and the feeling of never becoming a 'whole' in oneself. Thus, these communal ratifications about childbearing and motherhood, on the one hand, induce perplexing and everlasting feelings of rejection and emptiness and scarred notions of womanhood and identity among women experiencing infertility. On the other hand, they also perpetuate concealed suffering and silent repudiation of those females fearing to accept and live up to the ideals of motherhood, broadcasted as a mandate throughout the life discourses of every woman.

The findings also indicate a possibility of redefining the smothering narrative of motherhood and allowing women to re-position themselves outside the boxes of 'infertile' and 'childless'. The alienated body can be re-imagined as maternal, potent and desirous when these competing narratives of empowerment and motherhood are allowed to collide, confront and eventually coexist through interpersonal and intrapsychic dialogues. Thus, their claimed incompleteness is a 'fertile' site for rebuilding more cohesive imaginations of mothering and womanhood where, through affective solidarity, they depart from the overarching penalized and penalizing feeling that unfulfilled womanhood propagates.

The aim of this chapter is definitely not to disclaim the significance of motherhood or advocate its triviality. This line of research intends to bring forth a deeper understanding towards the 'experience of living with (in)fertility'. It attempts to unveil the 'psychic pain' of women who often live with 'psychic violence' for being infertile both within themselves and externally in the society, but fail to acknowledge and express it. Such insights call for strengthening the support system in the healthcare sector that refrains from addressing the 'being' within the patient. These insights also call for a more sensitive approach from the medical practitioners who work towards validating the assumptive consensual template of joy for these women while turning a blind eye to their existential angst. Prevalence of such cultural blind spots often leave deep impacts on the women's emotions, sometimes leading them to feel apathy towards the so-called natural maternal instinct. Hence, in order to understand the 'woman' in the 'infertile' state, there is a need to capture the multitude of experiences around maternal instinct lived by them.

REFERENCES

Ademola, A. (1982). Changes in the patterns of marriage and divorce in a Yoruba town. *Rural Africana, 14*, 1–24.

Atwal, J. (2016). *Real and imagined widows: Gender relations in Colonial North India.* Primus Books.

Badinter, E. (2012). *The conflict: Woman & mother.* Text Publishing.

Bagchi, J. (2017). *Interrogating motherhood.* SAGE Publications.

Domar, A. D. (2004). Impact of psychological factors on dropout rates in insured infertility patients. *Fertility and Sterility, 81*(2), 271–273.

Feldman-Savelsberg, P. (1994). Plundered kitchens and empty wombs: Fear of infertility in the Cameroonian grassfields. *Social Science & Medicine, 39*(4), 463–474.

Gillespie, R. (2003). Childfree and feminine: Understanding the gender identity of voluntarily childless women. *Gender & Society, 17*(1), 122–136.

Ginsburg, F., & Rapp, R. (1991). The politics of reproduction. *Annual Review of Anthropology, 20*(1), 311–343.

Hatem, M. (1987). Toward the study of the psychodynamics of mothering and gender in Egyptian families. *International Journal of Middle East Studies, 19*(3), 287–305.

Hermans, H. J., & Dimaggio, G. (Eds.). (2004). *The dialogical self in psychotherapy: An introduction.* Routledge.

Krishnaraj, M. (2012). The women's movement in India: A hundred year history. *Social Change, 42*(3), 325–333.

Larsen, U. (2003). Infertility in central Africa. *Tropical Medicine & International Health, 8*(4), 354–367.

Malson, H., & Swann, C. (2003). Re-producing 'woman's' body: Reflections on the (dis) place (ments) of 'reproduction'for (post) modern women. *Journal of Gender Studies, 12*(3), 191–201.

McLeod, C., & Ponesse, J. (2008). Infertility and moral luck: The politics of women blaming themselves for infertility. *IJFAB: International Journal of Feminist Approaches to Bioethics, 1*(1), 126–144.

McMahon, M. (1995). *Engendering motherhood: Identity and self-transformation in women's lives.* The Guilford Press.

Merleau-Ponty, M. (1982). *Phenomenology of perception.* Routledge.

Meyers, D. T. (2001). The rush to motherhood: Pronatalist discourse and women's autonomy. *Signs: Journal of Women in Culture and Society, 26*(3), 735–773.

Nandy, A. (1980). Woman versus womanliness in India: An essay in cultural and political psychology. In A. Nandy (Eds.), *At the edge of psychology* (pp. 32–46). Oxford University Press.

Oyewumi, O. (2000). Family bonds/conceptual binds: African notes on feminist epistemologies. *Signs: Journal of Women in Culture and Society, 25*(4), 1093–1098.

Penttinen, E., & Kynsilehto, A. (2017). *Gender and mobility: A critical introduction.* Rowman & Littlefield.

Peterson, H., & Engwall, K. (2013). *Silent bodies*: Childfree women's gendered and embodied experiences. *European Journal of Women's Studies, 20*(4), 376–389.

Peterson, H., & Engwall, K. (2016). Missing out on the parenthood bonus? Voluntarily childless in a 'child-friendly' society. *Journal of Family and Economic Issues, 37*(4), 540–552.

Ruddick, S. (1982). 'Maternal thinking'. In B. Thorne & M. Yalom (Eds.), *Rethinking the family: Some feminist questions* (pp. 76–94). Longman.

Ryan, R., O'Farrelly, C., & Ramchandani, P. (2017). Parenting and child mental health. *London Journal of Primary Care, 9*(6), 86–94. https://dx.doi.org/10.10 80/17571472.2017.1361630

Sáenz-Herrero, M., & Díez-Alegría, C. (2015). Gender and corporality, corporeality, and body image. In M. Sáenz-Herrero (Ed.), *Psychopathology in women* (pp. 113–142). Springer.

Sandelowski, M., & De Lacey, S. (2002). The uses of a 'disease'. In M. Inhorn & F. van Balen (Eds.), *Infertility around the globe: New thinking on childlessness, gender, and reproductive technologies* (pp. 33–51). University of California Press.

Spelman, E. V. (1988). *Inessential woman: Problems of exclusion in feminist thought.* Beacon Press.

Van Balen, F., & Bos, H. M. (2009). The social and cultural consequences of being childless in poor-resource areas. *Facts, Views & Vision in ObGyn, 1*(2), 106.

Wood, J. W. (1989). Fecundity and natural fertility in humans. *Oxford Reviews of Reproductive Biology, 11,* 61–109.

Young, I. M. (2005). *On female body experience: 'Throwing like a girl' and other essays.* Oxford University Press.

Chapter 11

The Experience of Vulnerability and Resilience of Adolescent Girls in Slums

Nandita Babu and Varuni Sethi

INTRODUCTION

The period of adolescence (age 10–19 years, as per the World Health Organization [2018]) has been identified as one that holds great impetus for growth and development, and holds within its fold a number of challenges, as well as opportunities. The stage of adolescence is marked by myriad changes that range from changes in physical development to changes in the emotional domain. The adolescence period, as per Steinberg (2014), 'begins from the phase where the child enters the stage of puberty and continues till the time the child begins to take responsibility of himself i.e. becomes independent'. The challenges faced in this stage do take on a positive connation when seen as leading to new learnings, if handled carefully, like learning to adjust well. However, for optimum growth to take place, it becomes imperative to face these challenges. The idea of the individual developing 'personal agency' at this stage has also been highlighted by researchers (e.g., Greenfield et al., 2003).

An important developmental psychologist who has worked in the area of understanding life span development is Erik Erikson. As part of the psychosocial stages of development proposed by him, Erikson described that on reaching adolescence, 'the individual strives to shape his own individuality, within the context in which he finds himself placed' (Erikson, 1968). This stage, as per Erikson, is one of 'exploration', where one tries to define for oneself what values are, which values are important to one, what one's goals are, etc. Further, as per him, just like any other psychosocial stage, this stage too is present with challenges, as well as opportunities. If successfully resolved, these challenges are likely to pave the way for optimum development to take place; however, if not resolved successfully, they might lead to uncertainties about one's role, perhaps hampering the development and growth of the individual (Erikson, 1968). Further, Erikson (1968) termed the 'late adolescence period as one of psychosocial moratorium', whereby the individual is free to explore and experiment before selecting a role for the self.

A dominant and recognizable trend that has come forth in adolescent research literature has been that of the differences in the unfolding of this stage for males and females. Research has suggested that strikingly different patterns emerge for the two groups. Researchers have reported that females might face more stress in their relations as compared to adolescent males in this stage (Hankin et al., 2007). For females, it has also been reported as a stage that 'may bring about greater internalising concerns' (Wade et al., 2002). Flook (2011) in his study found that adolescent females were more sensitive to such stressors or strain in the relationships and in general experienced a greater amount of stress. Nonetheless, such sensitivity also seems to have a positive connation, such as leading to greater learning of management of emotions (Morris et al., 2007). Some researchers have reported a 'higher level of emotional intelligence for adolescent boys as compared to girls' (Mishra & Ranjan, 2008), while other studies have reported a 'lower self-esteem among adolescent girls' (Baya et al., 2016).

Adolescent Girls in the Indian Context

While considering the phase of adolescence, it becomes imperative to consider the individual as situated in his/her culture. The person cannot be seen as acting separately from the context in which he/she is embedded. Therefore, in the Indian context, while gaining independence might be a characteristic feature of the stage of adolescence, such independence cannot be seen as overpowering over the interdependence that is found to be dominating across the varied subcultures of India.

Adolescence is a phase of exploration and one where an individual strives towards development of one's identity. The challenges that an individual is faced with during this phase have been well studied in the Indian context. It can be expected that recognizing these challenges is likely to help understand and develop ways for navigating through them and securing optimum development. Furthermore, young persons are the future of the country, and thus their own well-being first and foremost becomes important. A significant amount of literature in the Indian context has therefore focused on understanding the phase of adolescence and has focused on different aspects. While some studies have narrowed their focus and have considered more specific factors, such as the overall health, nutritional status and reproductive health of adolescent girls, other studies have focused on understanding the varied factors leading to possible vulnerability, as well as the factors that promote the development of resilience.

De (2017) in her research study highlighted the importance of an increased awareness around the nutritional needs of adolescent girls during this phase. The role of the sociocultural context on the development and growth of adolescents has also been highlighted in this context. Chandrakumari et al. (2019) highlighted in their research study carried out in Tamil Nadu that the development of anaemia is linked to the socio-economic status of an individual. Omidvar et al. (2018) suggested through their work that schools must take the initiative for designing sexual education programmes to aid adolescent girls and help develop adequate knowledge around menstrual health.

Other studies have focused on the impact of environmental or contextual factors. Researchers Chaplin and Kalita (n.d.) highlighted through their work the experiences of violence faced by adolescent girls residing in slum dwellings in the Indian capital city, Delhi. These were found to be caused due to the spatial constraints of the slum dwellings, which lack sufficient area for the construction of not just independent washrooms for the different households but also common public washrooms. Venturing into open spaces thus creates anxiety and concern in the minds of women, who have to leave their homes with a constant fear and the probability of being attacked. This problem was further found to be strengthened by the lack of responsibility by any member to bring about an improvement in the given situation, whether the sanitation situation or the security situation, with the latter being dependent on the former.

Vulnerability Leading to Resilience

Facing difficult challenges during the course of life may possibly be expected to pave the path for the development of resilience in individuals. The period of adolescence, which is accompanied by myriad changes, may make adolescents vulnerable, and the same has significantly been highlighted through past literature. For instance, as highlighted by authors, a number of adolescents have been found to develop body image concerns during this stage. Such concerns have been well documented by the researchers such as Ashikali et al. (2014), who showed that adolescents' exposure to certain programmes promoting bringing unnatural changes to one's body gave rise to body image concerns. As often cited in adolescent literature, parental relations are extremely important for an adolescent, as they helps develop a positive sense of who one is. Poor relations have been indicated by researchers as having negative effects on self-esteem, with authoritarian parenting showing similar effects (Yaacob, 2006). Being compared with other individuals of the same age, as well as lack of communication with parents, can also prove to be challenging. The vital role of communication with parents has been highlighted by a number of studies in the past. Communication promotes mutuality in the relation in terms of deciding rules, discussing concerns and problems, etc. (Lee, 2009). It is perhaps also likely to foster trust between members. Lack of communication is thus likely to create a distance, often an emotional one, and adds to the existing problems of an adolescent. A significant amount of studies have maintained the focus on challenges faced specifically by adolescent girls and have brought to light the issues such as safety concerns, absence of positive role models, body image concerns, gender discrimination, education- or career-related concerns, peer pressure, etc. (Kuruvilla & Nisha, 2015).

Fergus and Zimmerman (2005) have highlighted that resilience develops when an individual is exposed to risks but is also equipped with certain protective factors. Hence, despite being subject to vulnerable conditions, resilience can develop. The protective factors may be the strengths of the individual or may be factors defining the context. The bio-psychosocial framework also helps understand how there are unique contributory factors that lead to the shaping of an individual. One's unique biology, internal strengths and social support systems can be expected to influence the development of individuals, as well as their response to different life situations. Azam (2012) also highlighted that the school and home environment influence the development and growth of adolescents. These two domains serve as important support networks. Hence, an environment that fosters care is likely to aid in promoting positive growth and development.

Another line of research has focused on adolescents residing in slum dwellings, as living in a slum dwelling is marked by different challenges ranging from financial instability and lack of resources to an altogether different cultural and social environment often accompanied by traditional and stringent or restricting norms. It has been found that the number of unauthorized dwellings, and thus the associated challenges and struggles, are growing each year across the globe (Mahabir et al., 2016). These have also been stated as growing at a significantly steady rate. Many of these are urban slums, finding place in modern cities. Often behind or adjacent to high-rise buildings and structures equipped with all modern facilities, there are these growing slums where each day presents a new challenge. India too is one country where such a reality exists. Our country is witnessing a constant rise in the influx of people, but currently it seems to be unable to cater to the needs of all, thus resulting in the development of such squatter settlements.

Not only does the growth of slum dwellings impacts humans, but its effects also span to encompass the environment. It is challenging for humans, as they have to face the fear of abandonment and displacement and are challenged by the poor and often distressing living conditions (Napier, 2007). Such challenges have been well documented over the years. A 2015 survey on urban slums in Delhi highlighted the glaring facts and realities of urban slums in Delhi. The problems like 'lack of adequate washroom facilities and sanitation related concerns' were brought to focus (Government of National Capital Territory of Delhi, 2015). These challenges can either hinder positive growth or pave the way for the development of resilience. Given the same, a narrowed research focus has aided in highlighting the life of adolescents residing in slum dwellings.

One such study focused on adolescent girls residing in slum dwellings in Jaipur. They were found to face a number of challenges. These have primarily been related to the lack of timely understanding and awareness of menstruation, whereby researchers have shown the hesitation in encouraging such discussions. The problem has been found to be due to not just lack of awareness but also lack of facilities and resources in the slum dwellings. The same thus often gives rise to inadequate knowledge, a feeling of shame over this natural biological process, hiding of any difficulties in managing menstruation and related concerns and often the development of related health outcomes (Rajgopal & Mathur, 2017).

Kabiru et al. (2013) in their study found that adolescents living in slum dwellings are exposed to a challenging environment. In recent years, researchers have also shown that for adolescent girls, security is a matter of major concern, with fear of violence impeding their sense of safety (Kabiru et al., 2017). Sexual harassment is also a threat that narratives on adolescents have revealed. Researchers have also explained how the same hampers their motivation to succeed, thus highlighting increased vulnerability.

Suha and Haque (2013) reported that the increased degradation of environmental health is leading to poor health of adolescent girls, in turn affecting their capabilities in Tejgaon Railgate Slum, Dhaka, Bangladesh. Scorgie et al. (2017) have also brought to focus similar experiences in urban slums in South Africa, along with uncovering the glaring reality of the home being one of the most unsafe spaces for adolescent girls, as the above threat impedes the confines of home more than the outside world. The researchers also reported that concerns of violence due to a family member's abuse of alcohol were more prominent for girls as compared to boys. The effect of a financial crunch was also more prominent for girls as compared to boys, largely because the education of girls is compromised in such scenarios, who also at times fail to find positive role models to emulate in the home setting. Responsibility for household chores is also mostly placed on girls, who lack independence when compared to male adolescents (Scorgie et al., 2017).

Although the vulnerabilities of the adolescent stage have been highlighted in a considerable amount of studies, the literature has also indicated that this stage can have positive outcomes as well, such as adolescents reaching the stage of becoming independent (Greenfield et al., 2003). A synthesis of individual resilience and external environmental support can help the adolescent child blossom into an independent, mature and responsible adult. External support includes support in the form of close family ties, closeness with at least one parent, having an adult to confide in—all of which have been found to help foster resilience (Grossman et al., 1992). The literature has shown not merely the role of the family in promoting resilience but also the role of communities and the nature of interactions therein (Turliuc et al., 2013).

Thus, researchers have shown that despite the harsh lived realities, the adolescents try to look for opportunities to excel and grow. Factors in the environment, like social support, aid in the development of their resilience (e.g., Kabiru et al., 2013). Having social support, honing talents and developing an interest in activities, along with having a high achievement orientation, are likely to aid in fostering resilience. Given that the sociocultural context plays a major role in the development of resilience in young adolescent girls, it becomes imperative to understand the risk, as well as the protective, factors that form part of an urban slum context. Such studies also have implications for the development of interventions, as well as for policymaking, to improve the current status.

ADOLESCENT GIRLS RESIDING IN SLUM DWELLINGS IN DELHI: AN ANALYSIS

The current study was oriented towards understanding the experience of vulnerability and resilience in adolescent girls residing in urban slums in Delhi. The entire process of data collection was carried out in the natural setting, that is, community visits were made to the residence of the participants. All participants selected for the study belonged to a slum dwelling in South Delhi. The same was a squatter settlement, that is, devoid of legal rights over the land upon which the houses had been constructed. Following the qualitative paradigm and adopting a mixed-method approach, in-depth interviews and focus group discussions were carried out. The participants were interviewed individually, and a few were also invited in small groups for group discussions. Ten adolescent girls aged between 15 and 19 years (mean age = 17 years) were selected from the said slum dwelling. They were residing with their parents and were unmarried. Further, all participants were enrolled in a regular school or were pursuing an undergraduate/higher education course in Delhi and had been residing in the current slum dwelling for a minimum period of 3 years. The participants were found to be living in small 1–2 room houses, with the living space being limited to approximately 25 square yards. Each family comprised around five to eight members, with an annual income of approximately US $3,000. Access to basic household amenities, like drinking water, electricity, etc., was found to be present.

The research followed a multi-method approach to understand the experiences of the adolescents in detail. The study began with a thorough review of literature, based on which a semi-structured interview schedule was developed. The schedule was prepared to obtain an in-depth understanding of the experiences of the adolescent girls. The main points of inquiry included experiences across all major domains that can potentially play a role in shaping an individual, including family, peers, schooling, neighbourhood, body image, access to modern resources, etc. The adolescents were probed on the same areas, as part of the focus group discussions. Additionally, the level of awareness the participants possessed of their own developmental trajectory was briefly explored. Post the completion of the interview schedule, the researcher entered the field to gather qualitative data. The process of collecting data was spread over a period of 2 months. The participants were met in their respective slum dwellings. The duration of each interview ranged between 35 and 60 minutes (approximately).

Additionally, a few participants were met in small groups for the focus group discussions. The same were conducted with the aim of bringing forth the differing opinions and experiences of the participants, as well as to identify the converging point between their views. The discussion also provided a space to the adolescent girls to voice their opinions regarding the kind of challenges they experienced in their area of residence. The interviews and group discussions were audio-recorded, post taking consent from the participants. They were thanked for their valuable time and cooperation. After the data collection process was completed, thematic analysis was used as the method of analysis to understand their experiences of resilience and vulnerability.

The method of analysis selected for the current study was thematic analysis, which is a frequently used method of analysis for qualitative research and lends itself well to the understanding of data collected through the process of informal interviewing. It was used to identify the recurrent patterns emerging from the data. The current study adopted the six-step approach provided by Braun and Clarke (2006), which included 'familiarization with the data, generation of initial codes, searching for themes, reviewing themes, defining and naming the themes and finally producing the report'. The themes emerged from the interviews conducted with the participants and were not based on or guided by any prior theory. The themes thus obtained were looked at and explained holistically. In order to tap the nuances of the data, it was ascertained that each participant's voice was considered while the attempt was made to understand the data. The following section presents the themes generated from the interviews with the participants. All themes (as highlighted in Table 11.1) culled out have been explained holistically and supported with narratives and expressions from the interviews. The following section comprises the themes, first those highlighting the experience of vulnerability, followed by the themes highlighting the experience of resilience, both as experienced by the participants.

Barriers in Career Path

A salient theme emerging from the participant's narratives centred on the uncertainty of their career. Most participants opined on various

Table 11.1 *Themes Pertaining to Experience of Vulnerability*

Themes Related to Vulnerability
1. Barriers in career path
2. Apprehensions over probable future displacement
3. Apprehensions over finding the right life partner
4. Barriers in social relationships
5. Feelings of unsafety and insecurity
6. Feelings of marginalization and coping with the mainstream

Source: Babu and Sethi (2018).

perceived barriers on their way to success and development of self-sufficiency, yet the exact nature of these barriers differed among the different participants. While for some participants the barriers were restricted to personal challenges or limitations, others expressed financial barriers or the lack of family acceptance of their choice of career as a viable option. Given the contribution of their parents towards their growth through battling all odds and dealing with myriad challenges, the daughters felt responsible to provide for them in the future. Hence, their aspirations in this domain attained supremacy over other aspects of life. Any perceived barrier in this area hence seemed to act as a major threat for the participants. High meaning seemed to be attached to education by not just the adolescent girls but also by their parents, who seemed to struggle to provide for all academic needs, making the financial instability as invisible to their daughters as possible. For one participant, however, it was rather visible, especially owing to the recent loss of her father's job due to his drinking habit. She expressed, '*Mere ko aise lag nahi raha ke doctor bann paaoongi. Paise ki waise hi wo hora hai*' (I feel that I wouldn't be able to become a doctor…because of the financial constraints). Nonetheless, her achievement orientation seemed to be driving her towards achieving success through considering an alternative option of dance. Along with another participant, she expressed how the same might pose difficulties due to the generation gap between her and a few family members who did not consider this as a viable career option. Additionally, a participant spoke of her lost aspiration of becoming an air hostess owing to not having studied English in the 12th grade. It was learnt through the interviews that although such goal orientation is encouraging, it is not devoid of challenges.

Apprehensions over Probable Future Displacement

One of the major concerns affecting the participants stemmed from their knowledge that their slum dwelling was an unauthorized colony. They seemed to possess the knowledge of how each penny had been saved by their parents or forefathers in order to construct these houses. Given their current financial condition characterized by instability, and the lack of an alternate place to live in, a constant fear related to the impermanence of their residence lurked in the minds of the participants. One participant mentioned how she had witnessed houses being brought down in her vicinity and feared the future probability of losing her own. Moving to a new and modern city is often associated with a number of push and pull factors. The presence of greater opportunities and a more modern outlook perhaps tied the participants closer to the city as compared to the village. Thus the fear of dislocation or displacement seemed to be omnipresent. Another intriguing aspect was put forth by one participant who expressed her fear of losing the community bonding.

Apprehensions over Finding the Right Life Partner

The goal-oriented behaviour of the participants and the aspiration to achieve were found to be given greatest importance and priority by the adolescents. Nonetheless, concerns with respect to marriage were found to be existent, owing to marriage being a major milestone and especially an imperative one in the sociocultural context of a slum dwelling. One participant, for instance, indicated that she was worried about a relatively early marriage, as her sister had been through the same. Elaborating on it, she explained that in order to reduce the financial burden and buy an independent house, her parents were willing to marry her off early. Another participant expressed her underlying fear regarding finding a life partner, who mentioned, '*main darti hoon ki koi aisa insaan na aa jaaye life mein jo bahut hi aisa hota hai na ki mera…mera bhala nahi hoga toh main tera bhala bhi nahi hone doonga'* (I am scared over the possible entry of such an individual in my life who is very…like…if I can't succeed, I will not let you succeed'). The need to reach a stage of maturity before marriage was also expressed by one participant. Further, the participants seemed to possess an idea of the adequate age when a girl should marry. Although participants differed in their opinion, they did seem to agree with the idea that marriage should not be forced upon the female and that it is better to first settle down in one's career.

Barriers in Social Relationships

The current factor, operating as a challenge, was another found dominantly across interviews, yet once again the exact nature of these barriers differed. This salient theme thus subsumed a number of subthemes within its fold, spreading across social relations in the community to those in the family domain. With respect to the community, a number of participants expressed being affected by the interference caused by the community members. The same often seemed to have roots in the traditional notions held by the members of the community, especially the image of an ideal female child. A number of participants indicated the interference of the community members, such as through discouraging higher education of the girl child or through questioning a female child's use of the mobile phone.

A prominent sub-theme highlighted the experience of gender discrimination, owing to which the adolescent girls had to assume adult responsibility at a young age, especially related to performing household chores. The same also meant balancing academic work with such responsibilities. It was interesting to note that the same seemed to operate explicitly when such expectations or comparisons between the male and female child were voiced by the family members (*Kehte hain ki 'tu ladki hai, tereko karna perega. Wo ladka hai, usko nahi karna parega'* [They say that you are a girl, you will have to perform household chores. He is a boy, he will not have to]); at other times they were rather subtle. Additionally, a few participants spoke of the strains in the varied relations. These ranged from those due to existing generation gaps, for example, a grandparent restricting the choice of clothing, to sensing a lack of freedom from the parents. One participant highlighted her father's drinking habit that became the cause of frequent parental fights and harassment. The dwindling strength of the relation she shared with him was also expressed by her. Such aspects of relations seemed to be evident across the participants, be they close family ties or ties with extended members of the community.

Feelings of Unsafety and Insecurity

Another salient theme found across nearly all narratives pertained to the lack of safety experienced in the slum dwelling. Nearly all participants indicated that their immediate area provided a safe space while the neighbouring area posed a major threat to their sense of security, thus often binding them to their house at night time. Given the lack of an independent washroom in most homes, this problem increases in intensity, as access to the public washroom at night means facing an unsafe atmosphere created by outside entrants who seem to have created a drinking culture at night. Hence, the resultant fear or threat of eve-teasing becomes a major safety issue. Further, although the participants did not reveal any first-hand account of such victimization, they did express the fear related to the same, which does seem to curb their independence.

Feelings of Marginalization and Coping with the Mainstream

A few participants interviewed expressed a fear of being marginalized by the community. The need for peer acceptance was evident in the narratives of the adolescent girls interviewed for the current study, along with which came an underlying fear of being marginalized or being rejected as an outcast by the mainstream. The same seemed to place the burden of coping with the mainstream and becoming part of it while belonging to an altogether different socio cultural environment. The same was found to lead participants to keep knowledge of their place of residence hidden from their peers, perhaps reflecting an underlying sense of shame stemming from residing in a slum set-up.

An interesting insight was brought forth by another participant who did not fear marginalization per se but showed a resultant fear of receiving sympathy from others, or being seen as different from the rest in the event of her revealing her place of residence. Coping with the mainstream thus presented a major challenge, as it also perhaps involved underlying feelings of inferiority. The upcoming section will expand upon the themes highlighting the experience of resilience (Table 11.2).

Self-determination

The theme of self-determination, which is indicative of resilience, was found to run across all narratives. The participants were found to be driven by an internal and personal need to succeed. Despite the harsh living conditions and family difficulties that could function as possible barriers and blocks, they seemed to work through the challenges and limitations. Two primary sub-themes were revealed by the thematic analysis. The first pertained to the presence of self-regulatory behaviour, that is, the participants possessed the ability to observe, evaluate and exercise control over their behaviour. They were found to not only have an adequate knowledge of their strengths and weaknesses but also operate one step ahead of simply possessing self-awareness, that is, through engaging in self-monitoring. They were found to bring about required and necessary changes to reverse their limitations. For instance, a few participants verbalized their desire to improve in facing their academic challenges. The desire to improve academically

Table 11.2 *Themes Pertaining to Experience of Resilience*

Themes Related to Resilience
1. Self-determination
2. Reception of family support
3. Futuristic orientation
4. Community connectedness
5. Access to information and opportunities

Source: Babu and Sethi (2018).

was expressed by one participant as: '*apni English ko well-spoken karni hai*' (I have to improve my command over the English language). The same highlights how participants seemed to be aware that focusing on improving one's weakness is also vital, as it is likely to open up greater opportunities. Participants also seemed sensitive to the need to bring about an optimum balance between family expectations of assuming adult responsibilities, on the one hand, and the need to manage their academic work, on the other.

The second sub-theme derived from nearly all narratives was the intrinsic motivation that guided the participants and fuelled their efforts towards success. Living under such harsh conditions, the participants were found to be not just surviving but also attempting to thrive. The expressions like '*Bas ab yahi soch rakha hai ki kuch acha banna hai. Gharwaalon ka naam raushan karna hai*' (I have thought that now I have to do well in life. I have to make my family proud) highlight the internal psychological need of the participants to succeed rather than motivation from an external agent. The effort they put towards academics was seen as being internally satisfying and internally energizing. '*Life mein akele hi aage jaana hai*' (We have to tread the path of life alone) also beautifully sums up the same. A few participants also stated recognizing the essential role self-confidence plays in fulfilling one's dreams. It was also interesting to note that external demoralization too did not seem to interfere in the participants' desire to achieve. Rather, at times, it seemed to be interpreted by the participants as another motivating factor.

Reception of Family Support

The second major theme found to be consistent across interactions with participants related to the family unit as a major provider of strength. The dynamism and complexity of the relation shared with parents was reflected in each voice. The process of constructing and reconstructing the relation, constantly trying to make sense of the vast dynamics, became evident through not just the descriptions presented by the participants but also the shift in emotions at the time of interviewing, from a laugh on reminiscing positive moments to pauses and silence while reflecting on challenges. In the current study, complexity was captured in myriad ways. Despite such a multitude of existent emotions, the family unit, especially the parents, was found to function as an external factor contributing to the experience of resilience among the adolescent girls. Although this stage is associated with a growing need for independence and needs coming to be differently defined, most parents were found to be supportive of these needs. In a culture where traditional norms, often those inhibiting the girl child, prevail, the parents seemed to adopt a more modern outlook, hence bridging the barrier of generation gap. Given the near margins on which the families were surviving, where even certainty over the permanence of one's place of residence was absent, the parents seemed to financially support their children in all matters of education. Under circumstances of lack of money, they were found to rather compromise on other needs but rarely on educational or academic needs. One participant proclaimed how her mother was breaking all barriers and facing challenges to earn for the family since her father lost his job owing to his drinking habit. Despite disliking her job of providing household help, her mother continued for keeping the family intact. It was also noted that no difference in the education of male or female children was observed in nearly all the families considered.

Family support was not merely confined to the fulfilment of material or financial needs but rather extended to subsume and encompass other important needs, like those of providing emotional support to the adolescents. The family seemed to function as a pillar of emotional strength and provided an atmosphere of growth and enrichment. Hence, the parents were found to be contributing to their growing resilience, shaping and moulding them into potentially independent, competent and self-sufficient young women.

Futuristic Orientation

The futuristic orientation of the participants was found to exist at three levels: at the level of their own personal education and career; with respect to the desires they held for their family; and their desire to take initiative to bring about positive changes in their environment. The first encompassed both envisioning goals and engaging in goal-oriented behaviour, as well as the making attempts to attain self-sufficiency. All the participants aspired for higher education, and most had specific, attainable and measurable goals in mind, towards which they were found to be working. For instance, having completed her schooling and coaching, one participant was now preparing for her engineering entrances. The participants were found to have reached the stage where they were narrowing their career options and choosing between potential career options. They further seemed to be considering and developing sensitivity towards the other barriers that could come in the way of selecting a particular career path. For instance, one participant juggled between the desire to be a doctor and a dancer, owing to the financial constraints that could possibly interfere in the path of becoming a successful doctor. Other challenges, like the extended family's disapproval of dance as a viable career option, were also considered by her. The participants also expressed their aspiration to attain self-sufficiency and stand on their own feet rather than developing a dependence on others. This was especially shared in the context of prioritizing settling down in their career over marriage, so as to not be supressed.

With respect to the second level, the participants expressed an eagerness to enrich the relation that they shared with their parents, which additionally highlighted their perception of the relation as being characterized by reciprocity. The participants were found to acknowledge all that their parents had and continued to do for them despite the odds of their own life. Some participants expressed this in the form of the desire to provide their parents a comfortable life, a life in complete contrast to the prevailing hardships. Hence, perhaps they viewed the relation as ideally involving an investment from both ends, not only in financial terms but also, and more so, in terms of reciprocal emotional sharing. It was also observed that perhaps with this goal in mind, they seemed to remain high on achievement motivation and made efforts to achieve success in their education. Another domain where the participants maintained a futuristic orientation involved envisioning taking the initiative to eradicate existing problems in the slum dwelling. The same ranged from bringing about a change in the attitudes of the dwellers to managing the near water crisis, ensuring cleanliness, etc. This sense of responsibility towards the community was a probable result of the feeling of connectedness felt by the participants with other members of the dwelling.

Community Connectedness

In the event that the immediate family dynamics were found to be disturbed, the participants seemed to turn outwards. Being able to locate themselves within a community characterized by connectedness between the members facilitated the same. Hence, support not just stemmed from the family environment but could also be found beyond it. The same found space in nearly all narratives. Very few participants indicated feeling a lack of connect with the community; however, these largely found the same to stem from their own personal reasons. For instance, one participant acknowledged that a period of 3 years spent in the current slum dwelling could not ensure full faith in the community. Nonetheless, the majority of the participants indicated the presence of community bonding. Although fights among members were reported by nearly all participants and seemed to be a daily affair, the support provided to each other during stressful times seemed to overpower the same. Hence, this form of support, through the narratives of the participants, can be conceptualized as a protective factor.

Access to Information and Opportunities

Being part of the modern-day city, the participants were found to be making attempts to keep pace with the mainstream advances, despite the financial instability. Many of the participants indicated having access to either a mobile phone of their own or that of a family member.

Access to technology, and therefore to the dissemination of information through this platform, was thus found to be existent. The same allows participants' access to important academic information that is circulated by their school teachers through the modern-day applications like WhatsApp. While for some the desire to own a mobile phone stemmed from the need for access to such information, for others the same was important to maintain contact with their friends through social media platforms, like Facebook. It was interesting to note that the initiation of the use of such applications was not a result of peer pressure; rather, it was often a matter of desire for exploration of social media networks, as they are highly talked and heard about.

The results of the study highlight the experience of vulnerability and resilience of adolescent girls as embedded in the urban slum set-up. The participants' narratives are reflective of the challenges faced by them due to entering the phase of adolescence, while simultaneously bringing forth a developing understanding of the myriad ways in which these challenges become manifold when located in the sociocultural context of a slum dwelling. The practices existent in the sociocultural context of a slum dwelling seem to manifest as a 'culture' with its own norms and values, differing at times from the other sub-cultures of the capital city, and at other times merging with the more mainstream culture.

Adolescence has been recognized as a challenging and complex phase (Kuruvilla & Nisha, 2015), and such challenges have also been highlighted in the current study. Additionally, as research has indicated the power of resilience in turning challenges into opportunities, the current study's participants too seemed to be making attempts to navigate this stage in a way akin to those highlighted in a previous study (Greenfield et al., 2003). Their identity seems to be in the process of being moulded and shaped by their response of strength, resilience and hardiness in the face of much-evident stress in their life. Further, akin to the way Erik Erikson has conceptualized this stage as one of 'exploration' and 'psychosocial moratorium', the current study's adolescent girls have also been found to be engaged in making sense of their life circumstances and exploring aspects of their identity, such as career identity, family identity and community identity. The same can be expected to lead to the establishment of a coherent self-understanding, given that they are able to continue their movement across the barriers that they are currently faced with. It was interesting to note the unfolding of the complexities of human life through the narratives of the participants, especially the way in which the same factors took the form of probable risks for some participants and served a more protective role for others. Adding to the complexity, the analysis of the data also revealed that aspects of the same domain at instances seemed to protect the adolescents and at other instances, seemed to function as a risk factor. This was especially evident in the family domain, where the parents' financial aid added to the growing self-sufficiency of the daughter, whereas the lack of felt freedom and perceived gender discrimination added to their growing vulnerability. This also highlighted the importance of the microsystem in the growth and development of the adolescent.

Acknowledging the same, the above vulnerability needs be seen in light of this unique stage of adolescence where an adolescent is known to separate the self from the parents in order to establish an independent sense of identity. Penington (2003), for instance, mentioned that striving to attain independence, the adolescent often starts moving away from the rules set by her mother, with the resultant being her moving away from the mother herself and seeing the latter as someone undesirably present in the different domains of life.

For the current participants, the factors like lack of communication with the parents seem to be challenging, which have also found space in past research. Lee (2009), for instance, recognized the vital role of communication with one's parents. As indicated by the author, such a concern is likely to create an emotional distance with one's parents. The same was voiced in a number of current interviews. Although the lack of communication could also have been a result of other challenges in the family set-up, such as an existing generation gap, differential treatment of siblings or other concerns, like a parent's drinking habit, it could also be a possible result of perceived 'psychological control' (Aunola & Nurmi, 2005), a characteristic especially unique to the phase of adolescence.

Another major challenge witnessed in the family domain pertained to the experience of gender discrimination, which was voiced by a number of participants. The majority of the participants opined that they were expected to assume responsibility of the household chores while their brothers were not. Even communicating the concern to the parents did not lead to any changes in the gender role ideas. This is also likely since gender role perceptions have been found to be relatively fixed once formed. Kohlberg (1966) also stated that with increased age, 'gender constancy and fixed ideas of the roles expected come to be formed'. Thus, these perhaps become well ingrained into the adolescents' own personal systems. The same is also in line with the 'gender schema theory' (Bem, 1981).

Although the daughters were trying to break the barriers now that they were exposed to the more modern lifestyle of Delhi, these ideas were perhaps deep-rooted somewhere, and hence they confided to taking up household responsibilities and other gender-specific roles. Mensch et al. (2003) also indicated that as girls enter this stage, they begin to develop ideas of what can be conceptualized as appropriate behaviour and begin to develop an understanding of stereotypical thinking prevalent in society. Concerns, like those of unsafety and insecurity, also become more pronounced at this stage. Concerns of insecurity over eve-teasing have been pointed out in past literature as well (e.g. Leaper & Brown, 2008). Scorgie et al. (2017) also brought to focus experiences of urban slums in South Africa, uncovering the glaring reality of the home being one of the most unsafe spaces for adolescent girls. As also indicated by the researchers in the current study too, the responsibility for household chores was mostly placed on the girls, who seemed to lack independence when compared to their male counterparts (Scorgie et al., 2017).

Although the families of the adolescents have moved to a modern city in search of greater opportunities, restrictions continue to exist, as they continue to carry the traditional norms with them which often restrict the female. The same is further coupled with the already prevailing ideas of gender role assignment in the modern city. The factors like financial instability also visibly play a role in adding to the vulnerability. It is also imperative to look at the same in the light of Indian culture. In many parts of India, non-egalitarian ideas continue to exist, especially in the more traditional areas. Many of the participants hailed from such traditional areas and hence perhaps carried these ideas with them. It is possible that in this crucial stage, the negative effects and consequences of gender-based norms begin to slowly impede their lives and start becoming more and more visible, thus coming to be questioned.

Given the number of challenges witnessed in the domain of the family, the adolescents were found to turn outwards, either to their community or to their peer group. As cited in adolescent research literature (e.g., Steinberg & Monahan, 2007), adolescents become closer to their peer group, which arises from a need for belonging at a time when the individual is distancing the self from other caregivers, like parents. Given the supremacy of the peer group, and perhaps owing to a perceived inferiority, the participants preferred to keep their residence hidden from their peer group, thus attempting to adjust to the mainstream.

It was additionally noted that although the risk factors in the family domain were well recognized, the family also was found to act as a supportive network. A safe space is found to be created not only by the belief that the parent is physically close to the adolescent but also, and more so, by the belief that every time the adolescent slips, the parent would be there to pick her up (Kerr et al., 2003). The same is also likely to provide a buffer to reciprocity. The current study's participants realized the efforts of their parents towards their growth.

CONCLUSION

The study highlighted experiences of both vulnerability and resilience, seen as tied together in a complex web, either exerting its influence on the other. Despite the numerous challenges that the adolescent girls faced, there was hope and optimism in their voices. The study calls for changes that need to be brought in the family systems, as well as in the larger society, to make full use of the human capital that these adolescents are for the country, and more so to make their lives less challenging. It also has serious implications for the development of policies to better the existing state of slums in Delhi and make the lives of adolescent girls less challenging, thus allowing them to invest their energy, both physical and mental, into activities that enable their positive growth and development. The results also call for the development of appropriate interventions, once again for the betterment of the life of the adolescent.

The first step of intervention must include spreading awareness regarding the need for gender equality and educating the family members on the importance and capabilities of the female child. Several authors have proposed that facing gender inequality or perceiving such discrimination is likely to impact the adolescent female negatively, while perceived equality and support is likely to lead to encouraging outcomes, like academic success (Zysk, 2006). A number of policies and schemes have been proposed for the same in Delhi, like the Ladli scheme (Department of Women and Child Development, 2008). Although such policies exist, the interviews highlight that the participants were not quite aware of the schemes. Hence, strengthening awareness of these policies and on how to avail the benefits of these schemes can prove to be beneficial and is imperative. The study also has implications for spreading awareness about healthy adolescent development and the developmental trajectory that entails moving from childhood to adolescence. Family interventions can also be one area where efforts can be made to help counter the concerns in family relations. These can also possibly take the form of training programmes for parents. Interacting with adolescents around the need for healthy communication with their family members and understanding their views and positions, and remaining sensitive to the same, are also suggested. Further, the difficulties that come with residing in a slum dwelling, be they economic or social, call for change at a larger level.

The study also dispels the often cited idea that resilience is solely an innate capacity to 'bounce back'; it highlights how resilience is given impetus by the sociocultural factors like the amount of support available, quality of relations, etc. Future research should also endeavour to take into consideration the perspectives of adolescent boys and the nature of the challenges they experience. It should also focus on combatting the drawbacks of the current study, like through selecting a larger sample size and becoming immersed in the culture of the participants to capture their experiences in greater depth, thus making the process of development of policies and interventions more directed and goal-driven.

REFERENCES

Ashikali, E. M., Dittmar, H., & Ayers, S. (2014). The effect of cosmetic surgery reality TV shows on adolescent girls' body image. *Psychology of Popular Media Culture, 3*(3), 141–153.

Aunola, K., & Nurmi, J. (2005). The role of parenting styles in children's problem behavior. *Child Development, 76*(6), 1144–1159.

Azam, S. A. (2012). Resilience among adolescent girls in India: Role of home and school protective factors. *Journal of Educational and Psychological Studies, 6*(3), 45–56.

Babu, N., & Sethi., V (2018). *Exploring the Mother-Daughter Relationship in the Socio-cultural context of a slum Dwelling.* Voices of Mothers and their Adolescent daughters. (Unpublished doctoral dissertation). University of Delhi, India.

Baya, D. G., Mendoza, R., & Paino, S. (2016). Emotional basis of gender differences in adolescent self-esteem. *Journal of the Portuguese Association, 30*(2), 1–14.

Bem, S. L. (1981). Gender schema theory: A cognitive account of sex typing. *Psychological Review, 88,* 354–364.

Braun, V., & Clarke, V. (2006). Using thematic analysis in psychology. *Qualitative Research in Psychology, 3*(2), 77–201.

Chandrakumari, A. S., Sinha, P., Singaravelu, S., & Jaikumar, S. (2019). Prevalence of anemia among adolescent girls in a rural area of Tamil Nadu, India. *Journal of Family Medicine and Primary Care, 8,* 1414–1417.

Chaplin, S. E., & Kalita, R. (n.d.). *Infrastructure, gender and violence: Women and slum sanitation inequalities in Delhi.* Centre for Policy Research.

De, K. (2017). Study of bio-social behaviour of rural adolescent girls. *Journal of Community and Public Health Nursing, 3,* 172. https://doi.org/10.4172/2471-9846.1000172

Department of Women and Child Development. (2008). *Delhi Ladli scheme.* http://www.wcddel.in/streesakti_3Ladli.html.

Erikson, E. H. (1968). *Identity: Youth and crisis.* Norton.

Fergus, S., & Zimmerman, M. A. (2005). Adolescent resilience: A framework for understanding healthy development in the face of risk. *Annual Review of Public Health, 26,* 399–419.

Flook, L. (2011). Gender differences in adolescents' daily interpersonal events and well-being. *Child Development, 82*(2), 454–461.

Government of National Capital Territory of Delhi. (2015). *Urban slums in Delhi.* http://www.indiaenvironmentportal.org.in/files/file/urban%20slums%20in%20delhi.pdf

Greenfield, P. M., Keller, H., Fuligni, A., & Maynard, A. (2003). Cultural pathways through universal development. *Annual Review of Psychology, 54,* 461–490.

Grossman, F. K., Beinashowitz, J., Anderson, L., Sakurai, M., Finnin, I., & Flaherty, M. (1992). Risk and resilience in young adolescents. *Journal of Youth and Adolescence, 21*(5), 529–550.

Hankin, B. L., Mermelstein, R., & Roesch, L. (2007). Sex differences in adolescent depression: Stress exposure and reactivity models. *Child Development, 78,* 279–295.

Kabiru, C. W., Mojola, S. A., Beguy, D., & Okigbu, C. (2013). Growing up at the 'margins': Concerns, aspirations, and expectations of young people living in Nairobi's slums. *Journal of Research on Adolescence, 23*(1), 81–94.

Kabiru, C. W., Mumah, J. N., Maina, B. W., & Abuya, B. A. (2017). Violence victimization and aspirations-expectations disjunction among adolescent girls in urban Kenya. *International Journal of Adolescence and Youth.* https://doi.org/10.1080/02673843.2017.1345769

Kerr, M., Stattin, H., Biesecker, G., & Wreder, L. F. (2003). Relationships with parents & peer in adolescence. In B. I. Weiner & K. D. Freedheim (Eds.), *Handbook of psychology, developmental psychology* (pp. 394–412). Wiley.

Kohlberg, L. (1966). A cognitive-developmental analysis of children's sex-role concepts and attitudes. In E. E. Maccoby (Ed.), *The development of sex differences* (pp. 82–173). Stanford University Press.

Kuruvilla, M., & Nisha, P. (2015). Challenges faced by adolescent girls in the Indian context. *International Journal of Current Research, 7*(12), 23821–23829.

Leaper, C., & Brown, C. S. (2008). Perceived experiences with sexism among adolescent girls. *Child Development, 79*, 685–704.

Lee, S. S. (2009). School, parents, and peer factors in relation to Hong Kong students' bullying. *International Journal of Adolescence and Youth, 15*, 217–233.

Mahabir, R., Crooks, A., Croitoru, A., & Agouris, P. (2016). The study of slums as social and physical constructs: Challenges and emerging research opportunities. *Regional Studies, Regional Science, 3*(1), 399–419.

Mensch, B. S., Ibrahim, B. L., Lee, M. S., & Gibaly, O. E. (2003). Gender-role attitudes among Egyptian adolescents. *Studies in Family Planning, 34*(1), 8–18.

Mishra, R., & Ranjan, P. (2008). Emotional intelligence as related to self-esteem of adolescents. *Indian Journal of Human Relation, 34*, 13–17.

Morris, A. S., Silk, J. S., Steinberg, L., Myers, S. S., & Robinson, L. R. (2007). The role of the family context in the development of emotion regulation. *Social Development, 16*(2), 361–368.

Napier, M. (2007). *Informal settlement integration, the environment and sustainable livelihoods in Sub-Saharan Africa.* University of Montreal. http://www.grif.umontreal.ca/pages/i-rec%20papers/napier.pdf

Omidvar, S., Amiri, F. N., Bakhtiari, A., & Begum, K. (2018). A study on menstruation of Indian adolescent girls in an urban area of South India. *Journal of Family Medicine and Primary Care, 7*(4), 698–702.

Paul, B. K. (2006). Fear of eviction: The case of slum and squatter dwellers in Dhaka, Bangladesh. *Urban Geography, 27*(6), 567–574.

Penington, B. (2003). *Listening in mother-adolescent daughter relationships: A preliminary investigation into emergent themes using a multi-ethnic sample.* Paper presented at the annual meeting of the International Listening Association, July, 2003.

Piko, B. (2001). Gender differences and similarities in adolescents' ways of coping. *Psychological Record, 51*, 223–235.

Rajgopal, S., & Mathur, K. (2017). 'Breaking the silence around menstruation': Experiences of adolescent girls in an urban setting in India. *Gender and Development, 25*(2), 303–317.

Sati, L., & Gir, S. (2016). Emotional intelligence of late adolescent boys and girls belonging to nuclear family. *Journal of Humanities and Social Science, 21*(1), 37–40.

Scorgie, F., Baron, D., Stadler, J., Venables, E., Brahmbhatt, H., Mmari, K., & Moretlwe, S. D. (2017). From fear to resilience: Adolescents' experiences of violence in inner-city Johannesburg, South Africa. *BMC Public Health, 17*(3), 52–64.

Stafford, L., & Bayer, C. L. (1993). *Interaction between parents and children.* SAGE Publications.

Steinberg, L. (2014). *Age of opportunity: Lessons from the new science of adolescence.* Houghton Mifflin Harcourt.

Steinberg, L., & Monahan, K. C. (2007). Age differences in resistance to peer influence. *Developmental Psychology, 43*, 1531–1543.

Suha, S. M., & Haque, R. M. (2013). Adolescent girls in urban slum: Environmental health perspective. *The International Journal of Social Sciences, 9*(1), 91–103.

Turliuc, M. N., Mairean, C., & Danila, O. (2013). A multifaceted theory: Individual, family, and community resilience: A research review. In I. Rogobete & A. Neagoe (Eds.), *Contemporary issues facing families: An interdisciplinary dialogue* (pp. 33–53). Verlag fur Kultur und Wissenshaft (Culture and Science Publishing).

Wade, T. J., Cairney, J., & Pevalin, D. J. (2002). Emergence of gender differences in depression during adolescence: National panel results from three countries. *Journal of the American Academy of Child & Adolescent Psychiatry, 41*, 190–198.

World Health Organisation. (2018). *Adolescent health.* http://www.who.int/topics/adolescent_health/en/

Yaacob, M. J. B. (2006). Parent-adolescent relationships and its association to adolescents' self-esteem. *Malaysian Journal of Medical Sciences, 13*(1), 21–24.

Zysk, E. D. (2006). The significance of adolescents' relationships with significant others and school failure. *School Psychology International, 27*(2), 232–247.

Chapter 12

Managing Vulnerabilities of Institution Building and Organizational Change
The Role of Trust

Nidhi Prakash

INTRODUCTION

Institutions represent structural configurations in an organization, which are often taken for granted but have far-reaching impacts on the behaviours of members within the organization. Institutions help preserve stability, but at the same time they may also lead to obsolescence and possibly imminent chaos in the face of changing internal and external environments, particularly if the nature of these structural configurations are not dynamic. Organizations, therefore, can be vulnerable to a complex range of stability- and change-related issues in view of the institutions they represent.

One of the fundamental factors in maintaining these structural configurations and institutional practices, as well as successfully effecting change in organizational institutional arrangements, is 'trust'. This stems from the fact that many recent researches in the area of organizational psychology have found trust to have significant ramifications for a number of individual and organizational aspects, such as interpersonal relationships, intergroup behaviour (Insko et al., 1998), team management and leadership (Hasel & Grover, 2017), inter-firm interactions (Connelly et al., 2012; Lumineau, 2017), knowledge management (Hashim & Tan, 2015), innovation (Skard, 2017), organizational learning (Tirelli & Goh, 2015) and organizational effectiveness (Doney et al., 1998). These and many other researchers have paid greater attention to trust in the inter-personal context; however, the way trust interacts with the features and dynamics of organizational institutions, making them more vulnerable to change, is an area of notable importance which has remained unexplored. Therefore, trust, which is defined as a person's willingness to be vulnerable to others and 'openness to some kind of risks', and which can be related to the institutional organizational arrangements and vulnerabilities, is the subject of relevance which is examined in this chapter.

Thus, this chapter takes up a discussion on the process of institutionalization, followed by one on trust, vulnerability and institution-based trust in organizations and their interrelationships, and finally shares views on deinstitutionalization, organizational change and the institutional consequence of trust or the lack of it.

INSTITUTIONS AND INSTITUTIONALIZATION

'Institutions' are structures or structural arrangements that define normative patterns of individual and collective behaviour (Giddens, 1984) in an organization, community or society. They represent those rules of conduct, both formal rules and informal practices, which have acquired stability and legitimacy through being shared between and meaningful to the members of an organization (Bachmann & Inkpen, 2011).

On the other hand, 'institutionalization' refers to the set of processes that lead to the outcome called institution. Every institution fulfils two major functions: an objective function, through which the inherent rules are practised for the continuity of the organization, and a symbolic function, through which the consensual meaning and information about the organization is communicated to other members of the organization over and beyond what is explicitly stated (Meyer & Rowan, 1977).

According to Tolbert and Zucker (1996), three processes underlie the process of institutionalization. These are the process of 'habitualiza-tion', in which a particular pattern of behaviour is developed by the organizational actors to solve recurring problems, the process of 'objec-tification' in which behaviours associated with the problem-indicating stimuli are spontaneously enacted in response to those stimuli as the preferred course of action to resolve the impending situation (Tolbert & Zucker, 1996), and the process of 'sedimentation' in which the shared social meanings generated around the habitualized behaviours are transferred beyond the original contexts in which they were developed, becoming a fact, that is, an external reality that becomes independent of its original problem solving connotation. This exteriorized behaviour (Zucker, 1977) is then taken to the new entrants through the process of 'socialization' as a social given that is much contingent on the trust and vulnerabilities of the new entrants.

The process of institutionalization, thus, encompasses the process of 'legitimization' of a set of actions, practices or procedures, at the interpersonal, intergroup and organizational levels, which with repetition over time becomes the character of the organization. Legitimization, therefore, remains at the core of the institutionalization process, through which organizational structures, practices, policies and routines come to be accepted as inherent parts of the organizational culture (Oliver, 1992). Here, as per Berger and Luckmann (1966), the character of social interaction as a source of the norms and rules that define institutions and the interpersonal trust between the interactants is of paramount value.

TRUST AND VULNERABILITY IN ORGANIZATIONS

Trust Defined

The field of organizational behaviour has explored and understood 'trust' in multiple ways. Among the popular definitions of 'trust' is the one advanced by Mayer et al. (1995, p. 712), which explains trust as an 'unsaid contract' between two parties—the trustor and the trustee—where willingness of a party to be vulnerable to the actions of the other party based on the belief that the latter would reciprocate through performing an important and meaningful action for the trustor without monitoring or controlling them is of central value. Rousseau et al. (1998, p. 395), on the other hand, describe trust as 'a psychological state wherein a party is accepting of the vulnerabilities based on the positive expectations of a behaviour from the other party'. Fulmer and Gelfand (2012) identify two salient constructs in these and most other definitions of trust. These are: (a) positive expectations of trustworthiness, which is determined by three characteristics of the trustee—'ability', which is a domain-specific competence of the trustee, 'benevolence', through behaving in ways that are benign and harmless to the trustor by the trustee, and 'integrity' by the trustee through consistently adhering to principles and morals that appeal to the trustor (Mayer et al., 1995); and (b) willingness of the trustor to accept vulnerability, that is, willingness of the trustor to accept risks that are contingent on the trustor through their being dependent on the trustee. Thus, vulnerability is an important construct in understanding trust.

Vulnerability Defined

The term 'vulnerability' has its roots in the Latin term 'vulnerare', which means 'to hurt'. A person is said to be 'vulnerable' when he/she is susceptible or disposed to some kind of damage or risk. Depending on the context, vulnerability has been defined in many ways. In macroeconomics, vulnerability is defined as 'the conditions characterized by physical, social, economic and/or environmental factors or processes, which increase the susceptibility of a community to the impact of hazards' (ISDR, 2002, p. 7). In social sciences, it is understood as 'defenselessness, insecurity and exposure to risk, shocks and stress... and the experienced difficulty in coping with them' (Chamber, 1989). In the area of interpersonal relationships and communication, vulnerability is studied as 'uncertainty, risk, and emotional exposure' (Brown, 2012, p. 44). What is common to all these definitions is the notion of 'being exposed to or influenced by forces in the environment' or 'being open to some kind of potential risks'. Interestingly, at both the interpersonal and organizational levels, 'trusting others presupposes the exposure to a situation of risk to the trustor' (Luhmann, 1988, p. 97). This also indicates vulnerability, just as trust, exists at both the individual and organizational levels.

The discussion above demonstrates that on a theoretical level, the constructs of trust and vulnerability are closely intertwined. Both concepts are beyond the individual and are relational in nature. Members of a team or organization have mutual and/or shared perceptions and expectancies; thus, both trust and vulnerability offer a potential area for research within the realm of organizational psychology. Trust is the 'willingness to accept vulnerability' and involves exposing oneself to risk in interpersonal and organizational contexts. In the organizational context, these vulnerabilities are manifold. There can be functional vulnerabilities, in which one may be dependent on the trustee for attaining work-related objectives, failure of which may have important ramifications for task and organizational outcomes and processes. Alternatively, there can be social or political vulnerabilities, such that one may risk one's status, reputation, network access and/or other forms of social capital through participating in a trust relationship. In either scenario, institutions have the potential to impact trust through influencing the perceptions, nature and extent of vulnerabilities.

Both continuance and dissolution of the organizational routines, practices and behaviours of organizational members are heavily dependent on the level of trust shared by its members, as well as the level of trust members invest in the organization's institutions, and therefore the organization would begin to deinstitutionalize in the absence of this trust. These and other ramifications of trust and vulnerability for organizations are discussed in the following sections.

Institution-based Trust

'Institution-based trust' refers to 'a form of individual or collective action that is constitutively embedded in the institutional environment of the organization in which the relationship is placed, building favourable assumptions about the trustee's future behaviour vis-à-vis such conditions' (Bachmann & Inkpen, 2011, p. 284). This suggests that certain institutional arrangements in an organizational environment may serve as the backdrop against which the trustor develops willingness to be vulnerable. As per Zucker (1986), three sources have been found to contribute to the perceptions of this trust and willingness to be vulnerable in an organizational environment. These are: (a) process-based trust; (b) characteristic-based trust; and (c) institution-based trust. Trust is considered to be process-based when it is developed from past personal experience, often involving face-to-face interaction, or third-party experience accessible to the trustor, like the trustee's reputation. Characteristic-based trust is based on the personal characteristics of the trustee in particular sociocultural contexts, including the aspects such as age, gender and ethnicity, in which he/she exists. Institution-based trust is the third factor, which comes into play when first-hand information about the trustee is unavailable. In such cases, the institution becomes the medium to ascertain the trust of the trustor in the trustee. In the words of Bachmann and Inkpen (2011), institutions function as 'the third-party guarantors' between the trustor and the trustee which can establish a common ground through sharing explicit and tacit knowledge that may influence the willingness of the trustor to be vulnerable to the trustee. Thus, institution-based trust may signal reduced risk and low vulnerability for investing trust in another organizational member and facilitate trust even in the absence of direct face-to-face interaction or other forms of reliable information about the trustee.

VULNERABILITY, TRUST AND INSTITUTIONS: THEORETICAL PERSPECTIVES

Several theoretical perspectives can be applied in understanding how and when willingness to be vulnerable can be established and is facilitated by institutional arrangements and other organizational features that are directly tied to the institutions.

Social Exchange Theory

The 'social exchange theory' (Blau, 1964; Deustch, 1958) explains individual and collective behaviour based on what people put into and get out of their relationships. People enter relationships that they expect to be favourable and avoid those that incur greater costs than benefits. Imbalances in inputs and outputs can lead to dissatisfaction and conflict. The employment relationship can also be viewed as a social exchange relationship, wherein the employees expect to be treated fairly by their organization in return for their inputs. Organizations similarly treat employees fairly and respectfully, in the expectation that their employees would reciprocate with enhanced contributions (Aryee et al., 2002; Wayne et al., 1997).

The social exchange perspective has been widely applied in trust research, particularly in studies that focus on the role of justice and psychological contracting in trust (Aryee et al., 2002; Choi & Hartigan, 2008; Deery et al., 2006; Montes & Irving, 2008). Blau (1964, p. 98), in his original formulation of social exchange, states that 'the establishment of exchange relations involves making investments that constitute commitments to the other party. Since social exchange requires trusting others to reciprocate, the initial problem is to prove oneself trustworthy'. Thus, a social exchange relationship is expected to be initiated through fair treatment by the exchange party and maintained via trustworthiness developed over previous interactions (Aryee et al., 2002). This means that trust or willingness to be vulnerable to the trustee is grounded in the trustor's previous experiences with the trustee and his/her future expectations of fairness, equity and reciprocity from the trustee. This is process-based trust emerging from one's previous experiences of success with the trustee. When an imbalance is experienced between inputs, expectations and outcomes, dissatisfaction results, and trust is likely to decrease, with the willingness to be vulnerable to the trustee becoming low.

In the social exchange perspective, the nature of the exchange relationship between trustors and trustees determines this willingness to be vulnerable. Here, the trustee may not just be another individual but can also be an institutional arrangement, like a procedure or practice of an organization or the organization as a whole. For example, the quality of individuals' exchange relationships with their organization and their perceptions of organizational support have been found to mediate the relationship between institutions of procedural justice and organization-referenced but not supervisor-referenced outcomes, like commitment and turnover (Ambrose & Schminke, 2003; Masterson et al., 2000). Similarly, the quality of individuals' social exchange relationships with supervisors has been found to mediate the relationship between interactional justice and supervisor-referenced but not organization-referenced outcomes, like supervisory trust (Ambrose & Schminke, 2003; Masterson et al., 2000). In another research, Khazanchi and Masterson (2011) found that the perceptions of organizational and supervisory fairness promoted a constructive relational environment characterized by higher levels of willingness to be vulnerable and better social exchange relationships among organizational members. This shows that organizational members are likely to repose trust in institutions to the extent the benefits of maintaining the institutions outweigh the costs. And, when the organizational members' willingness to be vulnerable decreases, deinstitutionalization may result. Also, institutions are likely to facilitate willingness to be vulnerable to the extent that they signal the capacity of the trustees to live up to their obligations to the trustors.

Embeddedness

The 'embeddedness' perspective is built on the social exchange perspective. However, while the latter focuses largely on dyadic relationships between a trustor and a trustee, the embeddedness perspective recognizes people's embeddedness in 'a complex web of relationships, whether existing and/or potential' in organizations (Ferrin et al., 2006, p. 870) and, therefore, recognizes the role of third-party relations in the trustor's willingness to be vulnerable to the trustee. Drawing on Heider's transitivity principle (1958), Ferrin et al. (2006), propose that the trust between two people might be heavily influenced by a third party that may act as a 'missing' tie. This may be because the emotional tension between the two parties may serve as the motivation behind forming the missing ties through the third party in the case of a triad (p. 871).

The embeddedness perspective proposes two major ways in which the third parties can restrict unscrupulous or counter-normative dyadic behaviours. These are: (a) exerting sanctions that constrain behaviour

(Coleman, 1988); and (b) increasing the motivation for trustworthiness through providing inducements that have implications for individuals' reputations. Focusing on the integrity dimension of trustworthiness (Mayer et al., 1995), Ferrin et al. (2006) suggest three different forms of relations that fall in the latter category. These are: (a) network closure; (b) structural equivalence; and (c) trust transferability. Network closure refers to the number of third parties who are mutually connected via interpersonal communication with both the trustor and the trustee. The greater the number of mutual third parties, the greater is the probability that the trustee's reputation would be benefitted or impaired through her/his behaviour towards the trustor, thereby making the trustor more willing to be vulnerable to the trustee. Thus, in situations of high network closure, the trustor has greater willingness to be vulnerable, because the trustee has greater risk in behaving opportunistically and losing the trust of others with whom he/she has interdependencies. Structural equivalence refers to the extent of concordance between the trustor's and the trustee's relationships or the extent of similarity between the trustor and the trustee in formal and informal relationships that they have or do not have with the third parties in the organization. High structural equivalence implies that the two individuals share a similar social circle or fulfil similar social roles in the organization and are, thus, affected by the same structural and power constraints, for example, when employees are likely to be working under the same leaders, interacting frequently with the same teams and departments and operating under the same resource constraints. The interdependence resulting from such a situation is expected to facilitate the trustor's willingness to be vulnerable to the trustee. Trust transferability refers to the conditions where a third party simply communicates their judgements about the trustee to the trustor. In the absence of any direct behaviour verifying the trustworthiness of the trustee, social information accumulated from others regarding the trustee may be instrumental in developing the trustor's willingness to be vulnerable and be open to the various risks in trusting the trustee.

Social Information Processing

The 'social information processing theory' (Salancik & Pfeffer, 1978) explains how people make sense of and form attitudes based on their social environment. The underlying assumption of this theory is that people are adaptive organisms who transform their beliefs and actions to suit their social context, their past and present behaviours and their experiences. The theory, therefore, proposes that studying the social and informational environment within which a behaviour occurs is key to the understanding of that behaviour. Hence, any direct/indirect information from and about others can shape employee attitudes and behaviours in an organization. This is because people's interpretation of events is often dependent on social cues provided by others, and also the social environment provides information regarding normative attitudes and behaviours to others for a particular social context, that is, how acceptable or unacceptable a particular judgement, attitude or action is in that context. Thus, in the context of trust and vulnerability, the social environment not only directly provides information about the trustee but also dictates whether or not a person should trust and be vulnerable to the trustee. The social environment also alters the salience of the person's own past and present experiences, such that some thoughts, actions and statements appear to be more relevant and therefore attract greater attention than others in the trustor's decision to be vulnerable and open to risks. To summarize, the effect of social context on attitudes and needs statement is twofold. First, the social context provides a direct construction of meaning through guides to socially acceptable beliefs, attitudes and needs, and acceptable reasons for action. Second, it focuses an individual's attention on certain information, making that information more salient, and provides expectations concerning the individual's behaviour and the logical consequences of such behaviour (Salancik & Pfeffer, 1978, p. 227). In trust research, social information processing is widely used to understand the role of the factors like communication (Hill et al., 2009). Thus, the social context serves as a vital source of information about the meaning and value of institutions in organizations, especially during the socialization process, where this information is implicitly communicated to its members.

Attribution Theory

The 'attribution theory' explains how individuals attribute causes to events and behaviours. When a person chooses to invest trust in others, he/she is vulnerable to the latter, as trust involves risk-taking behaviours that can result in either a positive or a negative outcome. People take the outcome of their risk-taking behaviour into account to revise or update their levels of willingness to be open to risks in future (Tomlinson & Mayer, 2009; Weiner, 1986). They attribute causes to the outcomes of the initial trust decision based on their emotional reaction to the outcome (Weiner, 1986). The cause of this positive or negative outcome can be then attributed along three dimensions: internal or external locus, controllability and stability. Analysis along these three dimensions then determines the subsequent expectations regarding the trustor's future levels of trust. Attribution analysis can be particularly significant in the case of a negative outcome, that is, when the trustee has failed to meet the trustor's expectations (Tomlinson & Mayer, 2009). In such a situation, the trustor's readiness to be vulnerable decreases, because of the revaluations and perceived discrepancies by the trustor in the trustee's ability, benevolence and/or integrity (Tomlinson & Mayer, 2009). A major contribution of the attribution perspective is that not every negative outcome will cause a decrease in trust and in the trustor's willingness to be vulnerable to the trustee. The trustee's trustworthiness is likely to decrease only when certain types of attributions are made for negative events, that is, when the trustee's failure to meet the trustor's expectations is attributed to internal causes, such as his/her ability, integrity and benevolence. The damage is likely to be the greatest when the internal causes are also perceived to be stable and controllable. A second important contribution of the attribution perspective is that only voluntary behaviour is indicative of trustworthiness, as it is attributed to internal causes, as opposed to mandated or formally recognized behaviours that are attributed to external causes (Ferrin et al., 2006). The attribution theory has been used to examine a number of trust antecedents, like leadership (Gillespie & Mann, 2004; Korsgaard et al., 2002a) and the role of contracts (Ferrin et al., 2007; Malhotra & Murnighan, 2002). Thus, in short, this perspective suggests that as long as the cause of unmet expectations is not attributed to an institution itself, trust in the institution is likely to continue; however, when the intrinsic worth of the institution itself is questioned, trustees may take no further risk by being vulnerable through trusting the institution, eventually leading the organization into deinstitutionalization.

Social Identity Theory

The 'social identity theory' (Tajfel et al., 1979) proposes that individuals always strive to maintain a positive view of themselves and that both the personal identity and the social identity of a person play a role in their self-definition. Thus, people define themselves not only in terms of their individual characteristics but also in terms of the attributes of the social categories or groups to which they belong (Giessner et al., 2009). Accordingly, in order to maintain a positive self-definition, people often seek to identify with the groups that are valued in the society and distance themselves from groups that are devalued. In the area of trust, studies have found that the trustor's willingness to be vulnerable to the trustee may be enhanced if they share membership of one or more social categories, as in such case the trustee is likely to be evaluated more favourably and empathetically, resulting in greater trust between the two (Fulmer & Gelfand, 2012; Naquin & Paulson, 2003). Alternatively, when trustees are viewed as belonging to a high-status group within an organization (e.g., leaders or star performers), trustors are more likely to form positive opinions of them and find lower risk in trusting them (Giessner et al., 2009). A concept that has been particularly influential in this context is group prototypicality, that is, the extent to which an individual is perceived as representative of the group prototype (Hogg, 2001). People who are believed to be closer and similar to the group prototype are evaluated more favourably than those who are viewed as less similar. Thus, team members may be more willing to take risks by trusting a leader who is more proto-typical of a leader of a group than any other less prototypical leader (Giessner et al., 2009). This type of trust resulting from the identification processes associated with the social identity perspective is also known as identification-based trust (Naquin & Paulson, 2003).

The 'group-value theory' (Lind & Tyler, 1988; Tyler, 1989), a derivate of the social identity theory, further explains how the trustee treats the trustor and gives information to the trustor about himself/herself. If the trustor feels he/she is treated fairly and respectfully, he/she is likely to believe the trustee to be a valued group member, communicating symbolically that he/she can be proud of the trust relationship (Restubog et al., 2008), prompting further investment of himself/

herself in the trust relationship. On the other hand, if he/she perceives unfair treatment and/or unmet expectations, it may indicate his/her marginalized position in the group (Restubog et al., 2008) or that he/she is unworthy of identification, thereby prompting psychological withdrawal from the relationship (Kreiner & Ashforth, 2004). In the context of institutions, as long as organizational members perceive the trustees as having integrity, ability and benevolence, they are likely to identify with the latter. If the expectations are fulfilled, the institution might serve as a means of self-validation and identification (Restubog et al., 2008). However, failure to meet the expectations would reduce the trustor's willingness to be vulnerable to the trustee, which may cause the former to distance himself/herself from the institutionalized activity or practice, resulting in deinstitutionalization or the gradual breakdown of the institution.

Cycle of Mistrust

In another study, Oestrich and Ryan (2005) suggest that people behave in accordance with what is expected of them. This is in line with the self fulfilling prophecy that suggests that people's conduct towards others is based on their assumptions and expectations regarding them, and others in return behave according to these assumptions. In organizational settings, a 'cycle of mistrust' can be created and repeated between the supervisor and employees because of initial negative assumptions and lack of trust between them, or vice versa. For example, a new employee may not be completely trusted by the manager due to lack of information about the employee. Thus, the manager may choose to closely supervise the employee's activities, lest anything go wrong which may have serious repercussions for the organization. The new employee may perceive this act of the manager as a controlling behaviour and may resent it. Consequently, he/she may not share complete information about his/her activities. The manager may see this as verification of his earlier assumptions of mistrust, and this cycle of mistrust may get repeated. This suggests that institutions hold an important position during the setting of expectations between employees, influencing how social information is processed in organizations. This also explains how the cycle of mistrust can often continue in the absence of effective communication between the organization's members.

OTHER THEORETICAL PERSPECTIVES

Fairness Heuristic Theory

The 'fairness heuristic theory' (Lind, 2001) perceives that fairness between two interactants can be an important indicator of trustworthiness between those interactants. It assumes two basic processes: (a) fairness judgements—which serve as a proxy for trustworthiness in deciding whether to cooperate with another person or not; and (b) cognitive shortcuts—people use a number of cognitive shortcuts or heuristics for a fairness judgement in deciding whether to behave cooperatively or not. For example, employees often depend, consciously or unconsciously, on representative heuristic in judging their manager based on their cultural notions of a leader, which has implications on their judgement of the manager on the fairness dimension. Likewise, employees also perceive leaders to be fairer when they belong to the group prototype (familiarity heuristic). In the context of organizations, this perspective suggests individuals may be more willing to put their trust in and be vulnerable to the institutions when the latter are perceived to be fair.

Value Consensus Theory

The value consensus theory proposes that similarity or congruence in values between interactants underlies trust and willingness to be vulnerable. Since values define organizational cultures, the extent to which organizational institutions and cultures promote similar norms and values determines the agreement and harmony shared between group members (Jehn & Mannix, 2001). This decreases conflict and promotes trust and openness to risk between group members. This perspective particularly emphasizes the importance of cooperative goals, as opposed to competitive goals, in building trust and inducing willingness to be vulnerable to others. The institutional attributes like these promote value consensus, and cooperative goals may not only reduce unnecessary tensions between group members but also enable task-related conflicts to be expressed with greater ease, thereby facilitating trust (Jehn & Mannix, 2001). Whistle-blowers, for example, may be more trusting of the authority if they perceive their personal values to be same as the organization's core values.

Media Richness Theory

The basic premise of the 'media richness theory' (Daft & Lengel, 1986) is concerned with the role played by two forces—uncertainty and equivocality—in how information is interpreted in organizational contexts. Uncertainty can be understood as the lack or absence of information in an organization which is required to solve the organization's problems or perform tasks effectively. Equivocality pertains to the ambiguity of information, that is, the possibility of information being interpreted in multiple, varied and even contradictory ways. Different communication media are associated with varying levels of uncertainty and ambiguity characteristics. Thus, they differ in how effective they are in communicating information from the sender to the receiver. When a medium facilitates simultaneous communication of multiple cues and instant feedback, the trustor may be more willing to be vulnerable, because of the reduced uncertainty and ambiguity. Thus, any medium that is rich in social cues facilitates trust and willingness to be open to risks through reducing ambiguity and increasing the cognitive load associated with communicating a message (Rockman & Northcraft, 2008). While not exactly defined as a medium, it is possible to argue using the proposition of this theory that institutions also serve the function of reducing uncertainty and ambiguity in organizations through sharing meaningful social cues and, thus, are likely to promote trust and willingness to be more vulnerable among employees.

INSTITUTIONAL FACTORS THAT PROMOTE TRUST IN ORGANIZATIONS

Different studies discussed above have provided basis to assume a relationship between institutional factors and willingness to be vulnerable to others in organizations. Drawing from the social information processing theory, attribution theory and social exchange theory paradigms, the roles of reputation (Howorth & Moro, 2006), leaders' approval (Lau & Liden, 2008) and feedback mechanisms (Bolton et al., 2004; Dellarocas, 2003) in trust and associated vulnerabilities in interpersonal situations indicate the importance of institutions as third-party guarantors of the trustee's ability, integrity and benevolence. Moreover, institutionalized practices, like communicating a collective vision, promote team members' willingness to be vulnerable to the leaders (Gillespie & Mann, 2004), as do supportive mentoring practices, like providing task advice and career guidance, which indicate benevolence and increase trust between the mentor and the protégé (Young & Perrewe, 2000). Similarly, ethical conduct and loyalty have been found to increase willingness to be vulnerable (Bews & Rossouw, 2002; Rosanas & Velilla, 2003). Further, the institution of leadership is also directly relevant to trust and vulnerability, as indicated by the role played by different leadership styles, including transformational (Jung et al., 2009), authentic (Avolio et al., 2004), servant (Van Dierendonck, 2011) and empowering leadership (Caldwell & Dixon, 2010), in facilitating trust in leaders and between co-workers. For example, relational transparency is a key component of authentic relationships (Avolio et al., 2004; Gardner et al., 2009) which requires unmasked and open sharing of information and expression of one's true thoughts. Leaders are thereby vulnerable through being transparent, and through repeated interactions they create an experience of trust in followers and demonstrate trustworthiness in their followers. This has many positive organizational outcomes, such as followers' satisfaction, organizational commitment and extra effort. Other organizational institutions, such as reward structures and goal setting, also influence trust. For instance, cooperative organizational values, existence of reward structures, systematized recognition of individual achievement (Ferrin & Dirks, 2003; Hill et al., 2009), high-performance work systems characterized by the practices like job security and selective hiring (Zacharatos et al., 2005), cooperative conflict management procedures, compared to competitive ones (Hempel et al., 2009), perceived organizational support (Dirks & Ferrin, 2002) and profit sharing (Coyle-Shapiro et al., 2002) have been found to promote the readiness of referents to be vulnerable and open to risks within the organization. Relationship-oriented cultures and organizational practices have also been associated with increased levels of trust (Six & Sorge, 2008).

As predicted by the fairness heuristic theory, the experience of organizational justice is directly associated with trust and vulnerability at all levels in the organization (Johnson & Lord, 2010), and this finding extends to systems of distributive, procedural and interactional justice (Colquitt et al., 2012). In a similar vein, institutions of participative and consultative decision-making also help in increasing trust (Dirks & Ferrin, 2002; Gillespie & Mann, 2004; Huang et al., 2010), due to the increased perception of fairness resulting from having a voice in key decisions. An even more direct example of how institutions help in trust building can be seen in studies that indicate the negative consequences of the absence of institutions; for instance, when human resources (HR) decisions are made on the basis of personal relationships, organizational members perceive them as a contravention of procedural justice, resulting in a reduction in trust and resistance to be vulnerable to the leaders and the organization (Chen et al., 2004). Other institutions, like performance appraisals, may also contribute to reduced trust and willingness to be open to risks when they are perceived to be low on fairness (Choi & Hartigan, 2008).

Based predominantly on the value consensus, social exchange and social identity paradigms, behavioural integrity and/or consistency between espoused and enacted values is a significant antecedent of trust (Palanski & Yammarino, 2009) and readiness to be vulnerable. Convergence of individual and organizational values and principles has also been reported to be positively associated with organizational trust (D'Iribarne, 2003; Edwards & Cable, 2009). The extent of an employee's identification with his/her organization (Deery et al., 2006) positively relates to the employee's level of trust and willingness to be vulnerable in the organization. In accordance with the media richness and social information processing theories, the communication style promoted in an organization has a tremendous effect on trust levels and associated vulnerabilities. For example, face-to-face interactions have been found to increase the level of trust and openness to risk as compared to telephonic communication or online communication (Hill et al., 2009; Murrell et al., 2008). The extent to which an organization promotes positive and transparent communication, as well as informal communication unrelated to tasks, like gift giving or knowledge sharing, is also likely to be associated with trust and the trustor's decision to be vulnerable (Cameron & Webster, 2011; Dolfsma et al., 2009; Nguyen & Rose, 2009; Norman et al., 2010). Emotional cultures of organizations also have ramifications for trust, as emotional discomfort can reduce willingness to be vulnerable (Lee et al., 2006), while authentic emotional display and deep action (Gardner et al., 2009) on trust can help in promoting openness to risk among employees.

More formal institutional arrangements, like those of monitoring and contracting, have also been found to be related to trust and vulnerability. Specifically, if pre-existing contracts are removed, monitoring and contracting may result in lower trust and increased resistance of the trustor to be vulnerable to the trustee, as the trustee's prior trustworthy behaviour and cooperation are viewed as a result of the contract rather than their own trustworthiness (Malhotra & Murnighan, 2002). Monitoring processes are also presumed to increase trust and openness to risks in situations where they are viewed as necessary, for example, when trustors and trustees have no prior history together (Ferrin et al., 2007). However, in situations where a relationship exists, monitoring can also prevent the development of trust through ensuring that the trustor does not need to be vulnerable (Kramer, 1999).

At the macro level, legal and political institutions that regulate business transactions also promote interpersonal and inter-organizational trust and vulnerability (Balasubramanian et al., 2003; Hemmert et al., 2016). In the absence of legal structures, cultural institutions also play a similar role, as indicated by the practice of guanxi in China (Tan et al., 2009). Guanxi involves a highly personalized relationship where people are bound by social norms to maintain long-term relationships characterized by loyalty and mutuality (Tan et al., 2009), which promote trust and willingness to be vulnerable among members. The institution of corporate social responsibility is another such institution that increases trust in organizations (Du et al., 2011).

To summarize, the role of institutions in trust and vulnerability is both retrospective and prospective. Poppo et al. (2008) propose that both the past history shared by parties and expectations of relationship continuity are instrumental in building, maintaining and facilitating trust and willingness to be vulnerable. As indicated by the discussion above, within organizations, institutions not only provide the basis for meaningful sense making and reconstruction of prior experience but also serve as the framework within which expectations of the future are set and probabilities of trustworthy behaviours are evaluated.

DEINSTITUTIONALIZATION AND ORGANIZATIONAL CHANGE

As explained earlier, institutionalization includes the process of legitimization of activities, practices and procedures that become stable and result in the persistence and stability of the same behaviours and practices in an organization. These set of stable, repetitive and enduring activities or practices become 'infused with value beyond the technical requirements of the task at hand' (Selznick et al., 1957, p. 17), to an extent that they tend to generate organizational inertia, or what can be termed as the fundamental resistance to change.

Institutionalization gives rise to congruence in assumptions and values which defines an organization's culture (Schein, 1990), promotes conformity to commonly accepted routines and norms (Oliver, 1992) and gets naturalized to an extent that organizational members no longer question their utility or primacy. The institutional way then becomes the only natural and direct way to conduct an activity (Oliver, 1992, p. 565). This leads to institutionalized resistance to change.

To say that resistance is institutionalized means that 'it is embedded in and expressed through organizational structures and processes of legitimation, decision making and resource allocation' (Agocs, 1997, p. 918). Refusal by decision-makers to be influenced or affected by the views, concerns or evidence presented to them by those who advocate change in established practices, routines, goals or norms within the organization become the new norm under the institutionalized-resistance stage.

Thus, institutionalized practices or activities acquire a life of their own, such that they no longer need to be reinforced to be maintained;

instead, they become intrinsically valuable, and consequently, due to the changing dynamics, with the unquestioned assumptions, practices and rules of thumb, they become obsolete at some point and give rise to organizational entropy. In other words while institutionalization lends an organization its established character and sense of permanence, it also leads to loss of flexibility or rigidity and resistance to organizational change. As a result, the organization begins to perform suboptimally through continuing with its old, institutionalized practices, and its members perform activities as rituals rather than as functional, adaptive and agentic organizational behaviours (Donaldson & Grant-Vallone, 2002). Therefore, while institutionalization allows compliance with established rules and policies, it also retards unlearning of dysfunctional organizational routines and reinterpretation of outmoded structures, giving rise to 'institutionalised resistance to change'.

However, when forces in favour of change exceed the change-resisting forces (Lewin, 1951), in such an event or situation, the factors internal and external to the organization, the de-legitimation processes begin, and subsequently, changes in organizational configurations or deinstitutionalization (Greenwood & Hinings, 1988) may occur. Deinstitutionalization is 'the erosion or discontinuity of an institutionalized organizational activity or practice'. It involves 'de-legitimation of an established organizational practice or procedure as a result of organizational challenges to or the failure of organizations to reproduce previously legitimated or taken-for-granted organizational actions' (Oliver, 1992, pp. 563–564).

Several theoretical models have been proposed to delineate how deinstitutionalization occurs in an organization resulting in organizational change. These models focus on the role of internal and external pressures that disrupt the organizational status quo. For instance, Oliver (1992) identified political, functional and social pressures that lead to deinstitutionalization. These include changes in the distribution of power within organizations, performance crises, innovation-related pressures, emergence of visionaries or intra-organizational entrepreneurs, changes in the environmental conditions, technical changes, competition for resources, social fragmentation, historical discontinuity emerging from poor socialization of new organizational members and structural disaggregation through the events like mergers and acquisitions. These factors also indicate the competing roles of the forces of inertia and entropy in organizational contexts, as demonstrated by, for instance, Lewin's force field model, which posits the organizational status quo and possibility for change as functions of forces for and against change, respectively (Lewin, 1947). If the forces of entropy, that is, forces compelling the change, overcome the resistance presented by the inertial forces, that is, forces against the change, deinstitutionalization results, with the breakdown of long-held structures, processes, rules and practices.

INSTITUTIONAL CONSEQUENCES OF TRUST: DEINSTITUTIONALIZATION

Trust has obvious relevance for organizations. Several studies have linked trust with job satisfaction, reduced uncertainty, organizational commitment, support for leaders, creativity and increased risk-taking (Brockner et al., 1997; Colquitt et al., 2012; Dirks & Ferrin, 2002; Madjar & Ortiz-Walters, 2008). Among other outcomes that have been examined, trust and readiness to be vulnerable have been found to be beneficial for cooperative relations, knowledge sharing, help seeking, organizational citizenship behaviours, proactive problem-solving, collaboration and communication practices (Collins & Smith, 2006; Golden & Raghuram, 2010; Hofmann et al., 2009; Malhotra & Lumineau, 2011; Parker et al., 2006). Trust and the associated openness to risks have also been found to promote total quality management and commitment to continuous improvement in employees (Coyle-Shapiro & Morrow, 2003), as well as strengthening mentoring institutions through promoting supportive behaviours characterized by role modelling and career guidance (Wang et al., 2010). Trust also enhances alignment and adaptability in organizations (Gibson & Birkinshaw, 2004) and, in moderation, can facilitate innovation as well (Molina-Morales & Martenez-Fernandez, 2009).

While trust and openness to risks can help maintain institutions, their absence can lead to the breakdown of existing structural arrangements, causing deinstitutionalization. Since the creation and maintenance of structures often requires significant organizational resources and includes both tangible costs, like time and money invested in establishing the legitimacy of institutions, and intangible costs, like the activity or agency required to produce these social structures (Zucker & Kreft, 1994), unless organizational decision-makers and members believe that the institution in question is beneficial and would have positive consequences, it would be impossible for the institution to become embedded. Similarly, unless organizational members are willing to trust each other to share the implicit reality created by institutions, the institutions themselves are unlikely to survive. This suggests that trust and vulnerability are also connected with deinstitutionalization. This is because the breakdown of trust and resistance to be vulnerable in an institution is likely to result in counterproductive individual and organizational behaviours, such as secrecy, knowledge hiding and knowledge hoarding, leading to deinstitutionalization. When organizational members and decision-makers no longer believe that an institutional arrangement would serve them or the organization, they are likely to start doubting the functionality of the institution.

Trust again becomes the fundamental factor to the success of any organizational change effort following deinstitutionalization, as it can be instrumental in alleviating organizational members' negative responses to organizational change (Korsgaard et al., 2002; Oreg & Sverdlik, 2011).

REFERENCES

Agocs, C. (1997). Institutionalized resistance to organizational change: Denial, inaction and repression. *Journal of Business Ethics, 16*(9), 917–931.

Ambrose, M. L., & Schminke, M. (2003).Organization structure as a moderator of the relationship between procedural justice, interactional justice, perceived organizational support, and supervisory trust. *Journal of Applied Psychology, 88*(2), 295.

Aryee, S., Budhwar, P. S., & Chen, Z. X. (2002). Trust as a mediator of the relationship between organizational justice and work outcomes: Test of a social exchange model. *Journal of Organizational Behavior: The International Journal of Industrial, Occupational and Organizational Psychology and Behavior, 23*(3), 267–285.

Avolio, B. J., Gardner, W. L., Walumbwa, F. O., Luthans, F., & May, D. R. (2004). Unlocking the mask: A look at the process by which authentic leaders impact follower attitudes and behaviors. *The Leadership Quarterly*, *15*(6), 801–823.

Bachmann, R., & Inkpen, A. C. (2011). Understanding institutional-based trust building processes in inter-organizational relationships. *Organization Studies*, *32*(2), 281–301.

Balasubramanian, S., Konana, P., & Menon, N. M. (2003). Customer satisfaction in virtual environments: A study of online investing. *Management Science*, *49*(7), 871–889.

Berger, P. L., Berger, P. L., & Luckmann, T. (1966). *The social construction of reality: A treatise in the sociology of knowledge*. Anchor.

Bews, N. F., & Rossouw, G. J. (2002). A role for business ethics in facilitating trustworthiness. *Journal of Business Ethics*, *39*(4), 377–390.

Blau, P. (1964). *Power and exchange in social life*. John Wiley & Sons.

Bolton, G. E., Katok, E., & Ockenfels, A. (2004). Trust among Internet traders. *Analyse & Kritik*, *26*(1), 185–202.

Brockner, J., Siegel, P. A., Daly, J. P., Tyler, T., & Martin, C. (1997). When trust matters: The moderating effect of outcome favorability. *Administrative Science Quarterly*, *42*(3), 558–583.

Brown, B. (2012). Brené Brown: Listening to shame [video file]. https://www.ted.com/talks/brene_brown_listening_to_shame?language=en

Caldwell, C., & Dixon, R. D. (2010). Love, forgiveness, and trust: Critical values of the modern leader. *Journal of Business Ethics*, *93*(1), 91–101.

Cameron, A. F., & Webster, J. (2011). Relational outcomes of multicommunicating: Integrating incivility and social exchange perspectives. *Organization Science*, *22*(3), 754–771.

Chambers, R. (1989). Editorial introduction: Vulnerability, coping and policy. *IDS Bulletin*, *20*(2), 1–7.

Chen, C. C., Chen, Y. R., & Xin, K. (2004). Guanxi practices and trust in management: A procedural justice perspective. *Organization Science*, *15*(2), 200–209.

Choi, E. K., & Hartigan, J. C. (Eds.). (2008). *Handbook of international trade: Economic and legal analyses of trade policy and institutions* (Vol. 4). John Wiley & Sons.

Coleman, J. S. (1988). Social capital in the creation of human capital. *American Journal of Sociology*, *94*, S95–S120.

Collins, C. J., & Smith, K. G. (2006). Knowledge exchange and combination: The role of human resource practices in the performance of high-technology firms. *Academy of Management Journal*, *49*(3), 544–560.

Colquitt, J. A., LePine, J. A., Piccolo, R. F., Zapata, C. P., & Rich, B. L. (2012). Explaining the justice–performance relationship: Trust as exchange deepener or trust as uncertainty reducer? *Journal of Applied Psychology*, *97*(1), 1.

Connelly, B. L., Miller, T., & Devers, C. E. (2012). Under a cloud of suspicion: Trust, distrust, and their interactive effect in interorganizational contracting. *Strategic Management Journal, 33*(7), 820–833.

Coyle-Shapiro, J. A., & Morrow, P. C. (2003). The role of individual differences in employee adoption of TQM orientation. *Journal of Vocational Behavior, 62*(2), 320–340.

Coyle-Shapiro, J. A. M., Morrow, P. C., Richardson, R., & Dunn, S. R. (2002). Using profit sharing to enhance employee attitudes: A longitudinal examination of the effects on trust and commitment. *Human Resource Management, 41*(4), 423–439.

Daft, R. L., & Lengel, R. H. (1986). Organizational information requirements, media richness and structural design. *Management Science, 32*(5), 554–571.

Deery, S. J., Iverson, R. D., & Walsh, J. T. (2006). Toward a better understanding of psychological contract breach: A study of customer service employees. *Journal of Applied Psychology, 91*(1), 166.

Dellarocas, C. (2003). The digitization of word of mouth: Promise and challenges of online feedback mechanisms. *Management Science, 49*(10), 1407–1424.

Deutsch, M. (1958). Trust and suspicion. *Journal of Conflict Resolution, 2*(4), 265–279.

Dirks, K. T., & Ferrin, D. L. (2002). Trust in leadership: Meta-analytic findings and implications for research and practice. *Journal of Applied Psychology, 87*(4), 611.

D'Iribarne, P. (2003). The combination of strategic games and moral community in the functioning of firms. *Organization Studies, 24*(8), 1283–1307.

Dolfsma, W., Van der Eijk, R., & Jolink, A. (2009). On a source of social capital: Gift exchange. *Journal of Business Ethics, 89*(3), 315–329.

Donaldson, S. I., & Grant-Vallone, E. J. (2002). Understanding self-report bias in organizational behaviour research. *Journal of Business and Psychology, 17*(2), 245–260.

Doney, P. M., Cannon, J. P., & Mullen, M. R. (1998). Understanding the influence of national culture on the development of trust. *Academy of Management Review, 23*(3), 601–620.

Du, S., Bhattacharya, C. B., & Sen, S. (2011). Corporate social responsibility and competitive advantage: Overcoming the trust barrier. *Management Science, 57*(9), 1528–1545.

Edwards, J. R., & Cable, D. M. (2009). The value of value congruence. *Journal of Applied Psychology, 94*(3), 654.

Ferrin, D. L., & Dirks, K. T. (2003). The use of rewards to increase and decrease trust: Mediating processes and differential effects. *Organization Science, 14*(1), 18–31.

Ferrin, D. L., Dirks, K. T., & Shah, P. P. (2006). Direct and indirect effects of third-party relationships on interpersonal trust. *Journal of Applied Psychology, 91*(4), 870.

Ferrin, D. L., Bligh, M. C., & Kohles, J. C. (2007). Can I trust you to trust me? A theory of trust, monitoring, and cooperation in interpersonal and intergroup relationships. *Group & Organization Management, 32*(4), 465–499.

Fulmer, C. A., & Gelfand, M. J. (2012). At what level (and in whom) we trust: Trust across multiple organizational levels. *Journal of Management, 38*(4), 1167–1230.

Gardner, W. L., Fischer, D., & Hunt, J. G. J. (2009). Emotional labor and leadership: A threat to authenticity? *The Leadership Quarterly, 20*(3), 466–482.

Gibson, C. B., & Birkinshaw, J. (2004). The antecedents, consequences, and mediating role of organizational ambidexterity. *Academy of Management Journal, 47*(2), 209–226.

Giddens, A. (1984). *The constitution of society: Outline of the theory of structuration.* University of California Press.

Giessner, S. R., van Knippenberg, D. L., & Sleebos, Ed. (2008). License to fail? How leader group prototypicality moderates the effects of leader performance on perceptions of leadership effectiveness. ERIM Report Series Reference No. ERS-2008-066-ORG.

Gillespie, N. A., & Mann, L. (2004). Transformational leadership and shared values: The building blocks of trust. *Journal of Managerial Psychology, 19*(6), 588–607.

Golden, T. D., & Raghuram, S. (2010). Teleworker knowledge sharing and the role of altered relational and technological interactions. *Journal of Organizational Behavior, 31*(8), 1061–1085.

Greenwood, R., & Hinings, C. R. (1988). Organizational design types, tracks and the dynamics of strategic change. *Organization Studies, 9*(3), 293–316.

Hasel, M. C., & Grover, S. L. (2017). An integrative model of trust and leadership. *Leadership & Organization Development Journal, 38*(6), 849–867.

Hashim, K. F., & Tan, F. B. (2015). The mediating role of trust and commitment on members' continuous knowledge sharing intention: A commitment-trust theory perspective. *International Journal of Information Management, 35*(2), 145–151.

Heider, F. (1958). The psychology of interpersonal relations. John Wiley & Sons Inc. https://doi.org/10.1037/10628-000

Hemmert, M., Kim, D., Kim, J., & Cho, B. (2016). Building the supplier's trust: Role of institutional forces and buyer firm practices. *International Journal of Production Economics, 180*, 25–37.

Hempel, P. S., Zhang, Z. X., & Tjosvold, D. (2009). Conflict management between and within teams for trusting relationships and performance in China. *Journal of Organizational Behavior: The International Journal of Industrial, Occupational and Organizational Psychology and Behavior, 30*(1), 41–65.

Hill, N. S., Bartol, K. M., Tesluk, P. E., & Langa, G. A. (2009). Organizational context and face-to-face interaction: Influences on the development of trust and collaborative behaviors in computer-mediated groups. *Organizational Behavior and Human Decision Processes, 108*(2), 187–201.

Hofmann, D. A., Lei, Z., & Grant, A. M. (2009). Seeking help in the shadow of doubt: The sensemaking processes underlying how nurses decide whom to ask for advice. *Journal of Applied Psychology, 94*(5), 1261.

Hogg, M. A. (2001). A social identity theory of leadership. *Personality and Social Psychology Review, 5*(3), 184–200.

Howorth, C., & Moro, A. (2006). Trust within entrepreneur bank relationships: Insights from Italy. *Entrepreneurship Theory and Practice, 30*(4), 495–517.

Huang, X., Iun, J., Liu, A., & Gong, Y. (2010). Does participative leadership enhance work performance by inducing empowerment or trust? The differential effects on managerial and non-managerial subordinates. *Journal of Organizational Behavior, 31*(1), 122–143.

Insko, C. A., Schopler, J., & Sedikides, C. (1998). Differential distrust of groups and individuals. In C. Sedikides, J. Schopler, & C. A. Insko (Eds.), *Intergroup cognition and intergroup behavior* (pp. 75–107). Lawrence Erlbaum Associates Publishers.

ISDR, U. (2002). *Disaster reduction and sustainable development: Understanding the links between vulnerability and risk related to development and environment.* Background document for the World summit on sustainable development. http//:www.unis-dr.org

Jehn, K. A., & Mannix, E. A. (2001). The dynamic nature of conflict: A longitudinal study of intragroup conflict and group performance. *Academy of Management Journal, 44*(2), 238–251.

Johnson, R. E., & Lord, R. G. (2010). Implicit effects of justice on self-identity. *Journal of Applied Psychology, 95*(4), 681.

Jung, D., Yammarino, F. J., & Lee, J. K. (2009). Moderating role of subordinates' attitudes on transformational leadership and effectiveness: A multi-cultural and multi-level perspective. *The Leadership Quarterly, 20*(4), 586–603.

Khazanchi, S., & Masterson, S. S. (2011). Who and what is fair matters: A multifoci social exchange model of creativity. *Journal of Organizational Behavior, 32*(1), 86–106.

Korsgaard, M. A., Brodt, S. E., & Whitener, E. M. (2002a). Trust in the face of conflict: The role of managerial trustworthy behavior and organizational context. *Journal of Applied Psychology, 87*(2), 312.

Korsgaard, M. A., Sapienza, H. J., & Schweiger, D. M. (2002b). Beaten before begun: The role of procedural justice in planning change. *Journal of Management, 28*(4), 497–516.

Kramer, R. M. (1999). Trust and distrust in organizations: Emerging perspectives, enduring questions. *Annual Review of Psychology, 50*(1), 569–598.

Kreiner, G. E., & Ashforth, B. E. (2004). Evidence toward an expanded model of organizational identification. *Journal of Organizational Behavior: The International Journal of Industrial, Occupational and Organizational Psychology and Behavior, 25*(1), 1–27.

Lau, D. C., & Liden, R. C. (2008). Antecedents of coworker trust: Leaders' blessings. *Journal of Applied Psychology, 93*(5), 1130.

Lee, K. H., Yang, G., & Graham, J. L. (2006). Tension and trust in international business negotiations: American executives negotiating with Chinese executives. *Journal of International Business Studies, 37*(5), 623–641.

Lewin, K. (1947). Frontiers in group dynamics: Concept, method and reality in social science; Social equilibria and social change. *Human Relations, 1*(1), 5–41.

Lind, E. A. (2001). Fairness heuristic theory: Justice judgments as pivotal cognitions in organizational relations. In J. Greenberg & R. Cropanzano (Eds.), *Advances in organizational justice* (pp. 56–58). Stanford University Press.

Lewin, K. (1951). *Field theory in social science: selected theoretical papers* (Edited by Dorwin Cartwright). Harpers & Brothers.

Lind, E. A., & Tyler, T. R. (1988). *The social psychology of procedural justice*. Springer.

Luhmann, N. (1988). Law as a social system. *Northwestern University Law Review, 83*, 136–342.

Lumineau, F. (2017). How contracts influence trust and distrust. *Journal of Management, 43*(5), 1553–1577.

Madjar, N., & Ortiz-Walters, R. (2008). Customers as contributors and reliable evaluators of creativity in the service industry. *Journal of Organizational Behavior: The International Journal of Industrial, Occupational and Organizational Psychology and Behavior, 29*(7), 949–966.

Malhotra, D., & Lumineau, F. (2011). Trust and collaboration in the aftermath of conflict: The effects of contract structure. *Academy of Management Journal, 54*(5), 981–998.

Malhotra, D., & Murnighan, J. K. (2002). The effects of contracts on interpersonal trust. *Administrative Science Quarterly, 47*(3), 534–559.

Masterson, S. S., Lewis, K., Goldman, B. M., & Taylor, M. S. (2000). Integrating justice and social exchange: The differing effects of fair procedures and treatment on work relationships. *Academy of Management Journal, 43*(4), 738–748.

Mayer, R. C., Davis, J. H., & Schoorman, F. D. (1995). An integrative model of organizational trust. *Academy of Management Review, 20*(3), 709–734.

Meyer, J. W., & Rowan, B. (1977). Institutionalized organizations: Formal structure as myth and ceremony. *American Journal of Sociology, 83*(2), 340–363.

Molina-Morales, F. X., & Martínez-Fernández, M. T. (2009). Too much love in the neighborhood can hurt: How an excess of intensity and trust in relationships may produce negative effects on firms. *Strategic Management Journal, 30*(9), 1013–1023.

Montes, S. D., & Irving, P. G. (2008). Disentangling the effects of promised and delivered inducements: Relational and transactional contract elements and the mediating role of trust. *Journal of Applied Psychology, 93*(6), 1367.

Murrell, A. J., Blake-Beard, S., Porter, D. M., & Perkins-Williamson, A. (2008). Interorganizational formal mentoring: Breaking the concrete ceiling sometimes requires support from the outside. *Human Resource Management, 47*(2), 275–294.

Naquin, C. E., & Paulson, G. D. (2003). Online bargaining and interpersonal trust. *Journal of Applied Psychology, 88*(1), 113.

Nguyen, T. V., & Rose, J. (2009). Building trust—Evidence from Vietnamese entrepreneurs. *Journal of Business Venturing, 24*(2), 165–182.

Norman, S. M., Avolio, B. J., & Luthans, F. (2010). The impact of positivity and transparency on trust in leaders and their perceived effectiveness. *The Leadership Quarterly, 21*(3), 350–364.

Palanski, M. E., & Yammarino, F. J. (2009). Integrity and leadership: A multi-level conceptual framework. *The Leadership Quarterly, 20*(3), 405–420.

Parker, S. K., Williams, H. M., & Turner, N. (2006). Modeling the antecedents of proactive behavior at work. *Journal of Applied Psychology, 91*(3), 636.

Poppo, L., Zhou, K. Z., & Ryu, S. (2008). Alternative origins to interorganizational trust: An interdependence perspective on the shadow of the past and the shadow of the future. *Organization Science, 19*(1), 39–55.

Oliver, C. (1992). The antecedents of deinstitutionalization. *Organization Studies, 13*(4), 563–588.

Oreg, S., & Sverdlik, N. (2011). Ambivalence toward imposed change: The conflict between dispositional resistance to change and the orientation toward the change agent. *Journal of Applied Psychology, 96*(2), 337.

Restubog, S. L. D., Hornsey, M. J., Bordia, P., & Esposo, S. R. (2008). Effects of psychological contract breach on organizational citizenship behaviour: Insights from the group value model. *Journal of Management Studies, 45*(8), 1377–1400.

Rockman, K. W., & Northcraft, G. B. (2008). To be or not to be trusted: The influence of media richness on defection and deception. *Organizational Behaviour and Human Decision Processes, 107*(2), 106–122.

Rosanas, J. M., & Velilla, M. (2003). Loyalty and trust as the ethical bases of organizations. *Journal of Business Ethics, 44*(1), 49–59.

Rousseau, D. M., Sitkin, S. B., Burt, R. S., & Camerer, C. (1998). Not so different after all: A cross-discipline view of trust. *Academy of Management Review, 23*(3), 393–404.

Oestrich, D., & Ryan, K. (2005). *Driving fear out of the workplace.* John Wiley & Sons.

Salancik, G. R., & Pfeffer, J. (1978). A social information processing approach to job attitudes and task design. *Administrative Science Quarterly, 23*(2), 224–253.

Schein, E. H. (1990). Organizational culture. *American Psychologist, 45*(2), 109.

Selznick, P., McEwan, I., Yukl, G. A., & VanFleet, D. D. (1957). *Leadership in organizations.* Row, Peterson.

Six, F., & Sorge, A. (2008). Creating a high-trust organization: An exploration into organizational policies that stimulate interpersonal trust building. *Journal of Management Studies, 45*(5), 857–884.

Skard, S. E. R. (2017). Trust and service innovation. In M. Lüders (Ed.), *Innovating for trust* (pp. 17–30). Edward Elgar Publishing.

Tan, J., Yang, J., & Veliyath, R. (2009). Particularistic and system trust among small and medium enterprises: A comparative study in China's transition economy. *Journal of Business Venturing, 24*(6), 544–557.

Tajfel, H., Turner, J. C., Austin, W. G., & Worchel, S. (1979). An integrative theory of intergroup conflict. In M. J. Hatch & M. Schultz (Eds.), *Organizational identity: A reader* (pp. 56–65). Oxford University Press.

Tirelli, A., & Goh, S. C. (2015). The relationship between trust, learning capability, affective organisational commitment and turnover intentions. *International Journal of Human Resources Development and Management, 15*(1), 54–68.

Tolbert, P. S., & Zucker, L. G. (1996). The institutionalization of institutional theory. In S. Clegg, C. Hardy, & W. R. Nord (Eds.), *Handbook of organization studies* (pp. 175–190). SAGE Publications.

Tomlinson, E. C., & Mryer, R. C. (2009). The role of causal attribution dimensions in trust repair. *Academy of Management Review, 34*(1), 85–104.

Tyler, T. R. (1989). The psychology of procedural justice: A test of the group-value model. *Journal of Personality and Social Psychology, 57*(5), 830.

Van Dierendonck, D. (2011). Servant leadership: A review and synthesis. *Journal of Management, 37*(4), 1228–1261.

Wang, S., Tomlinson, E. C., & Noe, R. A. (2010). The role of mentor trust and protege internal locus of control in formal mentoring relationships. *Journal of Applied Psychology, 95*(2), 358.

Wayne, S. J., Shore, L. M., & Liden, R. C. (1997). Perceived organizational support and leader-member exchange: A social exchange perspective. *Academy of Management Journal, 40*(1), 82–111.

Weiner, B. (1986). Attribution, emotion, and action. In R. M. Sorrentino & E. T. Higgins (Eds.), *Handbook of motivation and cognition: Foundations of social behaviour* (pp. 93–130). Guilford Publications.

Young, A. M., & Perrewé, P. L. (2000). The exchange relationship between mentors and protégés: The development of a framework. *Human Resource Management Review, 10*(2), 177–209.

Zacharatos, A., Barling, J., & Iverson, R. D. (2005). High-performance work systems and occupational safety. *Journal of Applied Psychology, 90*(1), 77.

Zucker, L. G. (1977). The role of institutionalization in cultural persistence. *American Sociological Review, 42*(5), 726–743.

Zucker, L. G. (1986). Production of trust: Institutional sources of economic structure, 1840–1920. *Research in Organizational Behavior, 8*, 53–111.

Zucker, L. G., & Kreft, I.G.G. (1994). The evolution of socially contingent rational action: Effects of labor strikes on change in union founding in the 1880s. In J.A.C. Baum & J. V. Singh (Eds.), *Evolutionary dynamics of organizations* (pp.194–313). Oxford University Press.

About the Editors and Contributors

ABOUT THE EDITORS

Nandita Babu is a professor, Department of Psychology at the University of Delhi. She was awarded the prestigious Canadian Commonwealth Scholarship for her doctoral research in Ontario Institute for Studies in Education, University of Toronto. As a Fulbright Visiting Fellow, she has worked as an adjunct faculty in San Diego State University, United States. As a developmental psychologist, she has keen interest in areas such as socio-cognitive development in children, literacy acquisition during early childhood and adolescent psychology. Her passion for and expertise in teaching and research are reflected in her many publications and community outreach programmes.

Anand Prakash is a professor of psychology at the University of Delhi, and is currently the Head of the Department of Psychology. His academic career spans four decades. He received the Young Scientist award of the Indian Science Congress Association in 1987 and the Career Award of the University Grants Commission (UGC) of India in 1993. He is a Fulbright-Nehru scholar. He has worked in various committees of Government of India, such as the Expert Institution of Eminence and Special Committee of National Education Policy on Inclusion and Equity of the UGC. He was the chairman of the task force formed by Government of India for developing the National Aptitude Test. His publications in Hindi journals and magazines are widely appreciated for making psychology popular.

Ishita U. Bharadwaj is an assistant professor, Department of Psychology at the University of Delhi. With a PhD in existentialism, she is keenly committed to exploring the nuances of qualitative research for understanding the socio-clinical interface around the self and being, gender, psychology of margins, narratives of illness and alternative education. She has been actively engaged in building Manastha, the counselling centre run by the Department of Psychology, University of Delhi. Her recent doctoral supervisions have been in the area of woman and madness, suicide-attempt survivors, psychic pain and healing.

ABOUT THE CONTRIBUTORS

Alka Bajpai is currently serving as a faculty member in the Department of Psychology, University of Delhi. She obtained her PhD degree from the Department of Psychology, University of Allahabad, in the area of organizational politics. Her current interest areas include intergroup relations and peace.

Annie Baxi is currently working as an assistant professor at Jesus and Mary College, University of Delhi. Her PhD thesis was on the topic 'Exploring Discourses around Normalcy and Madness in Women's Lives: A Study of Contemporary Indian Society'. Her areas of interest include qualitative analysis, gender studies and clinical psychology. In her work as an academician and clinician, she attempts to unravel the social and intrapsychic patterns of identity and relational meaning making.

Supreet Kaur Bhasin is a doctoral scholar at the Department of Psychology, University of Delhi. She has been awarded a full-term doctoral scholarship by the Indian Council of Social Sciences Research (ICSSR) and has been a UGC-NET (National Eligibility Test) scholar previously. As a researcher, she has a keen orientation towards existentialism and phenomenology. Presently, she is engaged with exploring the meaning making and construction of being among suicide-attempt survivors, at Delhi University and Centre of Excellence in Mental Health, Dr Ram Manohar Lohia Hospital. This can aid in broadening the existing psychosocial discourses around suicide and in enhancing the clinical interventions offered to those presenting an imminent risk of suicide. She has previously been involved with Parkinson's disease caregivers and, through her research, has attempted to look into their journey of embodying the caregiver role and dealing with existential concerns.

Dinesh Chhabra is presently working as an assistant professor in the Department of Psychology, North Campus, University of Delhi. He was Post doctoral Fellow and visiting assistant professor at the University of Virginia (UVA), United States, for 2 years. In the past, he has also worked as research fellow and post-doctoral fellow at Defence Institute of Psychological Research, Defence Research and Development Organisation (DRDO), Ministry of Defence. He was awarded Raman Fellowship twice for his post-doctoral research in the United States, sponsored by UGC, and Post-doctoral Fellowship under the Cognitive Science Research Initiative sponsored by Department of Science and Technology (DST), Government of India. He has more than 12 years of teaching and research experience at national and international institutions. He has published 10 research papers in various national and international journals and presented more than 15 research presentations in national and international conferences.

Lokesh Gupta has been an assistant professor in Amity Institute of Behavioural and Allied Sciences, Amity University, Haryana, since February 2019. He has experience working in six different institutions (Defence Institute of Psychological Research, DRDO, Delhi, Indian Institute of Technology (IIT), Delhi, Kendriya Vidyalaya, Government PG College, Shree Guru Gobind Singh Tricentenary (SGT) University and Amity University). He has published one textbook, two book chapters in edited books and five research articles in referred journals. He has also worked as a research volunteer in a DST project, involved in the design of the project proposal, data compilation, data analysis, review of literature and report writing. He assists in the development and conduct of workshops on positive psychology, resilience building, disaster management, etc., for university teachers, defence services personnel, university students, etc. He has been conducting workshops on SPSS (Statistical Package for the Social Sciences) and Xcalibre (IRT [item response theory] analysis software).

Divyani Khurana is a licensed clinical psychologist working in the field of mental health for the last 5+ years and has worked as a clinical psychologist at All India Institute of Medical Sciences (AIIMS). She is experienced in working with adolescent and adult people with mental health issues. Her major areas of interest are psychological issues of females, minority groups and intervention modalities, such as cognitive behaviour therapy, dialectical behaviour therapy and acceptance and commitment therapy (ACT).

Revathy Kumar is a professor of educational psychology at the University of Toledo. She is a Fulbright Specialist scholar and a fellow of the American Psychological Association and is on the editorial board of *Educational Psychologist*. She earned a PhD in education and psychology from University of Michigan. Her research focuses on social and cultural processes involved in the construction of a sense of self and identity among adolescents and young adults in culturally diverse societies. She was a recipient of The Spencer Foundation's Major Grant and is co-principal investigator on grants funded by the National Science Foundation. Her works have been published in *American Educational Research Journal, Educational Psychologist, Journal of Educational Psychology, Journal of Research on Adolescence, Journal of Teacher Education, Contemporary Educational Psychology* and *Educational Studies.*

Padmini Ravindra Nath is currently an Associate Professor in economics (Women's College) and member, Academic Council, BHU. She is the editor of *Indian Journal of Nepalese Studies* published by Centre for Study of Nepal, BHU. She has also worked as an article editor and peer reviewer for SAGE Open. Her specific area of specialization is gender studies. She was also formerly the nodal person for the Internal Complaints Committee of BHU. Six candidates have so far been awarded PhD degrees under her supervision. She has authored two books and numerous research papers.

Nidhi Prakash is a faculty, Assistant Professor, in the Department of Psychology, University of Delhi. She has teaching and research experience of over 14 years in the department. Her areas of specialization include organizational psychology, communication research, persuasion, advertising, statistics and research methods. She has worked extensively in the area of social and psychological contracts at work to improve employee relations and resolve motivational issues. Other than the various research publications to her name, she has undertaken projects under UGC-SAP (Special Assistance Programme) on community capacity building and conducted training workshops in different universities and corporates on such areas as professionalism, self-development, competency building and building of a trusting culture, to name a few.

Pallavi Ramanathan is pursuing her PhD in psychology from IIT Delhi. Her key areas of interest lie at the intersection of identity and context. She is interested in how identities are negotiated within specific contexts and how they influence one another. She seeks to understand how various communities understand themselves both as individual members and as collective selves. She is particularly interested in the identity conceptualization of refugees and how they negotiate who they are, juxtaposed with where they are located.

Rajesh Sagar is a Professor of psychiatry at the Department of Psychiatry, AIIMS, New Delhi. His key area of clinical and research work is child and adolescent psychiatry. He has more than 23 years of experience in this field.

Sujata Satapathy is an additional Professor of clinical psychology, Department of Psychiatry, AIIMS, New Delhi. Her predominant clinical and research work is in the areas of trauma psychology and psychological interventions for children and adolescents. She has more than 20 years of experience in this field.

Varuni Sethi has been working as a project assistant (counsellor) at the Adolescent Guidance Service Centre (AGSC), National Institute of Public Cooperation and Child Development (NIPCCD), New Delhi, since October 2019. She is an RCI (Rehabilitation Council of India)-certified rehabilitation counsellor. Her work entails carrying out assessments and interventions with adolescents and guiding their families. Prior to the same, she completed an Advanced Diploma in

Child Guidance and Counselling from NIPCCD, New Delhi, master's in psychology from University of Delhi, North Campus, and BA(H) in psychology from Lady Shri Ram College for Women, University of Delhi.

Sarita Y. Shukla is a lecturer in the School of Educational Studies, University of Washington Bothell, where she teaches undergraduate students and preservice-teacher candidates in the areas of multicultural education, learning, identity and motivation. Sarita earned her PhD in educational psychology from the Educational, School, and Counseling Psychology programme at University of Kentucky. Her research focuses on the intersection of psychosocial and cultural influences with student motivation and learning.

Rajbir Singh has been a Professor and additional dean, Faculty of Behavioral Sciences, SGT University, since 2017. Before joining SGT, he served as Senior Professor of Psychology at Maharishi Dayanand University, Rohtak, from 1991 to 2016. Here, he had been Head of Department twice (1992–1995 and 2004–2007), Dean, Faculty of Social Sciences (2005–2008) and Dean, Student Welfare (2003–2016). Earlier, he has also served as faculty at Kurukshetra University, Kurukshetra. Professor Singh completed a UGC-sponsored project of 2 years (2000–2001), has been a coordinator of UGC's SAP in health psychology for 10 years (2004–2014) and has completed a 2-year DST-sponsored project (2015–2016). A total of 27 students completed their PhD degrees under his supervision. He has specialized in biology of behaviour and has taught for 36 years. He has authored three books and edited four volumes in the area of health psychology, well-being and research methods. He has published more than 65 research articles in various referred journals.

Ritu Singh is an Assistant Professor at Daulat Ram College, Department of Psychology, University of Delhi. Her doctoral work was on caste and class issues in the Indian context.

Chandrika Soni is currently an Assistant Professor in the Department of Economics at Gaya College, Magadh University, Bodh Gaya

(Bihar). She was also UGC Junior Research Fellow at the Department of Economics, Faculty of Social Sciences, Banaras Hindu University (BHU), Varanasi. She has a postgraduate degree in economics and also a PhD in economics from BHU. Her fields of specialization are industrial economics and gender studies. She has contributed numerous research papers in referred journals and has presented papers in several national and international seminars. She has worked actively in the field of student welfare during her tenure as Joint Secretary of the BHU Students' Council.

Index